THE VICTORIAN & EDWARDIAN
Schoolchild

PAMELA HORN

AMBERLEY

By the same author:

Life Below Stairs
Young Offenders
Women in the 1920s

First published 1989
This edition published 2010

Amberley Publishing plc
Cirencester Road, Chalford,
Stroud, Gloucestershire, GL6 8PE

www.amberley-books.com

British Library Cataloguing in Publication Data.
A catalogue record for this book is available from the British Library.

ISBN 978-1-84868-810-0

Typeset in 10pt on 12pt Sabon.
Typesetting and Origination by Amberley Publishing.
Printed in the UK.

Contents

Introduction

... notwithstanding the large sums of money we have voted, we find a vast number of children badly taught, or utterly untaught, because there are too few schools and too many bad schools, and because there are large numbers of parents in this country who cannot, or will not, send their children to school ... What is our purpose in this Bill? Briefly this, to bring elementary education within the reach of every English home, aye, and within the reach of those children who have no homes.

W. E. Forster, Vice-President of the Education Department, introducing the Elementary Education Bill in the House of Commons, 17 February 1870.

This book is concerned with the lives of that vast majority of English and Welsh children, the offspring of the working and lower middle classes, who attended elementary school between 1870 and 1914. Very few of them were able to proceed by way of scholarships to the secondary sector.

The 1870 Elementary Education Act ensured for the first time that every child would have a school place available to it in a building of reasonable quality and with a certificated head teacher. The book looks at the way this development affected the lives of the nation's children, but it goes far deeper than that. The welfare provisions for them which gradually emerged, the kinds of work many of them carried out alongside their schooling, the games they played and their relations with their teachers are all examined. Most of the teachers were, of course, themselves former elementary pupils. The large number of illustrations brings home just what these different aspects of life meant for the individual child, at a time when around one in three of the population was under the age of fourteen.

In writing the book I received much help and encouragement from my late husband, and to him my thanks are due. I was also assisted by many other people and institutions through the provision of photographs or information, and to them, too, I should like to express my gratitude. These include:

Mr Allan D. Barlow, Local History Library, Manchester; Mr K. Beevers, Farnworth Library, Bolton; Birmingham Public Library, Local Studies Department; Bodleian Library, Oxford; Bradford City Local Studies Library; British Library Newspaper Library, Colindale; Mr Brown, formerly of the Education Department, Oxfordshire County Council; Buckinghamshire County Museum; Trustees of Burston School; the former St Paul's College Library, Cheltenham; Dr Forrester, Wigan; Dr Malcolm Graham, Oxford County Council Libraries; Liverpool Record Office; City of London, London Metropolitan Archives; Hampshire County Record Office; Hitchin Museum; Mrs M. Horn, my late sister-in-law; Mrs J. Mayhew, Librarian, Lord Mayor Treloar Hospital, Alton; National Union of Teachers' Library; Northamptonshire County Record Office; Oldham Local Studies Library Collection; Oxfordshire County Record Office; Mr M. St John Parker, former Headmaster of Abingdon School; Mr Alastair Penfold, Hampshire County Museum Service; Pitstone Local History Library; Museum of English Rural Life, Reading University; Royal Commonwealth Society; Sutton Courtenay School; the late Miss M. Tyrrell; Welsh Folk Museum, Cardiff; the former Westminster College Library; High Wycombe Central Library; Working Class Movement Library, Salford.

Conversion Table

Shillings and pence and some illustrative decimal coinage equivalents:

1d	½p	11d	4½p
2d	1p	1s	5p
3d	1p	2s	10p
4d	1½p	2s 6d	12½p
5d	2p	2s 9d	14p
6d	2½p	2s 10d	14p
7d	3p	3s 15p	15p
8d	3½p	10s 50p	50p
9d	4p	12s 6d	62½p
10d	4p		

CHAPTER ONE

Schools and Scholars

There is no cloud so dark and dangerous in our political horizon, no blot so foul upon our social system, no stain so deep upon the Christianity which we all profess, as the existence of ... perhaps 500, 000 children ... who are growing to man's estate to be a curse instead of a blessing to the community in which we live.

George Melly MP in the House of Commons on 12 March 1869.

In the late 1860s most schoolchilden depended for their education upon instruction provided by various religious and philanthropic bodies, particularly those associated with the Church of England. At a time when a religiously based education was seen as essential for the lower orders, the State's role was confined to influencing the day-to-day curriculum and giving some cash aid to the voluntary organisations. The main school providers were the Anglican National Society, first set up in 1811, and the British and Foreign School Society, established in 1814. This last claimed to be non-sectarian but, in practice, enjoyed the support of Nonconformists. However, Church schools far outnumbered both their British and Foreign rivals and those belonging to other denominations, such as the Roman Catholics and Wesleyans, who also had their societies. In the late 1860s, about three-quarters of the total state grant to elementary education in England and Wales went to Anglican schools, and there was widespread acceptance of the view put forward by the Bishop of London that it was the Church which should be 'the authorised and recognised ... instrument of national education'.[1] Nevertheless, sectarian disputes and rivalries were to bedevil elementary education throughout the nineteenth century, as committed Nonconformists sought to ensure that their offspring were not subjected to Anglican 'indoctrination'.

Pupils at Deddington National School, Oxfordshire, in 1904. The school was built in 1853 and opened the following January. (*Oxfordshire County Council*)

The rector, the Revd A. J. Wilson, listening in to lessons at Tackley National School, Oxfordshire, on 30 June 1905. (*Oxfordshire County Council*)

The denominational schools depended for their funds upon the fees of pupils, supplemented by donations from well-wishers and by government grants. These last had started in a small way in 1833, but from 1862, under the terms of the notorious Revised Code, they were handed over on a 'payment by results' basis. This meant that the money secured by a school depended upon the success of its pupils in an annual examination in the three Rs (reading, writing and arithmetic), plus a satisfactory level of average attendance. Religious instruction also had to be given, though it did not earn any financial reward, and the girls were required to learn needlework. From 1867 additional 'specific' subject grants were offered for English grammar, geography and history, and in 1875 these were converted into 'class' subjects, with the grant earned by the proficiency of the whole group rather than of the individual pupils. During the 1870s the range of 'specific' subjects was also widened to include modern languages, Latin, mathematics, science and domestic economy. But these meant little to most pupils. In 1875 under 4 per cent of all children in elementary schools were examined for a 'specific' subject, and although in 1895 the taking of at least one 'class' subject became obligatory for all schools, the overall change in the curriculum remained very limited. As one of HM Inspectors of Schools commented drily, the tendency was for both teachers and pupils to concentrate upon 'the minimum of requirement ... What the State requires will be done: what the State does not require will generally be neglected.'[2]

For more than one generation of teachers and scholars, therefore, the daily routine became an unremitting grind in the three Rs, with constant repetition and rote learning the normal method of instruction. Individual initiative was crushed, as teachers endeavoured to meet the conditions of the Code, and discipline was severe. Charles Cooper, who attended a school at Walton in the West Riding of Yorkshire during the 1870s and 1880s, remembered the monotony of it all, and the frequent canings, as teachers sought to beat the required information into their young charges:

It was a cruel system ... Children were not regarded as mentally deficient. The idea was that every child could do the work if he tried hard enough. And he was made to try by threat of punishment.

For reading, the same books were used year after year until they were ready to fall to pieces ... For writing, Copy Books were used and the correct holding of the pen was insisted upon ... Blots and finger marks were punishable by cane ...

In arithmetic the addition and subtraction of simple figures came first and more difficult examples were gradually introduced ... All work was done on slates ... This type of work included boys and girls, but in the

RULES

To be observed by the Parents of Children attending the National

*School at*_____

Parents who **wish** to get their children admitted into the above-named school, **may** do so by applying to the Master **on** any Monday morning, at a quarter before 9 o'clock.

Parents are requested to pay particular attention to the following rules :—

1. The children are to assemble at the school on every week-day morning at a quarter before 9, and every afternoon at a quarter before 2 o'clock, except **Saturday**, which is a holiday.

2. On the **Sunday** the children meet in the morning at   , and in the afternoon at   o'clock.

3. The school hours are from 9 to 12, and 2 to 5, in the summer; and from 9 to 12, and 2 to 4, in the winter.

4. The children must be sent to school clean and neat in person and dress

5. No child **may** stay from school without leave from the Master.

6. Leave of **absence** will be readily granted, either by application personally or **by** note: this application must be made before, and not after, the child absents itself.

7. If any child come late or be absent, a ticket of suspension will be sent, requiring a reason from the parent.

8. If the ticket be disregarded, the child will not be allowed to attend the school until **a** satisfactory answer has been given by the parent.

9. Every child must bring   a week, to be paid in advance every **Monday** morning: if there should be three children in one family desirous of attending the school, the third will be admitted free.

10. No child **will** be admitted under the age of six years.

N.B. No child will be admitted until it has been vaccinated.

Sold at the **National Society's Depository**, Sanctuary, Westminster.

Rules to be adopted by schools in association with the National Society in the 1860s.

Burcot Church School, Oxfordshire, was built in 1869 to serve partly as a chapel of ease and partly as a school. Divine service was conducted there each Sunday. The photograph was taken early in the twentieth century and the school was closed in 1922, with the remaining pupils transferred to another school about a mile away. (*Oxfordshire County Council*)

Children sitting to attention at Spelsbury School, Oxfordshire, on 21 March 1906, under the eye of their new headmaster, Ernest W. Conduct. Under the previous head this small school had in 1902 produced the top two scholarship girls in Oxfordshire. A year before, Mr Holmes, one of HM Inspectors of Schools, had praised the teaching there: 'Brighter children I have seldom, if ever, come across.' (*Oxfordshire County Council*)

afternoons when the girls were sewing, the boys would work from cards. There were many packs of cards in the cupboard for each class, and sometimes when the master had a large batch of essays to mark, or other urgent work to do, all classes would work from cards at early periods. Then the marking of sums would fall to the monitors and the Head always came round with his cane to inspect and punish.[3]

No history was taught at Cooper's school and the smattering of geography he acquired consisted of memorizing lists of capes, bays, oceans and the like, which had then to be pointed out on a map of the British Isles or of the world. It was doubtless instruction of this kind that one inspector had in mind when he observed sourly that it was not uncommon 'to find a child able to indicate readily the exact position on a map of Flamborough Head or Airdnamurchan Point, and at the same time fail to give satisfactory proof that it understands the meaning of a map.'[4]

Not until 1890 did 'payment by results' begin to crumble, as the government phased out the rigid annual tests in the three Rs. However, the last vestiges of the system lingered for 'specific' subjects until the mid-1890s.

The yearly examination conducted by HMI was an ordeal for staff and pupils alike, with mock tests held for weeks beforehand in many cases. The nervous anxiety aroused in one teacher is indicated by the following extracts from a school log-book for 1864:

Jan. 11th. Must get on faster with the Reading to get through the course of reading prescribed for the next examination.
April 27th. Preparing for the New Code examinations is strange work. I believe it affects my nervous system, for many failures in Dictation or a sum makes me tremble, while a successful trial elates me perhaps beyond measure.
May 25th. The importance to them of a coming examination impressed upon the children. To be doomed to stay in the same class for another twelve months as the consequence of failure produces a very good effect.[5]

One HMI, A. J. Swinburne, ruefully admitted that before his arrival 'the children were stuffed and almost roasted ... the [teacher] had sleepless nights'. At a Suffolk school he visited the mistress collapsed while the examination was in progress because she thought, wrongly, that he was failing her pupils.[6]

The scholars also experienced much stress, with some youngsters brought to school even when they were ill if it was thought they would

Raunds School, Northamptonshire, *c.* 1911. The children are sitting with their hands behind their backs to maintain discipline. (*The late Mrs M. Horn*)

Lewknor National School at the end of the 1870s. The headmaster, Arthur Taylor, was assisted by his wife. (*Oxfordshire County Council*)

achieve a good result in the examination.[7] Best clothes and well-polished boots were likewise the order of the day. Joseph Ashby, who attended a Warwickshire school in the 1860s, remembered how he and the other children listened anxiously for the sound of the dog cart which heralded the arrival of HM Inspector and his assistant.

> In would come two gentlemen with a deportment of high authority, with rich voices. Each would sit at a desk and children would be called in turn to one or other. The master hovered round ... The children could see him start with vexation as a good pupil stuck at a word in the reading-book he had been using all the year, or sat motionless with his sum in front of him ... One year the atmosphere ... so affected the lower standards that, one after another as they were brought to the Inspector, the boys howled and the girls whimpered. It took hours to get through them.[8]

The teachers' desire to obtain a good result arose partly from the fact that, in the early days especially, their salaries often depended upon the amount of grant the school obtained.

Even in 1888, the newly-appointed headmaster of Charlbury Board School, Oxfordshire, received a basic salary of £80 a year, plus 20 per cent of the grant; his principal female assistant received £50 a year plus 10 per cent of the grant; and the second female assistant a meagre £15 per annum and 5 per cent of the grant. In most years the head's extra payment equalled over a quarter of his basic salary. Where these arrangements applied, a reduction in grant meant a salary cut and perhaps dismissal too, since school managers were reluctant to retain a teacher who could not secure the maximum cash return for the school. The fluctuations in the amount of money earned could be considerable. At Newtown near Newbury, Hampshire, the grant of £32 4s earned in 1872-3 had slumped to a mere £9 4s by 1875-6, with HMI noting there had been 'some five changes of teacher' during the course of the year – hence 'the school results are exceedingly low'. The following year they were little better, with rapid staff changes continuing. Not until 1879-80 did the grant return to what it had been seven years before.[9]

Meanwhile, with this mixture of government support and voluntary effort, by the early 1870s most people were able to read and write. In 1871 four-fifths of all men marrying and three-quarters of women could sign their name rather than having to make a mark.[10] Nevertheless, in the slum districts of major towns and in more remote country areas, where voluntary cash support was scanty, school provision remained seriously deficient. Many youngsters either attended private 'dame' schools run by elderly men and women of varying ability and efficiency, or they attended

EDUCATION.

Inspector of Schools. "IT STRIKES ME THAT TEACHER OF YOURS RETAINS LITTLE OR NO GRASP UPON THE ATTENTION OF THE CHILDREN,—NOT HOLD ENOUGH, YOU KNOW,—NOT HOLD ENOUGH——"

Lancashire Magnate (who takes great interest in the Educational Movement). "NOT HOLD ENOUGH! LOR' BLESS YER—IF SHE EVER SEES FORTY AGAIN, I'LL EAT MY 'AT!'"

In the 'payment by results' era HM Inspectors had great power in deciding the success or failure of a school and its teachers. (Punch, *Vol. 75, 1878*) no school at all. Although some 'private adventure' schools were favoured by parents because of their informality, especially for younger children, HMIs, accustomed to the regimented regime of government-aided schools, were doubtful of the value of the education they provided. A London survey in 1871 reported 'classrooms' where the washing of clothes took up more space than did the pupils, and where the 'teacher' occupied herself by turning the mangle. Sometimes the 'schools' were so crowded that children sat in passages or in the garden or wherever else there was space.[11] Likewise in the South Midlands, the Revd C. F. Johnstone, HMI, described 'dame schools' where the younger children rolled about on the floor in disorder, while the older ones, aged six or seven, sat round a board of letters. The mistress, often with her needlework on her lap, gave 'but small attention to the attempts at learning which [went] on around her'.[12]

In the northern industrial towns conditions could be even worse. In Manchester, where an estimated 1,750 children of varying ages were on the registers of private adventure schools in the late 1860s, there were complaints that many of them were held 'in premises in which it is injurious and improper that human beings should be gathered together for any purpose whatever'. Most were mere child-minding institutions, like the school conducted by a ragged elderly Irishman. Twenty-seven children were crammed into a small, smoke-filled, extremely dirty room. They sat on benches with no reading books and only a few copies of a spelling book and two or three slates for them to write upon. 'They learn a few prayers, and come up one by one to spell. Little else is done.'[13] For this parents paid a fee of 3d a week.

What particularly irked the inspectors, however, apart from the confusion and inefficiency, was the fact that at a time when much stress was laid on the need to 'reform' the working classes through education, these 'dame' classes lacked any consistent moral message.

But, of course, numerous youngsters in the larger towns and cities attended no school at all, or at best put in spasmodic attendances at charitably financed classes like Henry Blessley's Class for Poor Boys, which was still running at Portsmouth in the 1880s. Earlier, a government survey suggested that in Liverpool in 1869, of 80,000 children aged between five and thirteen who ought to have been at school, 20,000 attended nowhere, and another 20,000 attended places where the education was unsatisfactory. Similar problems existed in Manchester, Leeds and Birmingham.[14]

There was, as yet, no general compulsion for youngsters to attend school. Only pauper children, juvenile offenders and those working in factories and workshops were covered by special attendance legislation. For those outside the regulated trades or below the controlled industrial employment

A dame school in Norfolk. (*From P. H. Emerson*, Pictures from Life in Field and Fen, *1887*)

A class-room scene at Roath village school, Cardiff, in 1899. (*National Museum of Wales. Welsh Folk Museum*)

Henry Blessley's Class for Poor Boys at Portsmouth in the 1880s. Blessley was apparently in business as a music seller and pianoforte dealer. Teaching was clearly a part-time venture only. (*Hampshire County Museum Service*)

age, which was usually eight in the 1860s, there was no requirement that they receive an education.

Against this background, pressure groups like the National Education League, based in Birmingham, and the National Education Union, centred on Manchester, began to mobilize in the late 1860s to demand better school provision. On a broader front too, it was realized that Britain, once the undisputed workshop of the world, was no longer the industrial leader she had been. One of the reasons put forward for her relative decline was the inadequacy of the English school system compared to that of many of her European rivals. When W. E. Forster, Vice-President of the Education Department, introduced his famous Bill in 1870 he stressed the need for action on this account:

We must not delay. Upon the speedy provision of elementary education depends our industrial prosperity ... [I]f we leave our work-folk any

THE THREE R's; OR, BETTER LATE THAN NEVER.

Right Hon. W. E. Forster (Chairman of Board). "WELL, MY LITTLE PEOPLE, WE HAVE BEEN GRAVELY AND EARNESTLY CONSIDERING WHETHER YOU MAY LEARN TO READ. I AM HAPPY TO TELL YOU THAT, SUBJECT TO A VARIETY OF RESTRICTIONS, CONSCIENCE CLAUSES, AND THE CONSENT OF YOUR VESTRIES—*YOU MAY!*"

The disputes and delays which had surrrounded the passage of the 1870 Elementary Education Act are well captured by this *Punch* cartoon of 26 March 1870.

longer unskilled, notwithstanding their strong sinews and determined energy, they will become over-matched in the competition of the world.

The extension of the franchise in 1867 to all male householders living in towns also contributed to the upsurge of interest in elementary education around 1870. Men who were neither literate nor propertied could now exercise a vote and education reform came to be seen by some as an essential accompaniment of the change. 'From the moment you entrust the masses with power, their education becomes an imperative necessity', declared one critic of the wider franchise.

In conditions of mounting concern, therefore, the 1870 Elementary Education Act was passed, giving every child a school place in a building of reasonable quality and with a qualified head teacher. In deference to public suspicion of State intervention and the influence of the Church lobby in Parliament, the voluntary bodies were allowed six months to make good any shortfall in accommodation identified after a national survey of school facilities had been conducted. Only if they were unable or unwilling to 'fill the gaps' could new rate-aided schools be set up, under

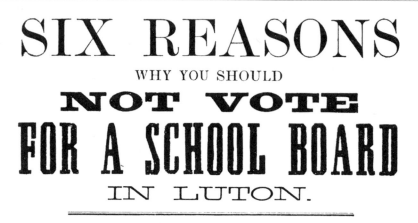

SIX REASONS

WHY YOU SHOULD

NOT VOTE

FOR A SCHOOL BOARD

IN LUTON.

1.—Because it is a leap in the dark.

2.—Because the Voluntary System is a complete success where it is adopted.

3.—Because the School Board is an untried scheme.

4.—Because when once you elect a School Board you cannot get rid of it.

5.—Because we are already burdened enough with Taxation.

6.—Because if you adopt that mode of working the Act, you may be compelled not only to Educate, but Feed and Clothe the Children.

FELLOW RATEPAYERS ponder well over the six Reasons and then ask yourselves who are the chief promoters of the School Board Scheme? Why men who are seeking place and power, men who have neglected their own duties, and now want to fasten the neglect on you.

No, Fellow Ratepayers, let us rather watch the working of the Board System in other Towns and Cities where it is really needed, and if there should be any portion of the Act worthy of being adopted, we can use it to Supplement but NOT TO SUPPLANT our present Voluntary System, which is the glory and boast of our Land.

January 25th, 1871.

There was much Anglican opposition to the establishment of a school board in Luton. The church party won a temporary reprieve by playing on parental fears of losing the children's wages in the straw-hat industry, but in 1874 a board was elected, under Education Department pressure.

the aegis of a board of locally elected ratepayers. In the case of London, however, the Act itself laid down that a school board must be established, for it was realized that the capital's problems were too severe to be met by voluntary effort. Eventually a quarter of a million new places were created there, and many temporary buildings remained in use to the end of the century – including prefabricated 'iron schools', which replaced earlier hired premises.[15]

In the nation at large though, up to the end of the nineteenth century more children attended denominational schools than those provided by the boards. In 1895, the respective figures were 1.9 million at board schools and 2.4 million attending voluntary schools of one kind or another.

To avoid inter-denominational bickering, the board schools were to be non-sectarian. But this did not placate many leading Anglican clerics, who were determined to 'fill the gaps' with Church schools. Typical was the reaction of the Bishop of Lincoln who declared they must do:

> all they could to try to maintain the voluntary and denominational system of education ... If they had a godless unchristian education they would have a godless unchristian people. If the system of School Board teaching was spread widely he would tremble for our civil and political institutions throughout the country.[16]

Elsewhere, as at Luton, clerical opposition delayed efforts to set up a board for several years.

Another 1870 innovation was the introduction of a 'conscience clause', allowing parents to withdraw their children from religious instruction in any government-aided school, either board or voluntary. In addition, school boards were empowered, though not compelled, to introduce attendance by-laws for children aged between five and twelve living within their area. They could also appoint school attendance officers to check on truants. A number, especially in the larger towns like London, took advantage of these powers and made the necessary appointments. In the capital the officers were euphemistically known as 'visitors'.

But not all parents welcomed these initiatives, since where they were applied not only was there a loss of income from the children's labour but school fees had to be paid as well. Although these usually amounted to only 1d or 2d per week, where there were several children in the family, this could represent a considerable outlay. Sometimes the charges were higher. At Basingstoke National Schools, parents earning £1 or upwards a week paid 4d for the first child and 2d for the remainder. Those earning from 16s to £1 paid 3d for the first child and 2d for the rest; and those with less than 16s a week paid 2d per child. These sums had to be handed

Punch mocking both the 'conscience clause' on religious education in the 1870

Pupils in the boys' department of Chaucer Board School, Bermondsey, in 1895, with their headmaster, Mr Shoveller. He stayed on at the school long enough to teach the sons of some of these boys. In 1897, the managers noted that many of the parents were so poor that they were 'obliged to secure the assistance of their children in earning the family daily bread. Sickness is very prevalent amongst the poor children.' This school was in one of the most deprived areas of London. (*London Metropolitan Archives*)

Boys wearing sisters' cast off clothing – an indication of family poverty – at Hill Wootton, Warwickshire, in 1890. (*Birmingham Public Library, Local Studies Department*)

over on Monday mornings, otherwise the child would be excluded and all 'absent weeks must be paid for, except in cases of serious illness or other urgent causes approved by the Secretary'.[17]

In London, fees were widely used to 'segregate' different sectors of the working classes. Thus, in the late 1880s the school board had 110,000 places at 1*d* a week for the poorest children, 180,000 at 2*d*, 100,000 at 3*d* and 60,000 at 4*d* or more. As John Hurt points out, in these cirumstances 'the artisan rate-paying father' could send his child to school 'secure in the knowledge that he would not come home harbouring lice from the children of the residuum'.[18] But some youngsters could not produce even 1*d* and although provision was made for the fees of the most necessitous to be remitted, in practice this was rarely done. Margaret Penn remembered how in her small Lancashire school, as the pupils filed past the teacher's desk on Mondays with their school pence, a few would hang back miserably, muttering that they 'hadn't got the money today, but would bring it next Monday for sure'.[19] But often parents reacted by simply keeping the youngsters away if they had no money for fees. Not until 1891 did an extra government grant at last make free schooling possible for virtually all elementary scholars.

Pupils at Bradford Church School, 1900. Note the ragged clothes of the children. One child is also without boots. (*Bradford City Local Studies Library*)

Lack of suitable clothing, and particularly boots, to attend school in was another cause of non-attendance. Many of the poorest wore cast-off clothing, which made them a target for ridicule and bullying by more fortunate fellow pupils. In one East End school cast-offs were publicly distributed to the worst-dressed scholars by the headmaster, much to their discomfiture.[20] Even during the First World War, Denis Gibson, an Oxfordshire labourer's son remembered his mother's anxiety as the time approached for him to start school, because she could not afford a suitable outfit. Eventually she managed to find some clothing, 'but I was exactly one week late in starting my education ... for this misdemeanour my mother had to give an explanation to the school attendance officer ... a day or two after I started school.'[21]

Encounters of that kind naturally added to the unpopularity of the attendance officers, and in the early days many of them faced violent parental hostility. John Reeves, who worked in the Shoreditch and Bethnal Green area of London, recalled parents standing at the street door and abusing him 'in the most dreadful language, and nearly all the people in the street would come out and see what was the matter and sympathise in their view'. Even locating the truants could present problems. Reeves would be told that youngsters were ill or dead, only to find later that they were at work, or up and dressed 'skipping in the middle of the floor'.[22] In some parts of the metropolis the officers had to work in pairs for protection.

But, of course, one of the major causes of absenteeism in both town and country schools was sickness, with epidemics of infectious diseases constantly mentioned in school log-books. Once such diseases appeared in a school the unhygienic living conditions of many of the pupils and the low resistance to infection caused by poor feeding meant that large numbers were vulnerable to attack. Thus at Whitchurch village school near Reading, a measles epidemic in the early months of 1886 was followed by an outbreak of scarlet fever and then by whooping cough.[23] Even milder disabilities could lead to absence, with log-books including such entries as, 'Several ... children at home with chilblains, "can't get their boots on".'

To add to the attendance difficulty was the fact that the 1870 initiative only applied to areas covered by school boards. The numerous districts served only by voluntary schools were outside its provisions entirely. Consequently in 1876 a new Act set out to make attendance compulsory for every child at least to the age of ten and thereafter to thirteen unless he or she could pass a special leaving examination or gain exemption in some other way. A new kind of local authority, the school attendance committee, was set up to cover the large parts of the country where there were only voluntary schools. Even then, some failed to introduce the relevant by-laws and it was left to the 1880 Education Act finally to make attendance compulsory for all children. During the 1890s the minimum leaving age

Oxfordshire school attendance medal for 1905-6. Medals were issued by many local education authorities to reward pupils for perfect attendance. London school board issued its first Queen Victoria Medal in 1887, and Oxfordshire Education Committee began the same procedure in 1903-4.

Gallery-type school in London in the 1890s. The pupils bending down on the left of the photograph are exercising with dumbbells. In the older schools it was common to have a single large room for the whole school. This could then be divided by movable partitions. (*London Metropolitan Archives*)

was gradually raised, to eleven in 1893 and twelve in 1899, although in certain rural communities, eleven was still accepted even after that date.

Some schools sought to improve attendances by offering medals or prizes. In London, where cards and books were given as rewards for good attendance in the 1870s, a local inspector thought these were responsible for the decline in truancy he had detected.[24] In the twentieth century similar incentives were offered by the new local education authorities set up under the terms of the 1902 Education Act.

Meanwhile, on a national scale the 1870 legislation led to the building of many new schools and the refurbishing of a number of the old. In London, the Fabian political and social reformer, Sidney Webb stressed the advances which had been made by 1904 compared to thirty years earlier. Instead of 'frowsy, dark, and insanitary rooms, practically destitute of apparatus or playgrounds, in which teachers ... ground a minimum of the three Rs required by the wooden old code into the heads of their scanty pupils', there were 'well-lighted and admirably decorated school buildings ... with pianos, school libraries, extensive playgrounds ... served by a staff of trained professional teachers'. [25]

After 1870, large groups of youngsters from slum homes entered school for the first time. Their presence created discipline problems for

Jews' Free School, Whitechapel, in 1908. Object lesson on 'the Dog' in a pleasant modern environment. (*London Metropolitan Archives*)

Children at Southfields Infants' School, Bermondsey, on 16 May 1906. From the 1880s kindergarten methods were applied in London infants' schools. Some of the children are drawing a caged pigeon 'from nature'; others are digging in a trough of soil in the playground – a poignant reminder of the scarcity of garden ground in the poor areas of large cities. (*London Metropolitan Archives*)

Brize Norton Council School, Oxfordshire, in June 1912. The school was built in 1876 by the local school board. Fees were fixed at 6d a week for the children of employers of labour and for other children, 3d a week for the first child in a family and 1d a week for the rest. However, after 1891 fees were abolished, as they were in most elementary schools at that time. (*Oxfordshire County Council*)

teachers, especially in view of the large size of most classes. Even such basic requirements as cleanliness, punctuality and sitting still had to be inculcated. HMI Parez, whilst welcoming the 'large influx of rough and ragged children' in bare feet and tattered clothing who had appeared in the schools in his Cumbrian district, recognized the difficulty posed for teachers by 'the reluctant presence ... of even a few ... embryo Artful Dodgers'; 'the additional labour of instruction which their total ignorance, as well as their want of docility involves, is a cause of serious complaint.'[26]

In the larger towns and cities the problem was yet more severe. In some of the poorest districts of London, schools had to face the disruptive influence of youngsters who had learned 'to swear, and lie, and pilfer, and in whom these habits seem to be rather fostered than checked by the example of their parents'.

Nevertheless, improvements soon began to be detected by inspectors, especially in the children's appearance, 'there being now a much smaller proportion of dirty faces ... while in some of the very poorest districts, the influence of the school is seen in the decreased numbers of children who formerly attended without shoes and stockings.'[27] In one school, anxiety among the girls to appear clean and neat led some of them to wash their pinafores in the dinner hour, and to put them on wet rather than wear

Boys at Oakes Street Council School, Liverpool c. 1914. They are learning to mend clothes and one, even at this late date, is without shoes. (*Liverpool Record Office*)

them to school dirty – the implication being that they had no spare clothes into which to change.

Academic standards among these new board school pupils were often very low. In the mid-1870s returns showed that only about one in five of the children in attendance in parts of London were above the level of Standard II of the school curriculum, while more than a third were below the level of Standard I. At that date, Standard I demanded an ability to read from a textbook including some words of more than one syllable, to write from dictation a few common words, and to do simple addition and subtraction of numbers consisting of not more than four figures, plus the multiplication table up to the number six. The fact that so many youngsters were unable to achieve this modest standard is an indication of the struggle faced by teaching staffs.

It is perhaps not surprising in these circumstances that a large number of teachers resorted to the cane in an attempt to impose discipline. This, in its turn, created ill feeling between them and their young charges. Daisy Cooper remembered with loathing the headmistress of her Liverpool school in the 1890s: 'The only words I ever heard her speak were harsh, bad-tempered ones ... It was the big girls of the school she vented her sadistic instincts on, and she would bring down her beastly cane on the palms, one on each hand, with such a full-arm action and sickening thwack that I was terrified that the hand would drop off at the wrist.'[28] In 1889 and 1911, at a time of labour unrest among adult workers, there were even school strikes in some of the larger schools to protest against the use of the cane, though they had little success.[29]

In the countryside feelings of hostility also existed. William Edwards, who attended school in the Huntingdonshire fens during the 1870s, recalled bitterly his relations with the teacher; 'they thought the on'y way to manage child'en were to frighten them to death.'[30] But some of his dislike may have been due to his inability to leave school as soon as he wanted. 'Arter I were about nine year old, I got real ashamed o' going to school when other folks went to work. One morning some men were working in a field as I passed on my way to school, and I 'eard one on 'ermsay "Look at that bloody grut ol' bor still a-gooing to school. Oughta be getting 'is own living." After that I used to get into the dykes and slink along out o' sight in case anybody should see me and laugh at me.' He eventually left at the age of twelve.

In squire dominated villages the teacher might also be used as an instrument of social control, to enforce obedience to those in authority. At Helmingham, Suffolk, in the mid-Victorian years, one girl who failed to curtsey to the squire's wife remembered being caned for it at school the next day, and that was certainly no isolated incident.

Sutton Courtenay Church School, *c.* 1907, with Thomas Yeates (1849-1940), the headmaster, on the left of the photograph. Mr Yeates remained at Sutton Courtenay from October 1877 until April 1916. He was also organist at the parish church for a quarter of a century and secretary of the village friendly society for many years. (*Sutton Courtenay Church School*)

But the 'intimidation' was not all on one side. Some of the older boys, in particular, acted violently towards teachers. Thus in the early 1880s at the village school at Sutton Courtenay then in Berkshire, where the head had recently taken over an ill-disciplined school, a pupil recalled seeing 'boys kick [his] legs and throw slates at him after having the cane'.[31] But in this case at least, the master, Mr Yeates, was able to restore order. He remained at the school for almost thirty-nine years before retiring in the spring of 1916. According to the school log-book, when he left he received 'a splendid writing case, the gift of Teachers & Scholars'.[32]

Parents, too, sometimes displayed violence to teachers. At Senrab Street Girls' School, Stepney, the headmistress noted on one occasion that she had been attacked by a father protesting at a small charge levied by the local council for medical attendance upon his daughter. 'He became very abusive & brawled,' she wrote. 'In the afternoon he was in the Hall at 1.45; as he repeated the offence the [School Keeper] gave him in charge.' The man was eventually taken to the police station, and the mistress hurried to the local council to ask for protection 'while in the execution of her office'. The following day she went to the police station in connection

Pupils from Sandford-on-Thames School, Oxfordshire, in May 1905. (*Oxfordshire County Council*)

Infants at Clifton Hampden School, Oxfordshire, in 1906, with the mistress, Mrs Creswell. She was wife of the school's head, William T. Creswell, who had come in 1891 and was to remain for about forty-four years. On the eve of the First World War he earned £115 per annum, while his wife was paid £35 per annum. (*Oxfordshire County Council*)

Anerley Residential School for the Deaf. Boys learning to make shoes, c. 1908.
Instruction for the deaf and blind began to be provided by the London School
Board from the mid-1870s. Note the emphasis on written instructions. (*London
Metropolitan Archives*)

with the case and had the doubtful satisfaction of seeing the offending
father fined 5s.[33]

More often, however, parents remained indifferent to their offspring's
schooling, perhaps because of their own limited education. Margaret Penn,
the adopted daughter of a farm worker, recalled her mother's impatience
when she found the girl reading. This she regarded as idleness – 'Satan allus
finds work for idle hands to do', she would observe severely, as she eyed
her daughter and an offending book.[34]

The 1870 Education Act, by drawing into school for the first time,
pupils from the most deprived sectors of society, highlighted the serious
scale of childhood poverty, ill health and physical (and mental) handicap.
Out of this came a recognition of the need for welfare provisions. Soon
after its establishment, the London school board began to provide
instruction for the deaf and blind for example. By 1898 it had twenty
centres for the former and eight for the latter in operation. Over the years
other boards followed suit, so that in 1900, Bradford had one school for
the deaf, one for the blind and five centres for the mentally defective.[35]
In 1899 the Elementary Education (Defective and Epileptic Children) Act

The uses of literacy! Two ragged boys reading a newspaper on the streets of Liverpool, *c.* 1900. (*Liverpool Record Office*)

empowered school authorities to force parents of children diagnosed as needing special education on account of mental handicap to send them to appropriate schools. Those failing to do so could be fined the considerable sum of £5.[36]

Consequently, although mass literacy had largely been achieved by 1870, it was only with the passage of the Elementary Education Act that the blackspots of ignorance, poverty and deprivation were tackled for children living in the slums of large towns and in the more remote rural parishes. From schooling, public attention turned to the broader aspects of child welfare and, for a minority, to the provision of scholarships to secondary education. It is to this changing approach to elementary schooling that we must now turn.

CHAPTER TWO

Widening Horizons

The purpose of the teacher is to prepare the child for the life of a good citizen, to create or foster the aptitude for work and for the intelligent use of leisure, and to develop those features of character which are most readily influenced by school life, such as loyalty to comrades, loyalty to institutions, unselfishness and an orderly and disciplined habit of mind ... The establishment of character must always be one of the main aims of Elementary Education.

Suggestions for the Consideration of Teachers and others concerned in the work of Public Elementary Schools (HMSO, 1912).

The purpose of the 1870 Education Act had been to 'fill the gaps' in the existing voluntary system and thereby to ensure that every child had a school place available to it. No mention was made of widening the scope of elementary schooling, since this was still conceived as something essentially for the lower orders. H. G. Wells called it educating 'the lower classes for employment on lower class lines', and as has already been seen, the three Rs remained the backbone of the system until the end of the nineteenth century. Nevertheless, as more school boards were established in the larger towns and cities, a change gradually occurred in the kind of instruction they provided. There was a growing acceptance of the view that education was a right to be made available to every child, not a privilege grudgingly to be offered only to those who could afford to pay for it. At the same time the Education Department itself began to encourage a broadening of the curriculum by increasing the number of subjects for which grants were paid and extending its requirements as to what should be taught in the schools. This was to become particularly important in the early twentieth century.

Metalworking class at Blackheath Road School, Greenwich, in 1908. This was a higher elementary school but similar vocational instruction was included in the curriculum of a growing number of elementary schools from the 1890s. (*London Metropolitan Archives*)

One of the initial problems to be tackled was that of school buildings, with London a notable pioneer in this regard. In 1870 the overall principle of design remained much what it had been a quarter of a century earlier, when voluntary providers were advised that a barn or a warehouse would offer a suitable model for a school. Children were taught within one large room, perhaps subdivided by partitions or curtains, but with little genuine separation between the different classes. The noise and confusion which resulted are easy to imagine. Joseph Ashby remembered the hubbub at his Warwickshire school when six different standards (or classes) worked together in the same room. 'Several children would be reading aloud, teachers scolding, infants reciting, all waxing louder and louder until the master rang the bell on his desk and the noise slid down to a lower note and less volume.'[1] It was easy for pupils to lose concentration as they watched friends in a different class. Inevitably, places were lost in the reading book or words misspelled, much to the annoyance of the teachers.

The practical difficulties faced by instructors in these circumstances were underlined by Albert Coles, master at Puddington School, Devon.

Mixbury Church School, Oxfordshire, was built in 1838 over cart sheds in the rectory drive and was still in use seventy years later. (*Oxfordshire County Council*)

He was responsible for teaching forty pupils of differing ages and levels of achievement. This meant that in arithmetic he had to dictate a sum to Standards I and II while at the same time writing problems on the board for Standards III and IV:

> In the intervals between these operations, give a lesson on compound practice to Standard V, and explain the relation between decimal and vulgar fractions to Standard VI ... taking care all the while to move about among Standards I and II for the purpose of seeing that the sums are correctly taken down and the figures well shaped.

As he ironically added, 'provided the teacher be able to do seven things at the same time, and withal a sufficiently clever athlete to be in seven different places almost at the same moment, it may be kept going.'[2]

It was to eliminate the difficulties of the single large classroom that in 1872 E. R. Robson, the architect of the London school board, produced a set of building rules which, in essence, governed elementary school construction into the twentieth century. They were based upon Prussian ideas and aimed to provide a separate room for each class. Wherever possible a large additional room with a roof light or high windows was to

Shipton-on-Cherwell National School, Oxfordshire, built in 1854 in the style of a small cottage. Even in the early twentieth century the only drinking water came from the village well across the road. (*Oxfordshire County Council*)

Girls saluting in a drill class in the playground of Ben Jonson School, Stepney, in 1911. This large school was in a very deprived area of London. In 1904, the managers noted that boots 'and clothing had been obtained from the charitably financed Ragged School Union for children whose parents were too poor to buy them'. (*London Metropolitan Archives*)

Infants playing the 'see-saw game' at Hugh Myddelton Infants' School, Finsbury, 1909. (*London Metropolitan Archives*)

be made available for drawing, and there were to be separate playgrounds for boys and girls. Although many old-style schools continued to be used for decades after this, particularly in country districts, Robson's views were widely adopted by urban school-builders.

London was also in advance of current opinion in its proposals for curricular reform. In infants' schools, for example, the obligatory lessons in the three Rs and religious knowledge were to be supplemented by music, drill and object lessons. These last were to require 'some such exercise of the hands and eyes as is given in the Kindergarten System'. Subsequently, object lessons, with their aim of stimulating the children's powers of observation and expression, were to become part of the government's own regulatory Code. For older pupils in the metropolis, instruction in science, history and geography was also suggested and was gradually incorporated into the daily curriculum. And to encourage an interest in reading among the pupils, in 1877 the board opened lending libraries at every school.[3]

Not all contemporaries, however, welcomed this broader approach to elementary education. Some felt it would give pupils ideas above their station and discourage them from taking up unskilled or semi-skilled manual labour when they left school; instead they would want to work as clerks or shop assistants. Others were anxious to prevent the development

Kindergarten at Millbank Infants' School, Westminster, 1907. The informality of this scene is in marked contrast to the old-style gallery classes for infants in earlier days. (*London Metropolitan Archives*)

of cut price secondary-type education which might damage existing grammar schools. *Punch*, in February 1871, mocked the new, broader range of 'specific' subjects for which grants were offered and suggested that dancing, etiquette, croquet, hieroglyphics and similar exotic subjects would soon be incorporated in the curriculum.[4] Three years later a still more rigid class view on the role of elementary schooling was put forward by the future Tory peer, Lord Norton, when he declared that state-aided education, like poor relief, was intended only for those unable to provide for themselves. Hence there should be no attempt to keep working-class children at school over the age of twelve, or to instruct them in anything beyond the rudiments: 'the educating, by the artificial stimulus of large public expenditure, a particular class out of, instead of in, the condition of life in which they naturally fill an important part ... must upset the social equilibrium.'[5]

Even in the early 1890s the question whether the capital's elementary schools should be equipped with pianos for use in singing lessons was an issue in board elections. One MP claimed that money had been spent unnecessarily by the board in purchasing 'pianos, harps, and other things quite beyond the children's station'.[6]

But while such attacks might slow down the reforms, they were unable to end them. Over the following decades the scope of elementary schooling continued to widen, as the Education Department's own perception of what should constitute mass learning underwent a fundamental alteration. As early as 1882 a new Standard VII was introduced into the Code to cater for children who wished to stay on at school beyond the minimum leaving age. This included the study of Shakespeare, Milton and other eminent writers, instruction on how to write a 'theme or letter', and, in arithmetic, the working of averages, percentages, 'discount and stocks'. Pupils were encouraged to take one or two 'class' subjects from a list now including English, geography, elementary science, history and needlework, while those who had achieved Standard V of the basic Code might take two 'specific' subjects as well. In 1893 a minimum of one class subject was required in all elementary schools.

Alongside this, older pupils in the larger and better equipped schools could enter for science examinations conducted by the Education Department's sister authority, the Department of Science and Art. In this way successful scholars not only improved their own qualifications but boosted the finances of their school through the grants they earned.

Gardening was adopted in an increasing number of schools from *c.* 1900. These pupils are in the garden at Sibford Gower School, Oxfordshire, in July 1906. The headmaster, Isaac Langley, had been at the school many years and was in his late fifties; he was certificated but not trained and was paid £112 a year. (*Oxfordshire County Council*)

The phasing out of 'payment by results' for the three Rs in 1890 led to further changes. In the mid-1890s visits to museums, art galleries and other 'institutions of educational value' were encouraged, and pupils were also instructed on how to collect their own 'museums' of interesting objects. These innovations proved popular in urban schools, with children taken on various expeditions.

Thus in 1896, boys from Orange Street school, one of the most deprived in the capital, visited the Zoological Gardens, Crystal Palace, the Tower of London and a Maypole Festival.[7] A year earlier some of the senior pupils at Chaucer School, Southwark, who were studying *The Merchant of Venice*, were taken by the headmaster to see the play performed at the Lyceum Theatre.[8] They, too, visited picture galleries, museums and the like, and their teachers were praised for the readiness with which they gave up their out of school hours for the children's benefit.

However, in the remoter rural communities these initiatives were difficult to apply. 'It is a very hard matter to cultivate the intelligence of our children', wrote the despondent head of Holbeton School, Devon. 'There is no foundation to work upon, they have seen nothing ... To talk of Railways, Manufactures, Telegraphs, or ordinary Arts of Civilisation is to make sure of not being understood at the very commencement.'[9]

An open-air lesson at Churchill and Sarsden Girls' School on a sunny July day in 1906. (*Oxfordshire County Council*)

In such quiet backwaters opportunities to benefit from excursions were almost non-existent. However, in part compensation, at the end of the century gardening was included in the curriculum of many schools. In Oxford the boys were said to be so enthusiastic about this that they were even prepared to continue work during the school holidays.[10] Overall, the number of pupils receiving a grant for gardening increased from under 5,000 in 1902 to nearly 30,000 eight years later.[11]

Although these piecemeal efforts at the end of the nineteenth century helped to broaden the horizons of elementary scholars, it was not until the introduction of a 'block grant' system of school finance in 1900 that a wide range of subjects was recommended for all. This was made clear by the Board of Education in 1904 when it defined the purpose of a public elementary school as forming and strengthening the character and developing the intelligence of the children entrusted to it. It was to assist both girls and boys 'to fit themselves, practically as well as intellectually, for the work of life'. To this end, teachers were 'to implant in the children habits of industry, self-control, and courageous perseverance in the face of difficulties; they can teach them to reverence what is noble, to be ready for self-sacrifice, and to strive their utmost after purity and truth.'[12] Such

Boys learning to knit at Walton Lane Council School, Liverpool, c. 1914. From their intent expressions they clearly found it an absorbing occupation. It was part of the Edwardian vogue for manual and domestic instruction in elementary schools. (*Liverpool Record Office*)

ambitious notions were a world away from the mechanical routine of the 'payment by results' era.

Hand in hand with changing official attitudes were improvements in the textbooks produced. They too became more varied and interesting. In the mid-1870s a London inspector had condemned the reading books used by some younger pupils as dull and nonsensical 'Why should children be called upon to learn such rubbish as ... "Do not nod on a sod," "Can a ram sit on a sod?" ... "Let Sam sip the sap of the red jam."' A decade later, under Education Department influence, poetry and adventure stories were being incorporated in reading books. Flora Thompson, who attended school at Cottisford in North Oxfordshire during the 1880s, recalled with pleasure the *Royal Readers* in use there:

> There was plenty ... to enthral any child: 'The Skater Chased by Wolves'; 'The Siege of Torquilstone', from *Ivanhoe*; Fenimore Cooper's *Prairie on Fire*; and Washington Irving's *Capture of Wild Horses* ... Interspersed between the prose readings were poems; 'The Slave's Dream'; 'Young Lochinvar'; 'The Parting of Douglas and Marmion; Tennyson's 'Brook' and 'Ring out, Wild Bells' ... and many more. 'Lochiel's Warning' was a

Girls learning to sew, mend and make clothes at Old Church C of E School, Liverpool, *c.* 1914. By this date virtually all girls in the city's elementary schools received some specialized instruction in cookery, laundry and housewifery before they left. (*Liverpool Record Office*)

favourite with Edmund [her brother], who often, in bed at night, might be heard declaiming: 'Lochiel! Lochiel! beware of the day!'[13]

Nor was this all. As more attention was paid to the role of education in fitting pupils for their future careers, so steps were taken to incorporate vocational instruction. This took the form of manual training for the boys and domestic economy for the girls. Manual instruction classes began informally in London in the mid-1880s, when senior boys at Beethoven Street School, Paddington, received lessons in woodwork from the caretaker, who was a carpenter by trade. But because this kind of instruction was outside the Education Department's official Code, the school authority was not allowed to finance it out of the rates. Instead money had to be raised from charitable sources. Not until 1890 did pressure from the Liverpool school board persuade the government to authorise the financing of manual instruction from official funds. Soon such lessons were provided in a growing number of elementary schools, with almost a thousand involved across the country by 1895.[14]

For the girls, meanwhile, lessons in domestic economy and general homemaking skills were gaining in popularity. They were seen as a way of helping to combat the high level of infant and child mortality then prevalent among working-class families, especially in the larger towns. In 1873 one HMI demanded that domestic economy classes be introduced

Grocery store conducted at Fairfield Council School, Basingstoke, in 1914-15. Pupils were receiving 'practical' instruction designed to fit them for adult life. (*Hampshire County Museum Service*)

Laying a fire at Dulwich Hamlet School's Housewifery Centre in July 1907. At this time domestic economy was taught at various centres throughout London, each serving a group of schools. The girls attended for half a day a week, and the aim was to teach them to become efficient housewives. Indirectly, the instruction also equipped them for domestic service – the major single employer of young girls in the late Victorian and Edwardian period. (*London Metropolitan Archives*)

Learning to lay a table correctly at Dulwich Hamlet School's Housewifery Centre in July 1907. (*London Metropolitan Archives*)

as 'part of the ordinary routine in girls' schools', even if this meant 'the sacrifice of fractions and decimals'. Over the years that attitude became more widespread.[15] Indeed, between 1878 and 1881 any girl who took a 'specific' subject had to include domestic economy. Clearly this limited the academic content of female education, particularly as all girls were also required to learn needlework as part of their basic curriculum.

With this official encouragement the number of girls taking domestic economy rose from 844 in 1874 to 59,812 in 1882. Alongside this, in the latter year a new grant for cookery was instituted, followed in 1890 by one for laundry work. By 1909-10 about a third of a million girls were learning cookery, and over 121,000 were attending laundry classes.[16]

The Board of Education (established in 1899 to replace the earlier Education Department as the controlling government agency) underlined the general commitment to female domesticity when it laid down in its 1905 *Suggestions for Teachers* that household management courses should 'be designed to fit girls to undertake, when they leave school the various household duties which fall more or less to all women'. At the same time the training should lead the scholars to set a 'high value on the housewife's position, and to understand that the work of women in their homes may do much to make a nation strong and prosperous'.

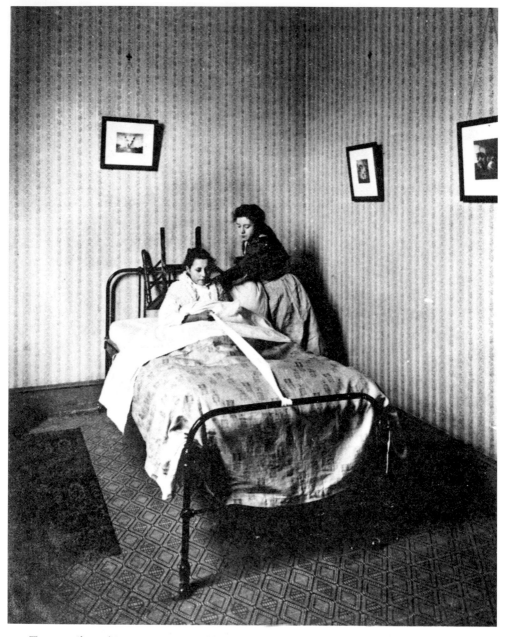

Two pupils making an improvised bed-rest, using a chair, in a housewifery class at Barnsbury Park Higher Grade School in 1908. (*London Metropolitan Archives*)

Cookery class at Eye and Dunsden Sonning Common Council School, Oxfordshire, in 1913. Although cookery classes were difficult to organise in rural areas, Oxfordshire had established a few cookery and manual instruction centres before the First World War. Children from nearby schools were taken to them by carrier's cart. This school had been built in 1912 and the boys were given instruction in gardening and woodwork. (*Oxfordshire County Council*)

School textbooks reinforced this general process of gender stereotyping. Girls were encouraged to be self-sacrificing, domesticated and highly moral. Even success in school work was to be subordinated to this vision of female service, with the cautionary tale told in one textbook of a girl whose father was quite clear that 'being top at school' was less important than her ability to carry out domestic chores and look after her mother when she was ill.[17] The *Domestic Economy Readers*, which proliferated from the 1890s, made much the same point – as in Longman's *Domestic Economy Reader*, Book II, published in 1900, which advised its young students that they should begin 'while young, *to learn to cook*, for this is mostly women's work'

Just how valuable the instruction was in improving homemaking skills must remain a matter for debate. One inspector in the north of England reported a lesson 'On Roasting Meat' in which a single chop was prepared and cooked by eighteen girls! In another case, a girl who attended a cookery centre in Barrow recalled the refusal of her family to eat the food she had prepared: 'when I think about it, and the messy way we carried on while we were doing these things ... I bet I didn't eat any m'self.'[18]

Cookery class at Eye and Dunsden Sonning Common School, Oxfordshire, in 1913. (*Oxfordshire County Council*)

But some girls took to the lessons with enthusiasm. In one Oxfordshire school the pleasure derived from cookery classes was so great that teachers of other subjects complained that the girls were 'being demoralised' as a consequence. '"They go to cookery all day on Monday", said one. "They can't sit still or settle to anything on Tuesday, and it is Wednesday before they begin to do any work. I can't possibly teach them the whole of the school syllabus in three days a week.'"[19] Significantly, older backward girls at Chaucer School, Southwark, one of the most poverty stricken in London, were put in a special class where they devoted half their time to practical work, including needlework and household management apparently with some success.[20]

These moves to improve the domestic skills of the nation's future wives and mothers were intensified at the very end of the nineteenth century by the outbreak of the Boer War. The health and physique of many would-be recruits from the larger towns were found to be so poor that large numbers had to be rejected. To the government, preoccupied with the security of an ever-expanding British Empire, the welfare of the nation's elementary schoolchildren became an immediate matter of concern, for it was upon them that the future defence of the Empire would largely depend. One result of this was growing State involvement in the provision of school

Pupils at Birley House Open-Air School, Forest Hill, learning infant care in 1908. (*London Metropolitan Archives*)

meals and medical treatment; but another was to ensure that all girls were instructed in infant and child welfare.

Other aspects of elementary education were also affected by this preoccupation with imperialism, notably the teaching of history and geography. While hostilities were still in progress, some schools displayed wall maps with the positions of friend and foe clearly marked. HMIs hastened to underline the link between elementary schooling and the growth of Empire.

Edmond Holmes, later to be Chief Inspector for Elementary Schools, wrote in 1899 of the village school as having a 'national, not to say imperial' role. 'Its business is to turn out youthful citizens rather than hedgers and ditchers ... preparing children for the battle of life (a battle which will ... be fought in *all* parts of the British Empire).'[21] Many pupils shared this enthusiasm. Walter Southgate, who attended Mowlem Street School in Bethnal Green, recalled that he and his friends played games like 'English versus Boers', and wore celluloid buttons in their lapels portraying their favourite generals. The relief of Ladysmith, and that of Mafeking, were occasions of general celebrations.[22]

Military drill, first introduced in the school curriculum in a minor way in 1871, was also incorporated on a wider basis about the time of the Boer War.

Musketry lesson at the Jews' Free School, Whitechapel, in March 1908. (*London Metropolitan Archives*)

The feelings of patriotism and pride in Empire, which were inculcated into many elementary scholars around the time of the First World War, are well to the fore in this display.

The aim was to promote discipline and smartness among the pupils, and to this end a *Model Course of Physical Training*, issued by the Board of Education in 1902, was largely based on army training methods. These close military connections, however, caused an outcry among teachers. T. J. Macnamara MP, a leading supporter of the National Union of Teachers, condemned the move as an attempt to make 'the elementary schools and the Board of Education a sort of antechamber to the War Office'. As a result of the protests, modifications were introduced, but even in its revised form the physical training course was heavily dependent upon military procedures. Teachers wishing to be informed on more advanced classes were, indeed, advised to consult the *Handbook of Physical Training* adopted by the Admiralty.[23]

Nevertheless, some schools took up these initiatives with enthusiasm. At Thurlestone, Devon, the boys were provided with toy guns, white sailor suits, and two airguns 'in the hope of making them good marksmen', under the direction of the local RNVR coastguard. In other cases servicemen were engaged as drill sergeants.[24] The Jews' Free School in Whitechapel was one of a small number of elementary schools which also established a cadet corps and provided instruction in 'musketry'. William Rogers, head of Washford Pyne School, Devon, noted the new developments with quiet irony: 'Took drill in the road, also took severe cold: still, we do not complain – our Country called us.'

More patriotism, *c.* 1914.

History and geography textbooks were likewise influenced by the burgeoning spirit of imperialism. Typical was Book Va in the popular *Highroads of History* series published by Thomas Nelson from 1907. It opened with a eulogy on the flag.

> No Briton can help being proud of the Union Jack. It flies over the greatest empire the world has ever known; and wherever it flies there are to be found at least justice and fair dealing for every man ... Men have fought to make it glorious, and have died to shield it from dishonour. Every British boy and girl will desire not merely to keep the flag unsullied, but to blazon it still further with the record of noble deeds nobly done.

The *Oxford and Cambridge English History*, published in 1906, also stressed the major territorial acquisitions which had occurred in Victoria's reign. 'The British Empire ... is so vast in extent ... that for the protection of British interests, and ... for the preservation of the very integrity of the Empire itself, the British army has very often had to fight in many wars on its own borders. These have led to its gradual expansion.' It was almost as if territorial annexation had been forced upon the nation!

Some of the geography textbooks, like Chambers's *Geographical Readers of the Continents: Asia* (1901), struck a similar note. This work extolled the virtues of British rule in India. 'No other nation but the British has ever held sway over a dependency so wide in extent, so dense in population ... Over those countless numbers of people Britain has established a system of rule that has spread the blessings of peace, security, and justice throughout the length and breadth of the land.'

Pupils, for their part, often came to share the pride – and the sense of racial superiority – which many of these books exemplified. 'They used to encourage us to be proud of the flag, salute the flag when we was at school,' recalled a former Bristol pupil. 'Yes, I was proud of being British ... We was the people of the world wasn't us?'[25] Similarly Robert Roberts remembered the heady imperial mixture doled out to him and his fellows at their Church of England school in the slums of Salford:

> Teachers, fed on Seeley's imperialistic work *The Expansion of England*, and often great readers of Kipling, spelled out patriotism among us with a fervour that with some edged on the religious ... What the undermass got materially from empire ... is hard to see, unless it was the banana ... which, exported from the colonies, began to appear increasingly in slum greengrocers' shops during the later years of the nineteenth century. Once instructed, however, the indigent remained staunchly patriotic. 'They didn't know', it was said, 'whether trade was good for the Empire,

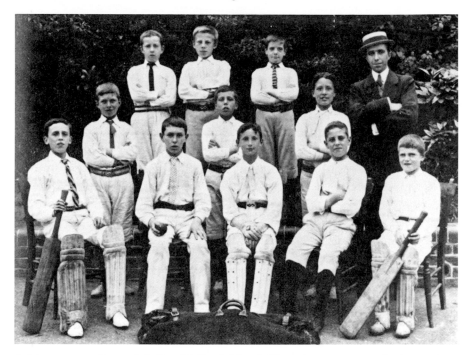

Cricket team at Rosendale Road Mixed School, Westminster, *c.* 1900. An increasing emphasis was placed on team games by the end of the Victorian era. (*London Metropolitan Archives*)

or the Empire was good for trade, but they knew the Empire was theirs and they were going to support it.'[26]

It was this philosophy which lay behind the growing stress on team games like football and cricket, which the Board of Education recommended to teachers as a way of creating 'an *esprit de corps*, and a readiness to endure fatigue, to submit to discipline, and to subordinate one's own powers and wishes to a common end.'[27] Such virtues were, of course, invaluable in time of war, and were without doubt partly encouraged for that reason, given the international tensions and rivalries so prevalent in the early twentieth century.

On a broader front, meanwhile, a few elementary pupils were gaining entry to secondary education, though efforts here were hampered by the general shortage of suitable secondary schools in the most heavily populated areas and by continuing family poverty, which meant most youngsters had to begin to earn as soon as they were able. Consequently, while well-to-do Leamington, Warwickshire, in the mid-1890s had about 16 per thousand of its population in attendance at secondary schools, in nearby Birmingham, where the population was overwhelmingly artisan, the corresponding figure was only about 10 per thousand.[28] Overall, in six selected counties of England, comprising about 30 per cent of the total population, a mere 3.6 per thousand of the population attended secondary endowed or proprietary schools. And many of these, even after a widening of scholarship opportunities under the Technical Instruction Act of 1889 and subsequent legislation, were from a non-elementary background. Thus while Hindley and Abram School, Lancashire, in 1892-4 admitted 93 per cent of its pupils from public elementary schools, Leigh Grammar School in the same county recruited only 20 per cent of pupils from that background. Likewise in Dunstable, Chew's Foundation admitted all its students from elementary schools but Bedford Modern School admitted only 12 per cent from that source.[29]

Scholarship pupils might also have difficulty settling into their new milieu, especially if, as at Abingdon School in Berkshire, they attended as day boys at a school whose prestigious side was that for boarders. In 1878 a reorganisation of Abingdon School's endowments led to the institution of five scholarships for boys educated for a minimum of three years at local elementary schools. This scheme was extended in 1904, when the town council provided finance for the school in return for a further award of scholarships to elementary pupils. The governors, pressed for cash to complete building developments, accepted reluctantly. But it is unlikely that the scholarship boys received a very encouraging welcome.[30]

So at a time when industry needed more clerks and technicians and when many better-off working-class parents were anxious that their offspring should stay on at school beyond the minimum leaving age, the overall provision for secondary education remained inadequate. In these circumstances some of the larger school boards began to provide quasi-secondary instruction in higher grade or higher elementary schools.

The first move in this direction came in the mid-1870s, when Bradford, acting on the recommendation of one of HM Inspectors, gathered together its few older full-time scholars into a single board school. Fees were 9d per week, the maximum allowed under the 1870 Act for elementary schooling, and along with a more advanced curriculum in the three Rs, lessons were also given in French, Latin, geometry, algebra and geography.

So successful was the venture that in 1879 a fourth higher grade school was opened in the city. Other boards followed suit, with Manchester claiming to have a higher grade school by 1877, Sheffield one by 1880 and Birmingham a so-called Seventh Standard school in 1884. The aim was for pupils, usually drawn from better-off artisan or small shopkeeping

Boys at Abingdon School, *c.* 1914. This secondary school was already accepting
a few scholarship boys, under the terms of its endowments, during the 1870s.
(*Abingdon School*)

Abingdon School Fours in 1870. The school boat club was one of the oldest rowing clubs on the Thames and was flourishing as early as 1840. (*Abingdon School*)

families, to study for the higher standards of the basic School Code and also to take additional subjects, including science, modern languages, mathematics, metalwork, carpentry, or, for the girls, cookery and laundry work. In many cases pupils were also entered for the examinations of the Department of Science and Art, since this brought added finance to the schools. Higher grade schools were particularly popular in the industrial north of England, where there was a growing need for technicians and yet where traditional secondary or grammar schools were relatively thin on the ground. In many cases the curriculum of these new schools became heavily 'science' based, some assigning as much as three-quarters of their time to scientific subjects. Elsewhere, as at Sheffield, a commercial department might be created for the study of French, German, English, shorthand and book keeping, to run alongside the science department, which included no language instruction.[31]

Some traditionalists, particularly within the Education Department, disliked the heavily scientific bias in the curriculum offered by most higher grade schools. Other critics considered they were exceeding the proper limits of elementary education, which was merely to provide children with the 'rudiments of learning'.[32]

Science lesson at Brownhill Road Higher Grade School, Lewisham, in 1908. The clothing of the pupils confirms that the school was situated in a more prosperous area of London. Science was an important part of the curriculum at most higher grade schools, especially in the nineteenth century. (*London Metropolitan Archives*)

Yet, despite the debate these schools provoked, their number remained small. Even in the mid-1890s there were only sixty of them in the country, outside London, and more than half the counties of England and Wales had none. Of the sixty, thirty-five were in Durham, Lancashire and Yorkshire, while London did not obtain its first higher standard school until the late 1880s. In 1899, however, the widening scope of education provided by the capital's school board was challenged by a district auditor named Cockerton. He disallowed all expenditure on higher elementary instruction provided by the board as *ultra vires* – i.e. beyond the power of the law. In the flurry of legal argument and fresh legislation which followed, the 'higher grade' experiment was curtailed.[33]

Meanwhile, scholarships continued to be offered under the terms of some grammar school endowments or, in London, under the aegis of the livery companies. From 1891 the newly-established county councils were also allowed to fund free places. It was in these circumstances that Fleet Road Board School, Hampstead, gained a reputation in the capital as 'the Eton of the Board schools' on account of the large number of scholarships

Female staff at Hugh Myddelton School, Finsbury, in 1908. Part of the school was higher grade and part not. This school also had a centre for deaf children, as well as centres for cookery, laundry work and manual training. (*London Metropolitan Archives*)

won by its pupils.[34] But in the nation as a whole the odds against a child from an elementary school being awarded a scholarship to a secondary school were still about 270 to 1 in the mid-1890s.[35]

In 1902 a new Education Act increased the provision of secondary schooling by substituting for the old school boards and attendance committees a national network of education authorities under the local councils, with powers to finance both the elementary, and secondary sectors.

As a result the number of grant-aided secondary schools more than doubled in the periods 1904-5 and 1913-14, and the total of pupils attending them nearly trebled, from just under 64,000 at the earlier date to almost 188,000 at the latter.[36] In 1907, this more liberal approach was taken a step further when the Board of Education required all grant-aided secondary schools to offer at least a quarter of their places free to children from public elementary schools. By 1913 the number of free places had reached 60,000.

However, within the secondary schools subjected to the Board's intervention, there was sometimes deep resentment. In 1912 one of the governors of Abingdon School resigned over what he called 'the crude and extravagant suggestions of the Board', which the schools were coerced into accepting. The headmaster followed suit six months later, giving financial stringency as one of the reasons, but making clear this was associated with the free place scheme, since Board payments did not cover the cost of the free places 'which its Regulations claim'.[37] On the eve of the First World War fees for non-scholarship day boys at the school amounted to about £14 a year.

Alongside these developments in England, a special Intermediate Education Act was passed in 1889 for Wales. This established secondary and technical-type education in every county in the Principality. By 1910-11 there were ninety-six Intermediate schools open and, unlike most English grammar schools, they combined academic work with a vocational aspect.[38]

Nevertheless, although secondary education was becoming available to a growing band of bright children from poorer homes, the main beneficiaries from the new schemes were the offspring of the lower middle classes. Sometimes, indeed, children from poor homes could not afford to take up the scholarships they had won. Edith Williams, who gained a scholarship to Cyfarthfa Castle Secondary School in 1910, was forced to leave, even though she was doing well, because her family, with eight children to support, could not afford to buy the textbooks needed. 'I was heartbroken and bitter, and my sense of deprivation was so great that I nursed this grievance for many years afterwards,' she later confessed.[39] Likewise George Birch, who was educated in Bethnal Green at the beginning of the twentieth century, was unable to take up a scholarship he had been awarded because his elder sister had already won one and their father could not afford to keep two children at secondary school. At fourteen, George found work as a tea boy in a printing business before eventually emigrating to Canada.[40]

On the eve of the First World War, one survey suggested that around 29 per cent of children attending the nation's secondary schools were the offspring of wholesale and retail traders, and almost 17 per cent more were the children of skilled workers; a mere 2.5 per cent came from the families of the unskilled.[41] And where such youngsters did take up their scholarship places, it was frequently because of the 'long hours of a sacrificing mother' or of sisters who went out to work to earn the extra cash needed.[42]

However, even in apparently unpromising family circumstances cultural attitudes might have a role to play. This seems to have been the case among Jewish children, whose parents were often willing to make considerable sacrifices in order to ensure they had a good education. Thus in Tower

Hebrew lesson at the Jews' Free School, Whitechapel, *c.* 1906. The school enjoyed a high success rate for scholarships. (*London Metropolitan Archives*)

Hamlets, where between 1893 and 1913 2,389 elementary schoolchildren were awarded scholarships to secondary education, more than two-fifths were Jewish, with the Jews' Free School alone accounting for 129 awards. The achievement this represented was all the greater since many of the youngsters were the offspring of poor immigrants from Eastern Europe, who knew little or no English when they arrived in this country. The Free School was particularly praised by HMIs for its skill in instructing immigrant children in the rudiments of English, so as to enable them speedily to take their place in the ordinary life of the school.[43]

But excluding such educationally ambitious and successful groups as these, for most elementary pupils, family poverty and limited scholarship provision ensured that very few were able to make the transition to the secondary sector. As Gerald Bernbaum has written:

By 1914, ... there were two separate branches to the public system of education. The majority of children attended elementary schools which had limited aims and offered few opportunities. A small number went to secondary education, thereby reflecting their parents' occupation and social position and at the same time almost guaranteeing their own.[44]

Detail from 'In the Scool Room' by Theophile Emmanuel Duverger. (*Fine Art Photographic Library*)

CHAPTER THREE

Health and Welfare

... there is no doubt that the school medical service ... taught the country to look upon the child, not as a unit for statistical record or clerical data, but as an individual to be trained in a hygienic way of life, preserved in health where he possessed it or restored to health where he did not. It taught the parents ... that ailments could not with impunity be treated, as trifling.

G. A. N. Lowndes, *The Silent Social Revolution* (first published, 1937).

Throughout the Victorian and Edwardian period epidemic diseases, such as measles, whooping cough, scarlet fever and diphtheria, posed major threats to the lives and well-being of the nation's children. Youngsters from poorer families, dwelling in overcrowded, insanitary homes, with a polluted water supply and, often enough, an inadequate diet, were especially vulnerable. In the 1860s and 1870s, half of the deaths from diphtheria were of children under the age of five, and of the remainder, four-fifths were among those between five and thirteen years.[1] Whooping cough, too, had a serious impact, accounting for two-fifths of all deaths under the age of five and being particularly lethal among little girls.[2] Another major killer, of young and old alike, was tuberculosis. Walter Rose, born in 1871 at Haddenham, Buckinghamshire, remembered 'consumption' as 'the dismal ogre that haunted the lives of scores of young villagers with perpetual menace'. He himself ate live snails because someone told him they prevented the disease.[3]

Overall, at the end of the 1890s nearly half of all deaths in the industrialised counties of Cheshire, Durham and Lancashire were accounted for by children under the age of five. Even in rural areas like

Orange Street Infants' School, Southwark, in 1894. The school was situated in a
very deprived area and a charitable meals scheme was pioneered by the head of the
girls' school, Mrs Burgwin, in the 1870s. (*London Metropolitan Archives*)

Herefordshire, Oxfordshire and Dorset, about a quarter of all deaths were
among the same age group.[4]

Public opinion was aware of this grim toll and over the years action
was gradually taken to combat it. During the first half of the nineteenth
century, a series of Factory Acts sought to regulate the hours of work and
the educational opportunities of children employed in the textile mills,
and to protect them from exploitation by parents and employers. (The
effects of this legislation will be examined in the next chapter.) In addition,
from the 1840s a vaccination programme to protect children against the
scourge of smallpox was embarked upon, although it was not until the
1870s that it was effectively implemented.[5]

The hardships endured by many poor children living in the towns were
likewise highlighted from the middle decades of the nineteenth century in
the novels of Charles Dickens and the writings of journalists and social
investigators like Henry Mayhew, George Sims, Charles Mackay and
many others.

On one occasion, Mayhew described a meeting with two girls, aged fifteen
and eleven respectively, who since their mother's death four years before had

The ragged clothing of these lads from the Hitchin area of Hertfordshire is mute testimony of the poverty of many labouring families in Victorian England. (*Hitchin Museum*)

cked out a living selling flowers and oranges on the streets of London. With these earnings they and their thirteen-year-old brother, who secured 1s 6d to 2s a week as a costermonger's boy, had managed to rent a room for 2s a week and to feed and clothe themselves. In another case, Mayhew encountered an eight-year-old watercress seller, who despite the coldness of the weather was clad only in a thin cotton gown, with a threadbare shawl round her shoulders, and a pair of large carpet slippers on her feet. Her head was bare and she had to walk with a shuffle to prevent the slippers sliding off. 'There was something cruelly pathetic in hearing this infant, so young ... talking of the bitterest struggles of life, with the calm earnestness of one who has endured them all.' When Mayhew asked her whether she liked visiting parks, she did not even know what they were. 'All her knowledge seemed to begin and end with watercresses ... She knew no more of London than that part she had seen on her rounds ... Her little face, pale and thin with privation, was wrinkled where the dimples ought to have been, and she would sigh frequently.'[6]

A similar message was conveyed in the final quarter of the century by another journalist, George Sims, both through his prose writings and through the popular ballads he published. Typical of them was *Billy's Rose*, with its theme of childhood death:

> Billy's dead, and gone to glory – so is Billy's sister Nell:
> There's a tale I know about them were I poet I would tell;
> Soft it comes, with perfume laden, like a breath of country air
> Wafted down the filthy alley, bringing fragrant odours there.
>
> In that vile and filthy alley, long ago, one winter's day,
> Dying quick of want and fever, hapless, patient, Billy lay;
> While beside him sat his sister, in the garret's dismal gloom,
> Cheering with her gentle presence, Billy's pathway to the tomb.[7]

There was a great deal more in a similar vein.

These accounts were reinforced by a whole range of governmental Royal Commissions and Select Committees concerned with child employment and welfare in a wide range of industries, including agriculture, textiles, metalwork, pottery and mining, and with the living conditions and

A Ragged School Dinner in Camberwell, *c.* 1900. This was one of many charitably financed breakfast and dinner schemes in operation in the capital. In 1904 it was estimated that over 120,000 children in London were underfed, and similar problems were identified in other large towns. (*London Metropolitan Archives*)

When miners went on strike at Wigan in 1893 the chief constable organised a soup kitchen for their children, supervised by his constables. Without such charitable aid many families must have starved. (*Dr Forrester*)

educational opportunities (or lack of them) of youngsters engaged in them.

The evidence thus assembled on juvenile ill health and exploitation touched the hearts and consciences of the mid-Victorians and led to pressure for further regulation of youngsters' working conditions, and to a proliferation of charities to assist and nurture the destitute child. By 1878, there were fifty philanthropic societies catering for children in London alone, including a number which ran homes for young orphans of the kind encountered by Mayhew.

But beyond this broad protective framework public opinion was reluctant to go, for fear of infringing parental rights and undermining the self-dependence of the working-class family

The intervention of the State directly to protect the health and well-being even of infants was opposed by many. 'I would far rather see ... a higher rate of infant mortality prevailing than has ever yet been proved ... than intrude one iota farther on the sanctity of the domestic hearth and the decent seclusion of private life,' declared Whately Cooke Taylor in 1874. [8] He made the comment at a time when about one in six of all babies born in England was dying before its first birthday. Fifteen more years were to elapse before the first legislation to protect children against cruelty appeared on the statute book. Significantly it came in the wake of the establishment of the National Society for the Prevention of Cruelty to Children and in the first five years after its passage 5,460 persons were successfully prosecuted under it. But there were still many loopholes, and it was not until the Children Act of 1908 that effective action was taken to protect children from ill treatment or neglect by their parents. This Act also outlawed begging by children on the streets and the imprisonment of youngsters under the age of fourteen. After 1908, as one historian has put it, children came to be 'properly regarded as wards of the community'.[9]

Meanwhile, the 1870 Education Act had also played a part in highlighting the scale of childhood need. The large numbers of malnourished and ill-clad youngsters who were brought into school for the first time ensured that the welfare issue was drawn to public attention. Teachers, in particular, realised that many youngsters in the poorest areas were too hungry to learn. As early as 1871 there were reports of pupils who came to London board schools without breakfast and then 'fell off the form fainting through hunger'.[10] It was in these circumstances that a Children's Free Breakfast and Dinner Fund was launched in 1880 in the capital with the active support of Mrs Burgwin, headmistress of Orange Street Girls' Board School, Southwark, and the journalist, George Sims. Mrs Burgwin had moved to Orange Street in 1874 and had begun to give milk to the most deprived children soon after. By the end of the nineteenth century the Free Breakfast and Dinner Fund she helped to found had an annual income of £4,000 and had become the largest and best known of the London societies supplying children with school meals.[11] In 1882 the London Board School Free Dinner Fund was also launched, and there were numerous similar initiatives elsewhere. The Birmingham Schools Cheap Dinner Society, formed in October 1884, for example, rapidly discovered that many scholars were so poor that they 'could no more find a halfpenny for a dinner than they could find a half-sovereign'.

In the mid-1890s managers at Chaucer School, Southwark, likewise reported that during the severe winter of 1894-5 charitable help had enabled teachers not only to provide some 400 meals a week for the pupils but also warm clothing and strong boots.[12] At this school over half of the children were regularly fed through philanthropic action, and many others obtained charitably funded meals away from the school premises.

Unfortunately not all needy youngsters enjoyed this precarious aid. In Liverpool, teachers who visited pupils' homes in 1905 to check on absentees found many asleep in sacks in unfurnished cellars. They were waiting for their parents to earn money to buy food and although they followed the teachers to school in the rags in which they had been sleeping – since they had no other clothes – it was to little avail. They were too faint from want of food to learn anything.[13] A decade later photographs of children in Liverpool still show a few attending school in bare feet.

In London too, youngsters continued to be sent breakfastless to school while their mothers went out to earn a few pence selling flowers or scrubbing steps. It was circumstances such as these which caused Dr Crichton-Browne, in a government report published in 1884, to recommend that liberal and regular feeding was essential if the most needy pupils were to benefit from their education. Movingly he drew attention to 'the quiet heroism' with which, 'when hunger [was] gnawing within ... they [sat] uncomplaining at their little desks, toiling at their allotted tasks ... These children want blood, and we offer them a little brain-polish; they ask for bread, and receive a problem.'[14] He proposed that two pints of fresh milk should be provided daily to each of them in order to ensure that they were properly nourished. But given the non-interventionist attitude of the government of the day, such proposals for assistance fell on deaf ears. Indeed, one of HM Chief Inspectors of Schools bluntly accused Dr Crichton-Browne of over-dramatising the situation. He argued it was not the purpose of a school to dispense milk to its pupils:

I trust the statesmen and philanthropists who are now considering this difficult and anxious question will think twice before complicating the problem of national education by mixing up with it the administration of food and medicine to the children of the poor ... the responsibility of caring for the food and health of young children belongs properly to the parent, and any public measures which relieved him of this responsibility might do far more mischief than is evident at first sight ... if once it becomes understood that the State, or any public authority, is willing to provide nourishment and medical attendance for all the children in the public [i.e. elementary] schools who seem to require it, the influence on a large number of parents in diminishing their sense of responsibility may become a serious public danger.[15]

Over twenty years were to elapse before Dr Crichton-Browne's ideas at last found favour. In the meantime, as the London school board's own investigations revealed, at the end of the nineteenth century around 55,000 children, or nearly a tenth of those in average attendance, came to school hungry.[16]

Some critics, despite the mounting evidence, even continued to deny that child poverty was a problem. They argued that it was the improvidence of working-class-life which was responsible for youngsters' ill health rather than low family incomes and bad housing.[17] The Charity Organisation Society, established in the late 1860s, was particularly opposed to the giving of casual help, claiming that only aid which made a family self-dependent should be provided. To this end it attacked the giving of boots to enable the poorest children to attend school, pointing out that if this became widely known it would encourage parents to keep their offspring away from school in order to qualify for the free boots.[18]

Nor were the problems of deprivation confined to towns. Similar difficulties arose in country areas too. In a typical case, a woman who attended school at Boughton Monchelsea, Kent, around 1906 remembered 'lots of children' being sent 'with no breakfast and quite often a child lost his dinner to a hungrier boy or girl'. She also recalled youngsters from poorer families arriving in broken boots that barely covered their feet and sometimes, even in winter, without socks or stockings. On wet days they were 'really soaked to the skin and as roads then were very muddy, some covered in several inches of it, they were in pretty poor shape for learning'.[19]

Poor country children were, indeed, worse placed than their urban counterparts when it came to obtaining help with meals, since almost all the charitable dinner schemes were urban based. The best that most village children could expect was the provision of a warm drink, perhaps supplied by the head teacher or a local worthy during the midday break. As late as 1914, there were reports of children in Bedfordshire, Hertfordshire and Gloucestershire being supplied with cocoa for 1d or so a week during the luncheon period.[20]

Churchill and Sarsden schoolchildren being taken home by the 'Cornwell conveyance' in 1906. Cornwell had lost its own school by closure in 1904 and pupils were then taken to nearby Churchill by wagonette. Country children often had to go long distances in order to reach their school and few enjoyed the luxury of a 'conveyance' of this kind. (*Oxfordshire County Council*)

School attendance, then, highlighted problems of malnutrition among children and in some cases stimulated action to relieve the deficiencies identified. But it also drew attention to other difficulties. After 1870 the ragged clothing and verminous heads and bodies of poorer pupils became matters of growing concern. At Orange Street School, attended by what one HMI called 'the lowest and most neglected class of children' in London, there were demands for the provision of a bath 'to wash the Boys' persons and of an oven to bake their clothes' so as to delouse them. 'Dirty heads' were a particular problem, with the entire scalp covered by vermin in some of the worst cases. Even in relatively prosperous Oxford there was, as late as 1909, not a single school entirely free from the problem of 'dirty heads'.[21]

At St Pancras, London, where the children were encouraged to use the public baths, teachers spoke enthusiastically of the improvement in the youngsters' health and academic progress which resulted. The skin improved, eyes were brighter and there was 'a disappearance of the horrid fidgeting, the result of irritation'.

But where such facilities were lacking, dirty, malodorous children appeared in the schools of the poorer districts of both town and country.

They also represented a nuisance to more fortunate fellow pupils. H. E. Bates, who attended school at Higham Ferrers, Northamptonshire, early in the twentieth century, recalled being seated next to a boy who stank: 'to this day [he wrote many years later] the peculiar acrid stench of the unwashed lingers in my nostrils ... Many of the children ... were in a constant state of itch and scratch, so that it needed all my father's vigilance and industry with soap and tooth-comb to keep me, as he would say, free of livestock.'[22]

But in urban areas the situation was far more serious. Dr Kerr, Bradford's first school medical officer, discovered when he conducted his initial inspections in the mid-1890s that more than a third of the three hundred children whom he examined had not had their clothes off for more than six months. The situation as it existed in Bradford at this time has been graphically described by G. A. N. Lowndes. He wrote of the matted, vermin-infested hair of the girls, the sore eyes and the 'open-mouths symptom of adenoids' –

the 'tallow candles' pendant from the nostrils of little children who had probably never heard of a handkerchief let alone possessed one; the evidence of rickets ... What you will not be able to perceive ... is how many of the children had been sewn into their clothing perhaps with pads of cotton wool underneath, for the whole of the winter months;

Cleanliness is next to godliness! Children in Bradford school baths in 1904. The baths were first opened in the 1890s as part of the city's child welfare programme. (*Bradford City Local Studies Library*)

Jonathan Priestley, headmaster of Green Lane School, Bradford, and Miss Maria Cuff, superintendent of domestic subjects, weighing children, c. 1908. Mr Priestley was the father of the novelist J. B. Priestley, and his son described him as 'not a born scholar but a born teacher, with an almost ludicrous passion for acquiring and imparting knowledge'. (*Bradford City Local Studies Library*)

> the number deprived of their birthright of sleep by the nightly attention of bed bugs ... the bags of sulphur sewn round the hems of the teachers' trailing skirts to prevent the vermin climbing, sidling or leaping up![23]

Kate Stearns, who taught in Hoxton from 1909, confirmed that it was common for pupils to be 'flea bitten ... many were verminous, bugs were often found in the school particularly amongst the needlework. I remember my class-room being closed in order that it should be fumigated.'[24]

Yet, despite the mounting evidence of childhood deprivation, there was still reluctance to sanction further state intervention in the welfare field in case this discouraged parents 'from discharging the most honourable and elevating duty of training their own children', as one MP put it.[25] Even those who favoured the provision of school meals included some who preferred the offering of breakfasts to midday dinners, partly from the humanitarian motive that this would ensure that the children had something to eat before the school day began, but also because it was felt that supplying a midday dinner would discourage mothers from performing their proper duties in this regard.[26] In 1914, Canon Barnett, a retired vicar of Whitechapel and former warden of Toynbee Hall in the East End, called for breakfasts of porridge, milk and treacle to be provided at 8 a.m. every morning to which all children should be free to come: 'on the mothers would remain the obligation of preparing some dinner. This obligation is a tradition of family life.'[27] He did not, of course, take account of the many mothers who were themselves out at work in the day time, helping to make ends meet.

Ironically, it was the growth of imperialist sentiment around the time of the Boer War which eventually led to effective action being taken in the school welfare field. As T. J. Macnamara, a Liberal MP and supporter of the National Union of Teachers, put it in 1904, while such a programme might sound like 'rank socialism, in reality it [was] first-class imperialism'.[28] It would be impossible for the country to defend itself properly if it had to rely on the 'rickety shoulders' of so many existing elementary pupils. The former Liberal Prime Minister, Lord Rosebery, was another powerful supporter of this view, declaring the Empire needed 'as its first condition'

White Abbey Feeding Centre, Bradford, 1908, with the children standing smartly to attention awaiting their school dinners. On the right, standing on a dais, was Mr Jonathan Priestley, and on the left, in an apron, Dr Dessian, a German master at Belle Vue Secondary School. (*Bradford City Local Studies Library*)

White Abbey Feeding Centre, Bradford, in 1908, with Mr Priestley and Dr Dessian
in attendance. Teachers were invited to assist with the serving of the meals on a
voluntary basis. By the spring of 1908 Bradford had thirteen dining centres in use.
(*Bradford City Local Studies Library*)

an imperial race, which could not be raised in the present 'rookeries and
slums'.[29]

The Boer War reinforced these concerns when recruitment statistics
revealed that about three out of every five men seeking to enlist in
Manchester in 1899 had to be rejected as physically unfit. Similar
evidence emerged for York, Leeds and Sheffield.[30] The government, in
alarm, appointed a special Interdepartmental Committee on Physical
Deterioration in 1903 to investigate the whole issue. It reported a year
later, and although in some respects its findings were reassuring, since they
showed that the most acute problems of ill health were confined to the
slums of the larger towns, it nonetheless recommended that a programme
to feed and medically inspect schoolchildren should be set up.[31]

Significantly, while these issues were being debated there was a growing
awareness that where Britain was failing to act, some of her continental
neighbours had already instituted welfare schemes, notably her great
trade rival, Germany, and France. In the 1880s, research into the health

of schoolchildren had been carried out in the newly-acquired German territory of Alsace-Lorraine, while the first school doctor was appointed at Frankfurt-am-Main in 1883. Two years later a similar appointment was made at Lausanne, Switzerland, and by the 1880s medical inspection of schools had been instituted in all the *departements* of France. By 1880 France had also established a well-organised system of school canteens. By contrast, England's first school medical officer was only recruited in 1890, when London took the initiative with a part-time appointment. Bradford followed in 1893, with the redoubtable Dr James Kerr the chosen candidate. He remained until 1902 when he moved to London to continue his reformist programme.

By 1905, in England and Wales as a whole there were forty-eight different areas making some provision for the medical inspection or supervision of schoolchildren. But the patchiness of the response underlined its heavy dependence on local interest and initiative.[32] Only the State could ensure effective action on a national scale.

It was against this background, therefore, that in 1906 and 1907 measures to provide for the public feeding and medical inspection of schoolchildren at last reached the statute book. The 1906 Education (Provision of Meals) Act permitted, though it did not compel, local education authorities to provide meals for elementary schoolchildren in their area. In so doing they could either work through charitably funded associations or make provision out of the rates. If they chose the rating option, the maximum sum they could levy was one halfpenny in the pound.[33] The Act also provided that pupils receiving meals could be charged for them and authorities might take defaulting parents to court to recover debts. In practice, this part of the legislation was a virtual dead letter.

Critics argued that such an indiscriminate approach would encourage parental irresponsibility and many authorities refused to adopt the school meals scheme. Among the laggards was Oxford, where the school medical officer declared in 1910 that if the city instituted the proposals it would do little good and might cause much harm.

> Bad nutrition is undoubtedly exercising a prejudicial effect on the health and the school work of a large number of children in Oxford but it is due in many cases as much to bad home conditions as to insufficient or improper food, though there are some really deserving cases where food alone is needed ... Something can be done by instruction at school to improve the home conditions and ... the nutrition and physique of the children, but the two lessons they must learn are to be self-reliant and to take a pride in themselves.[34]

If a few malnourished children suffered while those lessons were being absorbed, that was apparently just their misfortune.

Interestingly, though, not all children entitled to receive school meals wanted them. Some felt that to be selected was to be given a badge of poverty which they did not wish to wear. Among them was a girl who attended school in Norwich. As a member of a large family she could have had free dinners, 'but I couldn't lower my pride in accepting anything free. I also heard that boiled rice in water was sometimes served. This turned me completely from having school dinners.'[35]

In these circumstances the school meals scheme had a very limited success. By 1911-12 only 131 of the 322 education authorities in England and Wales had begun to provide the service and, of these, seventeen depended entirely upon voluntary contributions for support; nineteen used rate aid for administrative purposes only; and the remaining ninety-five used rate money for food.[36]

Bradford, a notable pioneer of child welfare at this time, was one of the ninety-five. Its central cooking depot, the first of its kind in the country,

Kitchen staff at the central cooking depot at Green Lane School, Bradford c. 1908. This central depot, the first of its kind in the country, was opened in October 1907 and from it cooked food was distributed to dining centres throughout the city. (*Bradford City Local Studies Library*)

Distribution of meals from Green Lane central depot, *c.* 1908. A motor wagon was especially built for the purpose by the city Tramways Committee and was hired by the Education Committee. (*Bradford City Local Studies Library*)

was constructed at Green Lane School in 1907. From it cooked food was distributed to dining centres throughout the city. When it opened in October 1907 the central cooking unit supplied 668 meals; within six months that daily total had almost trebled, and the number of dining centres had increased from six to thirteen.[37] Teachers were invited to assist with the serving of meals on a voluntary basis and so great was the response that no teacher was required to help more than once every three or four weeks. Breakfasts were also supplied to the most necessitous, and soon the education committee began to provide meals during school holidays as well, although it had no statutory powers to do this. Inevitably, the annual expenditure on meals exceeded the halfpenny rate product authorised, and, as a result, the authority was surcharged by the district auditor.

But these financial clashes with central government, reminiscent of disputes which have occurred between local and central government in the twenty-first century, did not discourage the Bradford councillors. They financed the surcharges out of profits earned by the Corporation's gas undertaking.

Elsewhere local education authorities which participated in the scheme began to make a virtue out of necessity by emphasizing that moral lessons could be given to the children along with the midday meal. As the Chief Medical Officer of the Board of Education solemnly observed in 1914, an orderly meal afforded 'an additional opportunity of teaching children good manners, kindliness to and consideration for others, and self-control'. This was the case in Halifax, for example, where the medical officer proudly reported that much of the training was being practised by the children at home. 'Parents have remarked: "The children wouldn't rest until I got them knives and forks to eat with."'[38] Likewise at a London cookery centre, some of the food provided for the infants was cooked by older girl pupils, who also made the bibs the children wore. The youngsters were seated at trestle tables decorated with flowers, and the older girls helped to wash the hands of their young charges before the dinner commenced. 'The children say Grace before the meal, behave quietly, and enjoy what they receive.'[39] This would seem to have been solid fare if the quoted menu of meat pie, vegetables and boiled rice with condensed milk and syrup sauce were in any way typical.

But in areas reluctant to take the initiative it was not until 1914 that the Board of Education was empowered to compel all authorities to feed necessitous children within their district. At the same time the halfpenny rate limit was removed from expenditure and government financial aid became available to help with the cost of meals.

School medical inspection was authorised in 1907. And, unlike meals, from the first an obligation was placed upon local education authorities to provide this service. They could also make arrangements to treat the children but many, anxious at the possible cost, or worried about annoying suspicious members of the medical profession, ignored that aspect. London, where medical care was already well established for schoolchildren, was one authority which took advantage of the opportunity to provide treatment. As early as 1910 a clinic was opened in Deptford as a result of a private initiative, and in 1911 the London County Council provided the clinic with its first grant for dental treatment. It followed this up a year later with grants for eye and ear cases and for the treatment of minor ailments.[40] By the end of 1912, eleven hospitals and seventeen treatment centres in the capital were caring for 54,000 children a year.

But often when illness was revealed as a result of medical inspection there was no treatment available. 'Many districts have nothing to offer but the local private practitioner and the poor law medical service,' anxiously commented the Board of Education's Chief Medical Officer in 1910. 'The fee of the former and the disadvantages of applying for poor law medical aid prove sufficiently prohibitive' for many. In Surrey, out of 1,991 children recommended for treatment (of 10,281 inspected) only 28.3 per cent actually received satisfactory medical attention. Likewise, in the Lindsey division of Lincolnshire a mere 24.8 per cent of 'defective' children were subsequently taken to the doctor. Overall, between 20 and 60 per cent of all the children requiring medical attention were estimated to be receiving

School nurse conducting an examination for head lice at Chaucer School, Bermondsey, in 1911, as part of the capital's school medical service. (*London Metropolitan Archives*)

School doctor examining the spine of a boy at Holland Street School, Southwark, 1911, in the presence of his mother. (*London Metropolitan Archives*)

treatment – which meant that a very high number remained untreated.[41] In 1913 the Chief Medical Officer also pinpointed the principal problems which the inspections had revealed. Out of six million children attending elementary schools in England and Wales, he estimated:

10% suffered from a serious vision defect
5% suffered from defective hearing
3% suffered from suppurating ears
3% had adenoids, or enlarged tonsils
50% suffered from injurious decay of their teeth
10% were unclean in their bodies
2% had tuberculosis
1% had heart disease
1% had ringworm[42]

As we have seen, the response of individual local authorities to these statistics was highly variable. While some provided effective treatment along the lines of that offered at Deptford in London, others took no action at all. Even in 1914, only just over three-quarters of LEAs made

Consultation with a parent during a medical examination at Holland Street School, Southwark, in May 1911. (*London Metropolitan Archives*)

Dental inspection at Deptford Children's Health Centre, 1911. This clinic had been established a year earlier, on an experimental basis, by Margaret McMillan and her sister. It received its first official grant for dental treatment in 1911 and for medical treatment a year later. (*London Metropolitan Archives*)

any treatment provision at all. These ranged from 204 dealing with 'minor ailments' and 195 with 'defective vision' to sixty-eight giving X-ray 'treatment for ringworm.[43]

Rural districts were particularly ill provided for because of their scattered population. In Devon a full-time dentist travelled around the schools with his portable equipment carried in the back of his car. He conducted inspections on the school premises and, in the case of small schools, the children were sometimes sent out to play while he carried out his work. In the rural areas of the West Riding of Yorkshire, dental apparatus was sent round from place to place by carrier's cart. This authority also provided cheap spectacles at prices ranging from 1s 2d to 2s 3d a pair, or entirely free in cases of necessity.[44] In Oxfordshire a determined attempt to tackle the high level of tooth decay among pupils led the Education Committee in 1909 to supply cost-price toothbrushes which parents could purchase from the respective head teachers.

Bradford, as ever, was particularly innovative. In 1908 it opened the first official school clinic in the country and one of its most notable developments here was the treatment of scalp ringworm by X-ray technique – a procedure which won wide acclaim. In 1910, the Board of Education's Chief Medical Officer described the Bradford school clinic as 'the most complete in England'.[45] It was part of the same approach that, even in the late nineteenth century, school baths and swimming pools had been established in the city.

By the early twentieth century almost two thousand Bradford children were visiting the baths each week, and certificates of swimming proficiency were being awarded. Swimming was, indeed, taken up in a growing number of urban elementary schools on the eve of the First World War.

Yet another child welfare initiative adopted by progressive local authorities like London and Bradford were open-air schools. They were set up to cater for children suffering from pulmonary complaints, heart trouble, anaemia or serious debility, and came at a time when over 3,000 children aged five to fourteen were dying each year from tuberculosis in England and Wales.

Like much child welfare, the first step was taken in Germany, where an open-air school was started at Charlottenberg near Berlin in 1904. In 1907, London began a similar experiment on land loaned by the Royal Arsenal Co-operative Society at Bostall Wood, Plumstead, with over a hundred youngsters nominated for admission from 9 a.m. to 6 p.m. on school days. They received three meals each day, served in temporary open buildings similar to those in which lessons were held. When the school closed for the winter after a three-month trial period, the pupils were considered to have benefited so greatly that the experiment was extended. In June 1908

Children resting at Birley House Open-Air School, Forest Hill, in July, 1908. The school was intended for children suffering from pulmonary complaints, heart trouble, anaemia or general debility. Rest was an important part of their treatment. (*London Metropolitan Archives*)

the London County Council opened three new schools, including Birley House, Dulwich, and Shrewsbury House, Shooters Hill. Each catered for about seventy-five children and instruction was given entirely in the open air. It was intended to combine education with treatment of the children, and initially the schools functioned only during the summer. However, in 1910 it was decided to keep Shrewsbury House open until the end of December, and a *Daily News* reporter who visited pupils in September contrasted their 'sickly appearance ... and languid air' on arrival in April with their current liveliness. They looked like 'ordinary ... London children ... recently returned from a country holiday'.[46] In order to ensure that they had plenty of rest, each pupil slept for about two hours after lunch in deckchairs or on the ground if the weather was suitable. Clothing was also provided where needed.

However, during wet weather the school sites became a quagmire, and in the winter the emphasis on open-air instruction was often uncomfortable. A girl who attended Birley House in 1917 recalled the discomforts of the winter months. She was the youngest of eleven children and went to Birley

Pupils resting at Shrewsbury House Open-Air School, Shooters Hill, in July 1908, under the watchful eye of a nurse. As at Birley House, the emphasis was on rest and fresh air. (*London Metropolitan Archives*)

Domestic science lesson conducted in the open air at Birley House, *c.* 1908. (*London Metropolitan Archives*)

Pupils at Bradford's first open-air school, opened at Thackley, in 1908. Nearly 300 children could be accommodated, travelling daily by tramcar in the charge of teachers, from the city. (*Bradford City Local Studies Library*)

The Forest School at Lord Mayor Treloar Cripples' Home (later changed to Hospital) and College, Alton, Hampshire, *c.* 1909. This was built in 1908 on the lines of the pioneering Forest School at Charlottenberg near Berlin. It was used as the summer class-room of the hospital school. This was itself an experimental venture which only came under the supervision of the Board of Education in 1913. (*Lord Mayor Treloar Hospital*)

House after receiving hospital treatment for TB glands. The class-rooms were spread around the grounds –

> I say 'classroom', but all we had was a covering over the top, so that we had fresh air all the time. It was agony in winter, we had to sleep out in the afternoons on hammocks, we had one blanket each, and had our outdoor clothes on all the time. These included hat, gloves and muff, which made writing difficult. We had to do gardening and lots of exercise. Our dining hall was also in the grounds and covered at the top only and we were made to eat everything, whether we liked it or not ... I travelled every day from home by tram, we were issued with tokens for the fare. When I was eleven, I was cured and went back to my old school.[47]

Pupils were examined regularly by a doctor whilst they were in attendance at the schools and there were always nurses on the premises. At a time when there was little effective treatment for TB sufferers, the spartan regime of the open-air schools, coupled with plentiful food, seems to have brought about a marked improvement in the health of many weak youngsters.

London's example was followed by authorities elsewhere, including Bradford, Sheffield, Halifax, Birmingham, Bristol, Norwich, Kettering, Lincoln and Aberdare. In all, twelve such schools were open by 1914, in addition to residential establishments like Lord Mayor Treloar Cripples' Hospital, Alton, Hampshire, which catered for youngsters suffering from tuberculous disease of the bones and joints. It was opened in 1908 as a result of the fund-raising efforts of Sir William Treloar, a Lord Mayor of London, and combined the role of hospital with that of school. By 1913 it was accommodating about 250 children from all over the country, of whom around a fifth were convalescent and able to be up and about, while the rest were confined to bed.[48]

Thackley open-air school, Bradford, also opened in 1908, was catering for around three hundred children six years later. Pupils came to the school daily by tramcar, and in addition to an open teaching veranda and a kitchen, a douche and slipper baths were provided.[49] Only the most delicate children were chosen to attend open-air schools because of their limited accommodation. But some of the benefits of open-air instruction were incorporated in the routine of the ordinary schools. Apart from the greater emphasis on outdoor physical exercise and gardening, open-air classes were conducted in a number of them. At Coventry, for example, shelters were erected at each end of the roof playground of one school, and here the regime adopted by the classes was not so strenuous or so rigid as in the rest of the school. After the midday break each child had to lie down on a resting stretcher for an hour and a half. In fact, so great

Crippled children on rheir way to the 'open-air' school at Alton under the watchful eye of a nurse, *c.* 1909. The Treloar hospital was opened in 1908 with the help of funds raised by Sir William Treloar while he was Lord Mayor of London. It treated children up to the age of twelve suffering from tuberculous disease of the bones or joints. They were sent to Alton from all over the country, with about 250 of them in residence by 1913. Around 90 per cent of the 900 children treated between 1908 and 1913 benefited from their stay. Each remained on average between one and three years. (*Lord Mayor Treloar Hospital*)

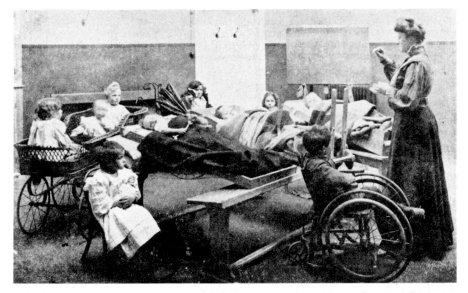

Young patients being taught in a winter class-room at the Lord Mayor Treloar Cripples' Home *c.* 1909. (*Lord Mayor Treloar Hospital*)

Children at the aviary at Lord Mayor Treloar Cripples' Home, *c.* 1909. Every effort was made to keep them happy and contented during their stay. Whilst in residence they were clothed at the hospital's expense. (*Lord Mayor Treloar Hospital*)

had the vogue for open-air instruction become by 1914 that the Board of Education's Chief Medical Officer declared that 'any scheme' to utilise cheap, temporary buildings for open-air schools or class-rooms would be considered by the authorities.[50]

By the eve of the First World War, then, a radical shift had occurred in attitudes towards child welfare. The health of the elementary pupil had become a matter of public concern, and initiatives were being taken on a variety of fronts to assist those who were now perceived as the nation's future. It was very different from the situation forty years before when a Chief Inspector of Schools could proclaim to general approval that it was the school's duty only 'to provide healthy and suitable buildings, and to place the scholar in the midst of proper moral and mental surroundings ... a school is established for the purposes of instruction, and not for the purpose of ... mixing up with it the administration of food and medicine to the children of the poor.'[51] Symbolic of the changing approach was the concern aroused in 1901 by the publication of Seebohm Rowntree's social survey of York. This revealed that boys from the poorest homes in the city were, at thirteen years of age, on average 11 lb lighter and 3 ½ in shorter than those even from better-off working-class homes. If comparison had been made with middle-class boys, the contrast would have been still greater.[52] It was to counter what Rowntree called the 'serious physical deterioration amongst the poorest section of the community' that the post-1906 welfare proposals were introduced.

CHAPTER FOUR

Children at Work

I began to work for my Aunt Alice, when I was nine and a half years of age. She and her husband were hand-loom weavers ... My job was to reach the threads in when my aunt was healding the warp ready for it being woven ... My first wage for a full day's labour was threepence for my mother, a half penny for myself, and a new-baked currant tea cake to eat on my way home. Wasn't I 'chuff' when I could swank home with a bit of wage!

Ben Turner, *About Myself 1863-1930* (1930).

In most working-class families in Victorian England it was expected that the children would contribute to the running of the household as soon as they were able. Often this meant helping their parents around the home, and up to the First World War domestic tasks occupied countless schoolchildren in their leisure hours. The boys usually took on the heavier jobs, carrying coal and water, sweeping the yard, running errands, helping in the garden and similar tasks. Their sisters were more likely to be engaged in domestic chores, with many kept away from school to help with the weekly wash, or to look after younger members of the family while their mother was at work. Mrs Wrigley, who was born in Cefn Mawr, Wales, remembered that when her mother went out sewing for 1s a day in the 1860s, she stayed at home to look after the rest of the children. At other times she had to walk to the pit bank two miles away to gather coal for the fire, carrying it home in a basket on her head. 'I also had to go ... to a farmhouse for buttermilk ... Clear water we had to carry on our heads from some spring well.'[1] On Saturdays she went out cleaning the floors and backyards of neighbours' houses for a penny a time, plus a piece of bread and butter, and on working

Most working-class children were expected to help with household chores, including the pumping of water. (*Museum of English Rural Life, Reading University*)

Helping to feed the family pig, 1910. (*Museum of English Rural Life, Reading University*)

days carried dinners and suppers to employees at the local iron forge for twopence a week.

Half a century later similar chores were still being carried out by young children. Indeed, a government report in 1901 claimed that the 'severest work, the longest hours, and the hardest conditions' were 'often to be found in the case of children ... employed without wages in doing housework in the homes of their parents'.

Particularly affected were the sons and daughters of women who took in washing. Whilst the older ones toiled at washtub, mangle and ironing board, the youngest sorted and packaged the laundry bundles, carried in dry clothes for ironing and helped deliver the finished bundles to their mothers' clients. One girl recalled how she and her sister worked late into the night turning the handle of the mangle, 'so as to have as many clothes as possible ready for delivering to the customers next morning before we went to school'. Of the mangle which dominated their existence, she declared, 'It wasn't only the clothes you pressed – you mangled out our young lives.'[2]

On small farms both sons and daughters were expected to help around the holding, with the boys involved in weeding the crops, haymaking and harvesting, while their sisters worked in the dairy, fed the livestock and helped to prepare poultry for market. On one typical holding in Cardigan

Farmer's daughter at Chinnor, Oxfordshire, assisting her elders to pluck geese for market, while her brother and sister look on, *c.* 1900.

A group of harvesters at Cwm Prysor, Trawsfynydd, Merioneth, in 1909. The children of small farming families were expected to lend a hand around the parental holding, especially at the busy seasons of the year. (*National Museum of Wales. Welsh Folk Museum*)

it was reported that the farmer's ten-year-old daughter not only helped to milk the cows and operated the cream separator but assisted her mother in making the butter. So widespread was this practice in the county that by the time girls reached the age of fifteen they were 'competent to perform all the lighter tasks that generally fall to the lot of women on farms'.[3]

But while this ready use of unpaid juvenile labour around home and farm continued up to 1914, in other areas of child employment a more critical attitude began to develop. Especially in the textile districts in the north of England, where youngsters were recruited into the mills in relatively large numbers, the age at which they should begin paid work was fiercely debated.

It was the growth of the factory system at the end of the eighteenth century which first turned public attention to the need to regulate child labour. In an effort to protect youngsters working in the new textile mills, and to ensure that they received a little schooling, a series of Factory Acts

Half-timers employed in Farnworth, Bolton, c. 1900. The photograph was taken by Mr J. W. Pickford, manager of the *Farnworth Journal* and a long-time critic of the half-time system. (*Farnworth Library, Bolton*)

Half-timers at Horrockses, Crewdson & Co. Ltd.'s Lorne Street Mill, Moses Gate, Farnworth, pre-1914. In 1899, the *Daily News* reported that the firm had the largest weaving shed in the United Kingdom and employed about a hundred half-timers. It commented also that many of them were under-sized and under-weight for their age. In the following year Horrockses were unsuccessfully prosecuted by the factory inspector for employing a boy from a very poor family who was under the legal age for half-time work. The magistrates, however, refused to convict. Half-time work finally came to an end in the early 1920s (under the terms of the 1918 Education Act). (*Farnworth Library, Bolton*)

was passed, commencing in 1802 with an ineffective measure to regulate the hours and conditions of young pauper apprentices. These led eventually in 1844 to legislation prohibiting the employment of any child below the age of eight in a textile factory.

Between eight and thirteen he or she must attend an approved elementary school for three hours a day. The 1844 Act also limited the hours youngsters could work to a maximum of 6½ per day, though over the years that was reduced. From 1874 the minimum working age was raised to ten, and four years later the same minimum age was applied to non-textile factories and workshops covered by the legislation. Thus was born the 'half-time' system, combining employment and education. With modifications it was to survive until 1918. Over the years the regulations it introduced were extended to a wide range of trades, including metalwork and pottery, as well as cottage industries like lacemaking, and strawplaiting for the hat and bonnet trade. Agriculture and domestic service, which were both major employers of juvenile labour were, however, not included and, in the case of mining, there was no requirement for youngsters to attend school. The prohibition in this case merely related to the age at which they might begin work underground, while girls were forbidden to work underground altogether.

The protection afforded young workers by the Factory Acts was very limited, but many recognised that without it the plight of the children would have been far worse. In 1864 a factory inspector described the 'half-time Act' as 'a godsend to the Potteries, it being the only opportunity whereby the poor children can gain any education'. HMI Tufnell put the matter still more starkly when he commented that 'the question with the parents frequently is, education on the half-time plan, or no education at all'.[4]

But by the end of the nineteenth century, as juvenile labour was reduced in major parts of the economy as a result of changes in production methods and a stricter application of educational by-laws, its continuation in textiles was seen as depriving many poor children of their schooling. In 1876 there were 201,284 half-timers at work in the nation at large, and that had declined only a little to 175,437 in 1890 (of whom over 52 per cent were in Lancashire).[5] Even in 1897 (four years after the minimum employment age had been raised to eleven), there were still 110,654 half-timers at work, of whom over 54 per cent lived in Lancashire. Not until the eve of the First World War did the total of half-timers move strongly and permanently downward, to reach 70,255 by 1911-12. Of this number, over 39,000 were employed in Lancashire and a further 19,651 in the West Riding of Yorkshire (with 8,355 in Bradford alone). The rest of England contributed a mere 11,402 youngsters.[6]

Meanwhile, although the Factory Acts had been intended as 'rescue agencies' for young workers, the regime they introduced, combining school and employment, was extremely arduous. One youngster involved was Ben Turner, who was born at Austonley near Huddersfield in 1863. After working for about six months for his aunt, who was a hand-loom weaver, he entered a local woollen factory at the age of ten. Like other half-timers, Ben began work at 6 a.m., and continued until 12.30 p.m. with a half-hour break for breakfast. 'We then had to go to school from 2 to 4.30 p.m.' The next week he went to school from 9 a.m. until 12 noon, and to work from 1.30 p.m. until 6 p.m., and this alternating pattern was continued in succeeding weeks. The morning stint at the mill was particularly tiring, with the youngsters rising at 5 a.m. in order to eat their breakfast of bread and treacle, before scurrying off to work. 'In winter we would creep into the boiler house, ... warm our frozen hands a bit and be in to work just on the stroke of six.'[7] For this he was paid the princely sum of 2s 6d a week.

Left: A little piecer at work in Oldham, *c.* 1900. Oldham, like Bolton, was a major centre of half-time labour. (*Oldham Local Studies Library Collection*)

Below: A little piecer working on a mule in an Oldham spinning mill, *c.* 1900. (*Oldham Local Studies Library Collection*)

John R. Clynes was another half-timer, this time in an Oldham cotton mill. He recalled the deafening noise of the machinery and the danger it posed. He began as a 'little piecer' in a local factory when he reached the age of ten. There he worked among the rows of huge spinning-frames, with their thousands of whirling spindles:

Often the threads on the spindles broke as they were stretched and twisted and spun. These broken ends had to be instantly repaired ... That was my job. I performed it, unresting, in my bare feet, since leather on those oil-soaked floors would have been treacherous. Often I fell, rolling instinctively and in terror from beneath the gliding jennies, well aware that horrible mutilation or death would result if the advancing monsters overtook and gripped me. Sometimes splinters as keen as daggers drove through my naked feet, leaving aching wounds from which dribbles of blood oozed forth to add to the slipperiness of the floor ...

Running in and out, straining my eyes in the gas-lit gloom to watch for broken threads, my ten-year-old legs soon felt like lead and my head spun faster than the pitiless machinery ... School somehow seemed less terrifying and revolting once I had become a half-timer in the mill. [8]

As late as 1908 factory inspectors were still prosecuting employers for illegally allowing children to clean spinning machinery whilst it was in motion, though the fines of £1 or so imposed by magistrates were hardly likely to act as a deterrent. Some young workers were also ill treated by foremen or overlookers.

To add to these hardships, half-timers employed in cotton mills had to endure the great heat and humidity required by the production process. Temperatures of 90° F were recorded in many spinning and weaving sheds, and it was common for lads to work only in thin trousers, while the girls wore a light petticoat. When the breakfast break came they would rush out into the biting cold of a winter's day still clad in these clothes. Their pallid, drawn features and stunted growth were commented upon by visitors. A *Daily News* correspondent in 1899 described youngsters he had encountered in Bolton as the 'veriest little mites indeed. Several little girls who gave me their ages as 12 and 13, looked more fitted to nurse dolls ... than to be engaged in the serious work of earning a living.'[9] And Dr Torrop of Heywood, Lancashire, lamented how soon the 'promising child of ten [degenerated] into the lean and sallow young person of thirteen ... insidious diseases settle in their lungs, the blood is squeezed out of their faces, their limbs lose their youthful straightness and vigour.'[10]

Yet, despite this, most youngsters were proud to contribute to family income and to feel they had entered the adult world. When a child became a half-timer, observed a report of 1909, it considered it was 'going out into the world ... It thinks itself grown up. It tends to care more for the mill than the school, and to copy the talk of mill hands.'[11] Inevitably, behaviour in school deteriorated, with teachers complaining of sullenness, bad language and general indiscipline. 'The half-timer has less pride in appearance,' declared the head of Moorside Mixed School, Halifax, in a typical comment.[12]

Many contemporaries, however, also noted the weariness of the young workers when they came to school after working in the factory. Allen Clarke, who had himself been a half-timer in Bolton before qualifying as an elementary school teacher, remembered excusing some half-timers their lessons because they were so tired. 'I have seen them fall asleep over their lesson books or tasks, after they have been in the factory all the morning ... it was often downright cruelty to force them along the curriculum fixed by the Education Code.'[13]

Meanwhile, numerous other occupations with large numbers of child workers remained virtually unregulated up to the 1870s. This was true of youngsters employed in agriculture, for example, save for those recruited into public gangs, who were covered by the 1867 Gangs Act. Even then, the restraints imposed were not very severe, the main ones being that children under eight could not work in publicly recruited gangs (though they could still work privately for individual farmers), while gangs of mixed sex were prohibited, and all gangmasters had to be licensed by the magistrates. This measure was passed in response to the findings of the Sixth Report of the Children's Employment Commission, which had revealed the appalling conditions under which many youngsters laboured on the large arable holdings of East Anglia during the 1860s. Cases were quoted of children as young as six being employed in weeding, hoeing, stonepicking and similar tasks from 8 a.m. to 6 p.m. during the summer months. In one case a little girl of four had to be carried by her father to the fields, and it was 'common practice' for parents to stipulate that if older children were hired the younger ones must be taken on too. If the gangs were working a long distance from home, the children might have to leave as early as 5 a.m. and not return before 8 in the evening. A little boy of six was said to have

regularly walked more than six miles out to work, and often to come home so tired that he could scarcely stand ... When the gang has a long distance to go the children become so exhausted, that the elder ones are seen dragging the younger ones home, sometimes carrying them on their backs. In winter, the children often return from the fields crying from the cold.[14]

Children working in an agricultural gang in East Anglia, *c.* 1860. Under the 1867 Agricultural Gangs Act it became illegal to employ children in public gangs under the age of eight or to recruit gangs of mixed sex. But young children continued to work on the land on a part-time basis to the end of the century.

Since the gangmaster's income depended on the amount of work he could extract from his young charges, beatings were administered to those who were slow or were not concentrating on their work. Although the size and composition of gangs varied from area to area, in most of them children predominated. Thus, in a Northamptonshire gang of seventy-two members, thirty-five of the boys and twenty-six of the girls were between seven and twelve years, plus six boys under seven (including one five-year-old).

It was to eliminate the worst aspects of gang labour that the 1867 Act was passed. Unfortunately, as we have seen, it did not apply to children employed in agriculture outside the public gangs. Nor did it prevent youngsters over the age of eight from becoming gang members. It was left to the education legislation of the 1870s and beyond to tackle this by establishing a minimum employment age of ten, and laying down that unless children could pass a leaving examination as specified in local by-laws, they must remain at school until fourteen. Partial exemption was, however, permitted to those who had made a certain number of attendances, and the restrictions were also relaxed for seasonal agricultural demands. One farmer from Hunmanby, Yorkshire, claimed that in his area as late as 1901 the requirements of the Education Acts were suspended for three weeks each year at the end of May and the beginning of June, so that youngsters over eight years could be employed in weeding the corn. He admitted that the three weeks were 'sometimes prolonged' well beyond this ostensible limit.[15] In other cases, the exact timing of the summer or 'harvest' holiday at school would be influenced by the ripeness of the corn, while areas engaged in pea-, hop-and fruit-picking arranged holidays to coincide with these.[16] Indeed, as school log-books show, if holidays were not granted, the children simply stayed away as soon as paid employment offered itself. For parents were anxious that their offspring should contribute to family income, and farmers wanted the use of cheap labour at the busy periods of the agricultural year.

Many farmers, too, doubted the merit of educating labourers' children anyway, believing that this filled them with unhealthy ambitions about their future employment and made them reluctant to take up land work in later life. There was also a belief that only those who began at an early age would become efficient adult labourers. In the 1860s some large farmers asserted that 'unless a boy begins to work at 6 or 7, or at the latest at 8, he will never grow into the man he ought to be'.[17] And as late as 1901 a Berkshire farmer claimed that the agricultural interest had suffered because boys were being kept at school until they were thirteen: 'by that time ... they know there is wide world, and it is

This 1903 photograph shows children gleaning, perhaps to gather grain for animal fodder or to be taken to the miller to be ground into flour for family bread making. (*Museum of English Rural Life, Reading University*)

not likely they will follow a plough and stay in a dull country village where there is so little chance of preferment, when so many are required for the Army, Navy, policemen, porters, and postmen.'[18] Men like him blamed education for the large-scale migration of young people from the countryside to the towns which was taking place in the final years of the nineteenth century.

With such hostile attitudes towards education among rural employers, there was often a reluctance among local magistrates to prosecute parents and employers for infringements of the attendance by-laws. HMI Howard sourly summarised the general position in 1898:

> So long as certain farming operations can be performed by children ... it appears that employers and parents will continue to break the law, magistrates will be slow to convict, school attendance committees will not press cases against employers and parents, managers will not furnish names of offenders for fear of ... making the school unpopular, and teachers will not make enemies by furnishing information.[19]

Only in the twentieth century, with changes in farming methods and a more critical overall attitude towards child employment, were these problems gradually eliminated. Prior to this, teachers faced difficulties like those experienced by the head of Westleigh School, Devon, who noted in

1880 that he had, 'Sent to one farmer for six boys employed in mangel picking. Received a message to the effect that when he wanted boys he should have them, and that I was not to enquire for them again.' Even a decade later things had hardly improved:

> It seems that parents take 'job work' at a reduced rate, reckoning on the assistance of the children. When I remonstrate, they tell me I must talk to 'Master', for they must either be better paid or have help from the children ... The Board Members will persist in employing boys under age. All are guilty alike, and of course they cannot summon when themselves are the chief offenders.[20]

One of the many youngsters who undertook part-time farm work during the school holidays was Fred Kitchen. His father had died in about 1902, when he was only eleven, and the following year he spent a fortnight at Whitsuntide and five weeks in the summer singling turnips at daily wages of 1s and 1s 6d, respectively. He later wrote:

> I shall never forget that five weeks – it was the longest holiday I have ever had. I worked from six a.m. to six p.m. and six days a week. But I stuck it, and proudly took home nine shillings each Saturday night ... I bent over the hot earth till the blood ran into my head and I couldn't see whether I'd left two plants or one. Day after day I stooped along the rows with the scorching sun blistering my neck.[21]

Kitchen finally left school in March 1904, and immediately got a job as a day-lad on a nearby farm at a wage of 1s 3d a day, working from 6.30 a.m. to 5.30 p.m., 'and proud I was to carry home on Saturday night three bright half-crowns'. At the 1911 census of population, when just over a fifth of all boys aged thirteen were recorded as in employment, one in ten of them worked on the land – though this was exceeded by more than one in four working as messengers, porters, etc. and more than one in five employed in the textile industries. Teachers often deplored the adverse effect on attendance levels of some of these attempts to earn money, yet sympathised with the children in their efforts to supplement an inadequate family income. In 1901 the headmistress of Ricardo Street Board School in Tower Hamlets, London, realised about a quarter of her pupils were earning wages in their spare time; yet she admitted that in approximately half the cases family poverty made this an 'absolute necessity'. In one instance the father was a helpless invalid and the mother was a trouser finisher, who was assisted by her daughter: 'the child works 60 hours a week ... I think when a child has reached the 6th standard ... she would be

Girls learning the skills of the cottage lace trade at Mrs Dobbins' lace school at Stokenchurch, Buckinghamshire, in 1860. (*High Wycombe Central Library*)

far better helping her parents than being at school'.[22] In another example, the headmaster of Vauxhall Street Board School, London, personally arranged Saturday jobs as a reward for boys who had attended well during the week. Twenty-five of them were regularly recruited as messenger boys, working from 9.30 or 10 a.m. until the late afternoon for a wage of 1s 6d.[23]

Occasionally, too, the education authorities bent their own regulations and allowed children who had not reached exemption standard to leave school permanently. Among them was Florence Plummer, the eldest of eight children, whose father had deserted the family. Her mother was unable to work, they were in arrears with their rent and were dependent on charity for their subsistence. Two of the children were permanent invalids, and if Florence were not allowed to work the family would probably have to go to the workhouse. The London Education Committee agreed to her exemption.[24]

Many parents therefore resisted attempts to limit the use of their children's labour and, often enough, evaded the restrictions where they could. In Lancashire, even in the 1890s, textile workers opposed attempts to raise the minimum working age of half-timers and, although a minimum of twelve was eventually introduced, it was in the face of what Allen Clarke, a former teacher, called the 'most strenuous opposition' of the operatives.

> Why was this? Because under the piece-work system the spinner or weaver is the employer of the child, and pays the half-timer out of his own earnings. Hence, the cheaper child labour is, the better pecuniarily for the spinner or the weaver.
>
> Money seems to be the first consideration with most cotton operatives; the health and happiness and even lives of their children are but of very minor importance ... Often in a Lancashire town you'll hear some coarse woman remark: 'Ay, So-and-so's not sendin' their Jack or Polly to t'factory; they're makin' 'em stuck-up an' consated. But *my* childer will have to go to t' spinnin' and weivin' whether they like it or not. I had for t' do it, and so must they' ... Many Lancashire mothers only love their children for what they can get out of them.[25]

Similar motives were attributed to the parents of youngsters engaged in some of the cottage industries, like pillow lacemaking, straw plaiting or gloving, especially in the 1870s. In all three, youngsters began to learn their trade at an early age, often as young as five or six in the case of lace and plait. A number of those so occupied were sent to learn their skills at special 'schools' conducted in a cottage by women (and occasionally men) whose only recommendation was perhaps their aptitude for the craft or, more likely, their ability to extract the maximum output from their young charges by the exercise of stern discipline.

Pillow lace was produced on a hard round cushion, stuffed with straw, which was supported either on the worker's knees or partly upon her knees and partly upon a three-legged pillow-horse or a bench. The parchment pattern for the lace the workers were to produce was fixed on the pillow, while the threads with which the fabric was formed were wound on bobbins about the size of a small pencil. In some lace schools as many as twenty or thirty children were crammed into a room only twelve feet square. Heating was provided by earthenware pots of hot ashes, known as 'dicky pots', which were placed at the feet of the young workers and emitted acrid fumes which added to the generally fetid atmosphere. There was little freedom of movement, as workers bent awkwardly over the pillow.[26]

Girls who did not progress with their work as well as expected would be beaten as they bent over the pillow, and during the winter months their eyes were strained by the effort to produce intricate patterns by the dim light of candles.

Even when the lace trade went into decline in the 1860s and 1870s, many young girls, like this one, learnt the craft from their mothers or sisters. Here the lace pillow can be seen, fitted up with its bobbins. (*Buckinghamshire County Museum*)

When completed, the lace was sold by parents to local dealers, often by a use of the illegal truck system, whereby items of grocery or drapery were accepted by the sellers rather than cash. However, families living in remote rural communities had little choice but to accept the dealers' terms, for they had no direct access to the urban dressmakers who used the lace eventually.

In 1867 a Workshops Regulation Act for the first time afforded domestic workers a protection similar to that previously given to youngsters employed in factories and the larger workshops. Under it, no child could be employed in a handicraft below the age of eight, while between eight and thirteen he or she could work only in accordance with the half-time system. Unfortunately, the legislation was difficult to enforce, given the scattered nature of the lacemaking villages and the fact that parents resented what they saw as an unwarranted interference by officialdom in their right to dispose of their children's labour as they saw fit. Long after 1867, an Assistant Factory Inspector observed bitterly of the Devon lace trade that there were 'still parents who think that they have brought children into the world to no purpose, if they do not become contributors to the family purse as soon as they can hold a lace pillow, or shuffle a lace stick', i.e. a bobbin.[27]

Although the Workshops Act may have thus reduced child employment to a limited extent, the main reason for the sharp decline in the number of young lacemakers which occurred in the 1870s was the collapse of the trade itself in the face of more intense competition from cheaper machine-made lace, and of changes in women's fashions. The education legislation of the decade reinforced that trend, and helped to eliminate the lace schools. Nevertheless, under parental pressure, a few youngsters continued to learn the craft during their leisure hours. Mrs E. Turney, who was born in about 1900 at Great Horwood, a noted Buckinghamshire lace centre, remembered starting to practise the craft when she was about five. At first she worked on the end of her mother's pillow but gradually progressed until she could make '8-pin lace ... As I went to school I used to take my pillow and there were five or six other girls ... who used to take their pillows with them to school and I used to teach them the right way to work it.'[28]

When she arrived home in the afterrnoon, she ate her tea and then 'the chair was put down before the pillow', and she had to make lace. 'Mother would always stand guard.'

Similar conditions applied in respect of straw plaiting, which was concentrated in Bedfordshire, Buckinghamshire, Hertfordshire and Essex, but especially around the principal hatmaking towns of Luton and Dunstable. Unlike the lace schools, where the threads and patterns

used were normally provided by the mistress, in their plait counterparts
the bundles of split and bleached or dyed straws needed were supplied
by parents, who purchased them from the dealers. Older children were
expected to make about twenty or thirty yards of plait a day, and if
they failed to reach their target they would be kept at work until they
had attained it. In both the lace and plait trades, girls comprised the
main body of child workers; at the 1871 census, Bedfordshire, with over
20,000 females working as plaiters, had about one in three of all girls
in the county aged ten to fifteen so occupied, while about one in nine of
Buckinghamshire girls in the same age group worked as lacemakers.[29] As
with lacemaking, it was only with the collapse of the trade from the 1870s
onwards, as hatmakers started to use foreign plaits on a large scale, that the
widespread employment of children came to an end in the plait districts.
In the interim, factory inspectors seeking to enforce the 1867 Workshops
Act bewailed the way 'children would slip out through the back door' of a
plait school 'when anyone in authority called', while the number working

A straw-plaiting school from *The Queen*, 9 November 1861.

at home was 'too great to be dealt with by the factory inspectorate or the police'.[30]

Teachers usually regarded the attendance of the half-timers with a marked lack of enthusiasm, even when they were sent to school. In part this was because they disrupted the normal routine. At Ivinghoe, Buckinghamshire, a major plait centre, where as late as January 1875 the majority of pupils in the village school were half-timers, the master bemoaned their poor attendance. Regular visits by the factory inspector brought about some improvement but, as the master wrote in his log-book in March 1877, most parents 'would not send their children to school if they could help, hence they keep them as much as they can. This is the great drawback to the progress of the children.'[31]

In the major textile areas, where the half-time system was most prevalent, these disruptions were, of course, far more serious. Teachers' anxieties were made particularly acute by the 1862 Revised Code and its successors, since the half-timers were supposed to achieve the same standard at the annual school inspection as their full-time fellow pupils, despite their reduced hours of tuition. The net effect was that the full-timers were held back in the interests of those attending part-time. In Bradford, where the half-time system was widespread in the worsted mills, those attending full-time were said to have 'no further advantage over half-timers than of getting the same lesson twice over. They are not carried forward to any new educational ground.' A similar situation applied in Oldham.[32]

By the 1880s educators were increasingly critical of the half-time system. *The Schoolmaster*, journal of the National Union of Teachers, was scathing about those who claimed that early contact with the world of work sharpened the children's wits and gave them a technical education. In an article published in February 1895 it asked ironically:

If there is anything in this technical education and 'wit sharpening' theory, why is it confined to the offspring of the worker? Millowners, daily in contact with the half-timer, send their offspring to Eton, Harrow, or Rugby, to Oxford or Cambridge. Why are the children of the rich denied the advantages of the 'wit sharpening' that comes from ... 'piecing', 'tenting,' and scavenging'?[33]

Yet the half-time system had its supporters. One such was a Bolton cotton manager interviewed by the *Daily News* in 1899. He claimed that the system was beneficial because it provided the children with a change of occupation during the day, between school and work. It also instilled manual skills which would be needed in later life. These must be acquired at the 'earliest reasonable moment ... there is no doubt that a child at

Girl plaiters at Titmore Green, near Stevenage, *c.* 1900. Although the plait trade had been hit by imports of foreign plaits from the Far East and Italy, some women and girls continued to practise the craft, selling their plait to local dealers for a mere pittance. They, in turn, disposed of it to hatmakers in the area. (*Hitchin Museum*)

11 becomes more dextrous than one first employed at 13 or 14.'[34] But by the 1890s the opponents of the system were gaining ground. At the beginning of the twentieth century, despite the opposition of textile factory operatives and owners, the minimum working age was raised to twelve and discussions were under way for phasing out the system entirely. In the event, these did not reach fruition until 1918.

It was in these circumstances that the Interdepartmental Committee on the Employment of School Children could observe in 1901 that child employment 'in most large industries' was now 'carefully regulated and in some dangerous cases prohibited ... while children [were] forbidden to do any [unregulated] work during school hours.'[35] However, it then went on to point out that, outside school hours, their employment in many occupations was still unrestricted. 'Provided they make 8 or 10 school attendances every week they may be employed (with a few exceptions and these little enforced) in the streets, in the fields, in shops, or at home, for the longest possible hours and on the hardest and most irksome work,

Street trading was a popular part-time job for children from the city slums during the Victorian and Edwardian period. This Manchester newspaper seller, c. 1903, bears all the signs of impudent defiance which so concerned the moralists of the day. (*Working Class Movement Library, Salford*)

without any limit or regulation.' At that date the committee estimated about 150,000 children attending school full-time were employed out of school hours for wages; of that total, around 40,000 worked for more than twenty hours a week.[36] In all, perhaps 6½ per cent of all elementary schoolchildren in London were working out of school hours, and 7½ per cent of those in Liverpool, compared to 4 per cent in the nation as a whole.

Most of these youngsters were casually employed as messengers, matchbox makers, street sellers, errand boys and, in the case of girls, as domestic servants. Their employment was, of course, not new. In 1872 when the Liverpool police undertook a street census of vagrant waifs, they picked up nearly a thousand youngsters. These included sixty-six employed as shoeblacks, 112 selling sand, sixty-one selling newspapers and forty-nine gathering rags. Most were helping to support their families, and less than a quarter had ever been to school.[37]

Just over twenty years later, similar motives of family poverty encouraged Walter Southgate in Bethnal Green to seek part-time employment, though in his case this was combined with exemplary school attendance. One way he earned a few pence was by offering to carry the parcels of people he

Another common part-time occupation for boys was helping in the delivery of milk. This Berrylands Farm milk cart was delivering milk in Surbiton, Surrey, c. 1900. (*Museum of English Rural Life, Reading University*)

Gardener's boy at work in Oxford with potato planter, *c.* 1900. (*Oxfordshire County Council Libraries*)

met in the street. Then in 1902, at the age of twelve, he became a barrow boy for a local milkman. He had to start work at 6 a.m. each day, pushing the heavily laden barrow along and carrying cans of milk to the doorsteps. Later he described the exhausting routine:

> I worked seven days a week and was engaged on an average 40 hours a week for 3/6 ... before and after school hours ... Although I kept my job for nearly two years I sometimes experienced great fatigue, dropping off to sleep about 3 o'clock on Sundays and sleeping round the clock until five o'clock the next morning. On Saturdays between the three rounds I was engaged in polishing up the brass-covered milk churns and barrow with brick dust and lemon. It became a habit with me to get up at about five o'clock and spend 15 minutes in the local coffee house ... swallowing a cup of hot tea and a slice of bread and dripping.[38]

Many similar cases were reported by the 1901 Committee on the Employment of School Children, including a twelve-year-old lad who rose between three and four each morning to knock up twenty-five working men. He then sold newspapers from 6 a.m. to 9 a.m. and afterwards attended school, 'but often slept during lessons'.[39] In yet another example, four sisters, aged 12, 10, 9 and 8, worked at home for between 44 and 50 hours a week chopping wood for sale.

Another variation on the street trading theme – shoeblacks by the Byrne Fountain, Scotland Place, Liverpool, *c.* 1895. (*Liverpool Record Office*)

Street hawking was also a common occupation for urban children, particularly in London and the larger towns. At the turn of the century both Liverpool and Manchester attempted to regulate entry to it by insisting that the youngsters be duly licensed, but, in practice, the restrictions remained a virtual dead letter.[40] The 1901 Committee was severe in its condemnation of the moral effects of such casual work: 'employment in the centre of many large towns makes the streets hotbeds for the corruption of children, who learn to drink, to gamble, and to use foul language, while girls are exposed to even worse things.'

It was in response to these findings that in 1903 a new Employment of Children Act prohibited the use of child labour between the hours of 9 p.m. and 6 a.m. and also in any occupations likely to injure life, limb, health or education. But such restrictions were easier to enact than to enforce, especially where children worked at home. In 1904, Robert Sherard found small children in the courts and closes of Birmingham engaged in wrapping hairpins in paper for 2¼d per thousand packets, or bending the tin clasp round safety pins for 1d a day. One evening, in a house off Jennens Row, he discovered three youngsters sitting at a table piled high with cards and a vast number of tangled hooks and eyes. They were working as quickly as

Children engaged in 'sweated' trades in the home were among the most exploited part-time employees in the early twentieth century. A mother and her children at work making boxes. (*Working Class Movement Library, Salford*)

Domestic service employed more young girls than any other single occupation up to the First World War. This thirteen-year-old maid-of-all-work was employed by an artist and his wife in London in 1911. Her wage was £5 a year.

AN EYE TO BUSINESS.

"NOW, THEN SEE WHAT YOU'VE DONE WI' YOUR LARKIN I WOULDN'T CARE
BUT—RIGHT AFORE THE CUSTOMER'S WINDER!"

An errand boy in difficulty as depicted by *Punch* in 1871.

they could. The eldest, aged eleven, and her sister, aged nine, were sewing the hooks and eyes on to the cards, while the third child, a small boy of five, fastened them together. They were too busy to raise their eyes from their task when Sherard entered the room.[41]

After they left school, such youngsters usually drifted into poorly paid unskilled jobs. For the girls, this often meant employment as a maid-of-all-work, scrubbing, polishing, preparing meals and serving at table, usually in a small household for a few shillings a week; or, in the north of England, employment in a textile factory. At the 1911 census of population nearly a third of all girls aged fourteen and fifteen years who were in occupations worked as domestic servants, while well over a third more were engaged in the manufacture of textiles or clothing.[42] For the boys, there was frequently short-term employment as messengers and errand boys before they entered the adult world as unskilled labourers. As a modern historian has put it, such a youngster 'passed from job to job' in an 'almost unconscious progress' which further condemned him 'to a life's work that would bring him as little personal satisfaction as it would financial reward'. Only the most fortunate gained an apprenticeship which gave entry to a skilled trade, or took up one of the growing number of clerical posts which were becoming available in commerce and industry. In 1899 a Board of Trade return of a representative sample of male school leavers in London revealed that 40 per cent were destined to become errand or van boys, while 14 per cent more became shop boys, and 8 per cent office boys or junior clerks. Less than a third took up apprenticeships leading to jobs classified as skilled. So it was that in England and Wales as a whole in 1911 nearly a quarter of all fourteen-year-old lads in employment worked as messengers, errand boys and the like; a mere one in thirty-five worked as a clerk.[43]

CHAPTER FIVE

Leisure and Pleasure

Errand-going, night or day, children found a detested chore, but during holidays many tramped miles on their own account. Our small posse would set off, taking the usual rations of bread and Spanish licorice water. On the way one met other little bands, similarly equipped ... En route, hopefully, one tried the locks of all vacant premises, chased cats, called up lobbies ... And ... on once more, past hedgerows now, and into the 'country'. There we made fires and marauded ... All day we ran wild through worn fields and scraggy copses that held their arms to the smut of Manchester, then traipsed home weary with the evening.

Robert Roberts, *A Ragged Schooling* (1976). *A volume on life in Manchester and Salford, c. 1914.*

Throughout the nineteenth century more than a third of the population of England and Wales consisted of children. Even in 1911 over 30 per cent of the nation was aged fourteen or less.[1] And although many of them spent at least part of their out-of-school hours at work, all of them were able to enjoy periods of play as well. Sometimes, indeed, work and pleasure could be satisfactorily intertwined. That was true of the large parties of inner city youngsters who moved out of London and Birmingham, for example, to take part in the fruit and hop harvests of Kent and Worcestershire/ Herefordshire during the late summer. It also applied to girls like Mrs Wrigley, the daughter of a shoemaker from Cefn Mawr, Wales, who recalled some of her happiest childhood hours as those when she and her friends went off for the day with food and the family's dirty washing to launder in the River Dee:

Children playing at Tysoe, Warwickshire, June 1891. They had probably just come out of school. (*Benjamin Stone Collection, Birmingham City Library*)

> We would take a bucket full of coal and get a few boulder stones and make a fire to boil the clothes in the bucket, and rinse them in the river ... Then, while the clothes was drying we had a good romp. We would take the babies with us as well, for there was plenty fields for them to pick the little daisies ... Some of our parents would come down to see if we was all right, and then we would fold the clothes and go home singing and rejoicing that we had had a good washing day and a good play.'

In the largest towns youngsters had to adapt their games to their cramped urban environment. For most, this meant playing on the streets, since there was no room for boisterous activities in the overcrowded homes, and parks and play areas were still in short supply. Or, during holidays, it could mean, as with Robert Roberts and his friends, arranging impromptu excursions to the surrounding suburbs or into the countryside.[3] Everywhere in the poorer districts of towns, noisy groups of children could be seen. Octavia Hill, engaged in a campaign for more open space for slum dwellers, recalled entering a court where the children were 'crawling or sitting on the hard hot stones till every corner of the place [looked] alive, and it [seemed] as if I must step on them if I [were] to walk up the Court.'[4] Likewise Henry Mayhew in the 1850s and 1860s described encounters with small groups

Even children too poor to have toys bought for them might amuse themselves, like these two, on an improvised see-saw. (*Museum of English Rural Life, Reading University*)

of boys playing at marbles, or gambling with halfpennies, farthings or even buttons in the streets. Near Drury Lane he met four or five of them gambling and squabbling for nuts.[5]

Those able to earn a little pocket-money could, of course, purchase simple toys or enjoy the quieter pleasures of reading books and comics, like the *Magnet*, *Gem* and *Popular*. Aneurin Bevan, who worked as a butcher's boy in Tredegar during his last months at school, spent part of his earnings in this way, to his father's disapproval. Eventually comics were banned from the home, but Aneurin, not to be thwarted, hid them in a crevice under a local bridge. Later he took the sensible step of joining a library, where he could read the popular novels of the day.[6]

For those children too poor to make even modest purchases there were games like blind-man's buff, tag, leap-frog, hide-and-seek and hopscotch, which did not need any equipment. Chasing games were particularly popular because of their spice of excitement. Often youngsters also improvised toys from odds and ends around them. Skipping ropes were made from a length of twine, hoops were filched from broken barrels, a plank and block of wood served for a see-saw, and spinning tops were made by fathers and older brothers from cotton reels, with hob nails used for the base. Pig's bladders were much in demand for football games. Ben Turner remembered that in his Yorkshire textile village, these were 'begged from the local butcher, blown up and covered over, and kicked here and there without any goal-posts at all. We played cricket with home-made bats, and balls made with twine, and our wicket would be a stone reared up.'[7]

Robert Roberts's parents, too, were unable to afford toys for their sizeable family – principally because of his father's heavy drinking but he recalled no sense of deprivation as a consequence. With a little imagination everyday objects could be turned into playthings. He and his older sisters 'borrowed' items from their mother's corner shop, constructing 'hamlets of thatched cottages' by covering gas mantle boxes with wisps of sticky straw gathered from the albumen-covered packing of egg crates. 'We borrowed lumps of washing soda from a sack under the counter to make cliffs ... using flour, sugar and salt sweepings from shelves to scatter creation with snow and ice, and peopled it with figures carved from pop bottle corks.'[8]

Practical jokes were common among the more mischievous. One popular trick was to tie together two door knockers across the street and watch the efforts of the respective householders as they struggled to pull the door open in response to a knock.

In the countryside inexpensive pleasures were even more accessible. Youngsters would roam fields and woodlands, searching for flowers, birds' nests, berries and mushrooms, according to the season, or they

Boys helping to beat the bounds of St Peter in the East parish, in Merton Street, Oxford, 1908. (*Oxfordshire County Council Libraries*)

would go fishing with an improvised net or line. For the more daring there were trees to climb and, in winter, skating and sliding on frozen streams or flooded meadows. Even toboggans or go-carts could easily be made up from an old box. Girls spent hours making chains of daisies, cowslips, primroses and buttercups, while a Norfolk girl recalled that her favourite toy was a popgun which her brothers made from an alder stick with the pith removed.[9] Sometimes they played formal dancing or rhyming games. At Juniper Hill in north Oxfordshire during the 1880s and 1890s Flora Thompson remembered the girls meeting regularly on summer evenings on one of the green open spaces. There they would 'bow and curtsey and sweep to and fro in their ankle-length frocks as they went through the game movements and sang the game rhymes as their mothers and grandmothers had done before them.'[10]

School log-books confirm how ready youngsters were to play truant if an unusual or exciting event presented itself. The arrival of a fair or one-man band, a local meet of hounds, the holding of church or chapel treats and friendly society celebrations – even the marching of soldiers along the high road – were all excuses for children to stay away. In the small market town of Banbury, it was the visits of a 'one-man band' which particularly attracted one child. 'Drum sticks to his elbows, triangles, cymbals, bells on

Local lads with a home-made 'go-cart' at Uffington Castle, Berkshire, on a Bank Holiday in 1899. (*Oxfordshire County Council Libraries*)

May Day celebrations at Ovington School, Hampshire, 1893. The multiplicity of garlands cannot disguise the pinched features and shabby clothing of some of the children. (*Hampshire County Museum Service*)

his ankles, pipe to blow.' Barrel organs also made weekly rounds, playing topical tunes and often accompanied by pretty Italian women wearing bright-coloured headscarves and shining earrings. 'On or by the organ would be a cage with ... budgerigars. If not birds, there would be a small monkey wearing a little suit of scarlet and perhaps a feathered cap.'[11]

Inevitably the children's schooling suffered as a result of these diversions. At Loddiswell British School, Devon, the head despondently noted in 1887 that he had never known 'such a village for holidaying, picnicing, etc. Every trivial event seems to be made an excuse for keeping home the children.'[12] Wider experience would have taught him that his was no unique problem. Certainly his colleague at Washford Pyne in the same county was more philosophical when he commented ironically in his log-book: 'This is the fifth (harvest) thanksgiving the children have left school to attend. Truly, we are a thankful people.'[13]

Elsewhere school managers bowed to the inevitable and granted half-day holidays. At St Thomas's Boys' School, Oxford, four such breaks were given between 25 June and 23 July 1903. Three were for different 'treats' and the fourth was in response to a visit by Buffalo Bill's Wild West Show to the city.[14]

At some schools special excursions were also arranged for the pupils. This happened at Overton, Hampshire, with the head escorting over forty older boys on a day trip to Bournemouth in the summer of 1900. They arrived at around 9 a.m. and spent the morning at the boating pool. After a 'good dinner', they went to the beach, where they bathed and enjoyed donkey rides. A walk round the town followed, before the party left for home. They arrived there at about 11 p.m. by the light of a full moon, and with 'all the boys expressing themselves ... highly delighted with their day's employment.'[15]

Cricket, too, was a regular feature of spring and summer activities at this school, and from time to time the pupils were invited to play a team of 'young gentlemen' recruited by the grandson of the owner of the nearby 'big house', Malshanger Park. One such match was arranged in April 1894, with the Overton boys travelling to the game by brake. Play began at 12.45 p.m., there was a break for a 'sumptuous lunch' at two, and the match eventually ended in the early evening. Perhaps fittingly the 'young gentlemen' won by eight runs, but the village boys acquitted themselves well and also enjoyed a 'splendid tea', to supplement the 'sumptuous' luncheon. To youngsters normally fed on bread and lard, perhaps supplemented by a little fat bacon and vegetables from the garden, the provision of a lavish meal was always a welcome part of any festivities.

In country districts, pupils were frequently given time off to celebrate traditional festivals like Valentine's Day, when they went round singing

May Day procession through Iffley, Oxfordshire, in 1906. (*Oxfordshire County Council Libraries*)

appropriate songs and begging for pennies, or May Day, when special processions were organised. For days before 1 May, the excitement mounted, as the May Queen was chosen and plans were made for producing the floral garlands to be carried by her entourage. At Cottisford, Flora Thompson remembered how, on the last morning in April, the children arrived at school with baskets, arms and pinafores filled with flowers. Then, while the majority worked away at the main garland, an older girl, perhaps the May Queen herself, would be busy in a corner making the crown, which was usually of daisies.

The final touches were given to the garland when the children assembled at six on May Day morning, and 'a large china doll in a blue frock was brought forth from the depths of the school needlework chest and arranged in a sitting posture on a little ledge in the centre front of the garland'. [16]

At nearby Lower Heyford, George James Dew, husband of the local headmistress, also noted how on the appointed day the pupils proudly marched round the village with flags flying and garlands borne aloft:

All [were] dressed up for the occasion, the girls in white & everyone with a goodly assortment of bright coloured ribbons ... Some of the poor women were up nearly all night I am told in washing & getting up their white frocks in the best style; and the clean, nay some of them most spotlessly pure, appearance they had spoke well for the general character of the Heyford poor. They had a tea in the School in the afternoon.[17]

Small wonder that Flora Thompson considered May Day the most important day of the year for the children: 'Christmas Day and the Village Feast came second and third to it.'[18] Elsewhere, particularly after 1900, when May Day was widely celebrated in urban schools as well, these processions were supplemented or replaced by dancing round the maypole. Lower Heyford acquired its first maypole in 1912 – a year which also saw morris dancing and country dancing added to the school's repertoire.[19]

In the early twentieth century, a new dimension of imperialism was added to the 'special events' held in many schools, with the celebration of Empire Day. This owed much to the efforts of the Earl of Meath, who was determined that the nation's youth should be imbued with feelings of devotion to King and Empire. To this end, in 1903 he founded the Empire Day Movement and by the following year had persuaded a number of local education authorities to adopt 24 May – the anniversary of Queen Victoria's birth – as a day of celebration in their schools. From this modest beginning, support rapidly grew. By 1907, over twelve and a half thousand elementary schools in England and Wales (well over half the total) were participating, and the movement continued to expand thereafter. The celebrations included hoisting and saluting the Union flag and singing the national anthem and other patriotic songs. Addresses were given to the children by visiting speakers on the duties of British citizenship and upon some aspect of the Empire itself. Recitation of a poem illustrative of 'heroic duty and of self-sacrifice on behalf of the nation' followed. Proceedings concluded with a rendering of Rudyard Kipling's *Recessional*, itself composed for Queen Victoria's diamond jubilee in 1897, and with the national anthem.

Sometimes more dramatic events were added. At Liverpool in 1909 a pageant of 'Britannia and her Possessions' was organised, with 480 children taking part, and ten thousand more forming a living Union flag. They were dressed in red, white or blue caps and jerseys and formed themselves into 'our Empire flag' in the short space of twenty seconds, according to a contemporary.[20] Likewise at Oxford in the same year, nearly one and a half thousand children gathered in the town hall to see a cinematograph presentation of 'Our Navy'. This was followed by an address by the Rector of Exeter College, in which he appealed to his young hearers to do their patriotic duty: 'The boys must learn to shoot straight and to be able to take part in the defence of their country in case of necessity, and the girls also had their duties to perform, and could encourage their brothers and

Children celebrating Empire Day at the Guildhall in London in the presence of the Lord Mayor, 1919. By this date 27,323 schools, training colleges and institutions in the United Kingdom were celebrating Empire Day, compared to the 5,540 elementary schools and six training colleges which had joined in on 24 May 1905, in the early days of the movement. In the photograph Britannia and Peace appear with their attendants. (*Royal Commonwealth Society*)

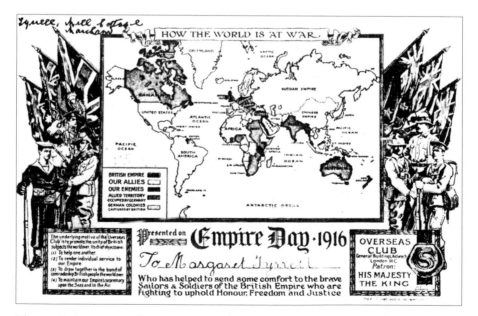

The patriotic message of Empire Day is clearly brought out in this certificate awarded to a pupil at Steventon Village School, Berkshire, in 1916. (*The late Miss M. Tyrrell*)

A DAY IN THE COUNTRY.

Little Tommy (who has never been out of Whitechapel before). "OH! OH! OH!"
Kind Lady. "WHAT'S THE MATTER, TOMMY?"   Little Tommy. "WHY, WHAT A BIG SKY THEY'VE GOT 'ERE, MISS!"

To children from the city slums a walk in the country was cause for comment, as *Punch* showed in this 1887 cartoon.

friends to take as much interest in handling a rifle as in playing football and cricket.'[21] His remarks were loudly applauded, and it is clear that many youngsters enjoyed the heady atmosphere engendered by these festivities. A boy who attended school in Fulham on the eve of the First World War described Empire Day as 'one of the happiest and [most] stirring memories of school'. He wore his scouts uniform for the occasion, and all the girls had their hair tied up with red, white and blue ribbons: 'children not wearing uniform were expected to carry a flag.'[22]

Later the Earl of Meath claimed that large numbers of the young men who 'rushed to the Colours' at the outbreak of the First World War had learned at school 'the watchwords of the [Empire Day] Movement' and had been inspired thereby to answer their country's call so readily. Many, sadly, were destined to die or to be badly maimed in that bitter struggle.

These events apart, both inside and outside school, charity continued to play a part in providing poorer children with entertainment. This was particularly true at Christmas, when well-to-do householders often supplied pupils from the local elementary schools with a tea and gifts of toys and fruit.

The *Reading Mercury* of January 1909 described a typical celebration at Pangbourne, when almost three hundred youngsters from the council schools enjoyed a lavish meal. They then made their way to a 'well laden and beautifully lighted Christmas-tree' loaded with gifts, sweets and oranges, which were distributed among them. Cheers were given to the 'ladies and gentlemen who had provided the treat', carols were sung and the evening concluded on a suitably patriotic note with the singing of the national anthem. Such events, pleasant though they were, nonetheless also subtly bolstered the class structure of contemporary English society, for the elementary pupils who attended were expected to acknowledge with suitable meekness the benevolence of their social superiors.

In the larger towns, special funds were often established to provide entertainment or holidays for youngsters. Some were attached to the schools. At the Jews' Free School in Whitechapel early in the twentieth century, there was a large charitably financed 'play centre' frequented by over a thousand children. It included classes in art, bookbinding and other crafts, Hebrew, music and gymnastics. Various clubs were organised, including those for rowing and photography, and excursions were arranged.[23]

On a broader base, in the late 1880s the socialist, Robert Blatchford, founded the Cinderella Clubs, which continued into the new century. They not only fed and clothed poor children, but arranged trips, concerts and social activities of all types. Country homes were established near London, Birmingham, Dundee and Nottingham, so that youngsters from town slums could enjoy unaccustomed fresh air and green fields; in other cases, as in Manchester, children were sent on holidays to the seaside.[24]

The Children's Country Holiday Fund similarly assisted youngsters from the poorer areas of London. During the summer of 1900, it provided help for a hundred deprived youngsters from Ben Jonson School in Stepney, and among the thousands of other Londoners who similarly benefited over the years was Walter Southgate from Bethnal Green.[25] Years later he recalled how the fund had enabled him and his sister to spend a fortnight away from their overcrowded home

> ... in the real country to us, at Stock in Essex. I was then nine years of age. My first impression was the smell of country air as something quite distinct from the smoky dust laden air of Bethnal Green. Here in rural Essex I saw field upon field of meadowgrass, numberless wild flowers, sheep and cows grazing, fields of vegetables, apples growing on trees and acres of corn waving their heads in the breeze. It was all very strange and exciting to a child from another world.[26]

On a less ambitious scale was the 'Fresh Air Fund' which financed London children on a day's outing to the country, with Loughton in Essex a popular venue.[27] But, despite the efforts of these organisations, the vast majority of London youngsters never obtained a holiday away from home. The only exception was if they and their families joined the annual exodus of East End families to the orchards and hop gardens of Kent.

In 1900 a survey of sixty board and fifteen voluntary schools in the capital revealed that 4,169 children were absent for an average of four weeks apiece, gathering fruit and hops. Hop-picking was especially common among pupils in South London and, providing the children went with their parents, no prosecutions for truancy were instituted by the authorities. Even the Board of Education accepted these annual absences with equanimity, one official commenting: 'I always thought that the annual "hopping" excursion ... is to the poor what going to the seaside is to the rich and I shd. not propose to interfere with it.'[28] Likewise HMI Eichholz, although critical of the scanty wages earned by the children and of the disruption to their education, nonetheless conceded that this was the only chance most of them had to enjoy an open-air country holiday.[29]

Some pickers travelled to Kent by special trains made up of old coaches and with cut-price fares. Often enough they arrived at their destination in the middle of the night and had to wait until the farmer arrived next day to collect them. Others, unable to afford the fare, came on foot, and

Hop-pickers near Alton, Hampshire, c. 1895. The hop harvest often provided the only 'holiday' that poorer town children could expect. Despite the hard work, there was a good deal of singing and joking while the picking was in progress. (*Museum of English Rural Life, Reading University*)

Hop-picking encampment near Maidstone in Kent. Accommodation was rough, with pickers sleeping on raised platforms covered with straw in the huts provided. But there were also the pleasures of meals eaten in the open air. 'I remember the delicious smell of smoked tea, mellow skies, and a whiff of baked potatoes sizzling in their jackets as they cook on the open fire,' wrote one woman who began 'hopping' at the age of seven.

that was, in any case, the usual mode of travel before the South Eastern Railway began to run hop-pickers' trains in the 1870s.

A Kentish girl remembered that many of the London children arrived in ragged clothes and had no shoes. They and their parents slept in crude makeshift huts or tents on the farms, with straw for bedding and meals cooked out-of-doors by camp fire. The working day lasted from 7 a.m. until 5.30 p.m. and those children too small to reach the top of the bins in which the hops were collected would pick into an open umbrella. Hands and arms became sore and stained with the picking, unless protective clothing was worn. Yet, despite the hard work, most youngsters welcomed the break with normal routine. Families often returned to the same farm year after year, with grandmothers and grandchildren all picking together around the same bin. Whilst they worked they sang popular songs and joked with one another. And when the day's labour was over, the young pickers would gather blackberries and mushrooms, or play cards, dominoes, 'conkers' and marbles round the camp fire. On Saturday nights impromptu parties were arranged.[30]

However, hop-picking involved a relatively small number of children for a few weeks only each year. Far more pervasive as long-term influences on Victorian schoolchildren were those organisations concerned with their religion and morals. As mentioned previously, links between education

Sunday school outing, Long Marston, Buckinghamshire, *c.* 1900. This was often one of the main events in a child's year. (*Pitstone Local History Society*)

and organised religion were already well established before 1870, so it is not surprising that attendance at Sunday school should form one of the most important events in the life of many youngsters. 'If there was a single experience common to the children of an agriculural labourer in Bedfordshire, of a stockinger or handloom weaver in the Midlands, or of a factory operative in south Lancashire, it was attendance at a Sunday school,' writes the historian of the movement.[31]

By 1851 membership in Britain had already reached 2.6 million and this increased to a peak of nearly 6.2 million in 1906. At that date about 16 per cent of the total population was enrolled in a Sunday school.

And although in the 1870s most schools concentrated on religious instruction, they also offered a wide variety of social activities, as well as links with other like-minded organisations, such as the Band of Hope, founded in the 1840s and incorporated into the Sunday school movement from 1874, and the Boys' Brigade, established in 1883. The Band of Hope sought to promote temperance among the impressionable young, while the Boys' Brigade aimed to inculcate a spirit of 'manly Christianity' into the aimless youth of the inner cities.

Many youngsters, of course, attended Sunday school not from personal inclination but because they were 'sent' by parents anxious to enjoy a peaceful child-free Sabbath or concerned to ensure that their offspring

Children being taken on a Sunday school outing by wagon at Fleet, Hampshire, c. 1912. (*Hampshire County Museum Service*)

were properly instructed in morality and religion. Although the schools were attached to both church and chapel, they were particularly popular among nonconformists. 'I used to be frit to death at the old men who run the chapel when I were a child,' wrote William Edwards of his experiences in the Lotting Fen, Huntingdonshire, during the 1870s and early 1880s.

> [They] were associated in my mind with the tales they used to tell us littl' uns at Sunday school about hell-fire and the bottomless pit, and the Angel of Death coming to fetch good children to heaven; and the Devil coming to fetch bad children to hell ... I used to sweat all over wondering which one on 'em 'ould come to fetch me, for I used to come out o' Sunday school convinced I coul'n't live till the next Sunday.[32]

However, other youngsters had happier memories, like Alice Moody, who attended Elm Grove Sunday School, Portsmouth, for twelve years during the 1880s and 1890s and subsequently recalled with affection its 'atmosphere of love, peace and joy, with teachers of good education and children like ourselves – well-behaved without being smug, and lively without being unruly. Lovely, lovely Elm Grove Sunday School. Every hour I spent in its walls was a foretaste of Heaven.'[33]

Even those whose attitude towards Sunday school instruction was less wholehearted than this, nonetheless enjoyed the annual treats and excursions offered, or the entertainment provided. 'We went', said a man

Boys' Brigade camp – display of equipment. The quasi-military nature of the
organisation is well brought out in this photograph.

brought up in one of the roughest districts of London, 'to see the magic
lantern.'[34] Likewise Robert Roberts recalled Band of Hope meetings
in Salford as the 'cultural highlight of the week' for boys and girls in
his neighbourhood. Meetings opened sluggishly with the singing of
temperance hymns, followed by a lecture on the evils of drink, but then
came 'galumphing young men, teetotallers every one' who tried to amuse
their young audience by 'capering on the stage in song and uproarious
sketch'. The children departed happy at 8.45 with 'little blue cards and the
promise renewed of a field day or Christmas treat. Wonderful value, we
juniors thought, for a penny a month. '[35]

   In the countryside, Sunday school celebrations were less sophisticated,
with outings often taking the form of a trip in a wagon or on foot to a local
beauty spot, to be followed by tea and games. At Tysoe, Warwickshire,
Joseph Ashby remembered the cake served at the special tea on the
vicarage lawn. It was 'a wonderful change from bread and lard'. Games
followed, with the older scholars staying behind for country dancing
before they departed for home, after consuming another piece of cake and
lemonade.[36]

   It was to promote the sterner qualities of self-reliance, firm discipline,
patriotism and 'manly Christianity' that quasi-military leisure
organisations like the Boys' Brigade and the Boy Scouts appeared. The
former was established in Glasgow in 1883 by a businessman and Sunday
school teacher, William Smith, who had also served in a local Volunteer

Regiment. He initially set up the Boys' Brigade in an effort to control the unruly lads attending his Mission Sunday School, and at first only Sunday scholars were recruited. In its very first session, dummy rifles, a club room and the familiar uniform of 'pill-box' cap, belt and haversack, which was to characterise the movement, had been adopted.[37] At the end of the following year, Bible classes were introduced, and Smith could then draw upon a wider range of recruits than merely Sunday school attenders. Soon the movement extended south of the border, until by 1899 over half its 35,148 membership was in England and Wales.[38]

The weekly routine consisted of drill, Bible class, and club room activities, interspersed with occasional field days to raise funds for the movement, and an annual camp. Bands were established, and so great was the success of the venture that other religious denominations followed Smith's example. The Church Lads' Brigade appeared in Fulham in 1891, the Jewish Lads' Brigade at Whitechapel four years later, and the short-lived Catholic Boys' Brigade in Bermondsey in 1896. The Church Lads' Brigade, in particular, was linked with the temperance movement and over the years tended to lay far greater stress on military activities than its Boys' Brigade forerunner. But in other respects it, and the others, followed the pattern established by Smith.

Many working-class lads were, however, hostile to the moral image the brigades were fostering and so early members (like the Scouts a little later) were faced with abuse and even physical assault from disaffected youngsters. 'Few drills went by without attacks from hooligans and the "discontents",' recalled an early Boys' Brigade captain; 'even officers in uniform were pelted with bottles and other missiles ... and the boys had to defend their uniform often with their fists.' Yet clearly they derived sufficient enjoyment from taking part in the various activities to compensate for the persecution they suffered from 'roving bands of "hooligans"'.[39]

By 1914, the United Kingdom membership of the Boys' Brigade had climbed to just over 60,000. But by then it was overshadowed by the most important youth organisation of the early twentieth century – the Boy Scouts – which in 1913 boasted a total membership of over 152,000.

The Scouts were established in 1907/8 by the Boer War hero, Robert Baden-Powell, with the aim of training boys 'to be more efficient and characterful citizens'. To this end they were introduced to woodcraft, camping, life-saving and similar manly activities. In drawing up his scheme Baden-Powell was influenced by earlier experiences in training young soldiers. But like many other social imperialists of his day, he was concerned about the alleged 'deterioration' of the British race and

Physical exercises at a Boys' Brigade camp.

Longworth Scout Troop, Berkshire, 1913. (*Oxfordshire County Council Libraries*)

the apparent decline in its physical fitness revealed by the Boer War recruitment statistics. Scouting was intended to arrest that decline. However, the immediate source of his inspiration was William Smith. In 1904, when inspecting a parade of seven or eight thousand Boys' Brigade members in Glasgow in company with Smith, Baden-Powell had commented on their smart bearing and alert appearance. Smith responded by suggesting that he re-write his book on *Aids to Scouting*, originally intended for military use, so as to appeal to boys. It could then be used by the Boys' Brigade and similar organisations as part of their training programme.

Baden-Powell took up Smith's suggestion but, in the meantime, he decided to hold an experimental Boy Scout camp on Brownsea Island in Poole Harbour, Dorset, during the summer of 1907. Twenty boys were selected with the help of Boys' Brigade officials from Bournemouth and Poole and, on arrival at Brownsea, were divided into four patrols of five members apiece. The senior boy in each was the patrol leader and, in Baden-Powell's view, this arrangement, which was later applied to the wider Scout movement, was the secret of its success. Not only was the patrol leader given responsibility for his group at all times, but a competitive edge was introduced into the proceedings. While on the island the boys learned various aspects of scouting, and every evening one patrol went on duty as a night picket, drawing rations of flour, meat, vegetables and tea, and then going to a designated spot to bivouac. Camp fires were lit and suppers cooked before sentries were carefully posted for the night. The next morning the camp was roused by a loud blast from a koodoo horn which Baden-Powell had captured on one of his African campaigns. Clearly, for the boys involved it was all a glorious adventure.[40]

With this success behind him, in 1908 Baden-Powell published *Scouting for Boys*. It was sub-titled 'A handbook for Instruction in Good Citizenship through Woodcraft' and was written in a lively style, with anecdotes and 'camp fire yarns' skilfully blended with useful information on scouting, camp life, first aid, signalling – and patriotism. 'You belong to the Great British Empire, one of the greatest empires that has ever existed in the world,' Baden-Powell told his young readers. 'I am sure that if you boys will keep the good of your country in your eyes *above everything else* she will be all right. But if you don't do this there is very great danger, because we have many enemies abroad.' Initially he had not intended to start an organisation of his own, but so great was the book's appeal that all over England youngsters began to form troops on their own initiative and then persuaded 'favoured adults to become their Scoutmasters'. Soon it became necessary to appoint local advisory committees as well as travelling inspectors, and a managing secretary at the new Boy Scouts headquarters at Westminster.[41] The movement was well and truly launched.

Among the early recruits was Paul English of Totton near Southampton. In the spring of 1908 he and a dozen other local lads, fired by the appeal of *Scouting for Boys*, formed two patrols – the Cuckoos and the Owls, since in accordance with Baden-Powell's rules, each patrol had to be named after a wild creature. (Members used the call of their patrol's emblem to signal to one another, especially at night.)

In this informal fashion the Totton troop was born. It had, as yet, no scoutmaster, and the youngsters provided the necessary items of kit for themselves. Within a short time they organised their first Saturday afternoon expedition, and at the rendezvous 'were soon indulging in various scouting activities'. Not until the early autumn did they acquire their first proper scoutmaster, when a Church Army lay reader, who had taken charge of the Totton mission church, also assumed leadership of the scout troop. During the following winter meetings were held for instruction in knot-tying, first aid, signalling and other scouting activities. They also acquired six bugles and two kettle drums, and soon found themselves in demand for church parades, flower shows and fêtes. 'By 1910', recalls Paul English, 'we had been firmly accepted in the community, having lived down the early catcalls, sneers and unpleasant remarks of the pioneering days.'[42]

Warren Scout Troop, Whitchurch, Oxfordshire, *c.* 1910. Troop members are sitting nervously waiting for tea at Hardwick House, Whitchurch, the home of Sir Charles Day Rose, Bt. (*Oxfordshire County Council Libraries*)

Children amusing themselves at Farnworth Park, Bolton, *c.* 1900. (*Farnworth Library, Bolton*)

Paul English and his fellow Totton scouts all came from relatively prosperous lower middle-class families, but the movement also appealed to those less fortunate. Robert Roberts in Salford remembered how he and a friend were determined to join the movement as soon as they had read *Scouting for Boys*. At first they were thwarted by lack of cash to purchase a uniform and by the fact that in their particular neighbourhood no troop had yet been set up. One day, however, Robert's friend discovered an obscure troop on the Manchester boundary which did not regard a uniform as compulsory. Immediately they decided to investigate:

> The scoutmaster ... welcomed us with surprising warmth. Dress, he said, didn't matter; that could come later. What counted in scouting was the spirit. 'Learn the Law!' he told us. 'Learn the knots!' They put us in the Eagle Patrol with boys much like ourselves ... We came home, a rather long trek across Salford, cock-a-hoop at our acceptance.[43]

For most scouts, the highlight of the year was the annual camp. Paul English's Totton troop in both 1910 and 1911 held its camp on the Solent

GORGEOUS SPECTACLE.

Sarah Jane. "OH, BETSY, COME 'ERE, AND BRING HISABELLER! WE CAN SEE THE 'OOFS
OF THE 'ORSES!!"

One way of seeing the show if you couldn't afford the entrance charge! (Punch)

about ten miles from home. Except for two or three of the younger ones, who rode on the baggage cart, they had to walk all the way. 'But we loved it ... apart from minimal scouting and fatigue duties we just enjoyed the holiday in sea and sun. We were given the use of a large boat ... and that suited our needs perfectly. The older boys had plenty of rowing practice and everybody was encouraged to swim.'[44]

Similar sentiments were expressed by Josef Morrell, member of a Fulham troop, who went to his first camp at the age of ten. For days before the departure his family had to endure his feverish excitement, since not only was the camp his first holiday but also his first visit to the seaside and the first time he had boarded a train.[45]

Most camps were also enlivened by having to repulse a night attack from another troop, probably in search of flags to decorate their headquarters, as trophies of their skill in camp raiding. Such events gave plenty of opportunity for mock skirmishing between the 'opposing' troops. They also formed part of Baden-Powell's overall aim of instilling scoutcraft.

But the majority of schoolchildren had to find their pleasures in less spectacular ways then these. Most probably shared the sentiments of Kate Edwards, when she summed up her childhood in the Lotting Fen during the 1880s and 1890s:

Living where we did and how we did, we used to make the most of anything a bit out o' the ordinary, and we looked for'ard from one special day to the next. Looking back on it now, I'm surprised to see how many high days and holidays there were during the year that we kept, and we certainly made the most of any that children could take part in.[46]

CHAPTER SIX

The Teachers

... as a whole, the present body of teachers are a very honourable class, and have a great sense of their duties to the children in regard to the formation of their character, and their moral guidance ... We are told that nine-tenths of the supply of elementary teachers is made up of those who have formerly served as pupil-teachers.

Final Report of the Commissioners Appointed to Inquire into the Elementary Education Acts, England and Wales, PP1888, Vol. XXXV.

In the early nineteenth century, elementary teaching was often taken up by those too old, too sick or too inefficient to earn their living in any other way. In North Wales during the 1840s a contemporary claimed gloomily that teachers were drawn

... from the lowest class in society which contains individuals competent to read, write, and cipher ... [The] majority ... are persons who were formerly employed in some petty trade or occupation ... as carpenters, joiners, innkeepers, assistants in grocers' or drapers' shops, retired soldiers or excisemen ... [The] class of schoolmistresses is composed of persons who have been employed as sempstresses, charwomen, and servants of the most humble description.[1]

He sourly added that since the average income of teachers was lower than the wages able-bodied labourers could command, few people were prepared to undertake the employment who were 'not incapacitated by age or infirmity for manual labour'. Similar criticisms were voiced by one of Her Majesty's Inspectors of Schools, the Revd H. W. Bellairs, when he

Teachers at Basingstoke National School, *c.* 1870. Seated in the centre of the photograph is Canon Millard, vicar of Basingstoke. Behind him on the left is Mr Skinner, head of the boys' department of the school. Sitting on the canon's right is Miss Goddard, head of the girls' department. The young man standing on the far left of the photograph was a pupil-teacher, as was the girl seated in front of him. (*Hampshire County Museum Service*)

pointed out that, whereas anyone seeking to become a shoemaker or tailor would expect to undergo training before he practised his trade, in regard to education, 'a man imagines that he may rush at once into it, and that no previous instruction or study is requisite'.[2]

At this stage the work of adult teachers in National and British and Foreign Society schools was normally supplemented by child monitors. They were drawn from the older pupils and taught their fellow scholars under the supervising eye of a single adult, who might have been briefly 'trained' for that role at one of the central schools run by the two societies. But often no such instruction had been given and, in these circumstances, teaching degenerated into a monotonous routine of repetitive chanting and rote-learning. Little attempt was made to arouse the pupils' interest or reasoning powers.

It was to end the monitorial system and to improve general educational standards that in 1846 the government drew up its programme for teacher training. Under it, youngsters aged thirteen and above were to be apprenticed for five years in an approved elementary school as pupil-teachers and were to combine a daily teaching stint with out-of-school tuition from the head and some private study. At the end of each year of apprenticeship, the pupil-teacher took an examination conducted by HM Inspector and, if successful, earned a government grant ranging from £10 a year for a first-year candidate to £20 for one in the final year. At the end of the apprenticeship, trainees could sit for a Queen's scholarship examination, to give entry to a training college, or they could remain in the schools as unqualified assistants, perhaps studying in their spare time for a teacher's certificate: from 1847 it was possible to take this qualifying examination as an 'acting teacher', while holding down a job in a school, and not merely by attendance at college. A large number of teachers chose this option and, in 1914, in a profession dominated by women, only 32 per cent of all the females employed in elementary schools were trained and certificated, compared to 27 per cent who were untrained (that is they had not been to college) but certificated and 41 per cent who were neither trained nor certificated.[3]

In 1877 the minimum age for apprenticeship was raised to fourteen and the training period was reduced to four years, while in 1900, at least in urban areas, the age limit was increased to fifteen and the training period became three years. This was intended to encourage would-be teachers to continue in full-time education for a longer period, but the shortage of secondary schools in country districts and the relatively high degree of poverty among many rural families made this higher age limit impractical in the countryside.

During their apprenticeship, pupil-teachers spent much time in private study and in receiving tuition from their head teacher out of school hours. This last was, of course, given at a time convenient to the head rather than the trainee. Thus Mary Banfield, a pupil teacher at West Hove National Girls' School during the 1860s, commenced her working day at 6.30 a.m., when she went to receive instruction from the headmistress. She then briefly returned to her lodgings for breakfast, before starting her stint as a teacher.[4] Most evenings were spent in study, but at the weekend she assisted her landlady with the household chores and with a catering business she ran, as part payment for board and lodgings. Mary's father was a farm worker and the family's already limited finances were reduced still further when he died during her apprenticeship.

Another pupil-teacher, Frances Goodway, who was born in 1874, the daughter of a coachbuilder and painter, served her apprenticeship at the Banbury school where she had once been a scholar. She and her fellow pupil-teachers had to arrive for instruction at 7.40 a.m. each day and remain for an hour. 'Then we started teaching. We had a class of fifty to sixty children or more.' Frances herself, at the ripe age of fourteen, was

Mary Dew (née Banfield), head of Lower Heyford Village School, Oxfordshire, with her husband and two children, c. 1893. Mrs Dew was born in Sussex and came to Lower Heyford in 1867. Her husband, George James Dew, was the poor law relieving officer and school attendance officer for the area. (*The late Miss D. B. Dew*)

Frances Goodway graduating from Stockwell Training College in the mid-1890s. She was head of Cherwell Infants' School, Banbury, 1898-1927 – a post she continued to hold after her marriage. She lived to be well over a hundred.

required to teach the third standard (children of about nine years), whom she particularly remembered taking for geography. 'You had to teach what the different towns manufactured. We used to stick a bit of cloth on where it was Bradford, and a bit of carpet for carpet-making areas, and pin them on the map.'[5]

Small wonder that Mrs Burgwin, head of Orange Street Girls' Board School in London, considered 'the five years which I spent as a pupil-teacher as being the hardest period of life that a girl can possibly have. I had to give up, during those five years, both music and painting ... because the work was so heavy, and we had so many home lessons to do.'[6]

Nevertheless, despite the disadvantages of these training arrangements, after 1846 school-teaching afforded men and women of relatively humble backgrounds a chance to enter a respectable profession with modest prestige. Earnings, particularly after the ending of government payments to trainees and qualified teachers under the 1862 Revised Code system, were not high. This made the profession unappealing to many qualified men who could earn higher salaries in commerce or industry. But for women, they were far better than could be obtained in domestic service, factory work or dressmaking – the most common jobs open to females. Equally, the fact that women teachers received lower pay than men increased their attractiveness to hard-pressed school managers (especially in rural areas) who had limited cash at their disposal. In 1870, while a certificated female earned, on average, about £58 a year, her male counterpart could expect to receive about £94. In the mid-1890s there were still over 1,200 country headmistresses who were paid under £50 a year, and even the advent of local education authorities after 1902 did not eliminate gender pay differences. In Devon, the annual salary scale of a trained certificated male assistant in 1903 was £80 to £110, but of his female colleague only £70 to £95. And in 1913-14 in the country as a whole the average £179 10s a year paid to male school heads was well above the average £126 18s paid to women at the same level.[7] Similar differentials applied to uncertificated teachers.

One of the principal objects of the government in drawing up its teacher training programme had been to establish firm moral and professional standards for the occupation. To this end training colleges laid great stress on students adopting an appropriate attitude of religious conformity. Typical was the view of Whitelands Training Institution for Schoolmistresses in Chelsea:

Whitelands professes to be a place of religious training. [The] officers of Whitelands ... believe that a young person, however clever, well informed, and free from ... obvious faults ... is not a fit person for a

Women at the Methodists' Westminster Training College, London, *c.* 1870, before their separate college opened at Southlands in 1872. (*The former Westminster College Library*)

training school, unless there be reason for believing her to be influenced by religious motives.

Overall, the student's future success as a teacher was felt 'to depend less on her literary acquirements than on her moral qualities'.[8]

An equally firm line was taken by the colleges over dress, particularly for female students. In the early 1870s entrants to Stockwell Training College, London, were informed that the 'Ladies' Committee wish it to be distinctly understood by all candidates for admission that they consider neatness and plainness of dress incumbent on those who undertake the instruction and training of the young; and it is the express wish of the committee that no flower, ornament, or other finery should be worn.'[9]

An allied concern of the training institutions was to make students aware of their precise place in the social order. It was recognised that most would themselves be ex-elementary pupils from a working-class or lower middle-class background who needed to be elevated socially by their training. But that social elevation was to be kept to the minimum necessary; all pretentiousness was to be firmly curbed. As the *Quarterly Review* observed in 1879, where pretensions were shown by teachers they 'must be crushed and checked without mercy'.[10]

Mrs Fielden of Todmorden, manager of a school on her husband's estate and a member of the local school board also condemned the 'very sad influence' of the colleges over students' characters. In evidence to a government commission in 1887 she commented scathingly:

> they come from poor homes, half educated ... and then they come out and get what, in my country, we call 'cocky,' because they know a little; but they do not know enough to show how little they know ... A girl ... goes up to a training college and she comes back ... exceedingly conceited, so that you cannot manage her.[11]

For this reason, Mrs Fielden refused to appoint training college graduates to any school with which she was associated. She preferred those who had gained their certificates by external study as 'acting teachers'.

A similar preoccupation with social status lay behind the requirement at St Hild's College, Durham, in the 1890s that each student must wash her own crockery, assist in sweeping and dusting, and take turns at ironing in the laundry once a week. At Lincoln, students referred bitterly to the blistered hands and aching backs which resulted when they had to turn the mangle for an hour at a time in the laundry. And when attempts were made in the mid-1890s to improve their living conditions, much anxiety

Recreation Room at St Mark's College, Chelsea, c. 1912. Recreation rooms were a relatively new development in teacher training colleges as college life became less spartan. (*The late Mrs M. Horn*)

Oxford Diocesan Training College,
CULHAM.

• General Rules •

FOR THE DIRECTION OF STUDENTS IN RESIDENCE.

1. Students must not go out of bounds, except after dinner till the following times :—on Sundays till 6 p.m. ; on Wednesdays and Saturdays till 6.30 p.m. ; on other days till 4.30 p.m.

The whole of the Quadrangle corridor is within bounds, so also is the Lane at the back of the College from the garden gate to the Railway Bridge, and the Eastern front Paddock. Both the Entrance Drives and the School Path are out of bounds. Those parts of the College grounds which are always out of bounds are shown in a plan in the Entrance Hall.

Students must not walk or study in the Grounds or the Lane after dusk.

2. No Student may absent himself from Chapel or Hall without permission of the Principal, or (in his absence) of the Vice-Principal ; nor from Lecture without the permission of the Lecturer. Strict punctuality is required.

3. No Student may go to the Dormitories during the day, except at the hours stated on the notice board, without the written permission of the Vice-Principal, or (in his absence) of the Senior member of the Staff in College.

4. Every Student must retire to his cubicle immediately after prayers at 10 p.m.

No Student is allowed to have a light in his cubicle, except the General Monitor, the Dormitory Monitor on duty and the Bell Monitor. It is strictly forbidden for any Student to enter the bedroom of another at night ; nor may he do so during the day except with the occupant's permission, and when the occupant is himself present.

The lights in the Dormitories are extinguished twenty minutes after retiring ; the Monitors may have their lights till 11 p.m.

Strict order and quietness must be observed in the Dormitories at all times ; no noisy conversation is allowed, and all conversation must cease when the Dormitory lights are extinguished.

Before leaving their bedrooms in the morning Students are required to strip their beds, and to open the window.

No boxes or luggage may be kept in the Dormitories.

5. In the Dining Hall, Lecture Rooms, and Dormitories, the Monitors are held responsible for order, quietness, and neatness, and Students are required to respect and support their authority. No Sporting materials are allowed in any of the College Rooms.

6. All Students are required to take some form of active exercise every afternoon.

7. It is strictly forbidden to enter any Public house for any reason, in Culham, Abingdon or the neighbourhood.

8. Smoking is not permitted in any part of the College buildings, except in the Common Room at stated hours, and in the Hut.

9. Students may not make or retain any acquaintances in the neighbourhood of Culham without the Principal's knowledge and consent.

10. Students are required at all times when away from College, whether in term or vacation, to conduct themselves in an orderly and gentlemanly manner, remembering that the reputation of their College is in their hands.

A. R. WHITHAM,
Principal.

Rules of Culham Training College, *c.* 1900. The importance of discipline, morality and religion is made very clear.

The chemical laboratory at Cheltenham Training College, *c.* 1900. Science became a more important part of the curriculum from the 1880s at all training colleges. (*The former St Paul's College Library, Cheltenham*)

Criticism lesson at Cheltenham Training College, *c.* 1904. The student was expected to give a lesson on a selected subject before an audience of staff and fellow students and had then to be prepared to receive their comments. The ordeal was hated by sensitive students. (*The former St Paul's College Library, Cheltenham*)

was expressed that this might harm their character. The college magazine, discussing the possible provision of a common room, expressed a hope that this 'may not, with its lounges and luxurious easy chairs and its general state of refined rest ... convert steady, working, industrious girls into mere imitations of fine ladies'.[12]

Male students, too, were expected to perform manual tasks in the interests of encouraging general humility. At Culham Diocesan Training College in Oxfordshire these included sweeping the class-rooms, fetching the coal and pumping the water required within the college. '"Duties" were numerous', recalled one ex-Culhamite, 'and various "turns" for sweeping rooms, fire lighting, corridor cleaning, garden, postman, chapel cleaning, and town messenger, &c., were the order of the day.' He also remembered the extreme cold of the dormitories and chapel during the winter months, and the poor quality of the food.[13] Nor did the principal mince his words when writing of students who had failed to meet his exacting moral standards. One man who entered the college in 1897, aged nineteen, was described soon after as 'Idle & desultory, bad influence ... morally weak & with no high standards. Untrustworthy.' Less than two decades later he became one of His Majesty's Assistant Inspectors of Schools![14]

The issue of status also affected relations between elementary teachers and many of HM Inspectors, thereby adding to the difficulties created by the 'payment by results' system. The problems experienced by the teachers were underlined by George Howe, head of Market Rasen Methodist School, Lincolnshire from 1876 to 1905, when he wrote despairingly in his log-book in 1883:

> I observe from the papers that a Master has committed suicide through overstrain, and I can truthfully say that I, and all the teachers of this neighbourhood are daily suffering from this same pressure. Teachers are expected to perform miracles and try to do so ... throughout the year I have felt underneath my work – I have sought change of air, Medical Advice, etc., but my doctor tells me nothing will do me good but complete rest. Query. How can a teacher obtain rest?

The following year he added gloomily. 'When I first entered my pupil-teachership teaching had its rosy hues: but alas they have all vanished.' Nevertheless, he laboured on at Market Rasen for twenty more years and, despite his fears, received generally favourable reports from the inspectors.[15]

At the same time it is notable that in 1911 the Chief Inspector of Schools described members of the elementary profession, in a confidential memorandum, as 'uncultivated and imperfectly educated' people who were for the most part 'creatures of tradition and routine', unworthy to perform an inspectoral role. In the furore his remarks aroused, the Secretary to the Board of Education was forced to resign, but there is little doubt that such views were held by many senior inspectors, who were themselves recruited from a higher social class and had been educated at one of the older universities.

Reinforcing these status problems was the fact that, especially in country areas, it was common for the local clergy or school managers to require teachers to undertake 'extraneous' or out-of-school activities, such as playing the organ in church on Sunday or training the choir, as part of their conditions of employment. Typical was the advertisement placed by a Kentish rector in *The Schoolmaster* of 3 January 1891, appealing for a certificated headmistress to take over a mixed village school with fifty pupils. She must be a 'Churchwoman. Energetic. Sunday-school. Harmonium desirable.' For these various duties she was to be paid £30 a year, plus the children's school pence, half the government grant to the school, and the use of a furnished cottage.

The 'extraneous duties' issue was one which involved the National Union of Elementary Teachers after its establishment in 1870 (it dropped the 'Elementary' from its title in 1889). A union survey of 1891 showed that around one in three of the sample of 1,200 teachers it had investigated depended for continuance in their post on the performance of outside tasks. Yet, despite union agitation, it was not until 1903 that the imposition of 'extraneous duties' as a condition of service came to an end.

Throughout the period, elementary teaching remained a preserve of the children of skilled artisans, shopkeepers and labourers, who were themselves products of the same school system. One HMI suggested that in country areas they tended to be 'the children of small tradesmen, yeomen, or the upper servants in gentlemen's families'. In the towns, and particularly in London, they belonged 'to the better and higher divisions of the operative classes ... They are the children of respectable artisans, silk-weavers, cabinet makers, etc.'[16]

One youngster who followed this path linking the elementary school with the training college was F. H. Spencer of Swindon. He was born in 1872, the son of a boilermaker employed by the Great Western Railway. As he freely admitted, he became a teacher not because of any particular interest in the profession but because in the 1880s it was almost the only avenue to higher education open to intelligent children of the upper artisan class. As a first step, at the age of thirteen, he was appointed a monitor, assisting an uncertificated master with the youngest children at a salary of 2s a week. A few months later he signed formal indentures as a pupil-

NATIONAL UNION OF TEACHERS.

OBJECTS OF THE UNION.

I. To unite together, by means of Local Associations, Public School Teachers throughout the kingdom, in order to provide a machinery by which teachers may give expression to their opinions when occasion requires, and may take united action in any matter affecting their interests.

II. To afford to the Education Department, to School Boards, and to other Educational Bodies, the benefit of the collective experience and advice of Teachers on practical educational questions.

III. To improve the general education of the country by seeking to raise the qualifications and status of Public School Teachers, and by opening out a career to the best qualified Members of the profession.

IV. To watch the working of the Education Act; to promote the insertion of such new Articles in the Code of Regulations as may from time to time be found necessary in the interests of Public Education; and to secure the removal of such regulations as are detrimental to the cause of educational progress.

V. To establish a Scheme, whereby retiring allowances may be secured to aged and incapacitated Teachers, and to seek the removal of such restrictions from the existing pension Minutes (1884) as were not contained in the Minutes of 1846 and 1851-61.

VI. To establish Provident, Benevolent, and Annuity Funds in connection with the Union, for the benefit of the Scholastic Profession.

VII. To establish and support in connection with the Union an Orphanage and Orphan Fund for the Children of Teachers.

VIII. To secure the representation of the profession in Parliament.

IX. To raise teaching to the dignity of a Profession by means of a Public Register of duly qualified Teachers for every class of Schools; by the appointment of a Representative Educational Council and the creation of a Ministry of Science and Education.

J. H. YOXALL, *General Secretary.*
C. JAMES, *Assistant Secretary.*

Objects of the National Union of Teachers, mid-1890s. The union was established in 1870 as the National Union of Elementary Teachers, but the 'Elementary' was dropped from the title in 1889. (*National Union of Teachers*) teacher. His father had discussed the matter with the headmaster and was attracted to the proposition because it meant his son would 'go to college'. This would bring more then purely educational benefits. Unlike most working men he would not have to jump out of bed at 5.15 a.m. each day in order to reach work by six, and he would have more than a week's annual holiday. Years later, Spencer recalled his experiences as a trainee:

> You sank or swam. Either you could 'hold' a class of thirty, fifty, or sixty boys or you could not. If you could, and you passed an annual examination of a rudimentary 'Secondary' level, you survived, and, in due course, at the age of eighteen to nineteen, proceeded to a training-college to take a two years' course ...
>
> So far as the academic side was concerned, my pupilage was largely a fraud. The Code laid down that a pupil teacher was to have at least one hour's instruction a day from the head master, who apparently could delegate this duty, or part of it, to certificated assistants. In our school these 'lessons' purported to take place every day from Monday to Friday inclusive from seven to eight in the morning ... In fact, [the headmaster], who took English [on Wednesdays] ... could be relied upon never to arrive before 7.30. On the other mornings things varied according to the conscientiousness of the various masters ... On Wednesdays, therefore, I would often struggle to arrive by 7.30; but I was not infrequently late. On the other mornings I turned up chiefly according to my interest in the subject taken and the degree of respect which each particular assistant master inspired. Sometimes sleep or laziness would ensnare me and I would not attend at all ... During the ordinary school hours, 9-12 and 2-4.15, I was quite a useful teacher; and after school hours I could be relied upon to play games with the boys, only too eagerly, and to take at least my share with all sorts of out-of-school activities.[17]

By diligent private study, Spencer passed his examinations and won a place at the British and Foreign School Society's Borough Road College. There he remained for two years and in December 1894, at the end of his course, was appointed to a post in a Nottingham Higher Grade school at a salary of £80 a year. Eventually he entered HM inspectorate.

But if Spencer's career appears to confirm the strengths – as well as some of the weaknesses – of the pupil-teacher system as a form of preliminary training, there were many critics who, especially from the 1880s, condemned its limited academic approach. Edmund Sargent, former secretary of the London Pupil Teachers' Association, commented in 1887 that most pupil-teachers had little interest in general reading or in cultural activities: 'all knowledge was valued according to its bearing on examination.'[18] Others suggested that the recruitment of trainees from more refined middle-class families would improve the overall 'tone' of elementary schools. This was a view put forward by the principal of Bishop Otter Memorial College for Elementary Teachers in 1886, when she discussed her attempts to recruit 'gentlewomen' to the profession. However, during the college's first ten years of existence, between 1873 and 1883, only 136 students had completed their training. Of these, twenty-nine were the daughters of clergymen, twenty-two of medical men, twenty-two of officers in the army and navy, and fourteen of merchants and manufacturers. Significantly, a high proportion were orphans who had been driven by economic necessity to seek employment as elementary teachers, rather than by any middle-class missionary zeal to regenerate the lower orders.[19]

Nevertheless, if attempts to recruit elementary teachers from a higher social class proved largely abortive, efforts were made with greater success to combat the profession's narrowness of vision by broadening the academic training of the pupil-teachers. During the 1870s some of the larger towns began to establish special centres where apprentices could attend for their daily tuition, instead of gaining it at odd moments

John James Graves, first President of the National Union of Elementary Teachers. Graves (1832-1903) was head of Lamport and Hanging Houghton Endowed School, Northamptonshire, from 1851 to 1901. He began his career in 1846 as a pupil-teacher at St Anne's School, Soho, and in 1900 the union presented him with £100 'in grateful recognition of the life-long services rendered to education'. He died in February 1903. (*National Union of Teachers*)

from their school head. The first was opened in Liverpool in 1876. There the school board had been induced to take the step by the examination successes of pupil-teachers from the city's Roman Catholic schools, who had received central class instruction from local nuns under a private arrangement. Similar experiments were instituted in London, but it was not until the 1880s, when the Education Department officially permitted central instruction, that the Liverpool and London experiments were able to function properly. By 1887 there were eleven centres at work in the capital alone, giving instruction to 1,636 pupil-teachers, and a number of other towns, including Birmingham, were following suit. By 1902 over half of all pupil-teachers were receiving part of their instruction under such arrangements.

Often, attendance at a centre meant a great rush for the pupil-teachers, especially when they had to spend the morning teaching in the schools. Leonora Eyles remembered having to cycle to the railway station and then take a twenty minute train journey, during the lunch break, in order to reach her centre. But she considered it worth the effort, despite the fact that family poverty made it difficult for her to purchase the books needed for the course. At the centre she gained her 'first taste of real music', and with staff help she made rapid progress. But it was at a price.

> I have often wondered if anybody was ever as tired as I was then; I suppose I never had more than five hours sleep in every twenty-four for more than two years ... I used to pin up Latin irregular verbs, French verbs, set poems and history dates with the music and learn them together. Whenever I hear certain pieces of Haydn I hear them to the accompaniment of irregular verbs.[20]

Despite the problems attached to the pupil-teacher system, it continued in operation up to the First World War and, indeed, beyond. Nevertheless, after the passage of the 1902 Education Act, further changes were made. From 1903, sixteen became the minimum age for apprenticeship in towns, although fifteen was still permitted in country districts. In addition, a specified number of hours' instruction had to be received by apprentices in pupil-teacher centres or classes. In order to meet the increased demand for tuition, many secondary schools became involved in this training process. Four years later, in 1907, fresh regulations offered special grants or bursaries to secondary pupils aged sixteen and above who were prepared to stay on at school to the age of eighteen and train for the elementary profession. The grant was to be available for a year and after it had expired the youngsters could either proceed direct to a training college or could serve for a year in schools as student teachers, so as to gain some practical

Terms of Agreement of a
schoolmaster at Kettering British
School, Northamptonshire, 1876.
(*Northamptonshire Record Office*)

experience of their future profession. By 1914 this 'bursary' method had
become the most common mode of entry. In 1911-12 there were 2,858
students training under the scheme, compared to 1,955 commencing pupil-
teacher courses. In rural areas, however, the scarcity of secondary schools
and the length of the unpaid training period made bursaries unattractive
to poorer trainees, and so it was accepted that there the 'ancient resource'
of pupil-teacherships must continue to be available.[21]

In many smaller village schools, indeed, shortage of cash meant that
it was still an untrained child monitor who provided the only assistance
available to the head teacher rather than even a pupil-teacher. An analysis
of Devon teaching records in 1903 shows that 30 per cent of all 'assistants
at that time were monitors, compared to about 12 per cent who were
pupil-teachers. Likewise in Oxfordshire a year later, 24 per cent of all
assistants were monitors as opposed to around 7 per cent who were pupil-
teachers. The relative cheapness of this option is indicated by the fact that
monitors might be paid as little as £2 2s per annum even in 1904.[22] They
included youngsters like Charity Finch in Flora Thompson's *Still Glides
the Stream*. At thirteen and a half she became a monitress, carrying, as her
badge of office, a short light cane, known as a pointer. This was ostensibly
for 'pointing out the letters of the alphabet on the big wall card to her class

A school group of Marhamchurch, Cornwall, *c.* 1900. The pupil-teacher is in a white pinafore on the left. (*Museum of English Rural Life, Reading University*)

of infants, but equally useful for banging the desk to give emphasis to her instructions'.[23] As a sign of her new status, her skirts were lengthened from her knees to her ankles, and over them she wore a small black, or coloured, apron in place of the white pinafore she had formerly worn.

Inevitably, many young monitors were too inexperienced and too ignorant to carry out their duties satisfactorily. Just as disquieting, however, was the continuing recruitment of large numbers of unqualified, uncertificated 'supplementary' teachers as well. This grade was first introduced in the mid-1870s with the aim of phasing out the monitors. In practice, both kinds of unqualified staff continued to be employed. The only requirements for a 'supplementary' were that she (supplementaries were virtually all female) should be at least eighteen years of age, have been vaccinated against smallpox, and be recognised by HM Inspector as 'employed during the whole of the school hours in the general instruction of the scholars and in teaching needlework'.[24] By 1900, there were 17,512 supplementaries employed in the nation's elementary schools – a total that had increased by more than 100 per cent over the proceding seven years. In 1909 the Board of Education sought to restrict their recruitment but, in fact, numbers fell only a little and in 1913 there were still 13,473 employed. At that date 'supplementaries' comprised about one in twelve of the elementary teaching workforce.

Finally, we must examine the relationships which grew up between the teachers and those whom they taught. As has been seen, most teachers were themselves products of the elementary system. But this common background did not mean that relations between them and their pupils were always good. Some were heartily disliked by the scholars because they were harsh disciplinarians or incompetent. Aneurin Bevan, himself a violent, self-willed child, recalled his Tredegar headmaster with deep dislike. 'He was a bully and a snob', writes Bevan's biographer, Michael Foot, 'and all the stories of Aneurin's schooldays centre round the physical combats between them.'[25] Even where contacts were less bitter than this, pupils and teachers, especially under the 'payment by results' regime, often regarded one another with mutual suspicion.

But happily there were many exceptions to this situation. Fred Kitchen, for one, considered his South Yorkshire schoolmistress 'the dearest old lady that ever kept school'. From time to time she would buy sweets for her pupils and, when the hounds met at the nearby hall, the children were taken to see them. 'One thing I shall always be grateful for is that she taught me to love and reverence good literature.'[26] Then there were teachers like Mrs Burgwin in London, whose sympathy for her pupils extended to arranging free dinners for the most necessitous and opening a creche so that older girls could bring younger brothers and sisters to school, instead of having to stay at home to look after them when their mother went out to work.[27]

Another much-loved and respected teacher was Mary Dew (née Banfield), who came to Lower Heyford School, Oxfordshire, in 1867 and remained its head until her retirement in 1913. Her concern for the children's welfare was such that, when necessary, she would go round to better off villagers to beg for cast-off boots for the poorest pupils. Out of her own pocket she provided milk at morning playtime for one or two delicate girls.

On a different level, she also purchased magazines to amuse and instruct her pupils, including the *Children's Friend* and *Chatterbox*, as well as providing occasional treats, like slices of cake on St Valentine's Day. She encouraged her pupils to keep in touch with her when they left, and many did so. In September 1875, a former scholar, then working as a nursemaid in nearby Woodstock, wrote to 'Dear Teacher' to describe her daily round. She admitted she did 'not like Woodstock near so much as Heyford and I long to come home again to see some of my friends and playmates ... Give my kindest love to all and accept the same yourself. I remain, your loving Scholar.' Another ex-pupil wrote from New York to tell her 'dear governess' that she was enjoying life as a maid there. When Mary finally retired in July 1913 she invited all the mothers of her pupils to a 'meat tea' which she herself provided.[28]

THE SCHOOL HOUSE,
LOWER HEYFORD,
BANBURY,
July 28th, 1913.

DEAR MADAM,

I have resigned my post as Head Mistress, after 46 years' work in this my only School, and shall have great pleasure in meeting you at a Social Gathering in the Schoolroom on Thursday afternoon, July 31st, 1913, at 3.30 o'clock.

I shall (D.V.) provide a Meat Tea, and hope all who are able will come and help us to spend a pleasant social evening.

After the tea there will be a small exhibition of work done by the children, and afterwards the children will dance the Maypole, and give other games.

I hope you will honour me with your company on this occasion, and that we shall have a happy time.

Believe me, dear Madam,

Yours very sincerely,

MARY DEW.

Please bring with you a plate, a knife and fork, a cup and saucer, and a tea spoon.

The invitation issued to pupils' mothers by Mrs Mary Dew when she retired as head of Lower Heyford School in 1913. (*The late Miss D. B. Dew*)

Jonathan Priestley, headmaster of Green Lane School, Bradford, with pupils, 1908. He was the son of a local millworker and was active in public welfare projects in Bradford. 'He believed in Education as few people nowadays believe in anything,' wrote his son, the novelist, J. B. Priestley. Not only did he take classes of adults in the evenings and at weekends but he also taught in his Baptist chapel Sunday school. He died in 1924. (*Bradford City Local Studies Library*)

But, without doubt, one of the most extraordinary displays of devotion by pupils to their teachers occurred in the small Norfolk parish of Burston in the spring of 1914, when almost the whole school went on 'strike' as a protest against what they considered the unfair dismissal of the school head, Mrs Annie Higdon, and her husband and assistant, Tom. In taking this action they had the wholehearted support of their parents.

The Higdons arrived in Burston on 31 January 1911, when Tom was almost forty-two and his wife five years his senior. This was not their first teaching appointment in Norfolk. In April 1902 Mrs Higdon had become head of Wood Dalling School and, under her guidance, standards had improved rapidly. But both she and her husband were angered by the failure of the managers to curb the illegal employment of pupils on local farms and by their neglect of the upkeep of the school premises. As a result of pressure by the Higdons, repairs were eventually carried out to the class-rooms but at the expense of creating friction between teachers and managers. Mrs Higdon, meanwhile, took a deep interest in the welfare of her pupils, providing gifts at Christmas and teaching the older girls to type and use a sewing machine, on equipment provided by herself.

Both of the Higdons were convinced socialists and they were much concerned at the poverty and bad housing of the local farm workers.

Mrs Annie Catherine Higdon (1864-1946) head of Burston School, Norfolk, from 1911 to 1914, and her husband and assistant, Tom (1869-1939), *c. 1900.* (*Trustees of Burston Strike School*)

Between 1906 and 1910 Tom actively promoted a branch of the Agricultural Labourers' Union in Wood Dalling. He also successfully encouraged some of the men to stand for election to the parish council. As a result, relations with the managers, several of whom were farmers, sharply worsened. Eventually, in 1910 the couple were threatened with dismissal when it was claimed that Mrs Higdon had called some of them liars, in a dispute over the timing of the school holidays and the heating of the school. Although Mrs Higdon denied this, she subsequently apologised for her outburst and, instead of being dismissed, she and her husband were transferred to Burston by the Norfolk Education Committee.

Prior to the arrival of the Higdons there had been a dozen teachers in the village in as many years. The last two heads had both applied for transfer after being in Burston less than three months, and it was generally agreed that, among other things, the school premises were cold and damp. Once the couple had settled in, conflict again developed between managers and teachers, as Tom Higdon took an active role in local political and trade union affairs and his wife demanded improvements to the school

Group of child strikers at Burston in April 1914. (*Trustees of Burston Strike School*)

buildings. These differences of opinion came to a head with the holding of parish council elections in March 1913.

As at Wood Dalling, Higdon set to work to get sufficient labourers nominated, along with himself and a sympathetic smallholder-cum-bricklayer, to win control of the council. Thanks to his energy, victory was secured but at considerable cost to himself. The rector, one of the unsuccessful candidates, and other members of the school management committee displayed increasing hostility towards the couple.

Eventually, Mrs Higdon was charged with having unreasonably caned two of the scholars. Although no satisfactory evidence was brought to support the claim – indeed, she was a well-known opponent of corporal punishment – she and her husband were dismissed. Many of the villagers suspected the charge was really brought because of Tom's political and trade union activity. Consequently when the couple were forced to leave the school on 31 March 1914, most of their pupils refused to attend any more. Instead the following morning they assembled on Burston Common under the leadership of one of the older girls, Violet Potter and marched round the village waving banners and placards inscribed with the slogans, 'We want our teachers back' and 'Justice'. As they marched, they sang to the accompaniment of Violet's concertina. In the days that followed they continued to boycott the official school and the replacement teachers sent by the Norfolk Education Committee. Instead they attended a temporary class established by Mrs Higdon, first in the open air on the village green, then in a tiny vacant cottage, and in a coalshed and copperhouse, before they eventually moved into a former carpenter's workshop.

Burston Strike School was built in 1917 on the edge of the village green. (*Trustees of Burston Strike School*)

And when the Higdons' belongings were removed from the school house, parents and children helped carry the goods from the premises and stored them in their own homes until the teachers obtained fresh accommodation. Nor did their loyalty waver even when some families were fined for failing to send their children to the official school.

The dispute continued to fester over the years and in 1917, with the backing of some of the trade unions and the help of villagers, a purpose-built 'strike' school was opened. It remained in operation until Tom Higdon's death in 1939, though by then the number of children in attendance had dwindled to a handful. The fact that Tom was himself the son of a Somerset farm labourer may have increased the couple's sympathy for, and understanding of, their pupils. But, whatever the reason, there is little doubt of the devotion they inspired among the scholars. 'I've seen her send out and buy children boots, if they came to school and their boots were leaking,' remembered one former pupil. Others recalled that Mrs Higdon laid particular stress on the importance of building one's life upon Christian values, especially the need to love and care for one another.[29]

Disputes of this magnitude were, fortunately, rare in the history of English elementary education. But the Burston dispute was not the only occasion when pupils went on strike in support of their teachers. Similar action was taken in Herefordshire early in 1914, when the local education authority refused to provide the county's teachers with a satisfactory salary

Ashperton children waiting to cheer their striking headmaster as he prepared to tour the county during the Herefordshire teachers' strike of 1914. (*British Library Newspaper Library*)

Pupils at Ledbury Girls' School surrounding the substitute headmistress appointed during the Herefordshire teachers' strike. They were barring her entrance to the school. (*British Library Newspaper Library*)

Not all pupils welcomed the Herefordshire dispute. This small boy was weeping because Ledbury Infants' School had been closed by the strike. (*British Library Newspaper Library*)

scale. The teachers resigned in protest and their pupils refused to attend schools where new staff had been appointed to replace those who had left. At Ledbury Girls' School, matters took a particularly serious turn, for when a new mistress came from Hertfordshire to take charge, a riot broke out.

Before the registers could be called, the girls dressed up brooms and affixed notices to them stating 'We are going to have our teachers back'. Desks were overturned 'to a piano accompaniment', according to one report, and the floor was 'bespattered with ink'. The new headmistress was chased out of the school by a crowd of children shouting 'blackleg' after her. Similar disturbances occurred in the afternoon and, according to *The Times*, these unseemly events were watched by a large crowd, composed mostly of the children's parents, who made no effort to end the uproar. On the walls and doors of the school the pupils wrote: 'We want our teachers back again and we mean to have them.'[30]

Similar unrest occurred at the boys' school at Ross, and in other cases it was decided not to attempt to reopen the schools. Faced with such scenes of pupil misbehaviour, some of the county's leading inhabitants pressed for an early settlement of the dispute and for the drawing up of a proper salary scale to match provisions in other counties at that time. In these circumstances, and under mounting pressure from the Board of Education, negotiations were entered into between teachers and local authority, and the strike was ended. Virtually all the teachers involved were reinstated in their old posts.[31] There can be little doubt that the scholars' action in supporting the demands of the teachers had helped in the speedy resolution of the conflict.

But Burston and Herefordshire were special cases. On a broader front, the period from 1870 to 1914 was a time when the blackspots of ignorance, poverty and deprivation were tackled among children living in the slums of large towns and in the more remote rural areas. From schooling, attention turned to the wider aspects of child welfare and, for a minority of pupils, the creation of a system of scholarships allowing free entry to secondary education. The school building programme inaugurated by the 1870 Elementary Education Act also led to a sharp increase in the size of the teaching profession. In 1870 there were 12,467 certificated teachers in England and Wales. That had almost trebled, to 31,422, a decade later. Pupil-teachers increased from 16,612 to 32,128 over the same period, while the number of assistant and 'additional' staff advanced from 1,262 in 1870 to 7,652 in 1880. The totals of certificated and assistant teachers continued to rise thereafter.[32] For women, in particular, the profession was, by 1914, a respectable and relatively attractive one, and they now made up three-quarters of the elementary labour force.

Meanwhile, within the nation as a whole the 'education of the people' had become recognised as an important responsibility of government, and the opportunity to attend school was regarded as the birthright of every child. Neither proposition would have been accepted without question in 1870. At the same time, the progressive raising of the minimum school-leaving age had also extended the boundaries of childhood. In the late 1860s factory legislation still allowed children to begin work at the age of eight, and in unregulated areas of employment, such as agriculture, an even earlier start might be made. By 1900, eleven or twelve was the accepted minimum working age, and that limit has continued to increase ever since.

Notes

PP = Parliamentary Papers

CHAPTER 1

1. Eric Midwinter, *Nineteenth Century Education* (1970), p. 37.
2. *Report of the Committee of Council on Education for 1869-70*, PP 1870, Vol. XXII, Report by the Revd H. B. Barry, HMI, p. 69.
3. John Burnett, *Destiny Obscure* (1984 edn), pp. 194-5.
4. *Reports Relating to Schools supported by the School Board of London*, PP1878, Vol. LX, Report by Mr Williams for 1875-76, p. 24.
5. Mary Sturt, *The Education of the People* (1967), pp. 272-3.
6. A. J. Swinburne, *Memories of a School Inspector* (n.d. *c.* 1914), p. 37 and pp. 40-1.
7. Margaret Penn, *Manchester Fourteen Miles* (1979 edn), p. 123.
8. M. K. Ashby, *Joseph Ashby of Tysoe 1859-1919* (1961), p. 18.
9. Newtown Church of England School Log-Book at Hampshire Record Office, 128M87/LB1.
10. Michael Sanderson, *Education, Economic Change and Society in England 1780-1870* (1983), p. 17.
11. David Rubinstein, *School Attendance in London, 1870-1904* (1969), p. 9.
12. *Report of the Committee of Council on Education for 1869-70*, Report by the Revd C. F. Johnstone, HMI, p. 146.
13. *Return for Birmingham, Leeds, Liverpool, and Manchester of all Schools for the Poorer Classes of Children*, PP 1870, Vol. LIV, p. 133.

14. John Hurt, *Elementary Schooling and the Working Classes 1860-1918* (1979), p. 55 and *Hansard*, 3rd Series, Vol. 199, col. 442.

15. Stuart Maclure, *One Hundred Years of London Education 1870-1970* (1970), p. 31. In 1899 there were still sixty-two iron buildings in use providing 8,000 places.

16. Quoted in Pamela Horn, *Education in Rural England, 1800-1914* (1978), p. 135.

17. Rules of Basingstoke National Schools as from 1 May 1876 at Hampshire Record Office 8M62/43. Children who left the schools and wished to be re-admitted had to pay an entrance fee of 1s and those absent on the day of the government examination were charged double fees or dismissed from the schools, unless their absence was due to illness.

18. John Hurt, op. cit., p. 71.

19. Margaret Penn, op. cit., p. 118.

20. John Burnett, op. cit., p. 155.

21. Denis A. Gibson, *Autobiography* (1986 typescript), privately communicated, p. 11.

22. John Reeves, *Recollections of a School Attendance Officer* (n.d. c. 1913), pp. 34-5 and p. 50.

23. Pamela Horn, *Village Education in Nineteenth-Century Oxfordshire* (Oxfordshire Record Society Vol. 51, 1979), pp. 116-20.

24. *Reports to the School Board of London by the Inspectors respecting the Schools supported by the Board for the Years 1876 and 1877*, PP 1878, Vol. LX, Report for 1876 by Mr Noble, p. 4.

25. Quoted in David Rubinstein, 'Socialization and the London School Board 1870-1904: aims, methods and public opinion' in P. McCann (ed.), *Popular Education and Socialization in the 19th Century* (1977), p. 231.

26. *Report of the Committee of Council on Education for 1872-73*, PP 1873, Vol. XXIV, Report by the Revd C. H. Parez, HMI, p. 111.

27. *Copy of Reports to the London School Board of Inspectors Appointed by the Board respecting the Schools supported by the Board in 1875*, PP 1876, Vol. LIX, pp. 1-2.

28. John Burnett, op. cit., pp. 199-200.

29. Stephen Humphries, *Hooligans or Rebels?* (1983 paperback edn), pp. 97-8.

30. Sybil Marshall, *Fenland Chronicle* (1980 paperback edn), p. 23.

31. John Burnett, op. cit., p. 154.

32. Sutton Courtenay Church School Log-Book for 1905-1939, consulted by kind permission of the head teacher.

33. Senrab Street Girls' School Log-Book at the London Metropolitan Archives, EC/DIV5/SEN/LB/3.

43. *Annual Report for 1914 of the Chief Medical Officer of the Board of Education*, p. 90.

44. Ibid., pp. 125 and 131.

45. *Education in Bradford 1870-1970*, p. 130.

46. Helen Allinson, 'Open Air Schools' in *Local History*, No. 18 (June 1988), p. 11; Hugh Broughton, *The Open Air School* (n.d. *c.* 1915), pp. 15-18.

47. Quoted in Helen Allinson, op. cit., p. 12.

48. *Annual Report for 1912 of the Chief Medical Officer of the Board of Education*, PP 1914, Vol. XXV, p. 79 and Annual Report for 1914, p. 160.

49. *Education in Bradford 1870-1970*, p. 134.

50. *Annual Report for 1914 of the Chief Medical Officer*, pp. 165-6.

51. *Report of Dr Crichton-Browne to the Education Department*, Memorandum by Mr J. G. Fitch, pp. 76-7.

52. B. Seebohm Rowntree, op. cit., pp. 210-14.

CHAPTER 4

1. Margaret Llewelyn Davies (ed.), *Life as We Have Known It* (1931), pp. 56-7.

2. *Report of the Inter-Departmental Committee on the Employment of School Children, 1901*, PP 1902, Vol. XXV, p. 14. Hereafter cited as *1901 Report*. Patricia E. Malcolmson, *English Laundresses. A Social History, 1850-1930* (1986), p. 21.

3. *Board of Agriculture and Fisheries: Wages and Conditions of Employment in Agriculture*, Vol. II, PP 1919, Vol. IX, Report on Cardiganshire, p. 412.

4. Quoted in Harold Silver, 'Ideology and the factory child: attitudes to half-time education' in *Popular Education and Socialization in the Nineteenth Century*, P. McCann (ed.) (1977), p. 144.

5. Brian Simon, Education and the Labour Movement 1870-1920 (1965), p. 290.

6. *Annual Report for 1912 of the Chief Medical Officer of the Board of Education*, PP 1914, Vol. XXV, p. 310.

7. Ben Turner, *About Myself 1863-1930* (1930), p. 39.

8. John R. Clynes, *Memoirs*, Vol. 1, 1869-1924 (1937), pp. 49-50.

9. *Daily News*, 3 January 1899; *The Schoolmaster*, Special Supplement on the Half-timers, 9 February 1895, p. 259.

10. *The Schoolmaster*, Special Supplement on the Half-timers, p. 259; Allen Clarke, *The Effects of the Factory System* (1899), pp. 102-3.

11. *Report of the Inter-Departmental Committee on Partial Exemption from School Attendance*, PP 1909, Vol. XVII, p. 6.
12. Ibid., Appendix 8, p. 256.
13. Allen Clarke, op. cit., p. 97.
14. 'Agricultural Gangs' in *Quarterly Review*, Vol. 123 (1867), p. 179. Peter Kirby, *Child Labour in Britain, 1750-1870* (2003), p. 60.
15. *1901 Report* Appendix No. 2, Comments of Mr J. B. Simpson of Hunmanby, p. 287.
16. Ibid., Comments by Col. Raikes of Alcester, p. 293.
17. *First Report of the Royal Commission on the Employment of Children, Young Persons and Women in Agriculture*, PP 1867-68, Vol. XVII, Report by the Revd James Fraser, p. 13.
18. *1901 Report* Appendix No. 2, Comments by Mr J. Tousley of Hampstead Norris, p. 279.
19. Quoted in P. L. R. Horn, 'The Agricultural Children Act of 1873' in *History of Education*, Vol. 3, No. 2 (1974), p. 36.
20. Roger R. Sellman, *Devon Village Schools in the Nineteenth Century* (1967), p. 120.
21. Fred Kitchen, *Brother to the Ox* (1963 edn), p. 26.
22. *1901 Report*, Evidence of Mrs Desprelles, Q.1739 and Q.1745-55.
23. Ibid., Evidence of Mr Foster, Q.1833-6.
24. *Minutes of the Education Committee of the London County Council*, September to December 1904, p. 1182.
25. Allen Clarke, op. cit., p. 101 and pp. 121-2.
26. Pamela Horn, 'Child Workers in the Pillow Lace and Straw Plait Trades of Victorian Buckinghamshire and Bedfordshire' in *Historical Journal*, Vol. XVII, No. 4 (1974), pp. 784-5.
27. *Report of the Commissioners Appointed to Inquire into the Working of the Factory and Workshops Acts*, PP 1876, Vol. XXIX, Appendix D, Report from Assistant-Inspector F. H. Whymper, p. 173.
28. Tape-recording of the late Mrs E. Turney in the possession of my late sister-in-law, Mrs M. Horn, to whom my thanks are due.
29. Pamela Horn, 'Child Workers in the Pillow Lace and Straw Plait Trades', ibid, p. 779.
30. Ibid., p. 793.
31. Ivinghoe School log-book at Buckinghamshire Record Office, E/LBI 1161/1.
32. Harold Silver, op. cit., p. 152.
33. *The Schoolmaster*, Special Supplement, p. 255.
34. *Daily News*, 3 January 1899.
35. *1901 Report*, p. 5.
36. Ibid., p. 6.

Index

Girl Reading

KATIE WARD

virago

VIRAGO

First published in Great Britain in 2011 by Virago Press

Copyright © Katie Ward 2011

The moral right of the author has been asserted.

*All characters and events in this publication, other than those
clearly in the public domain, are fictitious and any resemblance
to real persons, living or dead, is purely coincidental.*

A CIP catalogue record for this book
is available from the British Library.

ISBN 978-1-84408-738-9

Typeset in Horley by M Rules
Printed and bound in Great Britain by
Clays Ltd, St Ives plc

Virago Press
An imprint of
Little, Brown Book Group
100 Victoria Embankment
London EC4Y 0DY

An Hachette UK Company
www.hachette.co.uk

This is a book for David.

Contents

You can never say with certainty whether what appears to be going on in the collective unconscious of a single individual is not also happening in other individuals or organisms or things or situations.

C. G. Jung
'Synchronicity: An Acausal Connecting Principle'
(*Collected Works*, volume 8)

Simone Martini

Annunciation, 1333

She arrives glowing from the effort of running, strands of red hair coming loose from her kerchief (she tucks them in), marks on her neck like bruises on fruit. A few minutes late but not enough for anyone to mention it. Is almost surprised to find herself in the wards once more amid illness and suffering (on an evening such as this). Her mind is elsewhere. She accepts a dish, a spoon, instructions to feed a patient who rasps with each breath, whose sores stink, who has for eyes one piercing brown bead and one sagging black hole. Familiar and strange, ordinary and violent.

She does not smile encouragingly at the invalid to finish her meal, does not add to the whispered hubbub of the stone halls. They labour together in silence. The crone chews and swallows slowly despite the impulse of her body to reject what it consumes; the girl holds the spoon out, withdraws it, rests it; the food on the plate scarcely diminishes. Candle flames are

1

skittish in the draught, creating the impression of hasty movement.

The old woman speaks; the girl is roused from her private thoughts. Who are you?

My name is Laura Agnelli.

That is not what I asked.

A patient in a bed further along screams with pain. There is a disturbance. Some run to her aid, some are disgusted and afraid to be close by.

Laura offers one last mouthful to her charge, wipes the remnants from her bluish lips. I am a daughter of Santa Maria della Scala hospital.

You are a foundling? What is your history?

I have none.

You have a name though.

The rector himself named me Agnelli. It means 'lamb'. He is over there. Laura indicates, without pointing, Rettore Giovanni di Tese Tolomei, a man as wide as he is tall, his thumb tucked into his finery as he makes his inspection of the wards.

The woman swivels her eye towards him, then back to the girl. You were plucked from a crop of innocents by that man?

He showed me compassion because I was weak. He held me in his own arms and gave me his blessing, so I am told.

I am surprised he did not mistake you for a ham.

Laura frowns at the crone. He saved my life.

Did he?

And the lives of many foundlings, before and since.

But he bestowed his favour on *you*. It is not an honour I would wish for a daughter of mine.

The patient's pillow needs rearranging, the bedclothes have slipped down; Laura sets them right, noticing as she does so how cold are the limbs beneath.

The old woman winks her eye. What else do they tell you?

That it was Our Lady who inspired him. The rector heard me crying, held me and foretold that I would take religious vows – and that one day, I would bring rewards to Santa Maria della Scala hospital and the whole city of Siena.

The woman raises her good eyebrow, exaggerating the unevenness of her face; Laura covers the marks on her neck, uneasy.

What do the other children make of it?

They never say.

How did you come to be called Laura? Did your mother call you this?

I know not.

Maybe when she could provide nothing else, she gave you this name – Laura – hoping you would like it?

Yes, you might be right.

She did what she thought was for the best, like all mothers who bring their babes here and turn them over to Signor Rettore. *Suffer little children to come unto me.* (The woman shuts her eye, while the other socket hangs open still.) Yes, I can see her perfectly, even though she is doing her best to hide. Her head is uncovered, she lets her hair hang about her shoulders like the fallen woman she is. Pitiful. But we should not be too harsh on her; it is only because she is using every fragment of cloth to keep the infant warm. She is giving it her blessing before she parts with it: *I hope you will be spared the pain I knew.* Is that all? Such a small request, for such a small wriggling bundle! And yet it is worth a dozen of Signor Rettore's grand pronouncements. She looks tired . . . poor thing has not slept in days. She should sleep now, I think.

Laura counts the lengthening spaces between the woman's breaths, stays by the bedside for many hours until it is over.

*

What pretty feet you have. Like two pigeons with their wings folded and their heads tucked in. Do you dance?

Not often. Not well. When there is music, and I am moved to.

I imagine you bouncing and bobbing like a wheat stalk in a breeze, and afterwards I imagine you rosy and out of breath. What pretty knees you have too. There is no doubt about it, God intends you to be a bride. *My* bride.

You are making fun of me.

I would swear to it. Pretty legs. Where the heart goes, the body has to follow.

What did you say? What are you doing?

The magnificent cathedral is the envy of every city state. It matches the ambitions of those who built it, and the saints themselves would nod their appreciation. The Duomo is absolutely Siena's, and Siena is absolutely the Virgin's. How they flourish under her protection.

A man stands before the high altar but he is not here for mass, and he has no awe in his heart. He is inspecting something he has seen hundreds of times before, his objectivity strained. Wealth does not impress him, for he is wealthier than most. Lavish decorations hold few surprises these days. His arms are folded across his chest like a farmer's, his gargoyle features contracted in a scowl; a short lump of a man. Were it not for the fine weave of his tunic, the opulence of its colour, the ornate trim, he might be mistaken for a pilgrim or even a beggar. He senses a presence in this marvellous place (how it glitters, how it is still!) but it is no angel or deity: it is the laughing ghost of a man he knew extremely well in life.

The altarpiece is the *Maestà*, the enormous panel showing the Madonna and Child upon a throne, adored by a host of angels and saints. It is surrounded by smaller storytelling panels and drenched in gold. For the faithful, the *Maestà* is a channel to the

4

Virgin: she sees out of those very eyes, hears their pleas through it. On the day it was installed in the Duomo, there was a procession led by the bishop, the priests and friars around the Campo, attended by the Nine, the entire Commune, the citizens of Siena. Resplendent, it passed through the crowds. Bells rang, alms were given to the poor, prayers were made to Our Lady, our advocate. It is Duccio's (old master, old rogue). Simone Martini snorts.

Simone Martini? I've heard of him! He was Duccio's pupil.

This is the best accolade he can hope for now. One wants to be trained by the greatest living artist, and then to transcend him. That will not happen.

Simone examines the icon, trying to see it as a peasant would, as a monk would, as a lord, a foreigner, a child, a dog. He tries to see it for what it seems to be and for what it is. He tries to see its multiplicity in order to see its truth, but the truth eludes him like incense. It is before him, around him, above him, but vanishes into air. He is morose.

A new commission for Siena Cathedral. Something *different*. He is getting what he wants, and he does not like it. He does not like the serpent of his vanity being provoked by a bishop's crozier.

Vescovo Donusdeo dei Malavolti glides towards the artist, extends his hooked hand for Simone to kiss the episcopal ring. The bishop has an ancient face but his frailty comes and goes. Sometimes the sharp edge of his willpower is visible, which can be dangerous; sometimes he is as meek as a kitten, which can be lethal. When the formalities are over, he extends a trembling pat of reassurance to the artist's arm and wheezes, It warms me, Maestro Simone, to see that you have begun your work. That is what I like about painters, they always have their most valuable tool on their person: their imagination. You cannot help it, can you? You are making lines and filling shapes with pigment even

5

as we stand here. If I were a betting man, which naturally I am not, I would say you have made up your mind what the finished piece will look like. But I must rein in your impulses, though it grieves me to, for I would be intrigued to know what the farthest limits of your creativity can do. It is the Opera del Duomo, you see. You know what they are like. Some of them can be resistant to innovation. They mean well, of course, but it would be remiss of me not to repeat, for appearance's sake, the prescriptions they have made.

Prescriptions?

Prescription, guidance, what you will. You know best, and I trust you will interpret their expressed wishes suitably. They are not as brave as you and me. Were it my choice, I would say go and do your best, give to the cathedral whatever your genius can conceive of, and be as radical as you dare. They ought to listen to me, but they do not. I am too lenient with them. I sympathise, Maestro Simone, I do. Having someone restrict what you can paint must make you feel as I would feel if someone restricted my prayers.

I would not want my prayers inhibited either. What are the instructions?

Hardly worth mentioning. As I have stated already, you are to paint a functioning altarpiece which celebrates our principal protector, the Virgin, and represents an episode from her life. In due course there will be four new altars in the cathedral, each dedicated to one of Siena's auxiliary patrons, starting with Saint Ansanus – and then Saint Savinus, Saint Victor and Saint Crescentius. Each altar will feature a moment from Our Lady's history. Yours is the first commission. I insisted to the Opera del Duomo that you should have the honour.

You flatter me, Vescovo. So far, these are reasonable specifications.

I am glad you think so. The next point is one I am sure your

6

expert eye has already discerned: that the new altarpiece must be in harmony with Duccio's *Maestà*, and naturally in keeping with the traditions of the faith. How do you fellows say? The spatial relationship, the style, must not depart from his. There should be accord.

Simone takes some steps away from the bishop, and faces the spot where his altarpiece would be installed relative to Duccio's: to the side of it; smaller in size than it; dedicated to a relatively obscure saint instead of the Virgin herself; replicating his old tutor's hand. Vescovo Donusdeo is correct; the artist had indeed guessed as much. Simone says, What if I am engaged in another commission? I am in great demand.

The bishop laughs. Who in Siena would put his own interests above the needs of the Church? Tell me the name of the man who is attempting to commandeer you, and I shall personally intervene. It must be at the preliminary stages of negotiation in any case – I spoke with your brother-in-law, and know you not to be under contract at present.

Simone remains rigid, and silently curses Lippo.

Besides, the patronal altars of Siena will become supremely famous. After the first has been dedicated, artists will flock from miles around to beg for the next commission. People will expect it of you, Simone, as Siena's famous son, to make a panel for the Duomo. The question is not whether you paint one, but *which one* you will paint. I suspect that you would prefer to be the pioneer, and to have the freest hand. Have I not said, moreover, that what the Opera requires of you is something quite new?

You wish me to create an icon that maintains tradition, and yet is entirely original?

I am relieved you understand. You are capable of it.

The artist gazes at Duccio's legacy.

The bishop shares his contemplation briefly and sighs. It is a remarkable object, a singular tribute to the majesty of Our Lady. Do you think I am blind as well as old, my dear Simone? Do you think bishops arrive in office fully formed? Every day I walk in the footprints of my predecessors.

Have the Nine been informed of this project?

I am sure somebody has conveyed the news. You know how easily these things get about.

Are they aware the Duomo is appropriating some of their imagery?

Their imagery . . . ? I am not sure I follow.

Well, you say there shall be four altars dedicated to Siena's patrons – and citizens will come here to the cathedral to petition the saints through prayer, and the saints in turn petition the Blessed Virgin Mary and she in her turn is their advocate to God. True? I am simply wondering if the politicians could view this arrangement as – evocative.

You amuse me. What a cynic you have become. You have such a low opinion of people, and for what reason? I am sure such a misplaced and petty notion would not occur to any of the Council of Nine. And if it did, shame would prevent them from saying it aloud. And if they said so, I would answer, the Church is staking a claim only to that which she already owns.

Simone senses the bishop's enjoyment in being able to rehearse his argument.

But let me explain something to you, in strictest confidence. I know you will appreciate the spirit of it. Siena is a beam of marble supported by three columns: the Town Hall, Siena Cathedral and Santa Maria della Scala hospital. If one of these cracks or weakens, the other two must take more of the strain, so all is kept stable. Coincidental that you and I should visit this topic now, when I was debating it with Rettore Giovanni di Tese Tolomei just yesterday. He and I have had many productive conversations on this matter . . .

He notices how the bishop leaves the ribbon of his remark hanging in space, inviting someone to tug it. You have concerns about the Nine?

Certainly not. The oligarchs do a fine job. Legislating, scrutinising decisions, collecting taxes, arbitrating – how shall we say? – *disputes* regarding boundaries and livestock, and so on. Custodianship of these mundane matters is, I suppose, a necessity. And yet, even the ruling classes must acknowledge that truth is to be found not in the letter of the law but in the Word of God, and that the richest currency is not vulgar struck metal but what is scored into men's hearts. You count real wealth by good deeds and by saved souls, by charity and by faith. The Council of Nine, through no fault of their own, do not understand how transient they are. Their world is unstable, fickle. When the government of fair Siena has fallen twice-twenty times, the poor will still seek respite at her hospital, and sinners will still pray for salvation at her church. *These* are per-manent. *These* endure. I know it absolutely, and Signor Rettore is of the same mind. It is our moral obligation as Christians to act in accordance with what a perfect God has decreed, not with what imperfect and fallible men have frivolously decided. *Render to Caesar the things that are Caesar's, and to God the things that are God's.* (The bishop pauses, waiting for the other to concur, but Simone remains dispassionate.) I hear unsettling rumours.

Rumours are rarely of the reassuring kind.

I ought not to repeat them, because I do not believe them, they are too ridiculous. But you are a well-connected man and they will reach your ears sooner or later, so I really might as well tell you; apparently the Nine are planning an assault on the hos-pital and the cathedral. Not one of physical force, you understand – one of diktat. For Siena's hospital: a meticulous inventory of their assets and a regimen limiting their tax-free entitlements. For Siena's cathedral: the creation of a new 'official', a secular bureaucrat who would mediate between the church and the Nine, and be ever present. Well, it is very far-fetched.

And devilish?

Must you be so glib, Maestro Simone? I do not concern myself with the little schemes Siena's government might or might not be concocting, I have no time for it. But Signor Rettore and I agree that our institutions, or rather God's, could cooperate much more. We acknowledge that we can be of unique help to one another.

There. The bishop has all but told the artist he and Rettore Giovanni di Tese Tolomei have formed an alliance. No, Simone sneers inwardly, more than an alliance; they are in cahoots. He pictures the handshake: one hand gnarled and sinewy, covered in the spots of age, clasping the other, plump and pink, the jewels on their knuckles knocking together. What Vescovo Donusdeo dei Malavolti says next confirms his suspicions.

I understand you are planning a trip to Avignon, Maestro? If you manage to have a private moment with the Pope, please convey my personal greetings to him as his humble servant, admirer and brother.

You are misinformed. I have not yet made up my mind about going to Avignon. If I make the journey, I will of course pass on your message.

I hope you will also consider putting in a good word for Santa Maria della Scala hospital. The Holy Father is able to bestow favours on the agencies performing God's works, you know.

Yes, I am aware.

I was holding a light aloft for you. Our Lady would want you to remember Siena's hospital to the Pope, I guarantee it, and I shall entreat her to speak to your better judgement.

The painter re-examines the sallow features of the bishop, and wonders what precisely the rector of the hospital has offered him which has him so enthralled? Something more than mere strategic advantage. It has a filthy-dark quality to it, and moves Simone to change the subject. Tell me, Vescovo, when does the Opera del Duomo expect their new altarpiece?

By the feast of Saint Ansanus, on the first day of December.

That is less than two years hence, but not inconceivable.

Considerably less than two years. They want it by this coming feast of Saint Ansanus.

Simone Martini stares at Vescovo Donusdeo but does not speak. The acquisition of materials, carpentry and gold-beating alone would normally take at least a year.

If the bishop perceives a problem, his face does not betray him. He waits serenely for Simone's reply.

The artist's mind turns to the wife he will neglect if he accepts this commission, and intuitively he recalls her birthday and the gift he gave, her intake of breath when she saw it, the gratification to have chosen a present she adores . . . and his annoyance when she insisted on having her fortune told (it was her birthday, he could not refuse her whim) . . . A card was turned over for him, *La Papessa*. He says aloud, I have a condition before I agree.

A condition? The bishop crosses himself and mutters a prayer. Maestro Simone, I am not a well man. I cannot vouch for what will happen if you presume to make demands. But you may make a request, and I shall take the matter to the Opera for discussion.

I want to do an Annunciation.

He recoils. Oh, my dear Simone. Extraordinary. I am amazed. What an idea. Oh. I am struck by your audacity. Are you sure this is what you want me to tell them?

Do you not think the Opera will approve? Did they not specifically request something new?

11

The bishop's serenity appears to have deserted him; he succumbs to a vicious cough.

The artist does not enquire after the bishop's health, remarks instead, Funny that you should approach me now, when I am actively considering retirement from painting – did I not mention it before? – in order to spend more time with my wife. She tells me I have made my mark on the world. I take her views very seriously.

Vescovo Donusdeo puckers his dry mouth and draws his hairy eyebrows together, two caterpillars meeting on a leaf. Eventually he says, Can you do it?

Simone does not need to look at Duccio's *Maestà* any more; every inch of it is committed to memory. He nods.

The bishop throws up his hand in surrender and agitation. I do not know. I shall have to make a very thoughtful argument. Some may call it controversial, but if it were done correctly, if it conveyed Our Lady's obedience and piety . . . on balance I am cautiously optimistic that the officials of the Opera del Duomo could be – how shall we say? – *persuaded* to take a risk on a talent as unique as yours. After proper consultation and prayer, of course. An Annunciation, then! Congratulations, Maestro Simone, we are thrilled to have engaged you for this commission. There is one further detail I ought to tell you, although it is of such little consequence.

Three girls, including Laura Agnelli, kneel or crouch by baskets of almonds, shelling and grinding. It is hard, repetitive work. Imelda calls it peasant work, and moans that the land labourers should do it, not the daughters of Santa Maria della Scala. The almonds they have done are paltry in number, while the almonds left to do seem hardly to have reduced in volume. They will be at this for hours, aching and numb afterwards, sick of the sight and smell. The time would pass better were talking permitted.

The noise of the scraping makes discreet conversation difficult; nonetheless Imelda manages to mutter some of her complaints into Gisila's ear.

When I am married I shall have servants, and if they displease me I shall not flog them but make them grind mountains of almonds, then I shall feed the almonds to the pigs.

Servants and pigs? Almonds to dispense as punishment? What a daydreamer you are, Imelda.

Why should I not? Look at what they make us do. We are no better than slaves. As long as we are here, they own us body and soul. What have I to lose by indulging my dreams, when they take practically everything else?

We are the fortunate ones.

Are we? Do you think they love us as God's children? We embody our parents' sin. We are the offspring of harlots, beggars and adulterers – and they treat us as such.

What happened to Guido? I thought you liked him. He certainly fancied you. Or is a boy raised at the hospital not good enough for you any more?

I can do better than Guido. There are plenty of men outside this compound, you know. You just have to make sure you are not caught. (Laura quickens the rhythm of her labour to drown out Imelda's nattering.) Guido is immature, and his breath smells horrible. Is it too much to ask for a husband who has whiskers and a kiss which does not suffocate me? I expect at least that of a man – and that he will have a legitimate lineage and a fat inheritance coming his way.

Gisila laughs at her friend's bad temper. Then take comfort in your dreams. Think of the servants you will have one day, and how you can mistreat them, if it cheers you up. Think of your fine furs and your enormous house with a balcony, and your own mare to ride. Think of what your husband will look like, whether he will be dark or fair, whether he will be lean or broad. And

13

think of your father-in-law, who will be elderly and will dote on you.

I do, every day. If God loves me, he will send a rich man to save me from this hell. And when I am married, I shall definitely have a big—

Imelda stops short of naming the thing she will have, for the rector himself is visible in the passageway speaking to a gentleman neither of them recognises. The stranger is distinctly handsome, with black hair and brown eyes, dressed in a plaid kirtle and a red chaperon, with a buckle on his belt that gleams. Gisila cannot resist it and whispers, Your prayers have been answered, Imelda; here he comes now to take you to his mansion.

Imelda presses her attractive mouth to stifle the giggle, and permits herself a look of admiration at the man in conference with the rector, surely here to make a donation and so avoid paying unwanted duties. It is the rector's method to show off the charity and industry of the hospital, to emphasise the spiritual benefits of generosity to Santa Maria and to make people part with more than they initially intended. He is as skilful as a market pickpocket.

Then he does something surprising. He abandons his visitor momentarily in order to come over to the three girls (there is an increase in speed and purpose under his gaze). He clears his throat. Laura Agnelli, come with me, please.

Laura obediently wipes her hands on her apron, stands, follows.

Behind her back, the malign eyes of Imelda and Gisila meet, then separate. It is not unheard of that a man comes to the hospital and points to the young woman he wants as though selecting fish for the dinner table. Usually there is some semblance of paying court and an opportunity for the girl to refuse, followed by a wedding. *Usually.* However, Rettore Giovanni di

Tese Tolomei is fond of saying the well-being of the hospital is more important than the well-being of any one individual – many times his actions have demonstrated the sincerity of his belief.

Imelda murmurs savagely, I thought she was going into a convent.

The rector presents Laura to the visitor, who looks her up and down and answers yes, she will do. The rector continues, Laura, you are to go with this man to his master. You are to do whatever they ask of you for as long as they have a use for you. They will give you your meals when you are there. You will be submissive, patient, meek and conduct yourself as though the Blessed Virgin were standing at your side. This is a privilege and a test, and it will be a shame upon us all, not to mention a per onal offence to me, if your behaviour is not immaculate. In fact, it may have serious repercussions for your future. Do you understand?

Yes, Signor Rettore.

And Laura goes with the stranger. Perhaps, she acknowledges inwardly, into danger.

They do not walk far, up and down the city slopes, through the narrow streets, the stalls and relative safety of the Campo. He does not speak. It is when they go into a house and ascend a stairway into a private room (the door locked behind her) that Laura's heart jumps and she sends silent prayers to the Virgin to protect her, and if she cannot protect her then to limit her pain and suffering as far as possible, and if she cannot do that, then to grant Laura the strength to endure whatever is to take place.

The room is sparse though large, like a tradesman's workshop or rented storeroom, with enormous windows letting in Siena's glorious sky above and commotion beneath. It is occupied by a second man, significantly older, a hunched gnome who does not acknowledge them nor interrupt his inspection of documents. Laura looks for a bed, but there is none, just commonplace wooden furniture, scrolls and tools as though a great plan were being executed, a military campaign. That is Laura's impression. The ugly man is the general, the handsome one his lieutenant.

The younger man says, Maestro, will you see if you approve?

Simone Martini answers with a growl and puts down his parchment. As before, Laura's face and bearing are scrutinised, but this one pinches her chin to turn her head in profile and appears displeased with what he sees. To his subordinate he says, I have begun to think this is a terrible idea.

Signor Rettore was ... um ... quite *specific* that the girl ought to come every morning after Lauds and not return home before dusk, unless called for.

(Laura blinks at this news.)

We must have her here all day, every day?

Except the Sabbath.

This is unacceptable. You did not counter him, Lippo?

(Laura notices the assistant's fingers crossed behind his back.)

Well, it was not easily done.

Simone Martini is exasperated. Lippo, the keen and insecure patron will be constantly at your elbow, interfering, finding defects which do not exist. And now we have, in effect, *two*.

Lippo Memmi replies with more conviction, It is not too late to refuse the commission. I for one will not care about displeasing the bishop. We can go to Florence or to Venice, where your genius will be appreciated.

Simone grumbles indistinctly and returns to his plans, which Lippo interprets as a direction to continue.

For Laura, Lippo has further instructions, picking up the rector's refrain: You must sit in complete silence, for your very presence disturbs my master's work. You must let no one in without the master or myself being present, and ensure always this door is locked. Do you fear God? I said, do you fear God?

16

Yes.

Do you fear the flames of hell and the trident of Lucifer?

Yes.

I hope so, because I am about to make you swear an oath of secrecy. If anyone enquires about our panel, or asks you to report what has taken place in this room, if anyone – the rector, the bishop, anybody from the Commune, the Nine or the Opera del Duomo – asks you what is happening or is spoken about within these walls, you will cut out your own tongue before answering them and rot in hell when you do. Do you so swear?

Laura wavers. A promise of this kind is an extremely serious matter. If what you say is true, Signore, then what answer may I make to men such as these?

You may say the master works hard, and it appears to be going well, and that what you have seen of his design is extraordinary and confounds your understanding. You will furnish any details which distract from the substance of what they seek to know – describe the shoes my master is wearing, say whether it rained on your walk here, or that you had a splinter in your finger. You will tell them *anything* which protects the panel and my master from their scrutiny. Now, do you so swear?

Laura stammers, Yes, I swear—

Good.

– but there must be a mistake.

Child, they will all seek you out; yours are the most valuable eyes and ears in Siena. But remember, you belong to us. And while you are with us, you shall not chatter nor venture unnecessary questions; in fact, you would do well to make yourself invisible. Hush now, this is serious business.

A small chair has been set aside in the corner, and Lippo gestures for Laura to sit down. Uncertain what exactly is required of her, Laura Agnelli does so tentatively.

The two men turn away to confer in lowered voices. They

discuss names and plot dates, and estimate quantities and measurements and sums of money, extravagant sums of money (initially she thought she misheard), the kind of money Laura has never seen and will never see. She waits to be given another instruction, has nothing to occupy her except to sit alternating her attention between the gentlemen and the bustle outside which, unhappily, is out of sight unless she strains in her chair to peer over the sill. The older man is agitated, his fury sinks and rises over some problem or other, some unreasonable behaviour that maddens him. The assistant is unruffled by the master's shouting, suggests a solution, a different solution then, a compromise. Then he makes a note of their decision and does calculations.

At midday, a maidservant brings a basket of bread and tomatoes. Laura lets her in. The maid greets Signor Martini and Signor Memmi – this is how Laura learns their names – leaves the food and to Laura's dismay, departs forthwith.

Later Laura is sent home, unaccompanied.

And this is how the second day passes.

By the third day, Lippo Memmi is not present, sent away to procure materials and appoint workers. Simone Martini spends the day reading his books. The boredom makes Laura weary, but she does not complain. She has ample time to ponder how much longer she will be required to come here (a whole week? two?) and if her role is simply to sit quietly and observe, or if there is more to it that will be revealed later. At dusk, when Simone Martini lights a candle, she rises from her seat.

Maestro Simone, it is time for me to go, unless you have further use for me . . . ?

(This would be sarcasm if spoken by another girl, but Laura Agnelli does not mean it that way.)

18

The artist drags his attention from his research and appears startled to find her there. Yes, you may go.

She makes a small bow of respect.

What is your name, child?

Laura Agnelli.

Indeed, you are like a lamb, one that does not bleat. Tomorrow bring your spindle. You should not be idle.

Simone Martini has begun preparatory drawings, with each one his humour deteriorates further still. He sketches them out with a pen and red and black inks, bent like a monk in a scriptorium, his back giving him pain. Sometimes the modelli are more elaborate – he goes as far as making meticulous scale paintings. Laura watched with curiosity the first time he broke an egg into a cup, the familiar sound causing her to look up. He slithered the yolk in his fingers, pinched it, pierced the sac with a tiny blade, let the yellow liquid run out to mix with ground pigment. These are Simone's experiments in colour and design, but Laura knows them only as a flourish and a blur when he casts them aside as inadequate.

In the absence of Lippo, he finds reasons to bellow at Laura – for staring at him when she drifted off into a meditative state; for her stomach groaning the day she missed breakfast; for the clatter when she dropped her spindle on the floor. She begins to dread her next misdemeanour.

At noon, Laura rises to let in the maid but instead it is an elegant young lady, hair like the feathers on a rook, slim and exquisitely dressed, carrying an armful of cut lilies and a basket. Laura withdraws to her corner.

So this is where all the yarn comes from! I did not truly believe one person could make so much in a day.

Simone Martini huffs and Laura does not reply, assumes she is not meant to. The young woman lays down the bouquet, the

19

heady aroma of the lilies overpowering the warm space, and unpacks the basket: swathes of lavish fabric and wrapped parcels, which Simone stirs himself to sort through. He frowns. Why did you not send the maid, Giovanna?

Because Antonia is busy. And I wanted to come myself. To see you, my lord. To eat with you.

And yet you have brought no food.

Giovanna tilts her head in reproach. I thought I would bring the things you asked for first, then go to the Campo to buy some. If it is not too distracting for you, you can tell me what you would most like to eat.

Laura expects this tartness to be answered in kind, but Simone Martini's expression softens into paternal indulgence.

Figs, Giovanna, should do very well.

Figs. Then I shall bring you some. How is your work?

Simone sighs, waves the question away.

Giovanna picks up some of the studies – figures and triptychs – and looks them over. What is the matter with all these? Why can you not make a decision?

Do not concern yourself with it. Only one of us needs to be troubled.

Giovanna pouts, examines the sketches more closely, briefly glances at Laura, then murmurs, Not one of these Virgins is in the act of spinning.

Simone Martini takes them from her and shuffles the sheets together, grunting, I am getting to it.

My lord, the panel is within your reach. Your greatness is more than equal to this task. When it is finished, it will undoubtedly be the jewel of Siena. And yet ... I must protest, if it is affecting your health, if the sacrifices you are making are too much for you—

Simone kisses Giovanna on the forehead and she leaves the rest unsaid. Laura senses this is a longstanding family argument,

20

that he has mastered the girl's grievances and has gently reminded her of it.

Then I will go to the Campo for you. Would you like to come with me?

The question is not to Simone but to Laura, though he answers for her, *She* has instructions to stay.

The lady's voice has a note of weariness to it, Yes, from the rector, I know ... but he did not mean to trap her here, to deny her sun and air every now and then! What do *you* think?

Again this question is thrown to Laura rather than Simone. Laura forms the impression Giovanna often gets her way.

The gradient of the square slopes down to the Palazzo Pubblico. People are at work on the construction of the impressive tower, specks moving on the scaffolding. Laura waits to be addressed by Giovanna, who is preoccupied with the wares and produce on display. Finally she says, This must be strange for you. I expect you ask yourself why you agreed to do it.

I did not agree to it, I was commanded.

I see. Yes, that makes more sense. I suppose you are indebted to the people who raised you?

They saved my life, and gave me everything.

No doubt you are often reminded of it. Do you like it at Santa Maria della Scala?

The hospital is all I know.

It is your home but not your family, maybe? Do they tell you anything about your parents? Do you know whether yours are alive or dead?

No, they do not, and it is for the best, otherwise people would always be running away to try and find them. We have enough problems of that sort as it is. Oh dear, perhaps I should not have said that.

You do not need to worry, I shall not betray a confidence. You have been put in a position of trust while you are with us, so we must treat you in the manner we wish to be treated. Please feel free to say whatever you like, and be assured that I for one will not abuse you, and shall prevent others from doing so if it is within my power.

Laura Agnelli raises her eyes to Giovanna properly for the first time, notices her companion is a little older than herself but not by much, and despite her cool voice has a face which is not unkind. She also perceives a personality like a set of scales, reliable and balanced, speaking the truth. Laura licks her lips and continues: I used to try to feel whether or not my parents were alive. I would shut my eyes and let my mind wander through Siena and the contado and beyond, as far as the sea. I gave up when I was nine or ten. I am now quite convinced my parents are dead, and have been for a long time. I have made peace with that, but I should like to know who they were, where they came from.

Yes, I would want to know too. Tell me, what becomes of you orphans when you are grown?

We have some tuition. When the boys are old enough they can go into a trade. And the girls are given a dowry of fifty lire to marry or enter a convent with. Some stay to live and work in the hospital their whole lives. Some want to.

Not many, I expect. And what will you do?

Laura has the sun in her eyes, so she raises her hand to shade them. It has long been my intention to take vows and dedicate my life to God.

Giovanna does not reply – she is either struck by this revelation and covers it well, or is genuinely unmoved. I guessed before today the commission was faltering. My lord cannot hide his moods from me. He is struggling with the burden of choice. When a man has a decision to make, it becomes a great and weighty matter; yet if you or I behaved the same way, we would be accused of dithering, would we not? They would say, Woman, make up your mind! Excuse me, now you think I am being disrespectful. My poor husband gives me licence to say what I think, and I use his grace to make complaints. At least I am being consistent. I have spoken my honest opinions to him on many occasions.

Is your husband an artist too? The words are out of Laura's mouth even as she realises she has made a mistake.

Giovanna is amused. No need to feel embarrassed. After all, he is older than me. You let slip an innocent remark because you know no better; others are malicious about my marriage behind my back, which is far worse. You have not offended me.

Nonetheless, I profoundly apologise. It was thoughtless.

If it pleases you. But you are curious now, are you not? You think maybe there can be no genuine affection between an attractive woman like me and an old rich man like him? That the exchange must be one of convenience, not love?

Laura's face burns.

Convenience is not the worst reason to marry. It happens every day. Tell me, are the marriages of girls leaving Santa Maria della Scala all love matches? To many men, fifty lire is a lot of money, and maybe they wish to be looked after and to have children. For that, they need a wife. And I doubt many young women would choose a nunnery or servitude at the hospital over having a home of their own. Not you, I know. You are the exception which proves the rule.

Laura presses her temples as though to absorb Giovanna's words, as though this will make them fit comfortably in her head. I am not unsympathetic. To some, matrimony is an attractive proposition. To some, it means if not freedom then at least a preferable sort of bondage. The rule of a husband might be gentle and benevolent compared to the rule of a religious order.

That is not always true!

23

No . . . it is not always.

Are you all right, Laura? You look dreadful.

Yes thank you. I am relieved to be outside for a while. It was kind of you to invite me.

Giovanna answers it is her pleasure before continuing, I suppose all the children of Santa Maria are instilled with a sense of duty – a family one, or a vocation. That is the commonality. Duty is a powerful influence on people's lives, and would be a valid reason for my marriage to Simone, perhaps. So would you be scandalised if I said duty played no part in our betrothal? What if I told you that on our wedding day he gave me a generous financial gift? I am not teasing you. I am trying to show you how sometimes appearances are one thing and the truth another. And the truth is this: my brother Lippo was Simone's student, Simone came to our house on several occasions and was kind to me, and I grew to love him as though it had been written. He feared for my reputation. He said if we married, people would always gossip about us – and they do. He tried to put me off. I am extremely lucky to be his wife. If he were not wealthy and not a genius, I would still love him and I would still be extremely lucky.

Then yours is a good example to follow for those who are the marrying kind.

We are not perfect. There is an empty space in our lives, can you tell? We have no children yet, and it saddens us. I have tried various remedies and I have prayed my hardest, but so far we have not been answered. Money cannot buy everything—

Giovanna breaks off to buy the figs and some oranges.

They are over halfway round the Campo and Laura realises her time left alone with Giovanna is probably short. When they walk on she says, There is something which has been bothering me. Your brother told Maestro Simone I was instructed to attend his studio every day by Signor Rettore. But that is not strictly true. He did say I am to be obedient and present when I am required; however, since then the rector has expressed some surprise at my being needed so very often.

Giovanna flattens her lips together. I am afraid that was my doing.

How can it be yours?

I am sorry. I admit it: I made Lippo tell my lord this tiny white lie. Please try to understand, my husband is not very good with new people. It takes him a long time to trust someone. He needs to get to know them first. He has his method when he paints, and what they have asked of him is utterly unreasonable. And he is getting very . . . this commission is the worst I have ever seen him. It is affecting his health and his inspiration . . . and it makes me so angry! I rarely meddle in his work, I assure you, but we are living in strange times. I was certain your presence would hasten the conclusion, whatever that might be, *good or ill*. In fact I was convinced of it. Yet here we are, still waiting, still unsure what will happen.

Laura shivers despite the heat, hugs her arms across her body.

Giovanna puts her hand on her hip. Tell me, Laura Agnelli: how is he when he is working?

I hardly know.

Does he exhaust himself　? Does he rest? I know about the promise you made my brother, by the way, but a wife should know about her husband's welfare no matter what the oath is.

No, he never rests.

What of his temper? Is he content? Is he calm?

Laura hesitates before she replies. Generally his concentration is given over to his work. He goes for hours at a time without speaking, so I cannot comment on whether or not he is content. He is industrious, as you saw, makes many pictures. When he does speak, it is to scold me for disturbing him.

Does he shout at you?

I ought to be more careful.

You are afraid of him. I am right, he frightens you. This is very bad. (Giovanna takes an orange out of her basket and rolls it between her palms before continuing.) It does not matter how fate brought you to us; you are here now. Being afraid of someone is a terrible condemnation of his character. With Simone, you should know the dog that barks does not bite. He is a good man, and he needs your help.

I do not know what help I can possibly give.

He will need your assistance soon with the panel painting. At some point he will come to acknowledge it, and then you must be prepared. More than that, he needs you to be a friend because he does not have many. It might seem odd to you – he is so esteemed in Siena – but being admired and having friends are not the same, and even the greatest men need friends. Will you promise me that you will not judge him too harshly and, when the time comes, you will do whatever you can?

Laura is reminded of the promise she has already made to Giovanna's brother, struck by how alike the siblings are. She gives the lady her word, then ventures, Why me? Why not someone else?

Well, it was up to Signor Rettore to choose, and he chose you. He must have lots of reasons: your piousness, your gentle nature, your dedication. It is an enormous privilege, you should be pleased.

It is indeed a privilege to meet Simone Martini. But for what end?

Giovanna halts at this, then looks incredulous. To be in the . . . Wait. Tell me why you think you are made to come to the studio?

Laura shrugs. I sit while Maestro Simone works, and I spin to pass the time. I think I am his witness, or something like that. Signor Memmi said people would ask me about their progress and he was quite correct – Signor Rettore wants to hear news practically every day. Do not worry, your brother also told me how to answer, and it is basically the truth, so there you are. Today I will say I met Maestro Simone's wife and you brought us lunch from the market. This is what happened, and to say so is not a violation of my oath.

Giovanna shakes her head in disbelief. You actually do not know. Well, I did not think I should be the one to tell you, but if you are truly unaware, I feel I must. My lord and my brother Lippo have been commissioned by the Duomo to make a panel dedicated to Saint Ansanus celebrating the Annunciation. You know the story of Saint Ansanus?

Laura beams. But of course! His nurse, Saint Maxima, baptised him in secret and brought him up as a Christian. She was martyred through flagellation, but he survived and went on to convert and baptise many people here in Siena. Eventually he was martyred on the orders of Diocletian.

Yes. At the same time, the Duomo and the hospital have formed – how shall we say? – a partnership, because they are both anxious about the interference of the Nine in their affairs. The story of Ansanus is pertinent because he was raised to be a Christian and do God's work by his *nurse*, not by his own parents, who were members of the Roman ruling class. It therefore has a certain resonance. Through the altarpiece the Duomo will be, to an extent, restating its relationship with Santa Maria della Scala to show how the spiritual works of the cathedral and the charitable works of the hospital are joined, and are favoured and blessed by Our Lady. Siena's citizens will look at it and be reminded of how the Virgin bestows her protection on the faithful and the charitable.

How clever, I would not have thought of it.

It will encourage people to be loyal, and generous, to both institutions. It is also a veiled message to Siena's oligarchy, who will be capable of reading it quite clearly. Do you see? Government has been left out of the picture. And just for emphasis, an orphan of the hospital has been chosen to be a part of it: *you*. The politicians would have expected a daughter of one of the noble families to be given that honour. It is a snub. The Nine will be furious when they find out, and yet it will be unseemly for them to criticise it.

Laura considers. I do not understand politics. If it is as you say, I am sure the rector and the bishop know what they are doing. But what have I done that could possibly make the Council of Nine so upset?

I am not explaining myself very well. Your *likeness* is to be in the altarpiece.

Giovanna says it plainly and sensitively, concerned about how a young girl who has led a sheltered life might react to such news.

Initially, Laura Agnelli does not respond, except for her deepening frown and narrowing eyes. Then she mumbles she is hot, feeling dizzy; she sways on her feet.

Giovanna leads Laura into some shade, makes her sit and drink from a flask of wine until she has recovered her wits.

When the incident is over, Giovanna offers to take her home, but Laura is adamant that it is not her wish.

I apologise, Laura. I honestly thought you knew.

No. No one saw fit to tell me.

And you did not guess it?

Something like that would simply never occur to me. It is too unexpected.

Laura Agnelli offers a silent prayer, feels it leaving her and flying up into the sky beyond her reach, beyond even the reach of the new tower and the stonemasons tapping the stones with their hammers and chisels, the clicks answered with echoes.

*

Laura returns to the hospital while most are still at Vespers. Some have duties which excuse them from attending; some are sly and find ways to avoid it when it suits them. Laura rarely misses the evening prayer service, and to have been kept from it for days in succession is a trial for her. She needs these renewals even more than she did before.

In the dormitory, Laura finds Imelda and Gisila sitting on a bed, their heads close together in conference as they wind laundered cloth strips.

Imelda whispers to Gisila, whose uncontrollable giggle turns into a pig-snort.

Laura almost pauses to greet them, but even as she slows her pace their laughter dies. Suddenly they are absorbed in their work.

It would not hurt Laura, not normally. She would take solace in her prayers and think about the life she will have at Santa Marta. She is finding this more difficult of late. Because she is in halves.

A word, Laura Agnelli!

The shouted demand is from Rettore Giovanni di Tese Tolomei, whose pompous girth has appeared as abruptly in the girls' quarters as if he had followed Laura there. She turns to go with him, passes by the other two but a few steps before their joke resumes. Imelda sniggers into the back of her hand. Gisila drops her head on to her friend's shoulder, limp with laughter, tears forming on her lashes.

She has had enough practice at finding her way through Siena's streets in the dark, and takes the precaution of covering her head so that her red hair does not give her away at a distance. She knows from experience which entrances will still be unlocked and, once inside, which are the quietest passageways leading back to the dormitory.

The hospital is never entirely asleep. Individual candles are kept lit in alcoves; oblates keep watch in the wards and the pilgrims' hall; voices are still audible though fewer, muted, more urgent. Night is a dangerous time for the weak.

Laura traces her way close to walls and peers round corners before moving on. She has not been seen so far, but is not complacent either. She has tried to imagine what would happen if she met Imelda, or one of the other orphans, creeping around out of bed, too . . . and done her best not to dwell on the consequences if she were caught by a sister or Signor Rettore.

She listens. Blood thuds in her ears. Footsteps ahead send her back in the direction she came from and towards a main corridor. Rather than risk it, she is compelled down a stairway and when she hears them approaching once more – whether or not her mind is playing tricks on her – goes deeper into the underbelly of the hospital. The swinging flare of a lamp sends her hurrying away.

She tries to dampen her tread as she traverses the labyrinthine passages hastens down steps behind pillars makes stealthy progress. The tunnels are twisted and unfamiliar here.

She stayed out longer than she intended; it is so late it is almost early. Fatigue and fright and frustration and the need for prayer like thirst. She stops. She leans against an archway to steady her nerves, to get her bearings, to console her heart. It is futile to feel distress, or indulge unwanted thoughts at this particular moment: getting back to the dormitory undiscovered is what matters; ignore the rest of her troubles if she can.

Laura Agnelli looks about her. She decides on reflection she has been here before, years ago, can find a route which will bring her close to the girls' quarters from beneath. Here at least is one solution.

As to the rest (Laura summons her strength), I will try again soon.

And it is when she resolves this that she realises she has arrived almost at the door of the hospital's oratory. She lingers; turns away from it; is instinctively tugged back.

The rules are plain: the oratory is out of bounds.

Is it possible that a benevolent hand has steered her here? that a few minutes of solace and solitude will provide Laura with the guidance she needs?

She peeked within it once, when she was small, but has never been inside because she was never invited – or desperate – and remembers the ghost stories they told each other about the place, as children, for the cemetery and the charnel house are right next to it. These features made it fascinating and forbidding.

But the terrors are real enough now. And Laura Agnelli enters the oratory at last.

It is unlike any space in the sprawling warren of Santa Maria della Scala. Hewn. Enclosed. It exudes a dim glow of its own, a pulsation, a palpable intention, is ancient and potent as though the very walls had cognisance. This power presses upon Laura Agnelli, compresses her, makes her tingle. Is it evil? Is it sacred? Is this awe, or ecstasy?

The oratory is a stone vault with a simple altar, relics, bones, skulls, fragments of wood set in cases and embellished stands. A smaller doorway in the opposite wall is partially open. Beyond it, luminous and inviting warmth, an angelic figure retreating into the next chamber – its brilliance makes Laura shield her vision briefly.

Laura is lowering her head and following before the folly of disturbing the room's occupant prevents her—

She is in a narrow recess wide enough for a single person, a niche of several yards, and there at the end is a woman kneeling at a second tiny altar. A stranger. Her presence is somehow wrong, impossible, as if she does not belong here but has come for a special purpose. It is arresting.

Absorbed in her meditations, it takes minutes for the woman to perceive Laura. When she does notice, she does not speak. Instead the lady symbolically covers her mouth . . . then makes confusing movements with her hands, as though they contained a message.

She has fire in her. Laura can see the flames in the blacks of her eyes, can feel the heat emanate.

If this is a spirit sent to warn her, or a saint sent to comfort, then Laura is unprepared for it and baffled by the whole encounter. She leaves the oratory without uttering a single word of prayer, without the answers she craves.

Dawn rays find the edges of feet suspended in midair, fingers curled and stiff, a shape like a rag draped over a branch. Dew forms on the skin like stone. There she is, surprisingly small, discovered first by the sun, then by birds to be pecked at, then by a cart, then a staring multitude. The act was done with a red cord, it becomes apparent. There is one just like it tied round a curtain in the women's chapel of the hospital.

Laura opens her eyes, wakes without so much as a sigh, the vision still vivid. In the dark, the familiar outlines of sleeping girls huddled together and the sounds of their breathing flowing like a river. A stab of panic: which one of them did she dream about? In the haze of partial sleep she forgets. As she drifts off with the swell, she remembers; it is only herself, and there is no need to warn anyone.

Out of breath, she climbs the stairwell and pauses outside the room – tries the door, squeezes it open without the hinges squeaking.

The artist is standing by the window eating olives from a small dish, the people of Siena going about their day below.

It confirms her anxiety to find him thus, because each and

every day previously he has been at work with his back to the world and paid her no heed. But now he watches her secure the lock with unabashed interest. There is a moment ... maybe while she waits for him to summon his rage, or he waits for her to volunteer an apology. He breaks the silence first.

I bought us some olives from the Campo. I had to buy some eggs to make paint because I tend to run out without Lippo around to remind me. I am very fond of olives. Are you?

Laura Agnelli nods faintly, yes, she is.

Then it is good you came when you did, or I would have eaten them all, then there would have been none left for you. Here, you had better have some.

She cautiously takes one without eating it.

Simone pops another in his mouth making a noise of pleasure at the flavour, takes the stone out, drops it on another plate. He wipes his fingers on his tunic.

You did not come yesterday. (It is a statement of fact, and he declares it that way.) I waited the whole day for you to come, but you did not. It was disconcerting. In fact, I got no work done. I was going to send someone to Santa Maria to find out why, in case you had been taken ill, you see? Giovanna talked me out of it. She said if you were indisposed, someone from the hospital would have been dispatched to tell me about it and there was probably another explanation. That made sense. I said, then Laura is surely missing, and we should raise the alarm so she can be found! I was adamant.

Laura lifts her horrified gaze.

But Giovanna said we should not do that either – that if your absence was for a different reason, I ought not to draw attention to it in case it caused you difficulties. She said you would probably turn up in your own time if we left you alone. And look ... she was right. Giovanna knows much more about girls your age than I do.

Laura exhales, closing her eyes. I am sorry, Maestro Simone, to have caused you inconvenience.

Giovanna calls me *prickly*. She says I do not inspire confidences from the young. Huh. Eat your olives.

Simone gives Laura what is left, beckons her to take a seat, not in her usual corner but beside him for a while.

You disappeared for an entire day. I am not cross about it, but a child whose whereabouts are unknown is a cause of concern for any Christian.

Ashen, she apologises again.

At least you are here now, and your behaviour has been impeccable so far. I dined with the good rector at his palace last week. He artfully conveyed to me that he has a small mouse who squeaks all the newsworthy events into his ear every evening. He has really asked you, then . . . ?

Regularly.

I thought so. What a rascal. And what an appetite, for food and for intelligence. Somehow he has heard I am considering travelling to Avignon. He is trying to persuade me to petition the Holy Father for privileges for Santa Maria della Scala. He thinks I would make a good ambassador, and he has now offered as an incentive a new commission, to paint an exterior fresco for the hospital. A grand artwork, outside, where everyone can see it and admire it all the time.

It sounds marvellous.

Bah! – Simone flicks his wrist in a noncommittal gesture – he is appealing to my vanity. The hospital, the cathedral and the Nine are as bad as each other, what with their sumptuous art and their colossal architecture. They are all posturing schoolboys. Sometimes I think the wars we make with Florence are a blessing in disguise because if we did not fight the Florentines, we would descend into war with ourselves. However, he was vague on the details of the altarpiece, which I am pleased about, Laura,

34

especially when he was trying to create the impression you were his informant. You have done well to resist his coercion to reveal what you know.

I have an oath in heaven. It was not difficult, anyway, as I know so little.

Are you curious to know more?

Signor Memmi said I was not to ask questions unnecessarily, so I have not.

I see. Keeping your word is important to you.

I think it is important to anybody who is God-fearing.

I hear you are to become a nun someday?

Yes, Signore, at the convent of Santa Marta. At least, I hope so.

Ah – Abbess Emilia Pannocchieschi d'Elci.

You know her?

A very strict woman. Very devout. Extremely kind. You are fortunate if she takes you under her wing. She thinks novices should know scripture. Do you know scripture, Laura Agnelli?

How can I answer without sounding proud? or ignorant?

Be truthful. Do you read it regularly?

Laura fidgets. Ye-es. Some, at any rate. My Latin is not good, but I can usually identify the passages I need and have committed many more to memory. I often recite. I – cannot write.

Assuredly a woman has no occasion for writing?

No, I suppose not.

But many nuns are literate. If it holds a genuine attraction for you, perhaps you will have the chance to learn reading and writing at Santa Marta? Hmm?

Laura's blush deepens.

I think the rector unwittingly did me a favour when he inflicted you upon us. My wife tells me you are troubled at the prospect of your likeness being in the painting. I did not take it seriously before. Now I have talked with you, I understand a little better. You are naturally closed like a bud. (Simone Martini brings his hands together, fingertips pointed upwards as though in prayer, palms cupped as though protecting hidden contents.) I wish I could dispel some of your concerns. If you would care to look, I can show you some aspects of the panel, although you will have to use your imagination for some of it.

She frowns. Are you not worried I will betray what I see to the rector?

No. Neither should you be.

Simone retrieves some of the vellum leaves from the rest, studies of figures and objects, definite shapes and contours and pigments. I have settled upon these elements. Here.

She hesitates.

Go on, it will do us both some good. I would like to share the fruits of my creativity with someone trustworthy, for a change. Tell me what you see. Think of it as practice for when you are discussing theological questions at the convent.

Laura leans over to examine them. White lilies in an ornate gold vase.

Yes. Why?

White lilies are a symbol of purity and virginity. They are an obvious choice to represent the Blessed Virgin.

Quite right. A peasant could understand that, and it is a painting as much for him as for the bishop. They are pretty to look at as well, do you agree?

Yes. Very pleasing.

Do you have any other thoughts on the subject of lilies?

Laura says she does not.

They are a symbol of virginity, innocence and heavenly purity, as you mentioned, but some would say that lilies are . . . naughty flowers, that they suggest illicit passion and temptation. Have you heard that before?

No. People who say that are wrong. It is a flower of Our Lady!

36

Not necessarily. There are examples in pagan religions of this being the case, religions older than ours. Have you really smelled a lily before, Laura? It has an intoxicating and powerful fragrance, and the shape is uniquely alluring. I can see perfectly well how other cultures have bestowed upon it more dubious connotations than ours. So I, as the painter, need to consider whether the lily is truly appropriate for inclusion. And I think, on balance, it is, because through Our Lady as Theotokos, sin *is overcome*. Furthermore, lilies are used figuratively to remind us to trust in God's will and providence. *Consider the lilies of the field, how they grow: they toil not, neither do they spin.* We are told Mary was troubled and afraid when first the angel appeared, then she surrendered herself as the Lord's handmaid. These particular flowers add this wisdom to the Annunciation story.

Laura is astounded by the artist's elaborate construction.

Then he asks her about the vase.

The vase? Is it not a pot for the lilies to go in? (She chastens herself for her rudeness.) It is such a lovely pot.

I could have shown lilies planted in the ground, or cut stems being held, but I have chosen specifically a vase. Does this not strike you?

Laura shakes her head. I see only flowers in a vessel.

Aha. A *vessel*. Follow that line of thought.

I am ignorant, Signore. I have not studied these matters.

I think you are doing yourself a disservice. Do try for me . . . ?

I suppose the Virgin Mary could be called a vessel, in the sense that God chose her to give birth to Christ.

Precisely. Capital work. I can hear the Abbess's praises already.

Laura feels a spark of gratification.

A vase also means 'treasure' in certain traditions. And at the Annunciation, God gives us the most precious treasure of all, do you agree? The vase is a 'vessel' and it is a 'treasure' – but even an item as mundane as this can have more than two meanings. In alchemy, the vase is where miracles occur, as in the Virgin's womb. The mouth of this vase is open to God's divine influence.

Laura is taken by a new thought, one which would explain Maestro Simone's inclination towards layers of symbolism that are lost on her. Are you an alchemist scholar, Signore?

Ah, no. I find the toil of painting more than sufficiently fills my time without my attempting to purify the soul and turn base metals into gold. I do not mean to imply these things are impossible – who knows what can be achieved with enough study and luck? – only, that it would be futile for *me* to attempt such goals. I leave that task to those who are more fit for it. Although, being able to conjure gold would be useful just at the moment. You heard me and Lippo discussing it, of course, on the first day?

A lot of it went over my head.

I have charged Lippo with a difficult mission, to procure me a large amount of gold leaf in a short period of time. It is expensive but, believe it or not, affording it is the easy part. Finding an adequate supply and the gold-beaters who can make it fast enough – well, he has not let me down yet.

An altarpiece for the cathedral needs to be decorative.

This is true, and a man like Vescovo Donusdeo expects it. Nonetheless, I have the idea that I would like my Annunciation to *shimmer*. (Simone slides one of the sheets out from the sheaf and lays it on top for her to see. It is the angel kneeling to deliver his message in yellows and golds; the patterned cloak swirls and curls as though lifted by air, wings raised, mouth open mid-speech.) The angel will go on the left of the panel and face Our Lady, who will be here on the right, the figures set against a background of pure gold. I will not show a room as such, because in effect it has been swallowed up by ethereal light.

(Laura recalls her experience in the oratory – was it a dream?

Aspects of it feel distant and unreliable, when she turns her mind's eye towards the memory all she can see is light.) He is bearing an olive branch for peace. And for . . . ?

Victory, among other meanings. Have you heard this . . . ?

Simone Martini lifts a book from his collection. He wants to get it word for word.

God is the Light of the heavens and the earth;
The similitude of His Light is as if there were a niche;
And within it a Lamp: the Lamp enclosed in Glass;
The glass as it were a glittering star;
Lit from a Blessed Tree;
An Olive, neither of the East nor of the West;
Whose oil is nigh luminous, though no fire has touched it;
Light upon Light; God guides to His Light whom He will.
And God strikes similitudes for men, and God has knowledge
*   of everything.*

Do you like it, Laura?

It is beautiful.

I was recently reminded of this passage, and I had to look it up again. The light, the star, the olive: all of it is in harmony with what I am trying to do . . . even the niche. The triptych will be a sort of niche, will it not? And the painting is itself a similitude. I like it a great deal.

Where is it from?

A book called the Koran.

Laura opens her mouth in shock. The Saracen text? That is heretical.

First, they are not Saracens, that is a name which we have erroneously given to a people who do not use it themselves. Second, what is considered heretical is largely subjective, and we should be careful how we apply such an accusation. And third, you yourself just called it beautiful when you did not know its origin.

Laura bites her lip, burning at her inability to argue her point of view. He is too clever for her. Signore, I simply meant, what can that have to do with the Blessed Virgin? Theirs is a different god from ours. It seems to me you do not have time for these investigations. You should be concentrating on the commission for the cathedral, the church of our faith.

On the contrary, it has been extremely useful. I will leave aside the question of a 'different' god, or we will be here all day, and simply tell you this: Our Lady is exalted in the Koran; indeed, she has a whole chapter named after her. I have learned more about her here than from the entire New Testament.

Laura is uncomfortable with this conversation, and wishes to avoid more disagreement. Will the Virgin also be dressed in gold, Signore?

If she were, it would be troublesome to distinguish her at a distance on a background of the same material. No, she will be in a red gown with a night-sky blue mantle over it. I have a first-rate colour especially for this purpose. Her form will recede into the brightness, the eye will be irresistibly drawn towards her.

Laura leafs through the images. There is a preparatory sketch of a tondo for God the Father, and four more circular designs for the great prophets, Isaiah, Jeremiah, Ezekiel and Daniel, to be placed along the top of the triptych.

Simone explains that Lippo will be responsible for the side panels of two full-length saints, Saint Ansanus to whom the altar will be dedicated, and Saint Maxima his nurse. After Lippo's hard work, he should at least be allowed to paint something.

Laura lifts the last sheet, which is blank. Where is she . . . ?

Simone Martini laughs. You understand my problem.

But you have been working for all this time, I have watched you for hours. I thought you had made numerous pictures of her.

I have. None is satisfactory, none I can use.

The artist picks up an object wrapped in cloth, one of the items Giovanna brought. He uncovers it, a luminous codex bound in red leather, pages edged in gold leaf, thin black straps with intricate gold fastenings, the illuminated manuscript within.

This is my wife's own *Book of Hours*, which I gave to her on her last birthday.

Laura receives it, rests it carefully in her lap.

I know at least that my Virgin will be holding this, to show her as pious and wise – I knew it almost instantly when I was approached. As to the rest – the old man shrugs – how will her face be? How does one paint her receiving this strange and wonderful news? What can I paint that will be truthful?

Laura's heart aches, the guilt at her absence as fresh and sharp as a thorn, Simone's kindness in spite of it, and that he did not press her for an explanation. His need for friends precisely as Giovanna described; the position of trust in which she has been placed; a desire to do good. Laura feels these desperately.

What can I do?

It is a problem for me to worry about, young lady. I will solve it.

When? How?

Ideas are not rainbows which appear in the sky, at least not often; they can be worked on, planed like wood, improved with friction. Have I worn you out? You look quite unwell. Would you like to go home and rest?

I do not need rest. I want to be of service.

Simone taps his mottled cheek. Are you sure you want to offer your help?

Laura Agnelli insists she does.

Very well, then.

The painter gives her folded garments belonging to Giovanna, and bids her put them on behind the screen. The rich fabric, blue and red, is heavy in Laura's arms, the clothes cut slightly too big for her. Simone organises his materials: pen, brushes, ink, new parchment. Arranges chairs: One for you, and one we will pretend is the angel. He gives her the codex.

Laura is pinched by self-consciousness. How should she sit? How should she hold the book?

The man mutters for her to do whatever she thinks best.

Laura forces herself into stillness and grasps the *Book of Hours*. It is the most fabulous object she has ever held. Maestro Simone, is there a difference between a closed book and an open book?

A vast difference. (Simone breaks an egg and separates out the yolk, neglects to tell her what the difference is.)

Laura opens the book, then closes it. Open, it ought to be open. Randomly – it is a page from the Penitential Psalms, and what Laura recognises as *De profundis*. It used to be a favourite passage of hers. Her mouth dries. *De profundis clamavi, ad te Domine. Out of the depths have I cried unto thee, O Lord.* She sits upright, using her backbone in a pose she hopes is both modest and resolute.

Simone Martini commences a new Marian modello, the first he has made led by the instincts of an orphan. The novelty of the experiment reignites his enthusiasm.

They fall into a half-trance.

Time is measured for Simone by his progress, outline correction face hair feet chair blue gold. He is transfixed by the delicate doll which materialises – she has a sweetness, a primness and a restlessness – as though the figure on the page would drop her book on the floor, stand up, walk away. His experienced eye discerns it is not exactly right for the altar (it lacks drama, narrative, presence). He did not expect immediate gratification, but senses this is the closest yet he has come to his Virgin. He is on his way at last.

For Laura, it is oddly similar to sitting in private. She soon realises the painter is consumed by his work. Though he concentrates on her appearance so intently, he is barely aware of her person as long as she does not move. She finds this easier than the hours she endured when Simone was trying to ignore her and she so frequently irritated him. It is a relief. It is an opportunity to think, to untangle some of the mess.

De profundis clamavi, ad te Domine. Domine, exaudi vocem meam. Fiant aures tuae intendentes in vocem deprecationis meae. Out of the depths have I cried unto thee, O Lord. Lord, hear my voice: let thine ears be attentive to the voice of my supplications.

Laura, you are slumping.

The girl straightens, her muscles aching. Maestro Simone – her voice cracks a little – will your wife, will Giovanna, come today?

No, she is visiting her parents.

I should like to see her again.

You had a pleasant conversation, did you? I shall ask her to come by next week.

I should like to see her again very soon.

I am sure she would like to see you too.

Laura trembles. As soon as she can, please.

Simone Martini raises his gaze to her. Whatever is the matter?

Her skin has turned to a dreadful pallor.

The artist sets aside his tools and goes to her. He asks whether she is sickening, and she does not deny it. Should he send back to the hospital for a physician?

She refuses. It is true that Laura has the urge to cry, but she does not want to shed tears on anything which does not belong to her, least of all the precious *Book of Hours*. She rests the codex with her thumb to mark the page (it might be important for it to look the same when the study resumes).

I will be all right soon. I think we were doing well, Signore. We ought to continue.

No, we will stop. There is a burden weighing upon you, Laura Agnelli. Why not tell me what it is, and I shall see if I can help?

Laura mutely shakes her head, makes a brief and artificial smile.

It is why you want to see Giovanna, you want to confide something in her, I think. Regrettably she is away for several days. Whatever it is, can it wait for so long? To me, it seems not. To me, it seems you are suffering now.

It is unimportant.

Is someone hurting you? Are you in trouble? To confessor, doctor and lawyer, do not hide the truth.

Laura wrings the folds of the fabric with her free hand but does not, now, avoid his gaze. Which are you being, Signore?

Whichever you are most in need of. Just a friend, if it pleases you. I thought we had become friends today, you and I?

We have. We have.

Then tell me what ails you. Tell your babbo.

Laura's reply is a whisper. I am in despair, Maestro Simone. I have been robbed.

Who has stolen from you? What have you lost?

I have been seeing a man outside the hospital, and now I am sure I am with child.

There is a flicker of astonishment in the artist's face, and a glimmer in his eye like the breaking of day which fades as his features rearrange themselves into the mask of deep thought. Then your demeanour and your recent disappearance are finally accounted for. What can you tell me of your young man?

Laura fixes her suspicious stare on him. Why? What are you going to do?

Nothing. Not anything. Not one thing, without your express wish: you have my word.

At this, she relents. His name is Bartolomeo Pavoni. He is a citizen of Siena, I think. I had not considered marriage until I met him and he began paying me attention. He was very charming at first.

Yes. I see. Now I must be indelicate for a moment and ask a necessary question: are you absolutely certain that what you and this Pavoni did together can cause pregnancy? Because if you just held hands or merely kissed and touched one another—

Laura cuts across this speech. Yes, she knows what took place is the thing that causes pregnancy.

I had to make sure. Can you tell me the way this occurred?

We had a special place only we two knew about—

No, not that. I wish to be clear about whether or not this person physically harmed you. Did he force you?

Once again, Laura looks ill and for a minute is tongue-tied. He said he loved me. He made promises. He said I was too good for a convent, and he wanted me for his wife. I tried to reason with him, to put him off, but he was eager and impatient with me.

Was he cruel to you . . . ?

Laura covers her mouth, then composes herself. He was persistent, and I was deceived. He was kinder afterwards, and assured me no one would find out.

And no doubt he seemed mature to you. Did you see him again? Does he know about the pregnancy?

I did not wish to see him. I wished to break it off. I intended to do my penance and, God willing, to go to Santa Marta as I originally hoped. When I realised, I sought him out and told him. I said I accepted, I said I wanted to get married and to raise our child together. I thought he would be pleased because he had asked me often enough, but he just stopped coming. At first I thought he needed to get used to the idea, but I have since heard he has gone to Ravenna and I think it might be true because it is a city he talked about, and I have searched everywhere else I can

45

think of. In my heart I acknowledge he does not want to be found, but I do not know what to do without him.

Do you love this fellow?

You will think badly of me if I say it was his honeyed words which affected me most, the thought that someone cared for me and found me desirable. I have lost the life I might have had for *that*. (Laura's voice cracks.) I have been trying to think precisely which of my sins has merited this treatment. I have been trying to understand why God is allowing this to happen to me, and yet denies you and Giovanna the child you both yearn for.

Because God is either not as benevolent as we would like to believe, or not as powerful. Or maybe he has his own reasons.

I would have married Bartolomeo even though I do not love him, even though he would have made me miserable. I would have tolerated him and made do. (Laura covers her face.) I am on my own now.

Despair is also a sin.

If I bear this child and raise it as a bastard, we will be destitute. I have no income, nor the means to make one. We will be ostracised. I will never find a man who is prepared to marry me and take care of someone else's child. Shall we live on alms from Santa Maria della Scala until we are found dead in the street? Shall I become a prostitute as my mother probably was? I know I am complicit and I could have avoided this if I had behaved better, but why must I alone be punished when two people have sinned? Is it because I am the vessel? I am remorseful, Signore, but I am also angry. You will not tell anyone . . . ?

No. But nature is going to give your secret away unless you take your destiny in your own hands, young Laura. Clear-headedness must prevail over desperation.

Laura rises to pace to and fro.

Simone Martini sits with his fingers linked across his belly.

Would it be so terrible to entrust one more foundling to the care of the hospital that raised you? It would give both of you a chance.

A chance . . . it has not occurred to me before that my own mother might have been a daughter of Santa Maria della Scala, that I might be but a link in a chain. I always imagined I came from outside the walls, from somewhere else, was taken there out of misfortune. A chance? I might still go to a convent, then, perhaps not Santa Marta, but another may still take me. If not, I suppose I could marry, although it has never held much appeal. Eventually I may even be able to have the child back. (To Simone's surprise there is amusement in Laura's face.) We call that 'the lie'.

What do you mean?

It is the sentimental promise made by women when they bring their babies to the hospital. They give the infants tokens and trinkets to identify them by later on; engraved coins, rings, pins, buttons, embroidery – you would be amazed at the variety. But it has never happened, not once. The objects are disposed of and the women never come back.

You could stay on at the hospital and watch your child grow.

They would not allow it. Only one of us would be permitted to stay. But then, in all likelihood, only one of us would survive.

My child, do not think such morbid thoughts.

You have not seen it, Signore. You have not seen how many women and babies are killed by childbirth. By sickness. So many horrible ways to die. When disease ravages the wards, the smallest and weakest are the first to succumb. It is accepted, which is the same as saying it is acceptable.

You have lived to adulthood. Why do you doubt your offspring would?

Maybe it will. Maybe it will be a beautiful youth. Maybe one of the hospital's benefactors will take a fancy to it. You must have heard the rumours, Signore? I expect that you would recognise

47

one or two men from your social circle who are regular donors. Quid pro quo—

A hooked hand springs to Simone's mind; it repulses him momentarily, he forces it away.

I have been spared. If anyone's eye fell upon me, the rector steered them away because it was assumed I would be a nun and should be kept chaste. But some are too pretty for their own good. And stubborn. They draw attention to themselves. But I can see perfectly well why women who bring the children they cannot keep to the hospital believe it is for the best, for the slim chance you speak of.

What is in your prayers, young Laura?

That God will take this thing away. I know it is awful, but I would count it a blessing.

It is a risky strategy, simply to hope. Have you considered fully all your choices, or are you going to be a victim of fate?

She darkens, catching his meaning. I cannot undo one sin with another.

Not 'undo', but potentially limit the damage. It sounds to me that you are in a position where you must pick the lesser evil.

It would be wicked. I would be excommunicated if I was found out.

I am old now, but I was young once. Ought I to believe the thought has not occurred to you? Are these accidents new or unusual? There is nothing new under the sun. You are not the first young woman to be in this predicament, and you will not be the last.

But to harm an unborn—

Tell me where in the Bible it says that a woman shall not end a pregnancy if it appears the least harmful course of action?

Thou shalt not kill.

Simone Martini nods. Yes, it does say that. I cannot deny it.

The artist gets to his feet and turns his attention back to the plate of olives, which she has not touched. He takes one and offers them to her, and she refuses once more. He eats the olive and spits the stone back into the palm of his hand and holds it there.

Whenever I eat an olive I discard the stone. When you eat an olive, what do you do with the stone?

I discard it too.

Yes. It would be strange indeed if everybody attempted to plant the seed from every single olive fruit and grow a tree from it. The olive tree is sacred, you know. Myth has it that a goddess called Athena quarrelled with the god Poseidon, and won a competition against him to be the patron of a Greek city by giving its people the first olive tree. I like the idea of another great city with a powerful protectress like ours. Even if it is not true, it is a good story. It would be extremely destructive to cut down a fully grown olive tree without good reason.

It would be wrong . . .

Quite wrong.

But Signore, we are not talking about seeds and trees. We are talking about immortal souls. Your analogy does not hold.

I admit I do not have the flair of a bard, but I want to know whether you genuinely believe the cutting down of a tree and the discarding of a stone are of *equal* severity. Are they?

A simile is not reality.

But you agree that a grown tree and a dormant seed are not the same as one another? If you believe they are the same, have the courage to say so. *I* do not think they are. I think that one is life fulfilled, and one has the potential for life requiring soil, water, sunlight, time to grow and be actualised. That is my opinion. And I say these things to you because you have suffered much in isolation, because you have already been misled, because you have no parents to guide you. And a student of scripture really ought to know that on this specific matter, the Bible is silent. Why? Well, that is anyone's guess. Perhaps the authors do not pronounce judgement because they believe it to be a private matter, or a matter for society to decide. The Bible tells us *thou shalt not kill*, and yet we do, when there are sufficient reasons. Rather often, as it happens. What about defending one's city in war? What about the execution of a guilty man? Our *church*, on the other hand – the one that you and I are members of – is indeed vocal, and would call it a crime. But that is not the same.

Your words are hurtful.

I am sorry for that, Laura Agnelli. You ask God, why has this happened to you? I ask myself, why did God ensure you and I met? I believed at first it was for the painting, but now I am not sure. Be wary, Laura Agnelli, of anyone who claims to know what is in God's mind and what God wants us to do. *For my thoughts are not your thoughts, neither are your ways my ways, saith the Lord. For as the heavens are higher than the earth, so are my ways higher than your ways, and my thoughts than your thoughts.* Whatever you decide, young Laura, is up to you, because it is you who will have to reconcile your conscience and live with the consequences of your actions.

Laura murmurs, Graves are filled with after-the-fact wisdom.

Simone throws up his hands. Giovanna says that all the time, it is her favourite expression. My wife is a know-it-all.

Poor lamb. What shall we do with you?

Laura lays her head on Giovanna's lap. Giovanna rubs Laura's shoulder, pulls back the strands of Laura's hair so it does not fall into her face, tucks them behind her ear.

You know what I want most is a baby son or daughter, given to me by Simone. I still have hope that God will provide us with one.

Laura closes her eyes.

But I believe we can help you. We have connections.

*

If the Blessed Virgin gave but a moment of her attention to the prayers of the citizens of Siena, what might she hear?

A voice as thin and as sharp as a needle: Thank you for the new altarpiece. Let it bring to the Duomo many worshippers, regardless of its controversial design. Please do not be too displeased with it. Artists are wayward and unpredictable, and need your leniency . . .

A voice guttural and well fed: Ensure successful representations in Avignon on behalf of your beauteous hospital, and the privileges to guarantee its continuance and prosperity . . .

(These entreaties, and thousands more besides.)

A lady who renews her request every month: I know my life is rich, but give me this one blessing more and I shall never ask for anything else . . .

A girl whose pretty face is wrinkled with effort: Please bring me a husband who will take me away from here! Let him be talented in music so he can write me songs, and wealthy so he can buy me presents. Most of all, let him come quickly! I do not even mind if his breath smells . . .

(Not all requests shall be granted.)

Bless the new novice who has come to us, who seems troubled, who reminds me of myself . . .

Help me to be worthy to live here for the rest of my life . . .

What of the numerous pleas which are made without words, and to no one in particular? Does the Blessed Virgin distinguish between eloquent prayer and an infant's caterwauling? Would her eye fall, fleetingly, on a humble cot? Does she know one undersized baby from another? Recalling its history, is she moved to extend her protection to this one? Would a whisper from her to a flawed human heart be enough to save its life?

Many details go unrecorded.

Pieter Janssens Elinga

Woman Reading, 1668

They are friends, the two children. Children have a talent for making friends. They have not yet learned the inhibitions of grown-ups. The friendship between a woman and a man can be fraught with complexities, expectancy; but a girl and a boy may be friends and play together. Yes, let's play. What shall we play?

The girl is bossy. Girls are. They can be precocious and have fixed ideas. Girls like to think and feel, boys like to do. This girl is no exception: it shall be a game of dragons and swords – it is decided, she has decided it. Green dragons (the very worst dragons are always green) and golden swords with jewels in the hilt. We will use stinging nettles for dragons and sticks for swords. I shall be a knight and you can be my page. Or horse: you choose.

Boys can be ignorant, and here is a potential barrier to their friendship . . . he does not understand.

Patiently, Esther explains again. She is the knight, he is the page – or the horse – those nettles covering that bank are the dragons. And we are going to slay them.

Hugo responds to her instructions with bewilderment. She repeats herself once more, but his attention wanders. Rules and crafted stories are wasted on him. She resorts to pantomime, to dragging him by the arm to her chosen place, to exaggerated pointing.

Over *here*, Hugo – and this is your sword.

She forces a stick into his fist and picks up her own, hers is longer and straighter. He inspects their tools. His would make a useful walking cane and he tries it out.

This is the way we kill them.

She swishes her stick into the foliage and lacerates the leaves. Fleshy specks fly.

Boys are predisposed to destructiveness, so this game appeals to little Hugo. He has no idea of the romantic saga constructed around them; rather, he copies Esther (bossy girl) and their friendship strengthens – out of mutual hatred for nettles, out of shared enjoyment in smiting them. Heads of leaves chopped off, torn up, never to harm anyone again. *Swish smack*, for all the bumps and rashes, for terrorising the villagers with fire, for eating maidens. The children are ruthless in their work. The stems snap, excreting sticky resin – dragon's blood. Slice, poke, stab. Two small bodies doubled over like farmers, heads bobbing with effort, their sticks could be sickles harvesting the overgrowth.

A villager, unaware she has been liberated by the brave adventurers, approaches. It is Hugo's mother, her clogs kicking up dirt with each step. The knight and her attendant, the nettle-vanquishers, punish their prey without pause until she interrupts them.

Hugo's mother moves her lips. Hugo moves his lips. She moves hers again and Hugo stares at his toes.

Esther cannot fathom it.

The woman flares her nostrils at the little girl, her expression uglier than before. More lip movement.

Hugo, as though pulled on a string, waves goodbye to Esther and goes home.

Esther watches them leave and a familiar loneliness descends on her. Whenever she thinks of a good game, whenever she finds someone her own age to share it with . . .

She seeks solace in her task with more violence than before, but the spirit of Saint George deserts her. The dragons fade; the malevolent weeds take their place and counter-attack with invisible teeth, biting the backs of her fists, her bare legs, making her skin sore and scratchy. She bashes them down, *desist, surrender*, but they are winning. Without her friend, the battle is futile.

It is not fair. It is not fair.

And there is something else which hurts her horribly: how can Hugo – who is slow and unimaginative and needs commands and leadership – do this remarkable trick which Esther cannot?

Geertje is making pastry, sleeves rolled to her elbows, hands deep in the mixing bowl. She rubs the fat and flour together, lifts it up, lets it fall. This is the delicate process her mother showed her and she has shown Esther – who comes home. Her daughter's skirt has new stains on it, her hands and ankles are red and patchy, she is on the verge of crying. Geertje brushes off her fingers, wipes them on the cloth so she can sit with Esther, troubled child.

Now tell me what is wrong? I am sure I can make it better.

Esther recounts what has happened, leaving out some parts, but Mother can guess them.

Like this? Mother stills her hands and opens and closes her mouth like a trout.

Yes, exactly.

Then Geertje explains. You and I, we talk differently from other people. It is nothing to be sad about. God has simply decided that some people will talk using actions . . . and some people will talk with mouths. However, it often causes confusion. When we cannot understand each other's words, it can be very irritating. So we have to be tolerant, you see? We learn to manage and make the best of it. That is all we can do.

Does God not want everyone to talk to each other?

Yes, he certainly does. Yes, he would like that very much – which is why he made your father, who is especially talented and can do both kinds of talking.

Esther does not understand; she does not feel different from other people.

You are, my love.

The girl must check this with Father.

Christiaan is in the smithy, hammering a glowing bar with controlled force on the anvil, sparks escaping. It complies with his modulated strength, the blows softer, harder, softer, responsive and accurate. Esther stands clear as she has been taught her whole life to do, the wall of savage heat keeping her at bay. Christiaan slides the worked metal back into the furnace, a blade sunk deep into hellish fiery jaws.

Am I different?

The little girl implores the blacksmith to correct the mistake, to flatten it out, to reshape it. Yet if Mother is wrong about this, it will be the first time in Esther's life she has been wrong about anything. Geertje is commonsensical. Her ability to master the mysterious and fearful was one of the main reasons Christiaan married her.

Black. In her dreams, Esther sees a figure arriving at their village carrying a rake. It shuffles along passing the church, passing the well, passing the mill and the modest houses. It is not a man and it is not a woman. It is a creature. Old and covered, crossing an erratic path, touching walls and doorframes, windows and cradles, hearths and pillows. It touches what we touch and is guided by moonshine. Its robes are miasmic, seeping into cracks and crevices. It blows poisonous breath into lungs, on the napes of necks, under armpits, and dissolves stout hearts into nothing. It hears neither prayers nor argument. It sways with each step; it is bent, it is evil, the most efficient killer with the lightest caress. It leaves behind black footprints.

And Esther dreams of a land populated with skeletons. Skeletons which trip over fields, ride in wagons, crouch in boats, climb trees. They chase and hide and tumble. Bonfires are set alight in their names. They clatter their bones, they gnash their teeth. How quickly their abominable numbers swell, doubling doubling doubling.

All are equal, are levelled.

The blacksmith's forge is cold. Only one kind of work to be done: the ghoulish business of digging ditches and filling them in. Christiaan's arm is strong; he shoulders his spade and joins the volunteers. They improvise masks, communicate in single-word sentences. Here. More. Stop. Mounds appear beyond the boundaries of consecrated ground. Whole families laid waste, including Hugo's. People say, perhaps the whole village . . . ?

Geertje cannot hide the lumps under her arms and in her groin for long – she is bedridden in hours and dead within days. The brightest and kindest are as susceptible as any, and returned to the earth in a putrid heap.

The visions and smells and sounds penetrate Christiaan's mind, attractive to the daemons which Geertje's strength had kept at a distance. He recognises their advancing shadows and approaching tread. Their warnings.

Miraculously some do survive. Life grows back, gradually, like ivy, clinging on, breaking through. The peculiar blacksmith and his deaf daughter are long gone.

Where are we going?

Church.

You always say that. We passed a church this morning. We passed two yesterday. Churches abound. Do you really know where we are going? If you have lost your way, you ought to admit it and not be so proud.

Keep up.

I think we should go home.

We cannot.

Yes we can. Mother would want us to.

No. She would want you to have a future.

We can go back to the smithy and I will take care of you.

She would want you to have a husband and a family.

Maybe I will, one day. But if that happens, I will still be your daughter and look after you. We can turn round and go home, right now, if we want to. I could even find work.

Not safe there.

Safer than on the road. Safer than having nowhere to go.

We are going to church.

And what if the same thing happens when we get there? It might. It could. Who knows, it might even be worse.

Be quiet.

Do you have the pain?

No.

Are you sure? You promised to tell me when it comes. You made a promise.

No pain, and this is the way.

It must be some church, if we are going to all this trouble.

*

They arrive in Amsterdam. Suddenly they are walking along canals and through side streets and by the IJ Bay itself. Esther is in awe of the assault on her senses.

Here are the whalers, the ship-builders, the sugar merchants, the fishermen, the customs officials, the innumerable networks of contracts and dealings, the constant braying and barking of beast and hawker. Here are ropes, crates and kegs slung with force from deck to slipway, to cart, from man to man. Faces and arms cracked and browned from exposure to sun and salt.

Chinese porcelain held up and admired for its decoration and translucence; silk from Bengal; tea from Ceylon; Japanese gold and silver; cinnamon, mace, nutmeg, precious pepper from the Moluccas, the Banda Islands, Malabar and Sumatra; coffee and rice and opium and camphor: jealously guarded treasure. Even souls are bought and sold, written up in a numbered column by the slave traders.

The glitter of currency counted out of the port and immense wealth counted back in. Warehouses filled and emptied and refilled. A signature. Hefty mariners straining with physical work, men in expensive robes surveying progress, barefoot children chasing and climbing in dangerous places, prostitutes competing for trade. Boisterous inns. The rowing boats pass, and the shouting and the whistling, farewells and greetings. The pong of decomposition on the breeze. Flick of sails and twirl of smoke. Here in the grime, in the dipping and rising of vessels on the tide, in the maps of secret routes across the oceans, in the firm handshakes, in the bureaucratic structures, *here* is the most powerful agency in the world at work.

When they find the right church, it is in a shabby lane and indistinguishable on the outside from other Amsterdam houses. Hidden as it were.

Esther will never know for certain whether this was Father's last action as a sane man or the first action of a madman. But she will always be thankful for the day he brought her to a room noisy with conversations she could understand; will cherish the discovery that a place existed where people use their hands instead of their tongues for speech.

She tells him he is the cleverest of all fathers, he has got them here and now he can rest. But he is withdrawing into himself before her eyes, turns away from her entreaties, folds into a crouch on the floor.

Excuse me, lass, is your father all right? Would you like some help? You bring that chair over, we will pick him up.

Christiaan's imagination burns hot yellow and red, the iron of his personality is smelted. What is left is scorched and brittle: debris, the rubbish. His wife protected him when she was alive but now, after he has buried her in unconsecrated soil, the fiends are coming for him in hordes. It is Sunday again and they are here – the grotesques have come to stare at him and torment him (they demand their entertainment, they have paid their entrance fee). They wear civilised clothes and speak in refined voices but are plotting all the while, and will eventually drag him into a hole that is at once dark and aflame, smelling of rot, slithering with worms that will crawl over his flesh, eat him alive. He can feel them on him, in him.

His distress is amusing for the visitors. They find it hilarious when he makes funny gestures, waves his distracted hands in the air. What is he doing? Pumping pretend bellows? Carving with a pretend chisel? Striking a pretend nail on its pretend head? They believe he is miming the smithy he fantasises about. They do not know he is trying to communicate with the daughter he pines for.

The mute maid who has been taking care of Jurina's stepson must go and that is final. There was a period of grace following the wedding – Jurina Bos is no tyrant. But that was almost a year

59

ago and her baby is due any day. It is, she thinks, unseemly for a lady of her quality to have servants without the requisite skills and abilities. She has been charitable thus far, gracious in her acknowledgement of the maid's diligence and cleanliness, and yet the time has come—

Pieter Janssens Elinga, the painter and the husband, acquiesces. His adolescent moneyed bride shall have her way. He is beholden to her. The arrangement was supposed to be temporary anyhow, following the death of his first wife Beatrix van der Mijlen (whom they do not talk about). Esther, barely more than a child herself, was cheap to employ and all he could afford. An investment which enabled him to woo and remarry, for he was disadvantaged as a suitor: poor, widowed, a young son to look after. All he offered Jurina Bos was the prospect, the hint of a prospect, that his talent might be recognised in Amsterdam one day and prestige would follow. Will it do? Then he will give her as many children as she wishes to have, one or twenty or none, it is up to you. Is it enough for you, my sweet? He was artistic and persuasive.

More than enough. For Jurina this is a love match, and she is glad to share her wealth with him. With *him* and *their* children, in the home of *her* making, with servants of *her* choosing. She is a diplomat, has waited tactfully for the appropriate occasion. To be clear: the birth of her first child is the appropriate occasion.

Notice has been given to the girl despite Young Pieter's tantrums (that Elinga's son sometimes prefers sign language to speaking normally has grown tiresome). She is a benevolent mistress, intends to help Esther secure a post in a different household, a household more suitable for her.

That is all there is to it. Let it be done, let the matter be closed. For goodness' sake!

The labour starts.

The venerable doctor (handpicked by Jurina on account of his position within the surgeons' guild) does not hurry when called for. In this, at least, he turns out to be right. It is difficult, protracted; two nights go by and the baby does not arrive. Jurina has no choice but to be attended to by the silent, inexperienced maid who blends into the background. The lady sinks in and out of consciousness, barely feels the flutters of attentiveness, licks the water drops on her dry lips, has her hair pushed back from her forehead, squeezes the skinny hand holding hers. Unbearable. Agony. Exhausted, Jurina starts to pray. Not the prayers of the past nine months (let it be a son, let it be a strong bouncing son, let him be tall and gifted and rich). Those prayers no longer matter. A new prayer entirely erases all the old utterances: Please God, if you have any mercy, let it be over.

Does God answer? What, or who, will be his instrument?

Maybe it is the mercurial doctor who announces it is dead. It is worse than any of them thought; the baby is dead and in order to save the mother the legs and arms must be amputated inside the womb. He is taking the implements from his bag, reverently lays them out, eyes and blades glint with fascinating light.

Jurina screams, the mere sight of them sending her into histrionics.

It is normal to be apprehensive under the circumstances, but let me reassure you—

Elinga is beside himself. Helplessly he paces back and forth, nerves in tatters, allows bloody thoughts to overwhelm him.

A quack. Sheer quackery. At best the man is deluded; at worst he is a rogue. Yet it is this devil to whom they defer, his perverted expertise, his distorted sensibilities. Lack of sleep and food, anxiety, mortal pain . . . all have taken a terrible toll. Rationality is defeated.

Fortunately, amid turmoil, a vibration of good judgement can prevail. The shock is wearing off and Jurina succumbs

61

again to her body, disorientated, drowsy, making the surgeon's job easier so he thinks. But he is dismissed by the deaf-mute maidservant.

Absurd. He is insulted.

She cares not a whit for his indignation. Her gestures are unmistakable: Go! It is done before the master and mistress are truly aware of it.

A warm nutritious broth rouses the lady, carrots and beetroot and chicken and herbs, with Esther at the bedside gently feeding her. It is accepted gratefully, humbly. Two women from a neighbouring house answer the appeal for help (you should have come to us sooner) and the labour is resumed.

They deliver Baby Lucas, whole and perfect. For a time, Jurina will brook no discussion about Esther leaving.

Esther and Young Pieter sit by the Singel, feet dangling over the edge, shoes removed and laid beside them so they do not drop into the canal. They are playing their game, which involves pointing at what they can see. They take turns to be the teacher. Esther shows Pieter the sign and Pieter shows Esther the mouth shape. Practice and repetition help the lessons to stick.

Rope. Reflection. (Esther's hands form each one and Pieter copies.) Green. Fat. Wet. Canal.

And they make up phrases to test themselves. Pieter's goes like this: I saw a fat man wearing a green hat and he made a reflection in the canal. If I pushed you in, you would be wet and I would need a rope to pull you out.

I would like to see you try.

I would like to see you fall in. Basket. Old. Grey. Apron. Window. (Pieter says each word aloud and Esther studies his lips.) Flying. Fighting. Bone.

Esther's story is: I carried a bone in my basket to give to the old grey dog. People were fighting in the street and I looked out of my window, then I put on my apron and went flying over the houses.

Pieter exclaims, No you did not, that is nonsense.

I do fly, I do it when you are not looking.

It is a lie!

Esther assures him it is the truth and then gives him some words to do: Bricks. Woman. Fish. Parsnip. Short and ... Esther.

If the short woman who smells of fish sent Esther away, I would put bricks in her bed and I would never eat another parsnip.

The boy gazes at the maid loyally, unashamedly.

Esther reminds him he must treat his parents with respect.

Lucas, all of nine years and nearly ten, has an instinct for other people's crises. His knack for smelling the truth is so much a part of his nature he is barely aware of it ... and there is a new scent on the air. Not the ludicrous number of departing servants; anyone can see them for what they are, unimportant, uninteresting, unappealing. But what about the change in Esther? Stupid dumb Esther who prefers Young Pieter – of all people! – to handsome clever loveable Lucas. Who but a man with his father's weaknesses and a child as intelligent as he could detect a difference so subtle? Who in the household but canny, perceptive, astute Lucas could anticipate the chaos that will follow in its wake?

He sits alone deep in contemplation of the eddying currents at work in the family home.

Probably Esther is cleaning. Probably Father is drunk. Mother is out.

Then he is climbing the winding stairs before he thinks to do it.

Esther is a tall woman (taller than her mistress), adept at her role, has outlasted all the staff introduced above her. She sweeps dust into a pan in one of the bedrooms, oblivious of her master Pieter Janssens Elinga. Her head is bowed over her broom and her white lappet cap obscures her peripheral vision. She is concentrating on her work, and why would anyone have cause to stand and watch her without declaring themselves?

The artist, his back to the wall, tightening throat – what does he look at?

Her profile. The veins showing through her transparent wrist. The slope of her back under her jacket. A tiny scar where she once burned herself on a pan. Her poise, her purpose, her motion: he looks at that. The folds of her skirts, the hem moving to and fro. She goes into and back out of a corner, sweep sweep turn sweep, the floorboards will be spotless when she is done. That she pauses to scratch her nose, that she continues where she left off, it is endearing, has resonance. She is methodical and pretty in her way, and he cannot help himself.

Being alone in her presence fills him up. He feels it. He has experienced this sensation before, tastes the familiarity of it. He craves her body (he tells himself) to uncover her, to reveal her, to be in her. Yes he wants her, but no, not quite, not exactly.

Of course he would – if she ever came to him, he would. Though she is somewhat older and shapelier than he prefers, he would probably risk everything for her. He has imagined it often, imagined them together, imagined plenty of obscene details when he is fathering the children promised to his wife. Esther's face, Esther's skin, Esther's tongue, Esther's hips, on him, beneath him, bent in front of him. What prevents him then from having what he wants? If he has managed it before without compromising his reputation, made the arrangements before, found replacements, honed the techniques to make it discreet, enjoyable and perfectly possible from start to end?

She picks up a thread from the floor, displaying her angular ankle, and puts it in her pocket. She slips her hand under her cap to adjust the hair beneath. Upturned eyelashes.

He watches because he likes her spirit. He wants to be acquainted with it, intimate with it. He likes her for herself. He likes . . . her.

If she came to him, only if she came to him, only if *she* came to *him*. Even her silence is alluring – nothing to remonstrate or criticise or nag with – merely patience, admiration, empathy, the splendid qualities he attributes to her passivity. Regal and untouchable. He comprehends, finally, it would not be like the other maidservants, not a bit, and the feeling is familiar because it is the same as *Beatrix*.

Unlucky Pieter Janssens Elinga. Wretch. It has taken him more than ten years to discover this truth and when it happens, he is devastated, hardly anything left of a man. Your body tremors, Pieter Janssens Elinga.

At last the maid sees him, eyes vivid. Should she reproach him? A scowl?

He crosses the room, is too close to her too fast for her to believe it. All these years he has never shown any interest in—

Despite his high-minded sentiments and pure motives he reaches out to twist her hair, is touching her cheek, is drawing a line along her jaw with his thumbnail, construes her astonishment as curiosity, her reluctance as shyness. Would have her after all. This is part of the dream he has woven: their telepathy, their connection, the round pink open mouth which lacks a kiss—

She does not find it charming. That he has caught her off guard has contributed to her predicament, but composure is returning. How to repel him without turning him against her? She tries to pull away but Elinga tightens his grip, making indentations on her pale throat.

The absence of sweeping is most suspicious to Lucas. And he did not hear Father go to his studio at the top of the house, his sanctuary from his family. He wants to know what the grownups are doing, peers within rooms, finds them at last.

And what does Lucas see? Father holding Esther near to him; and the maid's hand reaching up to reciprocate, to clasp his, pressing her face into his palm like a cat.

Lucas's intake of breath alerts his father. Elinga stares at his treacherous son and while his guard is lowered, Esther peels away from him, dips down to pick up the dustpan and broom and escapes, strides directly for the doorway, straight at Lucas.

He squeaks (would Esther beat him with her broomstick for what he has seen?) and flees, hastening down, down the awkward staircase, running the whole way to the yard, heart pounding pounding out into the sunlight—

His little sister and baby brother are hunched on the ground playing with wooden clothes pegs. Anna does well to occupy Allart. The pegs are his toy army, she lets him give the orders in his burbled speech, sending them into war to be victorious, or killed, as he chooses.

Lucas crosses the yard to the opposite wall, presses his head to it with his arms around his face, as though counting for hide-and-seek, stays there a while. Then he appears to stop counting (did he reach his goal of 100?) and kicks the wall instead, once, twice, repeatedly, rams his fist against it as if he would knock it down. Allart pays him no attention, Anna pretends not to.

Lucas is not crying. Lucas never cries.

Then he stops and immediately assumes authority – he is the captain now and the captain musters his rabble crew (the smaller children) for inspection. They are for him and with him, willing and impressionable, deserting the wooden army on the battle-field in favour of stronger leadership and a better game. Get them moving seems the best plan, get them busy busier busiest.

66

Lucas resolves that his brother and sister will run around in a large circle with himself in the middle of it. He shouts his instructions.

Anna is seven (bonny and moon-faced); she screeches with delight, relishes the attentions of her admired older brother.

Faster if you can, lazy dog, chants Lucas.

Anna obediently tears about the yard. Waf-waf! Waf-waf! If she is the dog, Lucas must be the human.

Run, run, lazy dog. Catch the rabbit. Lucas encourages or reproves their progress.

Anna fizzes with excitement and chases Allart, who has been consigned to the role of prey.

Allart, too little to care about becoming someone's dinner, is enjoying the game. He nods his blond head repetitively, as though in agreement with every command and insult Lucas throws at him, while Anna still shrieks with pleasure. If Allart trips over he hauls himself up again on his chubby legs, bottom first, body following. Anna overtakes him more than once, doubles back when it pleases her.

In the yard (or is it a forest?), the dog captures the rabbit. The rabbit wriggles free but with further incitement from the human is apprehended again, giggling and hot.

Anna growls at Allart because she is thoughtful and knows how to inhabit a role.

Good dog. (Lucas pats her on the head.) Bad rabbit for trying to get away. (He wags his finger at Allart, and the rabbit laughs harder in response.) And now it is time to skin the rabbit.

Yes! Yes! Skin the rabbit! Skin the rabbit!

Anna says, But how can we when we have got no knife?

Simple, we will tickle him until his skin falls off. And then we will eat rabbit stew and I will have a new pair of gloves for the winter.

Lucas and Anna set to work. Allart is rolled on his back and transforms into quite a different animal, from a rabbit to a tortoise stuck on its upturned shell – he chuckles merrily and enjoys being the centre of attention. The laughter is shared by the three children, who have a pitch and pattern similar to each other. Anyone hearing them, like three bells ringing together, would think it delightful. Good fun and easy to join in with (at least at first). They grow louder, exhilarated, hysterical.

Eventually Anna feels the joke wear off, tires of it. As the only girl she has to be sensible. Her tickles have subsided, become less vigorous, less frequent, and then are finished. That is enough now.

Lucas does not agree, he is just getting started.

Allart's face glows and tears form in his eyes and still he laughs his helpless laughter, squeals belting out.

I think it is time to stop.

He likes it!

Allart is short of breath, gulps from the back of his throat, bursts of noise indistinguishable from cries. He is too small to fight back. Lucas tickles him all the more – some of the tickles resemble pokes, some are barely concealed pinches.

Lucas, I think you're hurting him—

But Lucas is determined.

Anna backs away. It is not fun any more, has turned quite nasty. (Why does Lucas have to spoil it?) She does not like being an accomplice and is now confronted with a horrid decision: to watch, to tell or to run away. She frowns at the cruelty of men while she considers her choices but is spared the anguish of committing to one – Esther is upon them in a trice, grabs both brothers, separates them, halts the attack.

Esther stands Allart up, loosens his buttons, rubs his back, checks him for bruises and lumps, dries his eyes. He recovers quickly, but is gasping, bewildered and flushed. Odd laughing sounds still escape him, as though, already shaken loose, they must all come out until he is empty.

The maid beckons Anna, puts her in charge of Allart. Anna will take him inside, splash cold water on his face, clean him up, calm him down. Anna does so without complaint because she reckons she has got off lightly.

Then Esther straightens to her full height, folds her arms, glares down at Lucas.

Normally Lucas would launch into his defence: they were only playing – it was an accident – it was someone else. Ah, but this is not a normal day . . .

Between them is the incident which took place upstairs, what was seen, what was perceived, what might be said or left unsaid, what consequences will follow.

Lucas looks back at her intensely, as though she has injured him, then he flings his arms round the maid, hugs her tight at the waist – too tight, he is strong for his age.

It is his turn to be patted on the head . . .

This child is difficult. He has long spells of moodiness and bad behaviour. When he is not having tantrums he is often serious and solitary. He has emulated his mother's dislike of Esther, is unafraid of showing it. Teasing, derision, spitefulness are his ways. Not neediness, not the offering of affection – it is atypical and uncomfortable.

Esther disentangles herself from his embrace. She would like to get away from him but he is dishevelled from his rough game, has mud on his knees, broken skin on his knuckles, his clothes are askew. And after all he is just a boy. She tends to the marks, brushes them off, dabs them with a hanky, straightens his collar and his garments in a matronly manner. She will not show him fear. She will not behave as if she has done anything wrong.

Something else which he never does: he never signs to Esther but always makes her read his lips. The only member of the family willing and able to converse fluently in her language is Young Pieter.

But Lucas is signing a sentence now, deliberately and correctly. I . . . want . . . to . . . lie . . . on . . . top . . . of . . . you.

Lucas has seen the private activities of his father, watched with fascination and revulsion from inside a closet and through a keyhole. It is the secret adults keep from children.

He waits.

For a moment, nothing. And with a flourish, abruptly, suddenly, making Lucas flinch at her speed, Esther turns on her heel and marches back inside.

Lucas is left alone again. He does not smile. He does not sneer. Of course he does not cry either.

He has a coin in his purse – one single coin. He does not yet know its full buying power but is certain he can only spend it once. The question is where to spend it, and on what? Where it will bring the most personal benefit? Or where it will cause the most damage?

It is sure to make her sister envious. In the lesser reception room, Jurina composes letters sitting upright at the desk, working with a quill pen. The bulge of pregnancy shows beneath her gown.

Her veracity has been tested of late. She has described in loving detail the accomplishment of Elinga's most recent still lifes . . . and omitted that his productivity has become erratic, the gaps between completed works wider. She has gushed about expectations for the new baby's health and possible names . . . but failed to mention the acute financial pressure it has put them under. Meditations on the exquisiteness of tasteful Delftware purchases have been replaced with inane chatter about coughs and colds. She has written herself into a corner. By naming their important guests, she will draw attention to the length of time since the last sale of a painting. Tricky. But, oh, Jurina wants to tell the witch about it, she will hate it!

Restraint, Jurina. Dignity. Best to stick to women's matters.

The baby has been moving and I wonder which sex it will be? It would be nice for Allart to have a brother near his own age to play with. And I think it might be good for Lucas to have two brothers.

She intends to write that another daughter would be an equally welcome addition when she realises her error. Not too late to save it – *it might be good for Lucas to have two brothers, to look up to him.*

There.

Allart is a bright and perfectly adorable child. If I can produce another little boy to match him, it would be an achievement indeed.

Too much, even if it is true. Her sister will find a snide remark to make about it, unfavourably comparing Jurina's modest brood to her own unruly flock.

(I know you agree that hyperbole is a mother's prerogative!) & a girl would be a welcome addition, so I find I do not mind.

The lady stretches in her chair, her back aching, perspires from the discomfort, massages it to bring some relief. Jurina could never have believed she would grow sick of pregnancy this quickly – how has her sister endured it eight times?

Carrying this child gives me more pleasure day by day. I shall be almost sorry when he finally arrives in the world and I shall have to return to my former self. By the way, please thank my brother-in-law again for the reference he wrote. My stepson and I are extremely grateful and will let you know of any developments.

Unusually, Jurina would like to write further about Young Pieter: that she thinks he may have left home by the time the new baby arrives; that without him Esther's employment will be untenable. She inhales a big breath at the prospect. Inside her womb her next child kicks. Despite herself, she continues—

It turns out Young Pieter is not as obtuse as he appears. He came

71

back from a market a week ago with a stuffed lizard. Quite the ugliest and strangest object you ever saw. & said we should make a gift of it to Rembrandt van Rijn – no need to put 'the painter', Rembrandt is a rare enough name – because the old bankrupt had to sell his collection of artefacts. He (Young Pieter) said Rembrandt still has valuable contacts in Amsterdam and at the Guild, and if Pieter Janssens gave him this thing as a present he would make some introductions with a view to arranging a sale or a commission. Here then is the surprising news. Not only did Rembrandt accept the gift eagerly, he & the prestigious art dealer Johannes de Renialme are coming to a viewing appointment at our home today. Who would have thought my stepson to have an aptitude for business and influencing people? Pieter Janssens insists that I be there, that he cannot do it without me.

Jurina rereads it, visualises her sister seething. So what if she guesses there has been a drought? It will be worth it. *Suffice to say, I find the whole thing an ordeal and would prefer a quiet afternoon with the children. How lucky you are not to have these burdens, and only the house and family to be concerned with.*

Esther enters, and Jurina is compelled to turn the letter over. She has brought a bowl of fruit and a cushion. The maid has noticed how her mistress neglects to eat and drink for several hours at a stretch when she is anxious; the meeting with the art dealer is clearly playing on her mind. The dish and a sharp knife are set down, and Jurina alters her posture so the cushion can be placed at her back. These kindnesses are infuriating.

Allart appears, rosy and dimpled, staggers into the room; Lucas lurks at a distance. Allart wants to be on Mother's lap so she lifts him up. Beloved Allart, darling prince, she kisses his temple.

Lucas, are you idle because you have finished all your lessons?

Lucas does not confirm or deny it but withdraws from his mother's sight.

Then she gives Allart back to Esther; the child whimpers as he is led out of the room.

Jurina attempts to pick up where she left off but the flow has deserted her. Instead she takes a pear, quarters it, eats it.

The mistress of the house has considered the matter in detail and her logic is infallible. She will argue it has become too much for her to cope with, that a lady of her status with four children requires a certain standard of help. And, she will say to her husband, if our situation means we can afford only one maid, then we must make a decision. Society has expectations for the wife and children of Pieter Janssens Elinga. Jurina's parents have expectations.

Jurina does not hate Young Pieter or Esther; that would be rather strong. It is more that they are anomalous in the life to which she aspires. Pieter is to join the East India Company, the VOC, like many of his class – they are not all bumpkins and street rats. Esther? Esther? Esther will have to accept what is what and find a new position. Nothing unusual about that. The girl has benefited from long service, twice and three times longer than normal. The obligation did diminish. Eventually. The maid can take no credit for the smooth pregnancies and faultless labours which followed Lucas, not one miscarried or stillborn. Jurina has grown hard-hearted about this, waited ten years, occasionally demeaned herself by resorting to petty tactics. The maid will be gone and a different, carefully chosen servant appointed instead. No more reprieves. No more dewy-eyed willows. And no more panting bitches. This time it shall be done properly.

She thinks of another topic to put in her letter. Her sister can be relied upon to relish complaints about the help. *Another flunky has left us. (A relief but obviously the Old Irritation persists.) I should like a mature maidservant to replace her, one with years of experience. Lots of years. I want her when my new son is born or*

soonest after to give me the support I need ~ what do you think, a
single solution to two problems? I know you know what I mean.

Jurina turns a blind eye, for her husband's and children's
sakes. It grieves her, yes, but if it is not flaunted, if she is not
humiliated—

Her pen nib hovers over the page. Were Elinga to turn his
attentions to Esther for a short while, were Jurina to have evidence of it, however flimsy, then she could send the packhorse
away immediately. She cannot confide this thought, though her
sister would certainly have sympathy for it.

I have realised I do not know where the Irritation attends church.
Not ours. I mention this because Lucas says It regularly visits the
Jewish quarter these days. But we would know if It was a Jewess by
now! Such a thing could not stay hidden for all these years! (Where
does Lucas get his information from? If he is making up lies, it
would not be the first time.) No, I am not worried about that.
However, I have grown concerned that we could be inadvertently
harbouring a Catholic. This is much more plausible. If I discovered
that It goes to a clandestine church of the old faith ~ in your opin-
ion would that be legitimate grounds for dismissal? Do write back
and advise, you are good at these knots.

When the two gentlemen are welcomed by the host and hostess, their presence fills the entire house. Johannes de Renialme
is the more loquacious, a tall serious man with a crisp white
collar, his clothes and broad hat expensively dyed black.
Rembrandt is dressed hardly better than an innkeeper, grey
locks and sprouts of whiskers, jowly and paunchy, he says little
and has a grumpy expression. Yet Jurina knows a fraternity when
it arrives in her home. They shake Elinga by the hand, pay him
respect as almost an equal, compliment him on his tasteful decor,
his elegant wife – expecting a fourth, are you? Jurina is prim by
nature but loves to be admired for her voluptuous belly. Esther
is instructed to fetch the good wine.

De Renialme surprises the party by accurately describing a domestic genre painting of Elinga's, which he saw in a client's home, of a maid sweeping. It was very pleasing. Have you got any more of those?

Not at the present time.

Elinga explains he has been concentrating on the medium of the vanitas still life recently – and the distinguished men are shown to the main room, where the paintings are hanging. There are two, displayed as pendants though conceived separately. Expertly done, remarkable, the objects look real enough to hold. One shows a perfectly formed wineglass half-filled, arranged with lemons in stages of decay upon a silver platter (even the reflections are perfect, *perfect*). The second is of a jug and some smoking materials. A pipe lies waiting to be picked up, the coal gutters in a cracked pot and the tobacco has been carelessly abandoned by the absent smoker.

Elinga asks the art dealer, How do you find them?

Maudlin.

Thrown, the painter starts to justify his choices. The fruit is bitter and disintegrates before our eyes; the smoke vanishes into the very air; as do we ourselves suffer and are ephemeral beings, mortals on the cusp of death.

Yes, yes, but will people like it? Do they wish to look at mouldy lemons every day while they are having their breakfast? (De Renialme has grown insensitive to artists.)

Rembrandt tries to defuse the situation by praising Elinga's skill and observation, but this irks his colleague further.

If you like them, Rembrandt, why don't you sell them in your own gallery, hmm? No, I thought not – and if this is how you repay a good turn, I shall remember it. Elinga, have you tried offering them to the Lottery? They might take them for runner-up prizes.

Jurina turns defensive. Are they not good? Since when did

liefhebbers, rich and knowledgeable connoisseurs, cease to appreciate superb Dutch painting?

The dealer explains the connoisseurs are as potty for fine art as ever they were, but there are phases, cycles you might say—

Fashions? the same as for hairstyles and dresses? for paintings? It is news to her. She thought fine art was timeless.

So it is Madam; *prices* of art, on the other hand, are a different animal and can fluctuate dramatically.

This is a blow to Elinga and his wife.

But Johannes de Renialme has not quite finished. His rudeness softens, One or two people come to mind who might be interested in your work, and a handful more will find the investment potential appealing. I think I can find someone to purchase your canvases, though if you take my advice and hold on to them, their value will appreciate.

The couple have discussed this beforehand. We cannot wait. We will accept reasonable offers.

Then – it is agreed, the arrangements follow, the tension dissipates. And, on time, the maid brings in a tray of wine and goblets, sets it down, pours. Johannes de Renialme notices her.

Are you sure you cannot muster the enthusiasm for some genre interiors, Elinga? Plenty of Amsterdam art dealers would have no problem whatsoever selling those. Pretty girls taking music lessons, pretty girls mopping floors, pretty girls cuddling pups – demand is ludicrously high. (He mentions some prices, depending on size and quality, of course.) Based on what I have seen, Elinga, yours are rather good.

Esther offers drinks to de Renialme and then to Rembrandt, then her mistress and master.

Would you sit for your master, for example?

The dealer directs the question to the back of Esther's head.

She cannot hear you, Elinga explains, and signals to the maid that one of their visitors addressed her.

Jurina bristles. Do not embarrass the girl.

Johannes de Renialme sips his drink, decides not to pursue it, is confident that if Elinga's family are as hard up as he thinks, the artist will soon come round.

The mistress dismisses her, and Esther takes the empty tray away (annoyed because they were talking about her).

To Jurina's consternation, Rembrandt van Rijn follows the maid, his feet flapping on the tiles all the way to the kitchen.

Esther knows who he is, folds her hands demurely at this breach of etiquette.

Rembrandt stands respectfully in front of the woman. In low tones he asks, Can you understand me, Miss?

She nods.

Rembrandt smiles, a wrinkly, mild, jocular smile that unmasks his severity, makes her smile back. I am very fond of faces, and I like yours. If ever you wish to be painted by me, if your mistress can spare you, come and see me.

The artist doffs his hat.

Esther beams.

Bodies crammed together surge into the East India House court-yard. On the threshold of ambition and uncertainty the men and boys thrust themselves forwards, a crush of folk, the strongest climbing over the weakest. From slums, villages, orphanages and foreign countries – brought here by poverty, bankruptcy, aspi-ration and pimps. Waves of meat. The crowd bottlenecks at the archway, regroups and scrabbles to the entrance steps of the VOC headquarters, where marshals struggle to hold the mob back so they can be seen individually within. The gang vents its frustration by jostling and grumbling at the front, by pushing and yelling at the back where they strain to see what is happen-ing. They press onwards. Desperation and conviction swell the throng, each applicant eager to catch the eye of the Committee, impatient to be signed up. Advance, advance, stand out from the masses. Be fearless. Many will be turned away.

The son of a painter, more timid than most, huddles down and presses between the shoulders and torsos of his rivals. He is kicked and punched. The new suit of clothes his parents gave him marks him out as middle class, may get torn before he is seen. His nose may get bloodied or his teeth knocked out. If he stumbles, they will trample him. He pushes towards the front of the multitude. He digs deep.

At the same time, elsewhere in the city, a maid works vigorously through the rooms of a house, brushing, scrubbing, shaking out. When she has finished a job she slaps the furniture or object, admonishing it for becoming dirty. Now she makes the beds, *smack* for being slept in. Now she empties a dustpan, *bang* for getting dusty. She picks up her mistress's shoes and drops them, *thud, thud*, find your own way back. It is only when she is standing on a chair forcefully rubbing at the window panes that her energy subsides, the glass gleaming, the latticed sunlight streaming in. She has expended some of her anger.

Esther can only be this way when she is on her own. Is it really the best use of her solitude? Closing the windows gently and stepping down from the chair, she looks about to see what is left to do in the lady's bedroom. Cushions to be set straight, jewellery to be put away, the mirror on the wall needs a polish. It is too early to move the cradle in, but perhaps time to sort out baby clothes from the storage trunks. She wipes her hands down her apron, tries not to think of Young Pieter.

Certain there are some in a chest here, she opens it and examines the contents. Jurina's dresses and petticoats are at the top; these Esther sets aside in neat piles. Beneath are the shifts, bootees and bonnets each of the children has outgrown; blankets, swaddling, a christening gown. Jurina should choose. Carefully Esther excavates the layers and separates this from that. A few family documents and letters and sheet music are kept here. Milk teeth in a jar. A perfume bottle from the Orient. Spare leather. Embroidery thread. And books. Only three, all unwanted gifts. The maid knows these. Jurina's books, literature, are neglected. She prefers her Calvinist Bible.

At this moment – when temptation invites, when it hurts no one and discovery is unlikely – a pause. Esther covets this. Not wealth, not the station of her mistress, not the person of her master. She covets *this*, the liberty to sit, to choose. A suspension. The awareness of an indistinct version of herself who comes into focus, who steps into the light.

The beautiful story of the knight Malegis, who won the famous horse Baiart, and undertook many wonderful adventures.

The rhythms of the story fill her up.

Esther does not have the disposition to dwell on who deserves what, and why she should be born to one class and not another, for reality is reality. She is concerned with her own spiritual well-being, and goes to church for that. She is good at her job, for if she has to work she will work well. But who is this other Esther, stirred into life when she is permitted to read stories? She remembers her from childhood – the girl who picked wild flowers for their magical properties, who had imaginary friends, who would stare at the fireplace alive with dancing, wicked goblins. This is the Esther to whom her parents would tell and retell parables and folk tales, and she would sit and listen without interrupting while their hands made dancing shadows.

The romance she is engrossed in has made etchings in her mind's eye; she retraces them easily. The wind that convulses trees, the coolness of a spring, the snort of hot breath from Baiart's nostrils, his stamping hoof, an outline of a castle on a hill. Esther's heart is with Malegis at each test of strength and virtue: do not drink from the poisoned chalice – hold fast – fight back. She fears for his safety, and wills him to win. They travel for miles together. Parts she has forgotten she rediscovers; the imprints of favourite passages burn bright with renewed colour and feeling. If she reads on, the horse will reveal his fabulous qualities and save Malegis's life.

It is time to stop at the end of this paragraph this page this chapter. She reminds herself she can return to a given point in the knight's journey another day. Malegis will not leave without her.

The shadow of Esther, the twin, the companion, has a stubborn streak. She wants more and has elaborate ways of keeping the world at bay – as he rides the hero looks over his shoulder, and has the face of a man outside the Portuguese synagogue.

The maid chides herself for her idleness. She cannot indulge in this any further, it is dangerous. Only in bed, in private, may she permit foolish thoughts. The practical Esther, her mother's daughter, is roused into action. She shuts the book. Still, a niggling, a reluctance. Rather than returning it, perhaps she could hide it in the kitchen under her pillow for a while? No, that is risky. It would not matter that the book is never read, that its absence has gone unnoticed. Were one of the children to discover it, were Esther to be accused of stealing . . .

Esther stands. Book, contents, lid, chair must be put back immediately and it is done. Cushions are beaten into shape. Garnet brooch and diamond necklace dropped into their case. Cleaning rags pocketed, the shoes she almost falls over reunited. She will take the baby garments downstairs for Jurina when she has given the mirror a quick clean. Esther wipes the looking-glass and sees behind her Pieter Janssens Elinga, watching.

This is the first time she has been on her own with him since he compromised her, and it strikes her hard. She does not wait to see what he will do next, does not consider how long he has been there or ponder his intention (good or bad). Practical Esther is in charge. She snatches up the baby clothes and hurries away, knocking past his open, insulting hand.

At the Company's headquarters Young Pieter signs a bond, takes possession of two months' wages in advance and an appointment to the VOC ship *Prosperous*.

Jurina wants Esther. To sew a button for Lucas, to buy some cloves because Allart might have a toothache, to lift a heavy object for her. Has she gone out? She must have done, and Jurina's bile gives her pain.

The lady has only herself to blame. Esther is doing what was asked of her, cleaning and tidying Elinga's studio while he keeps an appointment at Johannes de Renialme's office. Cups and plates have been discarded up there, some of his clothes have been draped and abandoned. Jurina said it offhandedly, Do the studio today, will you? Remember, the composition and the materials must not be disturbed.

Elinga is consumed by painting once again, has a project he is executing quickly, zestfully. It fulfils him and calms his mind, and he suspects the picture will fetch a decent price when finished. Jurina wants to encourage the optimum conditions for his creativity and yet has forgotten her instruction, or rather has fixated on the notion that the maid has gone out without permission.

Esther has felt the change in the atmosphere. Esther – who thinks always of self-preservation, who fears being blamed for accidents, who avoids going into her master's private space unless explicitly directed – is wary. She feels a threat from what she might see in there.

Jurina hastens from room to room in search of the maid. It is ludicrous that she cannot call her but must go and get her. She navigates the narrow stairs, up, up as far as the second floor, no further, then down, down back where she started, her pulse and breath increased. She will confront the maid about this.

Esther can carry out her task without necessarily seeing the work in progress. The easel, camera obscura and an arrangement of furniture are at one end of the studio, and by averting her eyes she need not discover the true content. Collecting the dishes, a cursory dab of the duster, and laying the stockings and under-shirts over her arm, she can circumvent the working area completely if she desires. But she does not quite desire. She prefers to know.

A knock at the front door, a figure visible through the window – and Jurina must answer it herself. No, she will not. She makes Lucas do it, adds this to the list of Esther's mistakes. Female voice. Lucas comes back to his mother, fiddles his fingers coyly. Well—? (Lucas grins without answering.) You are the least helpful sort of child. Jurina – impatient with her son, with her servant, with everything – goes to meet the unwanted person so she can send her away again.

Esther sets down her master's forsaken garments to inspect the scene unencumbered. From here, viewing the arranged furniture without proper sight of the canvas, what she can see is essentially a vacant interior. Two frames and a mirror hung up, a chair pulled near to the window at a peculiar angle, two more set either side of a closed chest with a cloth cover by the wall. There is a fruit bowl pertinently left on the upholstery (strange choice), a cushion and a pair of lady's shoes on the floor. She knew that Elinga had gone back to genres but from here, with-out a model and an activity to complete it, she cannot tell what the composition is doing. There is no musical instrument, no writing desk, no needle and thread, no foot warmer, no basket of linens, no clue about the story being told. Every picture contains a story, be it history, fiction, legend or myth.

In the hallway, there she is, with her back to Jurina, the back of her white cap, the looped bow of her apron down the back of her skirt. Jurina knows better than to bother saying her name. She strides up behind Esther and taps her hard on the shoulder. The maid turns but it is not Esther. Jurina has never seen her before.

At last, Esther steps in front of the easel, and it becomes clear. Though unfinished, the components slip into place like marbles dropping into holes. The artist's model, Margaretha, is being a maid reading a book. Jurina's book. (Esther throws her glance to her master's bench – there it is among his effects, waiting to resume its place in context.) Yes, it is, the moment when Pieter Janssens Elinga caught her in the act of reading her mistress's book. But it is not the same, not exactly. The artist has changed it, cleaned it, emptied it of domestic clutter. The sorted baby clothes and familial belongings have evaporated; the room is a fictitious one, not Jurina's. The eye is drawn to the patch of sunlight glowing on the floor, giving a sense of the personal and serene. Crucially, it is not Esther. She exhales with relief. She rests her hands on her hips.

In her haste, Jurina must not have looked at the woman properly. The woman has a similar height and build to Esther, but the cap is new cambric, the jacket a deep red. She has a spotty complexion and is not so attractive. When asked her name, she haltingly replies that she is Margaretha, working for the master in the studio. The model? – yes, he did say he was using a model this time. Jurina has not met her, she is always shown straight through.

No, not Esther. There is nothing in this painting to betray her. Nothing which puts her employment at risk.

(Lucas covers his mouth. He guesses this is not a coincidence but a street conjurer's trick – and his mother is the dupe.)

Esther looks again, properly. Not her; not Margaretha either. The woman in the painting has her back to the viewer, estranged and unidentifiable, her face and hair obscured totally by her white cap. It might be anybody.

Jurina berates herself for her lack of composure. The master is out on business. (What does this mean?)

What does this mean? Esther folds her arms. Could someone construe the subject to be her?

Lucas, go and see to your brother.

He scurries away.

Well . . . ?

Madam?

(Madam thinks, Silly bitch.) I said, the master is not here. Come back in an hour.

Margaretha shows herself out.

Jurina leans against the wall. What does it mean? She tries to assemble her thoughts and calm her body for the sake of her child. What, exactly, does it mean? Maybe nothing.

Esther wonders . . . could anyone have grounds to demand to know whether it is her or not? Then her future would rest on how Pieter Janssens Elinga chose to answer. He would surely reply that it is only Margaretha, a poor girl who sat for him playing the part of a negligent maid. He would surely explain it is a typical genre painting that panders to the tastes of the modern Dutch family.

Jurina decides that the girl has only a passing resemblance to Esther, the same resemblance most maids have to each other from behind when their heads are covered, their bodies hidden in frumpy clothes. She strokes her bump for comfort.

But he knows, and Esther knows. It is her. He has gone to some lengths to disguise the fact, but not far enough. What if Jurina should ask outright?

Esther, did you cause my husband to paint you by sitting on one of my chairs and reading one of my books when you ought to have been doing your duties? Did you allow him to stare at you, to

memorise your posture and shape, to watch you indulging your las-
civious fantasies? Did you ensnare him? Did you flaunt yourself?
Did you mean to seduce him?

The honest answer is no. Esther imagines herself denying it,
but Jurina is capable of twisting this into something terrible.

Then why has my husband admitted that you are the object of
this painting? Why does he dwell on your image in this way? What
have you done to captivate him?

Subject, Madam, *subject*. Not *object*. I am not, nor have I ever
been, his object. (The distinction will be immaterial.)

Is it a pious scene? Are you reading the Gospels so intently? No.
It is voyeuristic. It is fetish.

Esther will implore her to see reason—

Jurina will develop a mental block, conveniently forgetting
any sign language she once knew so that she can override the
maid's protests and play her trump card. *Lucas has seen you and*
my husband making love. He has seen it. Do you deny that some-
thing has occurred between you?

Evidence of a physical relationship – evidence of emotional
entanglement. Enough to send her packing twice over. When
Young Pieter has left, there will be no reason to retain her at all.
Esther shakes her head at the treacherous painting. It will not
matter that she has never encouraged Elinga. That he has all the
power, and has behaved improperly. That she is the victim.

She will get rid of me.

Downstairs, Jurina's temper has cooled and cold logic reigns
once more. Whatever has gone wrong here, the leverage of this
new baby will set it right.

I will get rid of her.

Lucas toys with his imaginary coin. He senses that its value is
not fixed, that if he waits too long it will turn out to be worthless.
And there is another question he has been considering in his

brilliant mind: Who will be the most eager to sell their wares? Who has the weakest disposition and will therefore put up the least resistance? Which transaction will give the highest yield for the lowest risk? The answer is obvious!

Lucas has decided what he wants – Young Pieter's bedroom. New shoes with buckles. A globe. His very own sword. And a pony. He is going to ask Father. No need to say why he wants them or what will happen if he does not have them. He will simply say, Father, I am too grown to share a room with the babies. I need my own room and a pony to ride. And seeing as the new baby will be showered with presents, I think I ought to have some presents because I am the older brother and have many responsibilities. Please?

After the farewell dinner will be the best time. Father will be drunk and suggestible.

Lucas is glad Young Pieter is leaving; anyone can see his half-brother does not really fit in. He also likes special occasions, because they have a way of making people less discreet. But it is in Lucas's interests not to be difficult tonight, so he has thought of some appropriate words to say: My dear brother, I will miss you deeply. Without you as my guiding compass, what path shall I follow into manhood? I will pray for your safe return every day.

He wants the family to hear his speech. After Young Pieter is gone, Lucas will be the eldest child, with all the rights and obligations that entails. Being held in higher esteem by his father and mother, for example. And perhaps ... a bit more tenderness from Esther (if she survives).

The meal is in Young Pieter's honour. The youth sits tensely, endures his stepmother's performance.

Let me toast our son.

The family obediently raise their glasses, apart from Allart, who picks through his food with his fingers.

86

I drink to you, Pieter. You will see wonderful sights, foreign horizons, I don't doubt you will return wealthier for it in every respect. If I could wish for anything, it would not be to keep you here, rather that we were all able to go with you and share in your adventure.

The children mutter their agreement, the supporting cast in Jurina's play, sip solemnly from their wine. Lucas has to admire their mother's flair. Elinga drains his glass and waves Esther forward to refill it and remove his plate. She steps out to the kitchen.

When Young Pieter does not make a reply, Jurina addresses her husband instead, and conversation turns to the buyers who have already expressed an interest in the genre piece without having seen it. Johannes de Renialme is running a whispering campaign and attracting a few nibbles. Jurina pouts – I knew it was only a matter of time – and flatters her husband relentlessly, going as far as biting his finger under the guise of a kiss. You must show it to me before it is taken away. She feels powerful. Is satisfied to count the hours until her stepson's departure, to count the days until her baby is due, and then—

(She leans over to cut up Allart's food, and prompts Anna to eat what they have provided for her.)

Jurina resolves to plant the seed with her husband this very night while they are in bed, her hands around his hard cock. It needs to have the appearance of being encouraging but contain the underlying point: I am so relieved good fortune is *finally* smiling on us, my love. I have put off searching for *qualified* help to raise our four children because – oh, now I can do so *confidently*.

And tomorrow, after Young Pieter has gone, it will be: My love, the baby is arriving imminently, it is time for us to prepare the house.

The day after, Jurina will initiate her husband's favourite

87

sexual act but she will find herself distracted, weeping, putting off his moment of climax because what if they cannot afford to pay two salaries . . . ?

Young Pieter's voice breaks over the hushed table, clear, unexpected: I will not see it.

The lady pushes a ringlet of hair from her face. Pieter, what do you mean?

I will not see my new sibling, it will be born after I have left. I will miss the first two years of his life, I will not be a part of the home he knows.

Jurina hesitates, putting her anxieties aside. My dear son, blessings on you, you are a credit to us. (She reaches over to briefly take his hand in hers.) Do you hear that, Pieter Janssens? Your eldest son would forgo his own future happiness in order to meet his baby brother.

Or sister!

Anna is the one who has chimed in. Mother soothes her only daughter's displeasure. Esther brings in grapes and cheeses, sets them down. Lucas indicates his own plate for Esther to take away.

Jurina thinks this would be a good time to reaffirm her generosity, asks Young Pieter if there is anything else he needs for the voyage, reiterates he must have whatever he wants from the house, that if there is anything left to buy Esther can be sent for it in the morning. She sounds firm, as though to mask her own pain. A loving mother putting on a brave face at her first child's departure.

He answers, Thank you Madam.

Jurina finds she has an appetite.

Father has advice to dispense, You must stay healthy, avoid contact with the sick whenever you can, avoid altercations.

The youth hangs his head. Yes Sir.

Anna declares, I promise I will talk about you to the baby so she will know who you are and know you are coming back one day. Then when you do come back, she will recognise you, and, and, we will look at maps of where you are. And I promise only to say nice things, I swear it by Jesus in the Manger.

Jurina tweaks her daughter's cheek. What a perfect idea! Anna will remind the baby of its big brother every single day.

Elinga Senior manages his first smile of the evening. Perhaps you can do the same for me, Anna?

For his part, Elinga Junior nods in gratitude at the person who, apart from Esther, has been his kindest friend.

Anna does not notice Lucas glowering at her and adds, We can write letters and save them for you. Would you like that, Pieter?

Lucas, not be outdone, Or put messages in bottles and throw them in the sea so they float all the way to Asia.

He replies that news will be difficult to come by and he should like to know, one way or another, what has been happening at home.

Anna asks, Ought I to come to wave you off from Silly Jack?

Jurina resumes her leadership. Partings are difficult, Anna, and best not done in public. You would not want Pieter worrying about you when he should be concentrating on the journey ahead and making a good impression on his first day. No, of course not, and you are a big girl for understanding. We can say our goodbyes here at home.

The child contains her feelings; the reality is taking hold.

And do call things by their proper names, Anna. It is the Montelbaans Tower; only ignorant people call it Silly Jack.

Lucas senses his moment has come. I have something to say to Pieter too.

Indulgently, Jurina focuses on his earnest face. What is it, my pet?

Lucas sits up in his chair and his expression becomes grave.

My dear brother, I will miss you deeply. Without you as my guiding compass, what path shall I follow—?

What is wrong with Allart? – Anna is the first to have spotted his contorted face. He seems pinkish and confused . . . something unexpected is happening to him.

Is he breathing? – Lucas's tone is curious.

Jurina's heart constricts, and inside her, the baby squirms. Allart makes a tiny gurgle.

Father announces, Yes he is fine, it is only wind.

Is it? Jurina, shrill. Are you sure?

In truth, he is not sure. Allart's face reddens further. The little boy mutely suffocates under the diners' gaze. Esther comes back to the awful tableau at the dinner table. She drops the ceramic jug – it smashes on the tiles, breaking the hypnotic spell. Jurina tries to move from her chair (she insisted they bought these huge carved chairs, she insisted upon it), hindered by heavy gown and cumbersome body.

Lucas wonders whether he is about to watch someone die.

The small body is jerked into the air by strong arms and struck on the back with controlled blows, *thump*, *thump*, for choking, *thump*, for not breathing. *Thump*.

Allart spits out a piece of maimed meat. The silence lasts a second more, then lifts as he wails his distress and the family give way to their own startled reactions. Jurina overcomes her enormous bulge at last, lifts Allart from Esther's grasp as though she were the real danger and this were the real rescue. There, there, my darling one, there, there. She coos and purrs, comforting him, coddling him. Allart bellows with all his might.

Father is pale and shiny. Young Pieter trembles. Anna tries to come to terms with what she has just witnessed by attending to her meal as she was urged to do before.

Esther sees she is no longer required, goes to fetch a bucket and a mop. (There on the floor a whole jug of the second best wine, shards of pottery, chewed food and a mouthful of vomit.)

And Lucas . . . Lucas's mind races, clicking like the beads of an abacus, and arrives at several conclusions in rapid succession, confirmed by the way Mother fusses over Allart and Father wordlessly leaves the room. First, Lucas has missed his chance to gain from what he saw and what he suspects; second, Father does not love Jurina's children the way he loves Pieter; and finally— Allart whimpers, rocked back and forth by Mother.

Lucas leans close to Jurina and whispers it: Now you will never get rid of her.

Please come in, Esther.

The maid lingers in the doorway of the studio.

Pieter Janssens Elinga beckons her, Do not be afraid, come in.

She hesitates then obeys, standing before him.

He sits by his workbench strewn with brushes, linseed oil jars, powders and paper. At the far end of the room, the painting, virtually completed, rests on the easel, drying.

I thought it was time for us to have a talk. Do you understand what I am—?

She nods.

For a time he does not speak. Perhaps this is the conversation that has been waiting to happen since she was first employed by him. Heaven knows it was not meant to last this long.

Remind me, I have forgotten, where is your mother?

She signs it and when he does not understand, fingerspells it instead.

Forgive me, I am out of practice.

He indicates for her to sit down opposite and take up a pen, which she does, reluctantly. He repeats his question.

paradise

And your father?

asylum

91

The one at Kloveniersburgwal?

She signs, Yes.

Elinga thinks this over. You visit him sometimes.

Yes.

He asks how her father is but she declines to respond, so he asks if she sends him money regularly.

Yes.

You always have?

A pause. Haughty, Esther raises her chin to him. Yes.

It must be hard seeing Pieter leave home. It is hard for me too.

The flash of rage in her does not go unnoticed.

You think I should have intervened by now, that I have sent him into the abyss. You think he is leaving because Jurina is making him go and because he does not want to disappoint me, that Pieter could be my apprentice or I could find him a trade if I tried. You think I have not done enough by him. Is that so—?

Esther does not disabuse him of it. He leans on his hand and she notices how old her master has come to look.

If you do think that, then you do not appreciate the extent to which we all rely on Jurina's income. (The master sighs, picks up a stained rag and wipes his palms.) Despite any bad opinion you have of her, Jurina has not been ungracious to Pieter. She is a tolerant lady, virtuous, constant, a devoted mother. She has the well-being of her own children to consider. Their futures. And despite what you might think of me, I do care what becomes of my son. However, I have made errors – and my wife keeps fastidious accounts.

Esther picks up the pen. *not too late*

I am afraid it is.

She shifts on her seat and flattens her apron then signs a complex sentence. Some years ago her master would have understood her meaning. She dips the nib into the inkpot. *you are not the man you were. what has happened?*

I am the same man, but I am worn down by the world.

She turns the paper over. *you have lost already one wife one son yet you risk losing much more. i say this as your servant & your friend*

Esther, are we still friends?

She barely nods. She could comfort him, in the past would have done. But always, now, she is thinking of self-preservation.

Elinga says, I do not want Pieter to go on his own tomorrow.

She signs that she is going with him. Then adjusts her apron, again unhappy at the way he watches her.

I meant to say, your idea to make a gift of that lizard to Rembrandt—

Esther jumps in her chair. No, not I.

It was your idea, I knew it straight away. Pieter would never have thought of it on his own.

Esther folds her arms.

You have given much to this family. And perhaps you have guessed already that you have inspired me to paint genres again.

No, not I. (It is quick, assertive.)

Elinga ponders for a moment then indicates the painting. Tell me, do you like it, Esther?

Yes. It is beautiful.

No one says that any more. In the art world it is 'sentimental', 'romanticised'. Beauty is out of fashion.

The maid shrugs her shoulders.

It is an old idea from my studies in Italy which I finally got round to. (He subdues his heart.) An old idea which I stole from an altar. I just wanted you to know that.

She exhales, and makes a simple sign that she knows he can understand.

Esther, have you never been inclined to find another job in another house?

She fingerspells deliberately, p, i, e, t, e, r.

93

Yes.

She touches both her ears in a mime.

But I am positive another family would appreciate you just the same. And if one of your employers or their children was deaf, well, your ability to communicate would be an asset.

My father.

His son used to address him using that sign, so it is fixed in Elinga's memory. It was hard to make him stop. The two of you depend on your salary? I see. Do you not wish to marry some day and have children of your own?

Esther explains: On Sundays and holy days, people go to look at the lunatics. For amusement. If the inmates' families can pay enough, they are given privacy and are not exhibited. The ones who rely on charity or whose families cannot afford the rates are exploited. I think it makes him worse.

Elinga glazes over until he speaks again, matter-of-factly. I remember all your kindnesses to this family, the grace you have shown us.

(Esther thinks he confuses grace with powerlessness.)

It is important at his age that your father is comfortable, that he has sustenance and medical treatment, whatever he needs. I propose making a charitable donation to ensure this is the case. And your years of unwavering service mean that you will be employed here for as long as you choose to remain. Your mistress and I are both extremely grateful to you.

Esther does not immediately react. She holds his offer in her mind and examines it for flaws. Is it tainted with additional expectations? Can Jurina be persuaded to honour it? Will it crack at the first test of its strength? She concludes it is the best commitment her master is able to make her, and thanks him for it.

After the interview, the maid returns to the kitchen, and Elinga is left alone in his studio. Prior to this evening, it would have been simple to send her away. He was merely waiting for his wife to bring it up. He tears up Esther's handwritten notes so his duplicitous son never finds them. It will be a painful promise for him to keep. His guilt. Fear of his own selfishness. He hates that Esther knows him so well.

He must quell his lust, or find more suitable outlets for it.

He must quell his heart, and allow its object to be free, to stay or go as she chooses.

There is a festival atmosphere around the Montelbaans Tower by the Oudeschans canal. Some people joke that Silly Jack will randomly peal its bells in honour of the occasion. This is an orderly version of the events at East India House – these are comrades for the time being, sharing empathy and excitement, brothers to look out for you. Some lads are cocky and unruly, sizing up their potential rivals, showing off. Rumours are passed on, blessings and superstitions are swapped.

The parents demonstrate their affection and grief. Embraces, kisses, pledging their prayers, their love, God speed. Wishes and presents are exchanged. Bystanders stop to marvel and cele-brate – or to pity them, the third that will not come back.

The Company Officers administer and direct the crowd from their ledgers. To the cutter do not dally we are racing the tide. Next soldier come forward.

As the small vessel fills with recruits, another cutter returns from the *Prosperous* having delivered the most eager, mast leaning to the tower, fat sails deflating, colours flickering, oars engaged, coming about. The full boat is pushed away to make room, the people cheer and whoop, family and strangers waving them off, hats and spirits lift when the boys aboard energetically wave back. Dozens of youths with nothing to lose but their lives. One starts to sing and the rest join in, sending their voices to those they have left behind. Children run alongside to the end of the jetty— They have gone out to the bay, are out of reach.

The empty craft is secured in its place, the boarding process is beginning again.

Esther is vulnerable, caught between shifting groups. Sunlight sears off the imposing form of an observer, it dazzles and disorients her (the highly polished breastplate and helmet of a pikeman, it must be), and she collides with another youth who could easily be a woman dressed as a boy, striking features, comely mouth; Esther bobs in apology to the prepossessing delinquent, finds Young Pieter's arm and links hers through it for security.

They hold back, there is no need to hurry.

Pieter has something on his mind, and this is his last chance to ask it. If there is an opportunity not to come back, should I stay for ever?

You mean permanent settlement at the Cape of Good Hope, or Batavia, or another VOC base?

Yes. Make a new life for myself. If I can, should I?

Esther does not answer immediately. You may find you want to come back. You may find you are homesick, you miss your family, the climate does not suit you. You may long to return to Amsterdam, marry a Dutch woman and have children with her. Life in a foreign country may be harder than it is here.

However?

However, if I were in your place and there was advancement or love for me on the other side of the world, nothing would induce me to return. Not even you.

Do you mean that?

Esther knows it hurts his feelings but adds, I would not give you a second thought.

Pieter does not respond. Instead he checks his bag, his document. Esther rubs a smudge from his cheek. She used to be able to pick him up; now he is a full head taller than she.

Pieter marks the accent of secrecy in her eyes, realises there is something else to ask, something important which he should have asked much sooner, but he has been insufficiently sensitive until now. Esther, are you in love?

She is stunned by his insolence. On any other day, at any other time, she would have denied it. Yes.

What is his name?

I do not know. We have never actually met.

Who is he then?

I think he is a student of medicine. Furthermore he is – Pieter does not know the sign so she has to fingerspell it – a Sephardi Jew. I am ashamed to admit that when I first noticed him, I followed him. He led me right into the Jewish quarter.

Pieter gazes at Esther in astonishment.

She says she has seen him several times since, always looks for him near the synagogue – would not dare go in, in case she caused offence. She describes the Jews she sometimes sees him with, chatting and sharing a joke, they seem like nice people.

Eventually, uncertainly, he says it does not matter.

Stop it.

But it does not. You have to meet him. Someone at your church can interpret for you. I would have done, if you had only asked me.

I insist you stop it.

Pieter is frightened by her sadness but persists. Esther, why should you not tell him how you feel, if he is your heart's desire?

Because.

She hides her face. Pieter puts his arm round her while some tears come, the way she used to comfort him when he cut his knee or banged his head. In a crowd of separations they do not stand out, and stay this way until her shuddering has ceased.

It is not only that I cannot speak to him. Even if I could, I have nothing to offer. He is well born and I am in service. He would prefer a woman of his own race and faith, I am sure of it. The obstacles are too big and too many to overcome.

But how can you live like this? My father loved my mother, Beatrix. They were happy and they had such a difficult time. I wish you had seen them. You would have liked my mother.

She smiles at his innocence. Yes. My parents loved each other too. Yet I can live like this, and I must. Besides, this way he remains perfect, this way I can never be betrayed or disappointed by him. He is just exactly what I hope and wish for.

To Pieter it seems tragic. He asks after her father.

Esther shakes her head. I do not think he knows who I am any more. Sometimes he acts as though he is pleased to see me, but I think it is the food I bring him which he is truly glad about.

Esther, are you going to marry one day?

One day I will be too old.

You there—! The VOC official is summoning stragglers.

Me Sir?

Say goodbye to your sister and get a move on. We need to fill all the spaces.

Pieter and Esther hug briefly. She kisses him on the cheek and finds a way to be pleased for him.

He presents himself to the Company Officer, gives his name, Pieter Janssens Elinga, the son of the painter.

Not any more, you are the company's son now.

Details are confirmed, the clerk makes a record. The young man boards the cutter and finds a gap where he can still see her. Other families can only shout or wave. Pieter and Esther continue their conversation.

Pieter, be careful.

I will. You too. Take care of Anna for me, she was upset.

I will look after her. She will be all right.

Will you promise not to tell anyone what we discussed?

Not a word, I swear it.

Commands and warnings as the cutter casts off. Friends and relatives bid farewell, handkerchiefs fluttering. Inspired by the example of the previous boat, a chorus strikes up of a different song, louder and ruder than the first. The Montelbaans bells ring out but it is only to announce the hour; Silly Jack is disappointingly punctual today.

Get a move on time is against us come forward. Next soldier—!

Thank you.

What for?

I will miss you.

I will miss you too.

I love you.

Good luck.

Goodbye.

Goodbye.

Angelica Kauffman

Portrait of a Lady, 1775

I looked everywhere for you, Frances!

But Frances does not appear to hear. She laughs, is running into the garden, following coloured lanterns down to the fountain, a bottle of champagne in her hand. They are at a wedding party, music drifting from open doors, intoxicated revellers.

Frances, I looked for you.

Come on.

Maria runs after her.

Come on!

Frances pauses, turns round, beckons. It is almost morning. She waves the bottle like a prize, mocking Maria.

Maria redoubles her efforts, lifts her dress in two handfuls to run faster. Frances slows to a walk, and with renewed optimism – she will surely catch her now – Maria sprints to her. But it is not right, as though she were underwater, as though her feet were floating several inches above the ground.

Coming, I am coming.

Drunk, Frances ignores Maria. She twirls on the spot; the lanterns blur, pink and blue and yellow, too fast, dangerously fast.

I wrote a poem for you, she is saying far away as she spins and spins.

New Year's Eve. They go to the masquerade as highwaymen, arm in arm, Maria holding her tight, feeling her solid warmth, the pair flashing their pistols, robbing ladies of their tokens. They wear breeches and stockings, the shapes of their legs revealed to the delight of the gentlemen, to the disapproval of the spinsters and chaperones.

Stand and deliver, Your Grace, we have taken a fancy to that decoration in your hair.

The duchess plays along, clutches her breast.

Villainous! What if I will not give it?

Then I will take your life, though it grieves me to deprive the world of such a beauty as yours (and Maria makes a bow to the excited onlookers' amusement).

Frances declares, Do not listen to him, Your Grace, he is a rogue. I will protect you and be satisfied to steal a kiss instead.

Her lips skim the back of the lady's hand to more shrieks and applause. Many allow themselves to be stolen from several times over – kisses trifles jewellery coin surrendered for the fun of it. The pair are sensational.

Did I tell you I wrote you a poem?

Did you? Is it in the bag?

Maria searches for it amid their booty; it is not there, and Frances is gone again, at the other end of the room, enthralled by the attentions of a gaudy matron dripping in frills and filigree. The woman's thick form almost bursts from her dress and she chuckles exuberantly as she pretends to read Frances's palm.

101

Maria's ferocious daggers of jealousy. She remembers this incident, it happened just as it is happening now: the other woman offers Frances a drink which looks like milk but gives off a nefarious green tinge. Maria wills Frances to refuse it, but she does not.

Mesmerised, they toast each other like lovers, and Frances tastes the mysterious liquid with the trepidation of a child taking an adult's medicine. Whatever is in that glass, it causes Frances to lean towards the wench and whisper into her ear. They share a secret moment of understanding, a connection.

Maria is helpless, watches them, horrified. What a row there was afterwards.

Have you seen the lady made of light?

Is it part of the poem you wrote?

Oh, here it is.

And there you are. I have been looking for you.

Maria has found her, is glad.

Now Frances is in the library bay window at home, her writing board on her knees, has been here the entire morning.

I am writing a poem for you.

Maria suspected as much; is nonetheless flattered. It is June, the smell of cut grass tells her so.

Please may I see it?

Frances holds out the paper and Maria attempts to take it once, twice; cannot, it dissolves at the touch.

Here it is. It says everything.

Maria tries again carefully but the sheet eludes her – a wisp.

Frances is radiant. Like a lady made of light.

Maybe Maria can make out the words from here? No. The words slip over each other, little black fishes swimming about.

What does it say? (It is her poem, Frances has written it for her.)

Everything I ever wanted to tell you.

Maria feels the edges of the world beginning to break apart and she guesses, or remembers, why it is imperative—

She is pleading with Frances to read it to her but her voice is muffled, will not be summoned. Everything is in it, she said. The room becomes as broad as a valley, the bookcases as tall as a forest, they are being swallowed by the sun. If only Frances would read it aloud, then she could memorise it, take it with her. Her begging is inaudible even to herself.

You read it, Maria.

I cannot. The words are moving. The paper does not like to be held.

And she tries once more, grabbing at space. The sun is getting brighter, draining the room of lines and depth. She is trying to shout, but the sounds take no form. She thinks, *I must not frighten Frances, she seems to have forgotten she is dead, and I ought not remind her.*

Read me some of it, Frances, because . . . because—

Frances is puzzled: Maria is rejecting it, something is amiss. Her face is impossible to see as the daylight blazes in.

Now – you might not have the chance again!

Maria reaches for her, has the parting perception that Frances is annoyed with her.

Just a few lines, Frances.

She is thinking it only, mentally imploring the fading vision.

Mrs Plett draws back the curtains and opens the shutters, the window, then another, and another, letting in fresh air.

My Lady?

The countess is deep in the middle of the mattress, a mess of bedding and auburn hair, asleep. Coward also, curled at the end.

Mrs Plett moves closer to her; firmly, My Lady?

Her breathing is regular, undisturbed.

103

Making no progress with the sleeping woman, Mrs Plett shoos off the black pug instead, who sneezes at the indignity.

My Lady?

The housekeeper cannot suffer it. She picks up one of the hard pillows and wallops it back down.

Maria!

Maria stirs not immediately, is groggy.

What is it, Mrs Plett?

She is here.

Maria knows that if she ignores her housekeeper, she will tire soon and leave her alone. Failed efforts to make her get up have become integral to their routine. The maidservants do not have the willpower to challenge the countess; only the housekeeper has enough authority to bully her for her own good. Already the tendrils of dreams ensnare Maria, pulling her back down (can still find out what is in that poem) but something Mrs Plett said peals like a bell.

Who is?

The Paintress.

Oh, nonsense.

You can tell her so yourself, My Lady.

Maria finds she is awake, narrows her eyes against the daylight, leans on one elbow.

Why would she turn up so early in the morning, unannounced?

The housekeeper stands to her full height, reaches the limit of her patience.

My Lady, it is almost three o'clock in the afternoon, and I would hardly describe the visit as impromptu.

The countess heaves herself up, gathers her thoughts.

Shall I bring tea to the drawing room and send Rachel to dress you?

The younger woman nods, and when Mrs Plett has left, she

steels herself to resist the comfort of her bed, rises. She finds she can remember her dreams most clearly in the dim seconds between sleeping and waking, can carry the figments with her by clinging fast, repeating them in her mind ... occasionally they survive the scorch of day and it is as though Frances has just left the room. And sometimes the images collapse like sandcastles.

Maria pours cold water from a jug into a basin, splashes her face. The Paintress is here, is she, Coward? And after Maria had given up hope. The dog watches his mistress with expressive eyes. Yet she finds she is not pleased, not pleased at all. She splashes again and dries herself with a towel. The glass tells her she is aging.

While she waits, Angelica Kauffman examines the paintings in the drawing room. Antiquities, mediocrities, noticeably nothing contemporary (someone told her once the Earl keeps the best for himself). The room is clean, elegant, fine, but old-fashioned and smallish. The Turkish carpet is beautiful but in need of repair, the furniture shabby, the stucco embellishments could do with touch-ups – opulence gone to seed.

The countess is dressed and wigged, though her bearing is sluggish, crumpled, unmade, shawl trailing, cameo askew. Coward follows, her little soldier. She sees the luggage as she passes through the hallway, greets the guest with a loose handshake, invites her to take tea.

Angelica is a beauty. Her hair is up in a turban of sorts, her mantua has sashes and accents of the pseudo-oriental in white and green. She is brown-eyed and slender, and her English retains hints of her European roots.

Your Ladyship looks well.

Thank you, Miss Kauffman, that is generous of you. Maria serves her, asks about her journey.

Long, Your Ladyship. I have come straight from London.

So far? You must have left early.

I did, it was still dark.

Maria lifts her own teacup and sips. She is nauseous, at sea, and this exotic creature perturbs her. She asks, Do you have business in the area, Miss Kauffman?

No, Your Ladyship.

Have you turned into the itinerant artist? Perchance this is a midway point on a longer journey up country?

No, Your Ladyship. Angelica frowns.

Then, Miss Kauffman, may I ask what has brought you here?

I came to see you, Your Ladyship.

Maria chinks the cup into the saucer. How sick she has become of society; how long it has been since she had visitors. She wonders if she will ever find it appealing again. Already this encounter is draining her.

Very conscientious of you, Miss Kauffman. And were the roads agreeable?

Dry.

Good. Wet roads are inconvenient.

The countess rises, a glance out at the garden, flattens her wig absent-mindedly. The artist, hungry after travelling, takes dainty bites from her biscuit. Coward, the spoiled baby, snuffles for crumbs.

What is the news in London, Miss Kauffman?

One topic dominates the rest: the American colonies are saying they want independence. From what I understand, the Loyalists are greatly outnumbered by the Patriots, who would declare the colonies a republic – are prepared to go to war for it against their king. They would risk mob rule, and even make alliances with France and Spain to shore up their cause.

How boring . . . To underline the point, Maria yawns and then adds, Do the Americans know that France and Spain are still monarchies?

I should not think it has escaped their attention, Your Ladyship.

Maria can see the delicate spine of the artist revealed by the
sunken neckline at the back of her outfit, reminding her of a bird.
What is your view, Miss Kauffman? Ought the king to surrender the colonies to the American people, and save everyone
a costly war?

Angelica sighs and answers, I have no interest in politics. One
cannot be both an artistic and a political being – not the kind of
artistic being I am, anyway.

She eats the meagre offering, while the countess circles the
room and asks if she has had enough.

Angelica replies she has eaten plenty . . . and hopes she did not
arrive at an inopportune time.

When I get headaches I sleep most of the day.

I am sorry to hear you are unwell, Your Ladyship.

Maria riffles through her correspondence, opens two letters
with an ivory blade, scans them, ignores the rest. She leans back
in her chair, head in hand, lifts her feet on to the ottoman and
closes her eyes for a few minutes. Eventually she rouses herself:
Miss Kauffman, may I ask how long you intend to be with us?
Naturally, you are welcome to stay as long as you like.

Though I came at your urging, I do not wish to impose, Your
Ladyship. I will remain only for as long as is necessary.

One month? Two?

No, not nearly so long. A few days at most. I have commitments in London.

Of course you do. While you are here, you must make yourself at home. You will want to settle in, recover your strength. I
will send a message when I need you.

Mrs Plett enters at just the right moment, announces the blue
room is ready.

Maria, anxious to go back to bed, gives her instructions

briskly. Mrs Plett, the day has been tiring for Miss Kauffman. Would you please show her there now? And arrange for the item to be taken out of storage and brought to her?

Yes, My Lady.

I shall leave it in your capable hands.

The countess bids Angelica good afternoon, and stalks away.

Angelica follows Mrs Plett through the house, up the expanse of staircase, allowing her hand to follow the curve of the banister, to the other wing and a beautiful guestroom in cerulean and gold brocade. The housekeeper leaves momentarily, returning with a footman carrying a canvas wrapped in gauze. She directs him to place it on the rosewood table and to leave.

Mrs Plett lifts the canvas easily, removes the cover and gives the unfinished painting to the artist.

I took the greatest care of it, Miss Kauffman. I had to hide it.

Angelica examines the portrait, holds it towards the light.

The face has some resemblance to the sitter (oval, aquiline nose, high forehead), though more work is required to bring it to life. The outline of the body is in place (flat and formless neoclassical garb), and some colour has been blocked into the background while other areas remain bare. Hardly more than a beginning of a painting – a false start. Angelica thought she had made more progress than this; recalls a portrait on the verge of completion, is disappointed by its feebleness. Then again, she is often disappointed by her own work. What is conceived of as sublime, an ideal, loses much in its execution and is eroded further still by criticism from her colleagues until at the end, the work can seem trite, trivial, even to herself.

Miss Kauffman, may I be permitted to speak in confidence?

Angelica inclines her head.

It was unfortunate, what happened. Believe me when I say

Her Ladyship has suffered terribly since, and has many regrets.

Each of us is human and deficient, Mrs Plett. I have not come to settle a score.

Your consenting to come at all is appreciated. I know you have many demands on your time.

As we are speaking in confidence, I am emboldened to say Her Ladyship is melancholy.

Yes, she is.

Then she is lucky to have you, Mrs Plett. We need our friends most when we are bereft.

Angelica Kauffman is in a residence which reminds her of a mausoleum, and she imagines herself its roaming ghost. She wanders from room to remote room, initially to discover its paintings, taking a lit candelabrum with her as the end of the day closes in. Ancestral portraits; other mismatched or uncared-for pieces bought but never appreciated; a handful of jewels from the Flemish and Dutch schools (her experienced eye picks out the ones made by copyists). She chooses one or two she might make sketches of, includes a composition of a maid sitting alone in a room with her back to the viewer. No face. But why?

She finds she is drawn to the vacancy, the stillness, the decrepitude of the place, the sounds of her heels reverberating along corridors. The ballroom, the dining room, the impressive library where Angelica lingers, running her finger along the spines, her gaze meandering along the titles. Unoccupied spaces. Haunted by sadness. It is a grand building, but Angelica has been in grander, and it is the absence of society, of comings and goings, that makes it feel enormous like a cavern, serious like a church. Her artistic mind responds to the atmosphere, gives fictional accounts for it – this is a palace, a forest of briars surrounding it, its occupants put to sleep by an evil spell. When she passes a servant on a wooden step straining to collect the cobwebs with her duster, these fancies blow away.

She strolls through the grounds during the late afternoon sun, then sunset, then twilight, around the rose garden and an orchard. It occurs to her that she may not be dining with the countess. It occurs to her that she should not have come, that she would like to return to London.

But they do have supper together by the drawing room fire, leftovers with port, Coward snoozing on the carpet, Maria being cordial—

And did you look round, Miss Kauffman?

Yes, Your Ladyship. I particularly admire your library. I should like to spend some time in there, if I may. For research.

By all means. I do not expect you to work during your entire stay, indeed I hope you will not.

Your Ladyship . . . ?

I mean, I want to hear all about the ton and their exploits! I have had no gossip for simply ages. You must tell me everything.

Angelica, having access to the fashionable ladies and gentlemen of London, is able to answer many of the questions Maria has about their mutual acquaintances, and shares some stories about the absurd height of ostrich feathers and the ridiculous width of panniers currently seen around town.

Suddenly the countess interrupts the artist, Actually there is no need for that.

For what, Your Ladyship?

That . . . or 'My Lady'. Just plain Maria will do, if you do not mind the familiarity?

It would be my pleasure.

And I prefer to call you Angelica, if you will indulge me?

Of course.

110

Or I can call you Miss Angel, as Sir Joshua Reynolds does.

The artist smiles at the mention of her friend, at the affectionate joke.

Angelica ... You are more accommodating than our Mrs Plett. I have known her my whole life, and still she will not call me by my first name, unless she is cross with me.

I should be afraid if your housekeeper were angry at me.

With good reason! And Maria smiles, yes, this is the way it was supposed to be, the way it had been. She goes on, Anyway, it is a convention that I do not see the need for in intimate company, and were we not on intimate terms once?

We were. We are. That is why I came here.

The ladies find this concession to each other makes a pause in their dialogue, the chink of cutlery on china, the gleam of candles in crystal, until Maria continues: I was thinking that you should use the orangery. It is warm and has the best light, very conducive to creativity. No one will disturb you.

For research?

For your work.

No. The orangery will not be necessary.

It was only a suggestion; you must work where you feel most at ease, wherever you like.

Maria, I think there has been a misunderstanding. I am not here to finish the painting.

You are not?

No. I am sorry if I gave you that impression.

But you turned up without sending a message. What else was I to think?

Angelica feels the sting of their previous encounter renewed, testing her compassion. You said it did not matter any more. You said other things were more important.

It most certainly matters. Besides, it is polite to state your intentions in advance, to say if and when and why you are paying

111

a visit to someone. You do not just appear one day and expect to be accommodated and entertained.

With respect, you wrote me sheets of letters imploring me to come.

Yes, to finish the painting.

You did not always say so. You would say one thing, and then something else. Some of your letters did not even sound like you. You seemed muddled.

I was upset. I was angry, and then . . .

Yes, I understand, but by the end I did not know exactly what you wanted from me, whether you would even see me. I came here expecting to be turned away.

Well, Miss Kauffman, I am telling you now, plainly: I want you to finish the painting of Frances.

That is not going to be possible.

Why not?

And the artist says it as gently as she can, Because you cannot afford to pay me, Maria.

The countess is thrown. Of course I can.

The whole world knows you cannot. If your creditors called in all your debts, you would not own even the gown you are wearing. It is only through the intervention of your husband that you have your home, your servants, your pin money.

The countess stands and turns away. I am sure we can come to an arrangement. I could pay in instalments. You can name your own terms for as much and for as long as you like.

You confuse me with someone else.

All right. You have refined sensibilities, I acknowledge that. You admire some of the artwork here? We have many interesting pieces. Why not choose a couple as payment in kind? That is a fair exchange, more than fair.

I have no desire to pillage your property, and I live in a tiny town house with barely enough room for the possessions I have.

112

Then what do you want? You are negotiating hard; you must have a price in mind.

No, I have not. I want nothing from you.

Miss Kauffman, my circumstances notwithstanding – though, by the way, I am appalled you presume to know about my private affairs, much less taunt me about them – I am still a person of influence. I have the ear of some of the richest and most powerful men and women in the country. I can help you. I can do wonderful things for your career.

Please stop this.

I can do terrible things too, if I want.

Angelica takes a moment to weigh these words, to be sure she has understood. She sighs. Maria, I am a woman of immense wealth in my own right. I am a founding Royal Academician. I have among my friends and colleagues Benjamin West, Francesco Bartolozzi, Thomas Gainsborough and Joshua Reynolds. My patrons include Johann Joachim Winckelmann, David Garrick, the king's sister and Queen Charlotte herself. Paintings, engravings, lady's fans, *teapots* for goodness' sake. They say I am one of the most famous artists alive; they say the whole world has gone *Angelicamad*. I do not need your patronage, Your Ladyship. I do not need your endorsement. A smear campaign would not hurt me. In reality, it would probably exclude you from society for ever.

An ugly silence follows. The fire spits and cracks. The countess's shallow breathing is audible, and then she speaks again: That was awful of me to attempt to threaten you, Miss Kauffman. I never used to be like this. If you did not come here to finish the portrait, then pray tell me, why did you come?

Out of friendship.

Then, out of friendship, go home in the morning. Goodbye, Miss Kauffman.

The countess picks up a candlestick to light her way.

*

She turns over, sits up; it is the morning, and last night is vivid in her memory. Coward, alert as a hunter, barks, wags the knot of his tail. Maria is wide awake and putting a robe on over her shift, hair unbrushed and uncovered, running down the great staircase to stop the carriage, but there is no sign of it. She checks the drawing room, the dining room.

We are too late, Coward (as though this were for his benefit).

She feels the nip of despair, loneliness digging into her ribs. She wishes she could escape her own company, if only temporarily; respite from this wickedness and sorrow. Damnable. Idiotic. Perverse. The frustration is a compressed spring inside her. The pressure chokes her.

Though it is unseemly and the morning is chill, she goes for a walk in the grounds in her nightgown and slippers with the pug, for the sake of movement, for the expenditure of the fidgets, for Angelica who was perfectly correct: Maria is a countess in name only. Because she might as well, as not.

This is Maria. This body, this mind, these emotions. This is what there is to Maria, and the sum of what she will ever be. She has had the best of her life: her youth, her marriage, her wealth, her children, her great love. The fabric has unravelled, only the filaments are left.

She breathes in the cool replenishing air, thinks how they used to love being outside. Picnics and walks and sunrises and swims and snowmen and drinking under the stars. It is a whole other person who was loved by Frances.

If you could see me now. If you saw me.

Maria's toes are wet from the dew. She moves fast, walks through the herb garden to smell the lavender and the rosemary, and then to the rose arch to sit on their stone bench, tapping the energy away. In the midst of her anguish it occurs to her how well Duncan, the gardener, has maintained the grounds practically single-handed.

It is on her way back that Maria is jolted into the present, as if by the glimpse of a fox between the trees.

In the orangery, Angelica is at work on the portrait.

She pauses when Maria enters.

My apologies. I do not mean to disturb you.

You are not. There is still some tea.

The artist points to the tray with the end of the brush.

Maria rests on the chaise longue, lifts the little dog (arthritic from the damp), enfolds herself in a blanket, speaks not another word.

Angelica Kauffman paints seated at her easel and has a talent for not spilling liquids or marking surfaces, putting the colours only where she wishes them to go. She is disciplined, methodical, with a strong work ethic. True, she was dissatisfied with her past efforts, but it is the way of creative temperaments that they find energy to turn around weak work, to view it as a stage in the development of better work – an optimism which is just short of delusion, persistence which is just short of obsession, self-belief which is just short of vanity. If this were a love affair, Art would be a brute, offering hope, making false promises; Artist would be a wronged and resilient victim, making excuses and accepting blame, always prepared to reconcile and try again.

Painting the face of a sitter from memory is tricky. At least she did the basics from life, has her preliminary sketches as a prompt. When a receptive mind observes and considers the minutiae of a face in order to draw it, the outlines and proportions stick. Angelica can remember what Frances looked like; that is not the problem. It is the soul which is absent, because that would have come later. The soul is the true likeness. The motion, the quickening, the particular expression of an individual caught off guard. That is what Angelica paints, that is her speciality. That is why she gets to know her subjects, uses her placid nature, her charm, puts them at their ease. Making people be themselves long enough for it to show through and yes, she gets it, holds it and, incredibly, records it (or something rather like it) – this is Angelica's gift. And she did not manage to capture Frances's essence before they parted.

Angelica has not mentioned this to Maria. The outcome will be inferior, is unlikely to meet Maria's fragile expectations.

Angelica Kauffman has decided not to accept payment. She makes this gesture out of friendship. And as a gift given by a friend, the picture has taken on more significance than a regular commission.

So she sets aside her worries, for now, and works on the parts she can do: the table with lion's legs, the Greco-Roman pillar, the chiton the figure is wearing. It takes time to give cloth a sheen and make it drape convincingly (Angelica has decided to make it the cerulean of the room where she sleeps). Even a lady's hands joined at rest, one elbow on the back of the chair, can be done generically. But this is not yet a portrait of Frances; it is a portrait of someone who resembles Frances. How to finish it without resorting to a map of features?

Coward likes Angelica. She gives him titbits, tickles his tummy, and the orangery is a warm place to lie. Switching his affection to another is not beneath him. When Angelica looks into his enormous eyes she can see a reflection of herself.

Angelica Kauffman is here, Frances, and I still make concessions to you. After what you have done! We made peace, so you have got what you wanted; she is finishing the painting, so I have got what I wanted.

I pace up and down for an entire morning, pace pace pace, deliberating over my apology, for now it must be done. One difficulty (I am ashamed of it) is recalling accurately what I actually said and did, and what was merely in my imagination. I remember

116

distinctly coming into the room during the sittings – you posing, she daubing – and being possessed by the notion that you had ceased speaking that very instant as if you were keeping secrets from me. This happened once, and I let it go. This happened again . . . and I felt a terrible heat in my chest.

We fought a lot around that time, did we not? Rather, I fought. You would wait for the torrent to subside, keeping your powder dry in order to wound me with a single shot. I could only make you cry by crying myself.

I caught Angelica holding your face, and you allowing it to be held. It looked just like a seduction. It looked as if you were giving to her something of yourself which you held back from me.

You defended her, saying that she is an artist and artists must look closely at the faces of their subjects.

You would say that!

Then you accused me of drinking gin, as if it made any difference.

This much is clear, but emotion blurs the rest.

Did I call her names, or accuse her of attempting to steal you? Did I, in fact, threaten to strike her, or did I daydream it? Did I shout and pick up a pitcher and hurl it against the wall? (Is that how it broke, in the end? Is that where the stain came from?) Or was my rage contained in the simple instruction for her to leave immediately, uncompensated?

I remember being ill afterwards, and you still furious. I remember you saying it was not the jealousy which was intolerable but that Angelica was one of the few real friends we had together, who knew us both as we really were, who accepted us. And I chased her away.

My skin puckers with shame, even now.

I do apologise to her. I try to.

The lady brooks not a word, soothes me, promises it was forgiven long ago. And, without my asking, assures me you were always loyal, and that doubting you was my worst offence. Confesses (if it be a confession) I caused you both to worry, and this was the only subject of your private conversations, the only concealment.

I am glad it is Angelica. I cannot think of anyone else, apart from Muriel, whom I could tolerate just now.

She works for as long as the light is good. I need not see her unless I wish to. We eat together, pass the evenings. These are surprisingly bearable. For all her elaborate tastes, she is understated as a companion, content to sit in quietude. I embroider, she sketches or reads. She asks bluntly if I will always be this way, and what will become of me? She senses no one can go on like this. *I will fade and die* – I do not say it but I think it. Then she says, And what would Frances want?

Indeed, what *would* you want? Your opinions and ideas have become a mystery to me, you who had so many. I look through your notes again and they seem so delicate, dropped leaves. I like the unfinished poems best because it feels as though you have been interrupted momentarily, called away to make a decision about the horses or the baking, will be back shortly to shine them up. I did not appreciate your calling enough. I am sorry for all the times I was flippant about it, or worse, tried to make you publish against your will. I am no poet, but I can at least keep them safe for you.

I have such black days. Whole hours are blotted out – what did I do? where did I go? was I alone? My nerves are in shreds.

I fear that before long I shall lose the ability to recall your voice and your smell and your advice. You have left a Frances-shaped hole. Everything familiar is falling through it.

Angelica wants to know how Coward came to be named, and if he was always mine or originally yours. I tell her I gave him to you as an anniversary present, that you called him Howard, that he constantly trembled, et cetera.

I like her. She is imaginative, thoughtful, like Muriel, like you (are these the qualities I value in women because I do not have them myself?). I like the way she asks about you, probing without being vulgar. But I cannot wait for her to leave.

The housekeeper fumes. She wants someone to read to her, My Lady, while she paints. You said we were to give her whatever she wanted . . . ?

Maria does not see the issue but is certain Mrs Plett will spell it out; she does enjoy a good gripe.

Miss Kauffman works in the orangery for hours at a time. I do not have time to sit and read to her.

Of course not. You are far too busy.

Mrs Plett is mollified, What ought to be done?

Make one of the others do it. Or are they unable?

William has no more time to spare than I do. And to have Rachel reading out loud would be cruelty to all concerned.

You will think of something. Is there not one task which could wait? for not even a single day?

Suppose Miss Kauffman requires to be read to tomorrow and the day after? Suppose she wants to be sung to, next?

I have heard your singing voice in church; it is adorable. Maybe I will ask you to sing for me while I do my needlework? (Maria is glared at for that.) Did Angelica ask specifically to be read to?

Yes, My Lady.

Then I realise our situation is not ideal, but we must give Angelica whatever she requires. It is a small request, considering what she is doing for me. I am sure you will manage beautifully.

Mrs Plett presses her mouth into a tight line.

What does she want to hear?

Poetry, My Lady—

119

Mrs Plett anticipates the effect of this detail on Maria. She pats her on the wrist ... and when Maria's eyes remain unfocused, lifts Maria's chin, encouraging her to stand the way a countess does. Maria will take the matter seriously now.

Yes, yes. I will look into it. Thank you, Mrs Plett.

So Maria must go to the library. She balances on the step, stretches to her full height to reach the shelves, turns books over, sorts them into piles and replaces them. New books and old books, books she has never seen before. Flicks and fans through pages. What would Angelica want to hear? What is Maria prepared to read?

Frances's favourite piece of furniture was a raspberry-red fainting couch. Maria had it moved into the library so Frances could be comfortable there. And she loved the door that looked like a bookcase, found it humorous and decadent. All the poetry books Frances either bought herself, or claimed as her own by virtue of her love for them.

You did not care for shoes and hairstyles and fashion. You said that your mind required decoration.

The memory tugs at Maria's heart. She selects some volumes haphazardly (this and that, and this Maria recognises and takes, and that she does not and rejects), feels as though she is invading her lover's privacy, carries them in her arms like babies.

Angelica does not stop painting or even look up when Maria enters the orangery but says, I think I annoyed Mrs Plett earlier, and she was exactly as fierce as I feared.

Not at all. She likes you, and I have brought you the poets.

Angelica sighs with satisfaction, Whom did you bring?

Alexander Pope, *The Rape of the Lock*. Milton, *Paradise Lost*. *Paradise Regained*. Shakespeare's sonnets. The *Iliad* and the *Odyssey*.

Do you have anything modern? Anything by Friedrich Gottlieb Klopstock?

Yes, but my German is so poor you might wish it was something else. I have a poetess called Phillis Wheatley: *Poems on Various Subjects, Religious and Moral*. She is fairly new.

I have not heard of her.

She is an African.

Do you mean she is a slave?

Yes. In America.

Angelica pauses, brush in midair: A woman and an African and a slave and a poet? And you have her book right there in your hand?

Yes. There is a picture of her on the frontispiece.

Let me see it.

And Maria shows Angelica the etching titled *Phillis Wheatley, Negro Servant to Mr John Wheatley, of Boston*.

How did you come by such a book?

Frances acquired it. Poetry was a particular interest of hers.

Angelica lowers her voice: Did Frances ever write any poems herself?

Maria answers with a sting in hers: Occasionally.

The painter suppresses the urge to ask more, senses she must choose the proper moment. Instead she says, And is Miss Wheatley very good?

I have not read her before.

Well, we must find out, mustn't we?

Angelica, would you not prefer to have a respite from your work?

Hearing Miss Wheatley's poems will be respite enough.

And Angelica says nothing else, resumes painting, lets the silence run on until Maria settles on the chaise longue and begins.

She starts with a poem about virtue . . . then one to the king. Poems about recollection, imagination, humanity, and a composition *To a Lady on her remarkable Preservation in an*

Hurricane in North-Carolina. Several are written following the deaths of children or loved ones, and after the awkward experience of reading one out she eschews these. But the poet has reinterpreted Niobe, from Ovid's *Metamorphoses*, And it says here, *from a view of the painting of Mr Richard Wilson*, which sparks Angelica's interest.

Familiar now with the poet's lyric style and metre, Maria comments: It seems Miss Wheatley is partial to artists; this one is *To S.M. a young African Painter, on seeing his Works* . . .

Here are two short poems like siblings, *An Hymn to the Morning*, and *An Hymn to the Evening* . . .

When Maria has read these, she realises Angelica is no longer painting but sitting at rest at her easel, listening.

Maria, reread me the last part of *Evening*? From 'placid slumbers'.

Let placid slumbers sooth each weary mind,
At morn to wake more heav'nly, more refin'd,
So shall the labours of the day begin
More pure, more guarded from the snares of sin.
Night's leaden sceptre seals my drowsy eyes,
Then cease, my song, till fair Aurora rise.

The artist sighs, Then you could read *Morning, Evening, Morning, Evening*, an infinite number of times in a cycle, inhaling and exhaling. Do you like her, Maria?

She is edifying. Do you?

I was just thinking of my glib assertion that one cannot be both an artistic and a political being.

You have fought some battles, no doubt. It is late, we should have some dinner.

Maria tidies the books, leaves them in the orangery for when Angelica wants them next.

Angelica slots her brushes into a pot, straightens her materials, stretches and then goes to her friend.

I meant to say it sooner, my condolences for your terrible loss.

Maria's grief grips her anew, sore and penetrating, yet she finds she is able to reply, Thank you; that is very kind.

You were half right about my debts, Angelica. When my husband intervenes in my affairs, he does so using money which was mine in the first place. He took it. My money, to pay off my debts – and yet I am supposed to be obliged to him? In a way . . . in a way I am, actually. He could set conditions or make demands, make me beg for his help. He does not. If he gets angry, he does not show it. When I see what other people have for husbands, I conclude he is not a bad sort entirely. Oh, he has plenty of faults, and I can happily enumerate them: he is a dullard and a glutton and sanctimonious, and he looks like a pig walking on its hind legs. But he is not cruel, and I have plenty of faults of my own. We have reached an understanding. He has his mistress, I am sure you know, but perhaps you did not know that he has had the same mistress since before we were married, installed with their children at Carsington. Her name is Dorothy, and she must be fifteen or twenty years older than I am and is apparently very fat. Then again, so is my husband. She lives in my place, sleeps in my bed, squanders my money on her chubby children. Copulating must be difficult, though at their age perhaps it is no longer an issue. My husband is going to die one day, and I know how she dreads that because my eldest son will inherit and the cuckoo will be out of the nest. I have two sons, Georgie and Augustus, the heir and the spare, and I thank God for them every day not only because I love them but also because, after three years of a dire marriage, they bought me my freedom. At least, a degree of freedom. My husband gave me this house, the least valued of the family's estates, and an

123

allowance. Said they were mine to do with as I wished. Plenty of women would exchange their lot for mine, I know it. I used to be enraptured with the ton – the parties, the operas, the intrigue, the gambling. Cards can undo a person; faro was the ruin of me. But even when we are in decline, we deal another hand and dress like parrots and drink like fishes because we know no better, because society is disparaging of the alternatives, because it is reinforced that if you do not do this or have this or behave in this way, you are deemed inferior.

What are the alternatives, Maria?

Finding harmony in one's domestic life. Investigating the inner world. Sharing it with someone who makes a restrained existence feel like a mountain range of possibilities. Frances was never seduced by the perfume and the lace. Oh, she could blend in, could even make herself the centre of attention – she had the wit and the manners for it. But she found it unsatisfactory, and dare I say a hardship. No matter how grand the occasion and how fashionable the company, she said, given the choice, she would prefer an evening at home with me. She would go only because I wanted to. Oh, we had such sport for a few years! We were invited simply everywhere. Our entrance was always antici-pated. People were curious to see if we would arrive dressed identically, if one or both of us would be in the garb of a gentle-man, whether we would bring a monkey with us and pretend it was our child, or a goat and pretend it was our lawyer. We spent hours devising and preparing our novelties. She was my comic heroine, my Viola, my Portia, my Rosalind. For a while we had them eating out of our hands. But a beast, if it is wild, if it is savage, will regress to its nature however tame it seems. You know what happened.

I have heard reports, but I was not there. And you do not have to repeat it for my sake.

Then I will tell you for mine. It was February, the coldest and blackest of nights, no moon, and the London fog thicker than I have known it. These were contributory, as if the scoundrel had arranged them. The cold meant that my coachman did not wait the whole night with the carriage; the dark meant that the deed went undiscovered until lights had been brought out and there was a crowd to behold his handiwork. We were in town for one of Lady Thetford's card parties, a genial and modest gathering by her standards. A number of us kept playing until the marquis entreated us to leave – we teased him for being an old man with no stamina. We assembled in the vestibule to wait for the carriages. Mine pulled up, the servants shone their lamps upon it – and Frances saw the offence before I did, and bade me avert my eyes. I pushed her aside, I had to see for myself what was provoking such horrified gasps among our group, and attracting more eager witnesses from within the house to stare in fascination and amusement and disgust. I was merry, quite inebriated, until I laid eyes on the message left for us.

I am afraid to hear it.

Along the side in white paint was the word TRIBADES.

Angelica catches her breath, then mutters, An enemy?

I suspected one of my creditors. In a single stroke we became pariahs. We were shunned.

You and Frances were the victims of a crime!

You do not know these people as I do. It gave them a reason to turn on us. It gave legitimacy to the disgusting and salacious thoughts they had kept hidden. We were lepers, we were the most obscene kind of joke. They relished our downfall. My downfall. Apparently, in England's brothels it became a fashion for a while to make two women perform 'The Countess and Her Companion'. Even my husband, aware some scandal had occurred, was obliged to visit me. He said, Maria, can you please explain why I am receiving notes from anonymous well-wishers telling me Sappho is in my bedchamber? (Maria manages to laugh.)

Remarkably, he did not get angry. I gave him my theory, that I believed it was to do with money, and he said, *With you, my wife, it is always to do with money.* He was thoroughly decent about it, settled my accounts and advised for the sake of appearances and for my well-being to give up Frances or to avoid society – one or the other. Interestingly, he refrained from explicitly forbidding me anything. And then he went away again. That was that. My porky, useless husband. Frances offered to leave if it would set me free . . . or to stay and live in disgrace. Whatever would bring me happiness, she was prepared to give.

And she did stay—

– and we did live! For a short time. Do you know what I realised in the end? They envied us, because by their standards we had no right to be happy. Because for them, happiness requires pomades and powders and ruffles and diamonds and concertos. And we required a roof, and a dog and a paper and pen, a candle at night and sometimes a sip of wine or port, and we were more than satisfied. They must have begrudged it so much. Why else would they desire to poison something harmless and beautiful?

They love each other, His Lordship and this Dorothy?

Yes, I think they probably do.

Then it probably follows that your situation, and His Lordship's tolerance of it, would have required at least her blessing.

Funny, she wrote to me once.

What did she say?

But Maria is done with this subject, so Angelica introduces another: I was not completely honest with you before, Maria, when I described the extent of my influence as an artist. I over-simplified it. (Coward raises his head and Angelica scratches his ears.) I endure a stream of commentary and pronouncements from my contemporaries. My portraits *do not bear a likeness*, there is one I have heard time after time, because I exaggerate the best features of my sitters, because I tend to flatter them. Well, show me a portraitist who depicts his patrons accurately and I will show you one in poverty who does not paint at all. We artists use some licence to ennoble our patrons ... at least I try to get beneath the skin of a person, to reflect back what is true about them. So, I ask myself, why am I disproportionately criticised for it? Why am I singled out? My portraits of men are *feminine*, they say – as though femininity were exclusively the reserve of females, and not a character trait shared to a greater or lesser extent by both sexes; as though the men of today's society were not a muster of peacocks, posing and prancing. They say the heroes in my history paintings look at best like androgynous youths and at worst like women wearing beards. They say, constantly, that I cannot draw the human body, that I have no knowledge of anatomy, and for this reason my work will always be inferior. Do you know why I have no knowledge of anatomy? Because, being a woman, I am not allowed to attend life-drawing classes. They deny me the opportunity to learn the techniques I need, then insult me for not having them. I have to make do with working from sculpture or other drawings and paintings, seeing the physical body through someone else's eyes, their bias, the limitations of their talent. Maybe the art of the ancients reached a summit of aesthetic beauty, but I can tell you it is a poor substitute for flesh and bones, for the work of God's own hand. Yet I want success and I play up to my strengths – colour and romance – and so I become guilty of the very defects of which I am accused. I always thank these experts for their insight because I know belligerence encourages them to repeat themselves, more loudly and with greater conviction. But if I am gracious, maybe they will be inclined towards generosity and one day the history books will say: *Miss Kauffman was a painter of middling accomplishment but delightful in conversation.* That is how I shall be remembered, as a dilettante and a moll. They whisper that I have got this far only because I use womanly wiles to advance myself, that I did not work for, and do not deserve, what I have achieved. Always eyes are upon me looking for fuel to add to that particular fire. I cannot form a friendship with a male colleague, however distinguished, without setting tongues wagging. Am I to form relationships only with lady painters? Must we, all three of us, sit in a room by ourselves? And now they do more than merely whisper it out of my hearing. Earlier this year, one of them made a painting which included a nude figure of me, flaunting myself, and exhibited it at the Royal Academy.

Did the members not act?

Joshua was incensed, and one or two of the others spoke up for me, but I suspect many of them found it satirical. It was a slur on my reputation, and hurt my pride more than I can tell you, and yes, it was removed when I wrote to them. After several days.

They are galled by your fame. You will be remembered. Your art is unparalleled, exalted. Your work – and that of Miss Wheatley – will survive. Your legacy means that artists in future eras will flourish, and they will thank you for it.

Is that why I endure such humiliation, Maria?

Why you both do, Angelica.

I almost became a musician, you know. I wonder what life would have been like if I had chosen that path.

You picked art over music?

Easier, perhaps. It was a dilemma, but art was the more urgent calling of the two. I fear that Miss Wheatley has picked the most difficult art form in which to thrive. And the barriers she has to overcome are manifold.

Frances said that many of life's skills can be taught – oratory, carpentry, agriculture, drawing too, by the sounds of it. But she was convinced that poets are born. So you may be right when you describe poetry as the more difficult art form, but you are probably wrong that Miss Wheatley knowingly chose it.

Angelica lies awake in the dark, her arm curved above her head. Her instincts prickle. Does she hear anything amiss, or is it only the sounds of the night scraping and rustling outside? Stepping into her shoes and wrapping a blanket about her shoulders, she feels no fear, only the ache of fatigue when one cannot sleep, the relief of giving up the attempt.

On the landing the moon casts rectangles. The furniture becomes stone, the picture frames are as dark as tunnels, eyes peering out of them. Blood rushes in her ears as loud as the wind. The house holds its breath. Nothing dangerous – just unsettling, vexing, a puzzle to be solved. Angelica leans over the balustrade and stares down into a space as impenetrable as an underground lake. She hears a disturbance coming from Maria's room.

She does not knock, lets herself into the chamber, is unsurprised by the sobbing woman. Coward is also awake; restless, grumpy. She does not talk, except to hush and hush the tired body buried in the pillows. She encircles Maria with a confident embrace, who responds with stillness, tears leaking down her face into her hair. Sheets and covers are pulled around, tucked in against the night, and Coward is the first to find repose. Then Maria, grateful for Angelica's company, feeling nonetheless alone in the world, sleeps with this pain like a pin in her chest.

Angelica lies awake, listens to their breathing, dozes for a few hours until the morning when the shadows are banished and the heartbeat of the estate increases in tempo once more.

It is consuming me. I feel nothing but this grief all the time. I find a wardrobe filled with gowns, and I think they must have been yours once, but they are mine. I had forgotten them because I have forgotten myself – literally the Maria I was. She is a foreigner. How did she do it – those parties, concerts, assemblies at court – when I cannot stand even to leave the house? I am afraid of the world, of its faces and jagged edges, of its venom. The thought of a journey brings on the terrors. I never want to leave here. I never want to make false conversation for as long as I live, or be judged by people I detest. I want to build a wall. I am falling so far, so deep, but I have yet to hit the ground. I could have killed you yesterday, for doing this.

The portrait is surprising. She is adding the bronze Minerva from the ballroom. A trick of composition to stop the eye trailing off the edge, she says. I almost collapse when I realise: of all the objets d'art she could have chosen . . . ?

You sent it back to me. You sent it back, saying I had misunderstood your motive, but I made you accept it, because you had misunderstood mine. I was not attempting to buy your body, or your silence. Honestly. I just wanted you to have something I knew you would like. I fully expected not to see you again.

I betray myself to Angelica, but will not be drawn out. And something else, though I do not know if you would approve.

Is it too late to make a change? to have a symbol to show—
My head hurts. Everything hurts.

I ask. I ask Angelica if she can show that you were a person who wrote.

I expect her to be annoyed. She is not, has anticipated my request, has already made a drawing of the hands in the painting adapted to hold a scroll and a pen. I remark that the scroll is rolled up, and she says she could include a whole legible stanza if I—

No, I like it that way, in the drawing.

I sense her disappointment; she wants me to share that aspect of you. I do not. The change is agreed.

Mrs Plett is suspicious. She has taken to ambushing me in the morning, flings petticoats and hats on me, hides things away. Of course I find them again.

All of it stays inside me, hissing and biting. I cannot, physically, sustain my anger at you, but if I stop there will be nothing left, just a void. I do not believe I shall be free of you in this life. Extraordinary – I can almost hear what you would say to that, an echo of it, a chime. You are wrong. Besides, you went away, so what you think no longer counts.

They picnic on the knoll overlooking the village, Angelica in a cream shalwar karmeez trimmed with burnished red, Maria in a white dress with a royal-blue hat and sash. The excursion has been forced on them by Mrs Plett, a means of restoring order, Maria explains. The potted meat is rich, the honey is sweet, the salad is sharp, the bread is wholesome. The sun radiates warmth until it is covered by a cloud turning the air fresh, then the cloud passes, the sun returns. Coward rolls on his back in the grass, plays like a puppy, investigates.

Maria complains aloud, She should be here. Why is she not here? – as though Frances is running late.

She is here.

And Maria shields her eyes to see her companion.

Do you believe in it when you say things like that?

I believe that when someone loves someone it leaves an impression after one of them has gone.

Have you ever been in love, Angelica?

What makes you ask that?

Because you speak knowingly.

Cannot a heart believe in something it has yet to encounter? (And Angelica turns towards the steeple of the church, the roofs of the houses, the hills.)

How have you formed such notions of love without

experience? – Maria narrows her eyes, not only because of the glare – Were you married?

I am married to my work.

And to a man, I think.

Angelica rises, brushes crumbs and grass from her trousers, steps away.

To a blackguard, then. And yet you still keep faith that love is unbreakable, conquering, enduring.

The Paintress folds her arms, gazes at the view around them, does not reply.

I had the best that love can offer, and look what it has done to me. You, I think, have had the worst. Somehow it becomes you, you have mastered it, turned it into a resource for your creativity. No wonder you are prolific.

I was prolific anyway. The only man who deserves any credit for my work is my father.

Ah, fathers. There is a different muddy puddle.

Who is that?

Climbing towards them is a blonde young woman raising her hand in greeting.

She is too far away to shout, yet she does, her hallo scattered by the wind.

Maria stands.

It is Muriel! My goddaughter – she probably heard you are here.

Maria trips and strides down the slope, meets the breathless girl part way, takes both hands in hers. Angelica watches them. The young lady is laughing, perhaps at her aborted attempt to run up the hillside, is explaining a complicated story to Maria, who clasps her round the shoulders, links arms with her. Both smiles are radiant.

– and this is Angelica Kauffman, the renowned artist and my good friend.

The girl exclaims, Can it be? Miss Kauffman, I am so delighted to make your acquaintance. Muriel Wyndham, but I should like it if you called me Muriel.

Thank you. You must call me Angelica.

What a wonderful costume, Angelica. Is that trousers? I never can keep up with what society is wearing from one week to the next. They look very comfortable, as if one could play in them all day, then go to bed without changing out of them. Hallo, Coward, you smelly animal.

She picks up the dog and fusses him. Maria leads the party back to the picnic.

Muriel talks fluidly: her parents in the village, a problem she had with her stocking this morning, a story from her childhood about getting stuck in a hayloft; and then, This honey is delicious, Maria (finally going quiet as she eats some).

And how are you, Muriel? I feel as though we have not talked for an age.

She nods emphatically, mouth full. I am so glad you have a visitor, Maria, and such a famous one at that. Were you going to tell me?

No need to tell you anything, you seem to find it all out on your own.

That is true. I have my spies. For example, Angelica is here to work on the painting of Frances, I believe. Is it finished yet?

Angelica says there is still work left to do.

I am desperate to see it!

This topic sets Muriel's mind alight with questions about Angelica's art. Where does she get her ideas from? What does she like to paint best? Who in society has she made portraits of? What is her favourite colour? I wish I could see every canvas you have ever touched!

If you are so enthusiastic, you must come to London and visit me at my studio.

Oh, may I?

But of course. Perhaps Maria can be persuaded to bring you? I shall show you round the Royal Academy.

Muriel turns to Maria, presses her lips together in supplication, urges with her eyes.

Maria murmurs, We shall see.

The younger woman kisses her in gratitude, as though it were settled.

Then Maria announces she has to speak to Mrs Plett, asks whether Muriel and Angelica would mind amusing themselves until she comes back?

As Maria heads to the house, Muriel becomes more reflective.

It was good of you to come; I was starting to worry. She seems better for it. She has not seen anyone since – you know – not even her sons.

They are estranged?

Not exactly. I think they have always belonged to their father. She has grown so very tired of society, become reclusive, exists with hardly any human contact. Poor Maria, and poor Frances, and praise God for the indomitable Mrs Plett. You must be especially dear to my mama.

Your . . . ?

It is a silly pet name, she asked me to call her it once. Maybe the others will follow now, and she will have a semblance of her old life back.

Angelica does not contradict the girl, so youthful and determined.

May I be candid with you? In the days that followed, Maria was completely devastated. It was dreadful to watch, and I . . . I had very bad thoughts. I stayed with her for a while because of it, because I could not shake the suspicions I had. She is my godmother and we are close, but still, it was presumptuous of me. I was overcome by these fears, overwhelmed by them, and I think

Mrs Plett thought the same, although she did not say so. I told myself I would only stay until her friends or relatives came. I ended up staying with her for a long time. No one came.

How did your parents feel?

My mother and father are simple people. They said the countess had shown me many kindnesses. They said I had a duty to help, if I was able to comfort a soul in need.

You shared her burden. That was kind of you.

That was when the portrait of Frances became important to her again. It became an obsession.

It is human nature to want ways of remembering the people we love.

What Muriel says next is hastily thought, hastily shared: Do you think likenesses of departed loved ones possess a special power?

I would have to say yes.

Like heathen idols? When the physical resemblance has been locked in paint or stone, is some aspect of the unique spirit also fixed, also sealed? Is the soul drawn to its image in life like a beacon on the shore?

What makes you ask these questions?

Muriel checks over her shoulder. Because I think, for Maria, the picture has an element of the occult. I think she has some plan for it when it is finished.

Angelica Kauffman decides it would be wise not to dwell on these ideas, and leads the conversation away: Did you know Frances well, Muriel?

Yes. And at first I did not like her. Rather, I wanted not to like her. It looked too much to her advantage. With hindsight, I now hold the opinion it was the other way round. Frances tolerated a lot. Maria can be demanding.

Angelica just smiles at this.

Maria may have been the countess, but Frances was definitely the adult. She was a force. Never bitter or resentful, always gentle, always sensitive. Maria seemed, what is the word . . . ? besotted? no, *smitten*.

What made you change your mind about Frances?

She visited me at home, arrived at the doorstep with some strawberries for my parents and one of your engravings for me. In a way, I was smitten as well, because I could see they were the right fit. You will never tell Maria any of this? I would be mortified if she ever found out.

No, I swear it.

I knew you would not be shocked. As an artist, you must be good at reading people. Creativity and perceptiveness are linked, I think. Both require one to see clearly with the mind.

Angelica is surprised by this creature, watches her pick at salad leaves without self-consciousness. What are your passions, Muriel?

Gardens. I like flowers and fruit trees and insects and earth and birds. The way it is all interconnected, a balancing act. I like the way everything gives something back. Maria's garden is wonderful. I spent a lot of time in it as a child. I shall have my own garden one day; it is what I require from a prospective husband.

You cannot be thinking of marriage already?

Muriel shrugs. Perhaps you will introduce me to a wealthy bachelor when I come to London?

There are plenty. Not all are desirable mates, and competition for the best prizes is fierce.

I do not need a prize for a spouse, only a man who is sensible and friendly and has a simply enormous garden which is mine to do whatever I like with. That is not too much to ask, is it?

Are you prepared to leave your home?

I shall have to one day.

The wind quickens, making both women shiver.

Muriel points, Look at that! Coward is dragging a stick in his mouth that is obviously too big for him. Enjoy it while you can, because you are not taking it back with you. Silly beast. Shall we pack this away?

I might get some work done, if we go back.

Do you know if Mrs Plett has made a cake today? I think I will ask.

Muriel carries the rug over her shoulder and they take a handle each of the basket.

We called this 'Jack and Jill' when I was little. (Muriel recites the nursery rhyme, which Angelica has not heard before, and makes Angelica do one in the German dialect of her childhood.) It was Penelope, by the way. The print Frances gave me. *Penelope at the Loom.* I look at it every day.

What am I doing, Frances? Caught up in the moment, giddy and – this is awful. No one will come, or if they do it will be out of morbid curiosity. I have forgotten how, what to do and say.

The way Muriel gasps at the suggestion, the reaction, yes, it makes me melt. Seeing the glow of pleasure. Giving her a reason to stay several nights with us, helping to plan it. That is why, I know it of course.

I say that I can send someone with a message to her father's house requesting his permission and to collect anything she needs.

She exclaims, Oh, let the theme be *Angelicamad*!

Angelica is mortified, but accepts gracefully. Then Muriel runs to find Mrs Plett, hungry for cake.

When we are alone, Angelica asks me, Does she know? that you are her mother?

I reply that Muriel is an innocent. Or maybe I do not say it aloud.

Muriel opened my eyes. You showed me the sky.

*

137

The ballroom is lit by tiny lights and swathed in curtains. Statues, objects and plinths are arranged like a set for a play – Roman ruins, or Atlantis, to Muriel's fertile mind. Pagan gods gleam and cast shadows.

But the incomplete portrait of Frances will not be displayed.

To avoid the expense of entertaining society and the inevitable flurry of refusals, guests have been chosen for their youth or for previous kindnesses or because they are admirers of the arts, and in a few rare cases, because they were once friends of both Maria and Frances together. They mostly accept. Maria is still a countess, after all; Muriel has a knack for galvanising the mannered young people of their parish; and the draw of Angelica's fame certainly swells the numbers. Assistance comes from Maria's uncle in the form of carriages and servants; gifts of sugared sweets arrive which supplement the repast. Muriel and Duncan gather peonies, gladioli, lilies, carnations, roses, poppies to make delicate and glorious arrangements, as though the garden has come indoors smelling delicious and wet. Maria finds she has little to do, with Mrs Plett attending to the practicalities, and Muriel and Angelica taking care of the aesthetics. Her idleness compounds her anxiety. Your job is to thank people, Angelica reminds her.

The musicians strike up. The guests mingle, greet and compliment each other, dashing praises for healthful complexions and ingenious ensembles. The spectacle of the fancy dress. Some have gone to great lengths: crowns, masks, flora, instruments, weapons and puppets. The company in the ballroom includes Mark Antony in a bed-sheet toga, Cleopatra with a crêpe-paper asp, Queen Eleanor, Cordelia, Prospero in emerald robes carrying a carved staff, Socrates in a horsehair beard, Troilus and Cressida, Ulysses, the Muses and allegories, a bevy of nymphs. A minority have resisted the impulse, dress conventionally or incorporate a single salient detail denoting their character. A woman who has brought an apple with her explains she is Aphrodite after the judgement of Paris; a priggish gentleman is dressed as 'a lord', one of Miss Kauffman's many portraits, he says, though is vague about which one. Muriel is most pleased with her costume, for she has come as a self-portrait, Angelica lending her one of her own exotic outfits; she proudly carries a palette and brush.

Among the gathering are Maria's second son Augustus and her daughter-in-law Harriet.

It is wonderful to see you both.

He kisses her hand.

How well you look, Mother.

Thank you. How are my grandchildren?

Harriet replies, A handful. They have sent you their love, and these letters and tokens . . . She gives a little bundle tied in pink ribbons to Maria.

There is a pause. Harriet raises her brows at her husband. He coughs.

Mother, it occurs to me you have not seen the girls for some time, and how nice it would be if you deigned to stay with us . . . (That appears to be his whole speech: either he has not prepared or cannot remember the rest.)

The daughter-in-law takes the initiative, The children would be very pleased, you would be welcome to come whenever you liked, either to the country or to town. If you had other appointments to keep in London, then a visit might be of particular benefit?

Maria wavers, promises to give it some consideration.

The rhythms and swirls of conversations, the swish and ruffle of gowns, the fragrance of hairstyles and snap of fans, the pounding of feet and the shower of clapping at the end of each dance. Muriel leads a game of Bluff – the blindfold is tied on her first,

139

and she is turned and turned, hands outstretched, giggles and jibes until she catches a young man (he does not try hard to evade her), then he is It and the game goes on.

Muriel flops next to her godmother, catches her breath from laughing hard, her hands over the twinges.

Is this what you wanted, my girl?

You have not called me that in a long time. Yes, it is splendid, perfect. Do you like it?

Maria kisses the young woman, uplifted to have given her something she enjoys, thankful there is at least this much beauty in the world. And so the party continues, peaks and peters out – warm-blooded jolly tipsy noisy fatigued. The chatter fades, the mood dims, the music concludes; they bid goodnight, the candles are snuffed out.

Angelica is to be found in the orangery early.

I wanted to finish this.

Maria is dishevelled and bleary, stands behind the artist to inspect the picture.

You have put a book on the table. One of these? She picks up a poet.

Writers are readers.

Initially Angelica refuses Miss Wheatley's book.

I said I would accept no payment.

A gift then, from one friend to another, as you have done for me, Miss Angel.

Angelica is uneasy about leaving, repeats her invitation for both Maria and Muriel to visit her in London. They embrace.

Maria waves at the departing carriage, Angelica's hand is visible waving back until the horses turn down the lane.

Maria pulls her tippet around her against the morning, walks to keep warm, follows Coward between the flowerbeds and high hedges, his tail disappearing through the rose arch. Sitting on the bench within is Frances in her red and black riding habit, a writing board and pen in her lap.

I am sorry. I do not mean to disturb you.

Frances sets the tools down by her feet, scoops the dog into her lap. You are not.

Maria sits by her, tears sliding down her face, how easily they fall. Why did you not come before?

I came when you called me. You waited for Angelica and Muriel to go home, you waited for Mrs Plett's sister to get ill so she went to her bedside, you waited until you and I would be entirely alone.

I am so glad to see you.

Yet you did not ask for me until now.

Where have you been?

Here. Nearby. Nowhere.

You are angry with me? You *are* angry with me! Why are you angry with me? This is your doing. You have done this to us, it is your fault.

Stop it, Maria.

Look at me – look at what you have done. I am a wreck, an invalid, I am broken into pieces.

You know I never chose this, so why do you insist that I did? What is it about being abandoned that pleases you? I treasured every second we had. I would not willingly have given you up. I fought to stay alive, and it is hateful to imply that I did not. Sometimes love is not enough to bind us to the world. What is beautiful may also be finite. It is written: *The Lord gave, and the Lord hath taken away.*

Well *you* were the one who was taken away, not the one who was left behind! Maria gasps, hardly composes herself . . . I changed everything for you, Frances.

Yes, you did.

141

You did not have to beg me or argue with me. I did it because I wanted to.

Yes, you did.

It is mortally unfair that what we had, what we made, was ripped from us.

Yes, it is.

You were the strong one, Frances, I was never made for this.

Then pray tell me, what were you made for, Maria?

To spend my youth and fulfil my duties, and after I met you my purpose was to love you.

Is that your purpose still?

More than ever.

A ladybird lands on Frances's skirt. She lets it crawl on to the tip of her gloved finger and fly away. I know that you hide my writings in your bedroom with a loaded pistol and a bottle of gin. Were you waiting for the portrait to be completed so my face would be the last sight you saw in this life?

And the first in the next.

Is this how you love me, Maria? Forlornly and destructively?

I have this pain, Frances, or I have nothing. I have told you enough times.

Does the painting resemble me, I wonder?

It is at once a pale reflection and speaks the truth.

Frances presses her temple, thinks. Maria, I shall speak the truth to you now. I shall tell you what I would have done if it had been the other way round. I would have mourned you desperately. I would have grown sick, I would tear my hair out and not sleep, I would weep and wail and despair and long for death and lament that it had been this way and not different, and scream until the ceiling fell in. I would break every glass within reach and knock over furniture and throw objects just to watch them smash. I would rage, I would blame you for leaving me, I would consider diving into a swift river or drinking poison. I would be shattered, I would be defeated, I would be mad, I would be the undead. And then, then – *the following day*, I would look into the glass and begin the process of healing. I would ... devise a tour with Muriel, yes, that is what I would do, to London to begin with, and the friends and relatives who will have us. She is a young woman who deserves the advantages being introduced into society can give, and perhaps under my guidance I can help find a suitable path for her. Share what small seeds of wisdom I have acquired. Bath next, then Europe. It would enrich her.

How would you afford it?

You will have made provision for Muriel and, though it does not match the wealth of the ton, I have my own income. Also, I did not squander all of your gifts. I worried that one day I might have to take care of you. Did not you know that already? I left the papers in your desk.

Maria pictures a mess of documents she has not yet faced.

Muriel's foster-parents should be consulted. Although she is not actually theirs, they love her just the same. It occurs to me, you would be a better tutor in the ways of society; how much more gratifying and extraordinary the world would seem to Muriel when viewed in your reflected light. Still, I would do my best. I would keep Mrs Plett with us. She has spent her life in service to you, saving you from yourself. What else is she to do? I would let her take charge of Muriel, and me, as a consolation. And I would visit your sons, if they would receive me, and your grandchildren.

Why would you visit my grandchildren?

Because they are yours. Because I would want to be an aunt or a friend to them. Whatever help I could give, they would have it – and who knows when they will need a listening ear or a sanctuary? A real grandparent would be better, but I would do my best.

I see what you are doing, Frances, and it is wasted.

Is it? And if he will hear me out, I would try to persuade

Georgie to make provision for Dorothy in the event that His Lordship dies first.

She has no right—

That is why I would raise it sooner rather than later. His Lordship's estate is enormous. It would not harm the legitimate heirs, it could prevent an embarrassing scandal and she will not need a pension for long, anyway. It is the clever and the moral course of action. That your son fears offending you is probably part of his motive for procrastinating. I would at least try to resolve it. And then I would never think of it again.

Why did you not say any of this before?

Because I was alive and – distracted.

Frances . . . I did not make any provision for you.

Then it is a mercy I died first.

Maria's tears swell childishly.

Oh Maria, it is only a joke! I would have survived, I would have made do. It would not have inhibited me, nor would I have been angry with you. Put it out of your mind.

Frances puts her arm round Maria's neck; Maria rests her head on her shoulder. A kiss.

Maria whispers, What else would you do?

I would honour your memory by living my life. I would explore whatever we would have explored together. I would regret deeply that you were not with me to share it, but I would let the pain go because I would be grateful each day that I had loved you and been loved by you. I would laugh at your wit whenever I recalled it. I would be steered by your precious influence. I would not even reject love if it crossed my path again.

Frances's voice becomes as indistinct as the breeze, her shoulder becomes Maria's own palm, the caress on her arm is only Coward's rough tongue, his black body warm at her side. A ladybird is on her knee, opens its shiny case to reveal transparent wings, flies away.

Featherstone of Piccadilly

Carte de Visite, 1864

Florence and Rosemary, the Gault twins – Flossie and Rosie to each other and their mother – dark-haired and green-eyed, are playing among the graves.

The little girls skip between the headstones, pausing to inspect the worn inscriptions, to pick at the lichen, to place twigs and leaves in mysterious shapes on the dirt of the dead. They commune with the sleepers, listen for the shriek of the magpie, the damp air making their frocks cling, the soles of their feet black. Their nails are clogged with filth.

Florence is the elder by a few minutes, considers herself to be wiser in the ways of the world for this reason, to have for ever an advantage over Rosemary. Rosie is fortunate to have an example to follow. They are bony and pale, but not miserable children. This churchyard is one of their 'best places'. They natter, they crouch, they chase and hide, they are identical guardians of the crypts.

One says to her twin, Let's do Our Secret. She likes to do that because the physical world warps into patterns, and the flow of sisterly understanding between them is powerful but *not at all* terrifying. Her sister does not want to, is content to be, runs along the row of mounds instead. They play and explore until their mother comes to fetch them.

Mrs Harry Gault – Isabella – the wan woman, sickly bearer of seven surviving children, five of them strapping boys destined for the Lancashire textile factories and coal pits. Her youngest are the twin girls who she had hoped would take up her mantle, for in her youth Isabella was both a great beauty and a brilliant dramatic soprano. Letters and gifts from enamoured princes, the whole of Europe her wardrobe and dining table and boudoir. The nectar of immortality was within her grasp, until a jealous rival (in love or in opera?) attacked her with a straight razor, leaving her face and career in tatters.

Isabella has known destitution, and in the end she could do no better than Harry Gault. The scarring is permanent and deep.

It was disappointing to find that her girls, though they can learn a song and some harmonies if they are repeated, have no special aptitude or inclination for music. And there is a house-ful of boys and men to attend to anyway, chores to do, the permanent threat of pregnancy—

Mrs Isabella Gault, wrapped against the weather in grey wool, makes her way towards the cemetery. She calls to her girls in her melodious voice.

One waves. She can see it is Florence (only Isabella could tell them apart at this distance). Rosemary is out of sight. The church spire points to a pale sky where starlings flock, swarming cloud shapes, pulsing presentiment, their mass contracting and expanding in collective consciousness. Isabella stops to watch the evening delight. Florence looks, then disappears from view further behind the graves.

Isabella climbs the hill, makes her way to her daughters, Flossie elevated on a grassy mound, Rosie huddled by a wall.

What have you been doing?

Flossie replies. We were talking to the beggar, he said the night was death.

Where is he now?

Flossie shrugs. Gone to heaven, I expect. You saw him too, didn't you? She addresses her twin.

Rosie turns, disconcerted.

Flossie scowls. Well . . . ?

Yes, I saw him. He had white hair and a staff. He had travelled far.

At first Isabella fears a criminal in their midst, then, Tell me, where was this man?

Standing there – Flossie points to the vacant threshold of the church where the thick oak door is shut fast. He was in pain. For a while. Then he left.

When was he here?

A moment before you.

Which way did he go?

Flossie looks to her sister to supply more details, but Rosie frowns. Flossie shrugs, Gone whence he came.

Isabella looks about her in case the stranger is nearby. He is not. She walks the perimeter of the building, determined to see in each direction so she can swear on the Bible she searched with her own eyes and found nobody. She has already begun to create the legend. She knows that twelve years ago an elderly man who had wandered for many miles seeking shelter in the depths of winter, finding the church locked and bolted, died of exposure on that very spot, his body frozen solid, his face locked in the grimace of pleas unanswered.

147

Florence goes to her twin. She and Rosemary whisper together.

Isabella Gault knows about the nurture of talent. She knows that finesse comes with rehearsal, that effortlessness requires effort.

The lamps are extinguished because the medium, Mrs Mortimer Solomon-Black, is giving a demonstration. She is an American, though her transatlantic tones merge with the furrows of another dialect. The participants at the séance hold hands round the table to ensure the authenticity of the experiment, the room so dark they cannot see their neighbours or the person opposite, or the lady herself. Listening to their own breath. They wait. Two of their number are avid spiritualists, thrilled to be in the presence of one of the most famous and proven mediums of the day. One man is an ardent sceptic, has come to figure out the trickery, deride the folly, denounce it as charlatanism. One attendee is bereaved, and three more are here for diversion, as though this were the music hall or a game of whist.

Mrs Solomon-Black is going into her trance: We are here as friends. Is there a spirit who desires to make contact with the living this evening?

The silence is painful. The members of the party attempt to repress the rustle of clothing, the whistling from one gentleman's hairy nose, the creak of the chairs they occupy. They grip one another's fingers tighter.

A clear, loud rap.

They react, shared relief and achievement. It came from above or beneath them somehow, from no discernible source in the room (which was examined in advance).

Two more raps.

148

Mrs Solomon-Black translates, Three for yes, we have broken through. May I remind you at this critical juncture not to break the circle. If the person sitting next to you lets go, you must draw attention to him immediately so that there can be no tampering or interference, and what happens here remains spontaneous and honest.

A man of city finance (and also the bereft son) asks whether it is his mother.

Mrs Solomon-Black puts the question to the spirit, Are you Hilda Merryweather? For there is someone here who wishes to contact Hilda Merryweather.

One rap. One rap for no. Then one more, then a third   it is she, after all.

Hilda, your son Phillip is here. He longs to speak with you.

Phillip Merryweather can hardly contain himself, and exclaims into the darkness, Mama! I am so happy. I have been lonely without you. But Mrs Solomon-Black, how do I know for certain it is she?

The medium agrees: We must make sure. Hilda, appear to me. Let me hear you. Let me bear witness. Show your love for your son by showing yourself.

The piquancy of the anticipation is heightened. Assuredly if the spirit is genuine, it will not deny her son solace? Assuredly if the medium is a fraud, she will expose herself now?

Aha. I see a most elegant lady, adorned in pearls, with white hair that used to be red. She holds a posy of thistles, and has been reunited with a white cat she is very fond of.

Phillip squeaks with emotion because this is an accurate description of his beloved mother.

She is giving me some names. She is saying Victoria and Albert. But that does not make any sense, Mr Merryweather; why should she be naming the Queen and her consort?

Because Victoria was her middle name, and Bert was the cat

she loved and lost. It is Mama's way of letting me know it is indeed her. (Some of the group murmur in amazement.) What is she saying now?

She is anxious about her pepper pot.

Oh dear. I gave it to Mrs Middleton after Mama died. Was I not supposed to? Does she want me to get it back?

It has some special significance.

I cannot think what.

And she is worried, fretful, about an unpaid bill from the butcher.

He raises his voice as though addressing someone across the road. We have settled your accounts, Mama, including the butcher's. He was saddened to hear the news, and gave us a ham for the wake.

The medium listens intently. I see. Was your mother one to accept charity in life?

Phillip Merryweather does not reply; senses disapproving eyes on him in the blackness.

I think your mother wants you to settle the outstanding payment.

Of course. How foolish of me. Mama, I am sorry, I was distraught. It never occurred to me—

She is saying that is no excuse. However, she is saying you were a good son to her, and she is proud of you. And she is saying a wonderful opportunity has recently come your way which you should take advantage of, with a Scottish connection.

Phillip Merryweather thinks instantly of his planned investment in a shipbuilding contract in Clydebank. The engineer's drawings were magnificent, the business model as tight as a drum, the potential returns fabulous. Uncanny!

She means Edward McClancy's proposal, of course. I am glad of her approval, for I intend to sign the papers tomorrow.

A single resolute knock.

Not McClancy's ship, Mama . . . ?

He considers.

Hmm. She cannot mean the loan Nicholas Nash asked me for, for his geological survey? (The cost of the project was enormous. Merryweather had laughed the man out of his office – it was a fool's errand, a lot of old rocks and marine fossils and glacial drifts and no money to be made whatsoever.)

Three distinct knocks. Yes.

Mama? Are you positive that Nash is the man I should be financing, not McClancy?

Hilda . . . ? The medium strains in her chair. She is being called away. She is leaving us.

Phillip Merryweather is peeved, but the two experienced spiritualists, Miss Langdon and Miss Mellor, can be heard twittering with excitement, for Mrs Solomon-Black is thoroughly convincing and there is still more to come.

This is most unusual. I see a bold spirit-light taking on the form of a maiden, an Amazon princess made of white spirit-energy . . . wait . . . it is making a pathway for someone else, it recedes and is replaced by another female – I see her with total clarity – she comes forward with intention. She is drawn, dishevelled, she has lost her good looks but has determination and an exceptional mind. She is adorned with a single precious stone that resembles the deep sea . . . and it is as if she is falling into it, the blueness swells up, it covers her head. She has turned her back on love. Poor, fragile lady, what a frightful waste.

No one present claims ownership of this woman.

Mrs Solomon-Black persists: This vision is vivid. Will nobody speak up for it? There is nothing to be ashamed of.

When no reply is forthcoming, the medium suggests to the ghost that she allows a soul with a more urgent message to come forward . . . and concentrates.

151

A different spirit is attempting to communicate, a gentleman called G, wearing a fetching waistcoat in bright colours, carrying a carved-bone-topped cane and with him is – what is this? an exotic bird, if I am not mistaken.

The gasp of recognition comes from Mr Thomas Hubbard, the cynic, here to pooh-pooh, here to call it all bunkum.

The medium senses a conquest.

Do not furnish any details, Mr Hubbard, allow me: the G stands for Godwin, am I right? And in life, he was a great intellect, a distinguished man of letters. He may even have worked in the law, for I see justice and fairness are imperative to him.

Good gracious. Thomas Hubbard perspires in the darkness, unable to mop the moisture away without breaking the séance circle.

And so on. The spirits are willing and talkative, until all in the party but one have made contact with a friend or relative who has passed over – Miss Langdon fails to reach her late Aunt Mildred, but does not mind as she spoke to her only last week.

Mrs Solomon-Black's style of clairvoyance is calm. Her job is, she says, to foster peace by aiding the spirits in their communiqués so they may be restful, and to reassure the living that they might live. Towards the end of the demonstration, she briefly loses control and the séance gets out of hand: the table levitates and turns, the participants feel spectral fingers on their faces, scratches, jabs in the ribs, tweaked knees and yanked hair. An object flies from one side of the room to the other and smashes. (My poor shepherdess, says the hostess who has arranged the entertainment.) The medium is angry at the disruptiveness of those spirits who are trying to sabotage their civilised meeting; one enters her body and begins speaking through her to someone present: I know you, I know what you have done. You think you have covered your tracks, but I shall unmask you and ruin you, monster, fiend, wretch—

There is bedlam, during which the person who thinks this warning applies to him is stricken with fear, relieved his peers cannot see his horror at being found out.

Mrs Solomon-Black fights back, sends the wicked spirits away, is shaking with exhaustion afterwards and apologises: When unfriendly spirits upset proceedings it is very draining, and even if my mind is able, my body is weak. I shall have to bring this evening to a close. I do hope you understand.

Her clients do not feel short-changed; on the contrary, the excitement of the malevolent spirits has added flavour to the experience. All present are persuaded of Mrs Mortimer Solomon-Black's authenticity, all (apart from one) are extolling her extraordinary abilities for weeks afterwards to any who will listen.

In the photographer's studio, all must be done at the critical moment while the glass is dripping wet with light-sensitive chemicals. Not one of the steps can be blundered or missed. The paper print with which the client is presented, at which they exclaim out of pleasure and fascination, that is the easy part – the very last part, the sprint to the end. One can make dozens, hundreds of reprints with barely any skill. But the innumerable difficulties that arise before, the inordinate potential for things to go wrong – being heavy-handed or hurried or less than systematic or simply unlucky – and behold: blemishes, ridging, specks or possibly nothing whatever where the portrait should be. And when the entire intricate process has been conducted flawlessly to make an image that is as naturally near to perfection as possible, and the sitter *moves* during the exposure, it is enough to send one into a fit.

In the cramped darkroom, the photographer can do little

more than arrange the bottles in order of use, labels outwards, and lay the equipment in readiness so it can be accessed by the dimness of a single orange window pane.

Not all photographers are as meticulous. The sheer number of studios in the towns and countryside suggests that virtually anyone is capable of making a photograph, that there is no mystery to discover, no alchemy to master, no craft. Some call it sneeringly 'a trade'. But see also how inferior their pictures are? Nasty. No doubt they employ a tout to browbeat passing customers, especially on Sundays when people are dressed for church and should be observing the Sabbath. Let them part with their guinea, and may it bring them luck.

Featherstone of Piccadilly is a superior establishment. Mr Amos Featherstone, a schooled painter, accomplished, gentle, genteel, maker of fine photographic portraits, and the most amiable of companions to the end. On his deathbed he whispered to his wife, I deeply regret it is time for me to go. I wish I didn't have to.

Amos Featherstone's widow checks the workbench where her son has prepared some plates; he has smoothed the edges with the sharpening stone and polished the surfaces with tripoli. Jem has done it thoroughly, but each will need to be cleaned again with a soft brush, because any dust particles whatsoever will show as spots on the final image. Jem has been busy mounting albumen prints for collection in the morning, and has replenished the stock of collodion solution which will ripen next week. He is a good boy.

She hesitates, places her hand upon her breastbone. Heaviness, that dratted heaviness. The tightness of a vice. Pain in her shoulders and neck. In minutes it subsides.

Mrs Amos Featherstone did not imagine having to take on the studio at this age – at any age. She was her husband's helpmeet.

Her role was at home raising their children. The moral paradigm, the pillar of virtue, the protectress of domestic order. Two sons and two daughters grew into adulthood, the girls safely married off. It had been intended that their eldest boy Robert would run his father's business, though his heart was never truly in it, though he longed to join the British army, though he was clumsy and made errors and spilled and damaged. But it was a moot point because Robert was lost to cholera. This left Jem, whose delicate disposition was perhaps better suited to photography . . . but who did not have long enough with his father to learn the art, whose nervousness with the public and naivety as regards money meant it would have been irresponsible to give him full control just yet. Therefore Mrs Featherstone became the custodian of Featherstone of Piccadilly. It feels like a failure on her part. Her daughters believe as much; indeed, she has raised them to.

A lady of mature years, the decades have added bulk to her body. The wearing of a corset and crinolette provides a more fashionable silhouette, and her gowns are of the plainest, black or grey, and spattered with chemicals. Amos's pocket watch on a chain pinned at her waist is entirely practical, for the timing of exposures and so on. Her hair, mainly still dark, has a straight parting at the front and is gathered in a net snood at the nape. By the end of the day wisps of it escape, reminding her when she looks in the mirror that she is not a dowager but a woman who must work. She has fat cheeks, a severe mouth, hooded eyes. Which episodes in her life have done this?

She could have sold the business as a going concern. It would be worth a small fortune, for the premises alone are ideal and neatly formed. On the ground floor is their shop, where clients may browse a gallery of glossy brown-reddish, brown-purplish portraits of ladies, gentlemen, children, families, couples – a testament to the quality of the company and the satisfaction of the clientele. The shop displays some of the choices on offer: the range of poses, the size of prints, the design of mounts. Here is the counter where the first consultation and final transaction are conducted. There is also a selection of royalty, nobility and celebrity *cartes* which can be added to a private album for a shilling apiece (the Prince of Wales and Princess Alexandra are doing exceedingly well, as is Mr Charles Dickens). The first floor is the archive – some of it, at any rate – for the studio retains the negative for at least a year from last use; miscellany storage. The photographic studio itself is on the top floor, has a northern aspect and a roof the length and breadth of which are windows windows windows, the light modulated by curtains and blinds on a matrix of pulleys. And, as in a theatre, there are backdrops and props: tables, potted plants, a section of a banister, a faux mantelpiece, chairs, a rocking horse and so forth, used for creating the scene. These are muddled with the backstage equipment and tools, the various chemical jars and beakers, the posing stands, the wet-plate multiplying camera – a box of wood and brass with bellows for focusing affixed on a tripod, its various lenses and appendages – and the sectioned-off darkroom is here too. Amos spent years accumulating and perfecting this. Selling was never an option.

Neither was installing a man to run it, not only because the halcyon days might be coming to an end, but because Amos wanted Featherstone always to mean Featherstone. Wanted it this way. He was a good father and provider, and so his wishes have been respected.

Jem in his waistcoat and loosely knotted necktie, his sleeves rolled up like a grocer's, his hair untidy as though he has just risen from bed. Humble by nature. Aware of what his mother is doing for him. Honoured that one day he shall be Featherstone of Piccadilly, having believed for most of his life that it would be Robert. He asks if there is anything she needs?

Mrs Featherstone has made a list. As it is quiet, he can run these errands for her, and she will see him at home for dinner. She can hold the fort for the last hour or so. As Jem puts on his jacket and billycock, she tells him he has been a help today.

He then ventures, Mama, perhaps we can take a walk to Regent's Park and visit the Zoo? We might enjoy the aquarium and the hippopotamuses. What do you think?

Jem has made a suggestion for an outing nearly every week since his father died. Parks, museums, exhibitions, strolls to take in landmarks and monuments. Initially it irritated her, initially she rejected these trivial distractions from her duties and adjustment. Then she remembered how young he still was, took pity on him, thought she would humour him once, because he was in mourning as she was.

The lecture on electromagnetism was followed by an evening at the Haymarket to hear a comedy, an omnibus to Richmond for lunch, a day in Greenwich. She came to understand why he had persisted, came to acknowledge the wisdom of these trips, to see how they helped them both and restored normality of a kind.

When he had suggested taking the train to Brighton and staying overnight, his mother simply said what she is saying now, We will not know what it is like until we find out for ourselves. They had walked arm in arm along the esplanade, taking in the views. The sea air was cleansing after the effluvia and fetid vapours of London. Mrs Featherstone found the illustrations exhibited at the Royal Pavilion especially diverting, charming, quaint. She bought a souvenir print very cheaply, telling Jem the figure in it was probably an allegory of poetry.

Hippos in Regent's Park? She can manage them with ease.

Jem touches the brim of his hat to her and goes to his tasks, the shop bell ringing on his way out.

After watching him disappear down the road into the crowds and smog, she turns the sign over to read *CLOSED* and sits at the counter to peruse the *Morning Post* until—

The shop bell rings again, and a lady enters. She is dressed grandly, dramatically, in violet and black with stripes on the bodice, crimped trimming and a velvet coat. The voluminous silk ties of her bonnet make an enormous bow. She is adorned with jewellery in a way some would find vulgar: an enormous locket, lengths of beads over her bosom, earrings that glitter. Two spots of rouge make her look like a painted doll.

And she is, in every physical detail, the exact replica of the lady at the counter.

Hello Flossie, says Mrs Amos Featherstone.

Hello Rosie, says Mrs Mortimer Solomon-Black. You do not seem very surprised to see me.

The *Morning Post* announced you were in London. I expected you to drop by.

Really? Do go on.

Your profession means you still keep late hours, and were therefore bound to visit in the afternoon. And I read that this evening you are to give a demonstration at rooms in the White Hart, which is close by. I said to myself, Flossie will come today.

Florence shakes her head in disbelief – her sister can tell what she is thinking.

The twins regard each other. It has been eleven years since they last spoke, an interval of four years before that, and an ocean between them. Yet it may as well be eleven hours. In a moment they have become the Gaults of Lancashire again, their relationship with one another longer and deeper than with anyone else – parents, husbands, children. Each was her twin's first experience, what she first saw, knew and understood about the world, a copy of herself.

Florence takes in the displays of photographs, turns a page or two of a made album, says, I am sorry about Amos and about Robert. How sad.

Thank you, and thank you for your kind letter. You are married *again*, aren't you ... ?

Yes. No need for that tone, little sister. I have been divorced only the once, don't-you-know.

You did not keep your name.

Mortimer's name carries weight in its own right. He is with me here, in London. We always travel together. You can meet him if you like.

Is America still making you happy?

It is home, even with its faults.

You are not in any danger I hope ... ?

Oh no, we will be all right. What a thoroughly despicable war! This is a nice shop, Rosie, it rather suits you.

This does not please Rosemary Featherstone; she does not respond.

And Jem – it is Jem? – how is he working out?

He has a natural eye and a steady hand.

No magnetism though ... ? Perhaps it skips a generation – or it is simply that none of the Gault menfolk has it. Have you heard from any of our kin? (Florence pauses long enough to realise Rosemary will not rise to that.) Come on, Rosie, don't look sad. If you are sad no good will come of it, except perhaps that people will be able to tell us apart.

Rosemary smiles at the truth of it, at the innumerable mix-ups and misunderstandings of the past. As girls, they encouraged the confusion, dressed the same, wore their hair the same, lied frequently to cover for the other.

I have also come to bring you business – don't panic, not the kind you dislike. I have been in England for only five minutes, and people are swamping me with their *cartes de visite*, but I cannot reciprocate. So I wondered if you would oblige? I do not require a special rate, just whatever you would normally charge, but I will need several dozen, maybe a hundred or more if I am inundated. Would it be possible?

It is possible to oblige immediately, and Rosemary leads Florence up to the studio and hangs her bonnet and coat on the hat stand, revealing her twin's black hair tightly braided and styled with oil.

The visiting sister takes in the room. What a marvellous place. What a pretty view of the city. If I were you, I should live here just to be able to see it.

I practically do.

Rosemary has Florence try out some poses in front of the camera. Initially Florence wants full-length standing portraits, but Rosemary can see that even with the aid of a posing stand under her skirt or a prop to lean on, her sister is too much of a fidget, so they agree upon a three-quarter-length seated pose. The Featherstone studio makes eight images of standard size to a plate. Florence is keen to experiment; Rosemary persuades her just two poses of four each will be sufficient variety. She makes Flossie practise, first sitting in the mode of reading a book for the duration of one exposure, fifty seconds at this time of day and in this weather—

Mrs Beeton . . . ? Really, Rosie!

Don't move please, Flossie.

Florence holds her tongue and herself while Rosemary explains her lady customers are usually happy to be photographed with it, though the title on the spine will not actually be visible.

– and then the switch to resting her elbow on the table and looking over her shoulder for the same length of time, for a second exposure. Rosemary angles some mirrors so Florence can see and maintain her facial expression.

Well done, Flossie, but I am afraid that was only the rehearsal. Are you ready for the real thing?

Without waiting for a response, Rosemary takes up the glass plate by one corner in her white-gloved hand, pours some collodion into the centre – yellow like castor oil – and begins flowing the plate by gentle tilting to cover it evenly in the liquid.

The photographer says, You will have to bear with me, as I am doing this without assistance.

You haven't changed.

Rosemary goes into the darkroom and places the plate upright in a bath of silver nitrate. She then brings the pocket watch up to her ear and starts counting. A few minutes later—

Rosie, what are you doing?

Prepare, please.

Florence gives herself a stretch, then opens Mrs Beeton's *Household Management*, affecting interest.

Rosemary comes out of the darkroom with the sensitised plate inside a wooden holder to protect it from light. Some of the solution leaks out of it. She slots the wooden plate holder into the back of the camera and pulls out the slide, saying she is about to make the exposure. Taking her twin's silence and stillness for assent, she removes the lens cap and times it, counting down aloud. Florence breathes shallowly, does not blink, does not read a word of the page but stares quite through it. She could be mistaken for a waxwork. Then Rosemary replaces the cap, directs Florence to alter her posture and adjusts the wet plate. The second exposure is taken. Florence has proved to be a good subject after all.

In the darkroom once more, Rosemary gently pours developer on the glass plate to make the image appear – silver and grainy. When her eyes were stronger she was able to discern the image materialising, halt it at the optimum second; now she must rely on her experience. Water stops the development of the negative, and at last Rosemary can take it out of the darkroom and submerge it in the bath of sodium thiosulphate fixer. She waits while the eight images become clear and vivid. They are not unsatisfactory thus far.

Rosie, we ought to go to Mama's grave together while I am in London. You and I haven't done that since we buried her.

Will your engagements permit it?

Will yours?

Rosemary gives the plate a wash in water and lays it out. The negative is extremely delicate. She lights the paraffin lamp for warmth.

Rosie, have you been to Mama's grave since she died?

Rosemary's face is hidden. She busies herself at the workbench.

You must stop being mad with her. She was doing what she knew, what she thought was best for us.

Mama was doing what pleased her most. If we had been born joined at the hip she would have put us in a circus.

Florence cannot deny this. Didn't you enjoy any of it? At times it seemed you did.

Rosemary sighs, pauses her activity, sits on the just-for-pretence sofa. It is not a part of my life I think about any more, and I have forgotten a lot of it. I look at a city on the globe and realise I cannot remember if I have been there or not. Cities, and even whole countries, have merged together in my memory. Maybe it was because there were so many, and maybe it is because I do not revise them in my mind's eye – and maybe it is just because one's faculties tend to diminish. Anyway, it is history to me. Why should I dwell on my past when there is Jem's future to consider? I really do not think on it.

You must know if you enjoyed it? Can you not recall a single minute of pleasure?

I don't remember. I know that I did not enjoy the limelight as much as you.

I adore it. I mean the work, not the attention. Mama did right by at least one of us.

Then who am I to criticise? (Rosemary picks up the plate, practically dry, and gently warms it over the lamp flame.)

Her twin says, However, if I had to identify something I disliked about it—

Heats the bottle of varnish next until it is blood warm.

– it would have to be that it emphasised what was different about us.

I don't know what you mean, Flossie.

Yes, you do. I liked it when we were as identical as two people can be, when we looked the same and spoke the same. I liked it when we were following the same road and having the same adventures and thinking the same thoughts. I loved sharing it with you as much as anything else, as much as the novelties and the trappings. You made me secure about my place in the world. I am very happy you got the family you wanted and the home you deserved. It turned out wonderfully for me, so I can't complain. But it was a blow to find out we were not as alike as I thought we were – that one of us was fulfilled and one of us was not.

Rosemary holds the glass by the same corner, pours the tepid varnish – yellow like urine – into the middle and flows the plate as before to coat the negative. She finally lets it rest.

You are putting on quite a show over there. Maybe it is not such a different vocation as you would have me believe . . . ?

This is not my vocation.

If you are doing it for Jem, which you are, then it is. You thought it was beneath you, didn't you, Rosie? You thought it was degrading.

Public exhibitionism and parlour tricks are degrading.

163

Affectation, performance and insincere speech are demeaning for a lady.

The medium shrugs: And yet you have given a performance every day since, as a spouse and a mother. Isn't that demeaning also? To pretend to be less than what you are?

Less?

Florence continues, Was our mother more than, or less than, what she once was after she married our father? It was not the attack which broke her spirit; it was what it reduced her to. Anyone can marry. Anyone can bring children into the world. But you are unique, and you gave it up for the sake of dreary convention.

Rosemary stares at her twin. Florence has done exactly what Rosemary expected; found a way to spite her.

Well, Flossie, what you see as sacrifice, I see as freedom. What you call convention, I call stability. My greatest achievements are being obedient to my husband and setting a good example to my sons and daughters.

Florence is nonplussed. But you admit it is all for show? It is not what you really are. I do not mean to cause offence, Rosie, just to speak the truth. Being 'mistress of a house' requires putting on an act, does it not? And dressing in costume. And speaking lines. And doing what is expected.

You would say that, Florence, because you have never had a family.

On the contrary, I have had a family. I have had more than one. I have never had any *children*, is that what you are referring to? I was merely pointing out that you have exchanged one role for another.

You disapprove.

No more than you disapprove of me.

I have never given you reason to think such a thing. (The photographer removes her gloves, businesslike.) I am afraid I

164

cannot make you any prints until tomorrow because the negative is wet. And it will be better to do duplicates in stronger sunlight.

I am grateful.

Would you like me to have Jem deliver them?

No need, I will send someone to collect them. By the bye, where is my nephew?

Doing errands for me.

The spiritualist replies, Strange . . . you guessed I was coming today . . . and when I arrive, he is out running errands.

Life does go on, Flossie.

I tell my clients exactly the same, Rosie.

The carriage of Mr and Mrs Lennox, a young couple, pulls up outside Featherstone of Piccadilly, and Jones the valet enters the shop, presents Mr Lennox's card and speaks to Jem. His employers require some *cartes de visite* of their daughter Edna as a matter of urgency. They are waiting to be received.

Jem smothers his nerves, affirms it can be done this instant, and while Jones returns to his master to convey the acceptance of the commission, Jem calls to his mother.

Rosemary Featherstone greets Mr and Mrs Lennox, both pinched and dressed head to foot in refined black tailoring. Mrs Lennox, a blonde, watery woman, wears crêpe and an exquisite jet brooch. Mr Lennox carries his top hat, occasionally touches his moustache as he speaks. This type of portrait is always problematic. The photographer assesses the couple, and it is as she fears – he is exacting, suspicious, has expectations, is enumerating them.

Mrs Lennox is mute until she spies a portion of the display set discreetly in one corner. Mrs Featherstone, you have done child *cartes* of this kind before? These are they?

Mrs Featherstone replies, Yes, Mrs Lennox, we have plenty of experience and testimonials from parents pleased with the outcome. A photograph of a child is a highly cherished possession.

Mr Lennox examines the pictures himself, nods.

Jones loiters outside, awaiting instructions, and Rosemary sends Jem to assist.

The sofa and a selection of satin cushions are chosen for the little girl to rest on. Edna turns out to be blonde like her mother, dressed in white, piously holding a crucifix in her fragile ivory hand. A pale cherub. But it is not an easy photograph, not nearly as easy as it ought to be. The parents are anxious, determined to supervise, obstructive. Jem has yet to acquire the skill of diverting unwanted onlookers and keeping them at a distance; his attempts to assist Mrs Featherstone are a hindrance. Jones the valet serves no purpose, none, gets in the way. And the child herself . . .

It is down to Rosemary Featherstone to manage the situation tactfully without making any errors. It will be disastrous if she has to take the portrait a second time. She must patiently accommodate the patrons' needs, lead assertively and diplomatically, trust in her abilities, ignore the distractions.

Tiny footsteps across the floorboards – investigative fingers – a shrill giggle.

Rosemary prepares the wet plate, laments not for the last time how many things can go wrong.

When the picture has been taken, the Lennox party leaves. Mr Lennox carries Edna in his arms.

An hour later, and Rosemary is able to make the proof in solitude. She puts the glass negative into the printing frame in contact with the albumen paper and exposes it to sunlight. The eight identical pictures emerge; she watches it to arrest the exposure and fix the print. Here, then, is the first proper sight of the Lennox child's *carte*. She looks carefully. It seems to be all right.

She will have Jem make the duplicates. No need for her to do it herself. But—

She takes out her magnifying glass because she does not trust her weakening vision and examines the paper proof again, each eighth, carefully, looking not at the girl on the sofa but around her, in the background, on the curtain, for imperfections, for—

Edna Lennox, you naughty child.

Rosemary scrutinises now the plate negative. She sighs with exasperation, puts the magnifying glass down with a clunk. She cannot face having them back in the studio for a second attempt, and even if she wanted to, it is probably too late. It will just have to be retouched.

Amos Featherstone was a purist, outwardly opposed to retouching. But in private he, like the majority of his colleagues, would paint out unwanted spots and markings which detracted from the finished result (but, unlike some of the less scrupulous studios, he stopped short of improving the sitter's personal appearance). Amos, a trained artist, used watercolours or India ink on the negative. Rosemary uses instead a soft lead pencil. She makes the corrections using the magnifier, bends over her task, her hand trembles with concentration.

Jem appears at her elbow. He is grinning.

What are you so happy about?

He shakes his head. 'Stonishing.

Apparently he does not mean the proof, he means the lady standing in the studio.

Rosemary, startled: Why are you here? You said you would send someone.

I sent myself. Are you glad?

Yes, I am rather.

Jem looks at the two women, shakes his head again.

Rosie, we have not been formally introduced . . . ?

Flossie, may I present my youngest, Jem. Jemmy, this is my sister, your aunt, Mrs Mortimer Solomon-Black.

He dips in a bow. How d'you do?

Florence says, What a handsome man you have grown into. You were a baby when I last saw you. Now look at you.

He blushes at this – and coming from such a lady in jewels and polka dots – he finds the resemblance intriguing. Would you like some tea, Mrs Solomon-Black?

That would be very nice. (Jem goes to boil the water, Florence follows him out with her eyes.)

You have made a beautiful boy. He looks exactly like her – does he sound like her, too?

He would be horrified at the very notion of singing on a stage. Thankfully none of my children was that way inclined. He likes this – Rosemary gestures about her.

I am surprised you told him about me.

Well, why shouldn't I?

What about the girls? Do they know about me? about us? about *you*?

Rosemary is nettled. They know what they need to, which is more than they care for. If you try to see them, of course I would not presume to prevent you. On the other hand, you oughtn't take it to heart if you find they are not at home.

They would turn me away . . . ?

I doubt it would be their decision. One is married to a lawyer, the other to a man of industry. They are directed by their husbands, as they were brought up to be, and have reputations to maintain. Mary read that you were coming to London. She hopes your trip is a success, but said it was a shame that your public engagements would keep you from visiting her.

Florence wonders how Rosemary could have permitted this, yet her sister is unrepentant. Rather than forcing the issue,

Florence says, I have brought you and your son an invitation to dine. (Gives her sister the short letter in a looping script.) If you decline, I shall not question it.

Mr and Mrs Mortimer Solomon-Black present their compliments to Mrs Amos Featherstone and Mr James Featherstone, and request the honour of their company to dinner on Thursday, et cetera.

Rosemary notes the venue, replies quietly, The gesture is extremely kind.

It was Mortimer's idea. For some reason he wants to meet you before we leave.

I intended to invite you both to our home.

You did not mention it yesterday.

No, I suppose I did not get to it. Your *cartes* are printed. Rosemary lays the letter down, shows Florence a finished picture mounted on card from a boxful.

Florence opens her tortoiseshell lorgnette. Superb. This is much better than what I have been using.

Rosemary offers to send a bill, but Florence wishes to make payment now. The transaction is done. Rosemary wraps the box in paper.

It is while she is doing this and counting out change that Florence notices the Lennox proof and examines it through her spectacles, remarks, This photograph is post-mortem. She looks as though she is sleeping peacefully.

Rosemary represses the urge to take it back. That is our job, sometimes.

My God.

Florence gazes hard at it. The recognition is twofold; what is on the proof and what Rosemary is now doing to the negative. You are unbelievable.

It is just a mistake on the film.

It is not. If it were, it would appear only in one place, but it

169

is identical on each image. Do you know what you have got here?

Give it to me please, Florence.

Do you know how many fakes are out there? Photographers making double exposures, painting in figures on the plate, lurkers in bed sheets coming out from behind curtains when the subject's head is in a posing apparatus and he cannot see what is going on behind him. And yet, here you are—

Rosemary snatches the print away at last.

Let me buy it from you. You can name your price.

No.

You have a responsibility.

No such responsibility exists. She is someone's child, the parents are grieving. It would be indecent.

Are you going to show it to them? They have the right to know.

Rosemary does not answer.

I assume this has happened before. How many times, Rosie? Rosie, how many times?

I have said it is a mistake on the film, and I have said no. I am sorry, you will have to do without.

Florence sighs, knows she cannot change her twin's mind, collects her package. As you wish. Let me know about Thursday, will you?

As she turns to go, Jem returns with the tea tray. Are you leaving already, Mrs Solomon-Black? I was looking forward to hearing about your life in the United States. It does sound a fascinating place.

Florence and Rosemary exchange glances.

I was looking forward to telling you about it. Regrettably, I have more engagements.

The shop bell rings downstairs. Jem, unable to hide his disappointment, says, I should see to that anyhow.

His mother intercedes. I shall see to it. My sister has a few minutes to spare for some refreshment before her next appointment. You two can stay—

Rosemary takes the proof with her, out of temptation's reach.

Mortimer Solomon-Black shuffles off his frock coat, undoes his floppy cravat, discards it, groans as he pulls off his shoes. He takes off his waistcoat, undoes the studs on his stiff collar and some more on his shirt. He has mutton-chop whiskers and a resonant New Yorker's diction.

Fire is going out. I'll do it. Got to do something – so damnably damp in this country.

He rebuilds it with coal and a poker while his wife, sixteen years his senior, begins to undress, peeling off her outer layers, stepping out of the dress, out of the crinoline, plucking hairpins from her hair, remains in her corset and undergarments. The fire grows lively, warming the room.

Mortimer admires his wife, her shapely body, her hair long and loose. You were a marvel tonight. There wasn't an empty seat in the house.

That was your doing.

Your doing. They were captivated.

Florence settles on one of the chairs, rests her feet on a stool. Without being asked, Mortimer kneels down to remove her boots. He kisses one of her ankles and begins to massage her tired foot. They stay this way for a while, Florence growling with pleasure, the tension dissipating. Perhaps Mortimer does not want to chat, wants to go straight to bed ... ?

Mortimer would like that very much. But he is the kind of man who likes to have his mental faculties as well as his physical senses stimulated. His wife was sensational this evening, note-perfect, saw off an attempted sabotage by a heckler, hit each target first time, every time, like a sharpshooter.

171

The audience was spellbound. He loves how they admire her, the stirrings of awe, the way doors open for her and people jostle to be near. All the same, he loves to have her for himself and when they are touring these hours become rare and precious. He will make love to her, but first they will have this – their conversation, when they share or spar or pontificate. Mortimer shows her an emerald bottle – she smiles, removes her earrings – then pours an ounce of absinthe, dragonfly green, into the bulbous reservoirs of two glass goblets. The scent of the holy trinity, aniseed, grande wormwood and fennel, escapes. He balances a perforated spoon on the rim of each vessel, and on the spoon a lump of sugar. Slowly, hardly more than a drop at a time, he pours iced water from a carafe over the sugar which begins to dissolve, the white solution dripping into the absinthe at the bottom, swirling and merging as the liquids meet like living creatures. He does this for her, this ceremony; they are forced to wait until the transparent green spirit is absorbed by white cloudy water. When the last trace of liquor is gone, the process is not yet complete, for three more parts of water must be added, gradually, until the drink is a fluid fog with a faint green tint.

To us.

They sip.

He says, I have begun to wonder whether it is time to phase out the smaller venues. No more parlours and tea parties, except for patrons of quality who can be a help to us. We can do private demonstrations at the beginning of a tour, find a scientist or conjuror who wants to test you, to generate some publicity, but that is it. Focus on larger venues – eight hundred seats minimum – fifteen hundred seats should be the norm, not the exception. You can do it. You outshine anything to be seen on stage in Britain or the United States. No intimate gatherings any more, unless we can have who we want and charge what we like.

We need you to conserve your energy. Do bigger shows, better shows, fewer of them.

Florence visualises it in the mist of her glass.

He continues, I wonder if it is time to revisit the idea of a bill of acts, with you at the top?

I have been doing this on my own for a long time now. I don't need anyone else.

That's fine by me, if it's what you want. But it will be hard to grow if we don't make some changes.

Look at me, Mortimer. How much more growing do you think I have left to do?

He sneers at the implied suggestion. You are svelte-like, and young and beautiful. You also have a special talent, and you owe it to the world. You can become the most famous spiritualist that ever lived if you want to. Nonetheless, I think we should talk about touring with other psychics. Lesser-knowns, up-and-comings. They provide the support act – they will be inferior to you, of course – they will do it to make their own names and to learn from the best.

Florence shakes her head. She says, If we put other mediums up there, we run the risk of being undermined. They will over-reach, crack under pressure, especially in front of large audiences. At the very least they will steal my best marks from the front three rows before intermission, and then I will have to work twice as hard. We are as likely as not to get some magician's apprentice trying to make a name for himself by disproving me, like that fellow tonight.

You handled him splendidly.

I don't care for it.

As you please. No other spiritualists, then: they are your rivals, they are unreliable or they are frauds. There is not anyone we can trust enough. So be it. (Mortimer drinks from his absinthe.) You have not told me how the second encounter with your sister went?

Ha. Florence feels the absinthe filling her, tingling. Unbelievable.

Why so?

She looks at her husband over the rim of her glass, perceives something in his attitude, makes a decision. My nieces are prigs, is all. I have been waved off. She practically forbade me from trying to contact them while we are here. She said they will not be at home to me.

Preposterous. Shun you? You are the toast of the town. I'm astounded.

It is not important. Her son is a decent sort, anyway.

Did you give her the invitation after that?

Yes.

Will she come?

Who knows? I think she is lonely, I sense that from her.

Mortimer begins to feel the absinthe taking effect. It makes him bold. He ventures, I did have another thought about the act.

Florence leans her head on her hand to listen.

What if the Gault twins were to make a comeback ... ? Eighteen months in the United States, starting in the small towns and backwaters to correct any teething problems, then Canada, nine months in Europe and then Australia. Then we'll take six months off for a vacation and to perfect a new routine, followed by a second tour of just the very finest venues in the finest cities of the world, and the odd audience with royalty thrown in for good measure. In four years, maybe less, we'll all be millionaires. What do you think?

To his chagrin, Florence bursts into laughter. When she comes to herself again she says, That's it? That's the big idea?

Is it so absurd?

I'm afraid it is, Mortimer. My sister would be appalled. (She drinks more absinthe.) You should ask her at dinner, though, then I can sell tickets for people to watch that.

I was only trying to help.

You are a help, I could not do it without you (she reaches forward to tweak his chin, pouting her lips at him). And if Rosie says no, you can always go back to catching bullets and pulling doves out of your sleeves.

Mortimer Solomon-Black sulks. Well there's no need for sarcasm.

Poor old Rosie. You know, she is still cross with our mother. Florence dips her finger into her glass and sucks the end of it.

He answers, It can be hard on a child from a theatre family. You are either centre stage, a part of the act, or you are in the wings of your parents' lives.

Like my brothers were. Like my father.

My folks made me perform practically from the day I could stand up. I whistled tunes and took the cap around the saloon while they did the songs and skits.

How old?

Four? Honestly, I don't know.

I bet you were darling.

Difficult to leave it behind, though. Incredible she managed it after all those years – such success, such an ingrained way of life. She must have hated it.

She did. It was why she left, but not why she got so angry. I thought so at the time, but now . . .

Mortimer frowns. What else happened?

Rosemary broke Isabella's heart . . . and then Isabella died. I have come to realise my twin hates her even more for that.

Guilt is a sickness, it can kill you. What about you? You could have given up this game years ago, enjoyed comfort and respectability.

There is wickedness as Florence makes her answer. But I settled for you, didn't I?

Florence's first marriage was adequate in many aspects,

175

except for her husband's habit of beating her. After this experience she resisted overtures from a number of bachelors and spurned two proposals. Then it dawned on her that Mortimer Solomon-Black, her trusted business associate, was also pursuing her. He did not press the matter – or rather, pressed it lightly, indirectly, deferred his own gratification. She kept him at arm's length for several years, insisting she would never remarry, while always keeping him near at hand. Out of pity maybe, out of grace for his tortured heart and somewhat against her better judgement, the wedding came to pass, in a green haze like the one surrounding them now. How startling to discover marriage to Mortimer had an unexpected recreational quality.

In bed they bounce and bound, uninhibited, at liberty, manifestly themselves. The mattress squeaks like a wheelbarrow, the headboard bangs against the wall like a locomotive, their exclamations and moans audible to the landlady passing in the hallway.

Obaysch dozes in the afternoon sun, what muted beams there are. He lies in squalor, fat and dense, his skin shining and hot breath exhaling from his nostrils, bristly muzzle. It causes a ripple of amusement to see him yawn. A hint of personality. His teeth yellow, protruding, the enormous mouth pale and textured compared to his smooth, thick hide. Dormant fellow he is. Nonchalant. Ignores his admirers. No further action until one of his ears twitches and then is at rest. He is as broad and as grey and as motionless as a boulder. Tame, not wild. He has a wife, Adhela, who wallows in the pool. The onlookers are dismayed when she submerges for minutes at a time, gleeful when her facial features appear on the surface in another spot, and she sinks again. Bigness, solidness, laziness. Popular with the children, who like to ascribe to them human characteristics (he is taking a nap because he has had a busy morning and a large lunch; she is going under water because she is shy and having her bath).

The girls, boys and nannies lean on the railing to watch them, the hippopotamus enclosure out of their grasp, compounding the wish to be able to touch or feed one.

Rosemary and Jem have seen. Stroll on. Families and friends promenade in their finery, hats, umbrellas, on show like flamingos.

He says, Do you think it would be a notion to make photographs of zoo animals? the hippo or camel or quagga?

What do you think, Jem? What would be the virtues?

He licks his lips with thought. That they would make nice pictures. People might like to buy them for their albums.

What do you think the Zoological Society would have to say about it?

Jem considers. You would have to ask. They might want good photographs of their animals for posterity and science and such. They might want to sell prints themselves. And other people, ordinary folk, may want photographs made of their pets and livestock, horses and cattle, not just cats and dogs.

What would be the disadvantages?

Jem swallows, and does not answer.

Rosemary persists firmly, When you are in charge one day, you will need to think of ways to make Featherstone prosper. The suggestion of taking photographs of animals has some merit. Examining ideas for faults and problems to solve is an important skill, don't-you-know.

If you say so, Mama. Well, animals would be difficult subjects, wouldn't they? Making them lie still, or getting close enough, and that. Developing the plate would be tricky, too. You would need a portable darkroom, like the itinerants have. And then there is the cost of it.

She tries not to show her relief. Rosemary has been drilling

Jem with the need to consider expense and economise when possible.

He presses on. If it were affordable, you could do both. Featherstone of Piccadilly could do studio portraits and sort of itinerant photography in London. Then you would be able to do other pictures of, of anything, really. Shops, carriages, people standing outside their shops, houses – anything.

What should you do first?

Find out whether people want it . . . ?

Yes, I think that would be a good starting point.

His confidence deteriorates. Maybe not, though? Maybe people only like their *cartes de visite*. No point going to so much trouble if no one likes it.

Maybe so. And maybe tastes will change someday? and people will want to try something new? and you shall be a pioneer?

It does not sound like him, he thinks. Sounds as if it would go wrong before it started. He hangs his head, discouraged, unaware how he has pleased his mother.

In fact, she intends to tell him that it is precisely this kind of thinking which will benefit the business in the long run and ensure its continuation—

But she cannot. For the sensation has come back: a weight, a strain, a constraint. It is hurting. It causes her to sweat and struggle for breath.

Jem supports her under one arm. A gentleman on an outing, somewhat unwilling to manhandle a widow, is prompted to help by his wife (Right you are, m'dear). Together they lead Mrs Featherstone to a bench where she can compose herself until the distress has passed. Jem thanks the Samaritans, assures them he will be able to take care of her. Mother and son sit in silence.

Rosemary blames it on indigestion, feels better, expresses her enthusiasm for visiting the reptile house.

Jem grips his knees and knits his brow. He would like to see the snakes himself (serpents move infrequently, and space in the building could be used temporarily for a make-do darkroom) but decides they should take a hansom cab home instead, decides not to seek approval from his mother first in case she overrides him, which she is more than capable of doing.

Turtle soup is set before them. Jem has not eaten turtle before, has not seen the interior of the Café de l'Europe until this evening. Thus far, his most formal experience of dining out was Dolly's Chophouse in St Paul's Churchyard. And apart from in correspondence, no one ever called him James until he met his uncle.

It is a delicacy, James. Exquisite.

Jem observes Mortimer sucking a spoonful of meat and gravy, some of it sticking to his moustaches, humming with appreciation. Jem tries his. The meat is dark and chewy, reminds him of offal. It is not unpalatable, though overpriced in his private opinion.

What do you think? Come now, be honest, James.

The women also pause to hear what Jem will say.

Very tasty.

They murmur their agreement. Mortimer beams. Wait until you try the oysters, they are the food of kings.

The effect of the twins' similarity on Jem has begun to wear off. Although they sit to his left and right, facing each other like a mirror image, he can discern differences not only in their apparel (one elaborate, one modest), not only in their accents. There is something altogether contrasting, even opposite, about the sisters that is almost visible – in his mother's case beneath the eyes, in his aunt's case at the corners of hers. Two carriage wheels, weathered differently. He eats the soup fearing for his constitution, which is unused to rich foods.

Today Jem paid visits to his two older sisters, Mary and Winifred, to inform them that their famous aunt was in town, and to ask would they not like to see her? was it not an occasion for the whole family to celebrate?

Mary flummoxed him by explaining that much as she would like to, she was occupied with a string of entertaining commitments with her husband's partners and clients, and it was vital she not let them down; and no doubt Mr and Mrs Solomon-Black would be sympathetic to her plight because they were busy people themselves.

Winifred blanched at the suggestion, before explaining that she and her children had been ill of late, were not quite recovered – indeed, she felt the chills coming on once again and gave a cough – she would not want to risk her aunt and uncle's health unnecessarily.

These reasons seemed fair and frank in their own right, but taken together even Jem, ignorant in the ways of society, harboured the discomfiture of suspicion. Curious, he cannot fathom why Mary and Winifred would choose to distance themselves from such a friendly and interesting lady.

Mortimer kisses his wife on the wrist, then leans to whisper something in her ear. She sniggers.

Jem assumes this must be what all Americans are like, that the United States must be a jolly country if you are free to marry whoever wins your heart and to express your affection in public. He cannot recall meeting an English couple like them – concludes he would be most satisfied with a wife who is kind and wise and jovial like his aunt.

Mortimer is telling Jem about a demonstration he saw the Gault sisters give when he was a young man, younger than Jem is now, before he had the privilege of making Florence's acquaintance. Rosemary politely listens as though the story relates to someone else entirely.

It was at the Walnut in Philadelphia, Pennsylvania. Have you heard of it, James? It is a fine theatre – we have fine theatres in Manhattan too, of course, but the Walnut is historic. I was just beginning to establish a reputation as an illusionist. I come from a family of variety singers and comedians, knew how to work hard and rough it with a volatile crowd but, seriously, I have an inferior singing voice, and telling jokes is not my forte. Conjuring, however, can be practised and perfected and has all the finesse and excitement of professional gambling, except you are not playing for money, it is pride which is at stake: the audience's pride that they are intelligent, observant people who cannot be fooled; your pride as a performer that you can deceive and entertain them. An impresario on the circuit, a man I respected, advised me to go see the Gault twins from England who were in Philadelphia at the time doing the best stage magic he had laid eyes on, packing houses, he said. Part of the job of an entertainer is to monitor the competition – what has he got in his act that you should have in yours? how can you steal it from him and make it better? I went along just to see what the fuss was about. There they were as alike as two people can be. Feminine but still authoritative, in control. I can even remember what they were wearing. Very beautiful, very strange to see and hear. All manner of peculiar occurrences – furniture tipping over right there in front of you, people in the balcony complaining of being touched by invisible hands. For me, though, it was the amount of detail, the specifics, which were incredible to hear, the reactions extraordinary to behold. The number of people moved to tears, ladies weeping, and even uptight old men sniffing into their handkerchiefs. When a medium picks you out of a crowd, when she accurately describes someone you have loved dearly and lost, when she tells you about yourself using words and phrases only you would recognise, well . . . (Mortimer lets his point trail away.) I don't know what that fellow was talking about because I have been to literally hundreds of shows, seen thousands of performers, and that was definitely not regular stage magic. That was something entirely *other*. James, there are two obstacles which prevent spiritualism from becoming acceptable to society. The first is the amount of fakers. If they are hearing voices at all, which is questionable, it is due to a disturbed mind and not discarnate spirits. While they persist in muddying the reputation of spiritualism, real mediums will never gain the respect they deserve. Second, this era is uncomfortable with a movement where the individual emotional experience is so pervasive – not to mention the consequences for science and religion as we understand them in the modern world. Society is far from ready to embrace spiritualism. But I don't worry. Revolutions happen. And when someone comes along with a gift, like your Aunt Florence here, it is incumbent upon all of us to help her do what she was put on the earth to do.

Jem observes Florence Solomon-Black squeezing her husband's hand, her face shining with admiration. Jem observes Rosemary Featherstone adjusting the napkin on her lap as though she did not hear all of it, as though weary – bored, even.

If this is the opportune moment for Mortimer to broach with his sister-in-law a business proposition – to make the argument for her to join them on a world tour that would make her wealthy and independent, bring guidance and relief to the bereaved and hapless, and for a great number more, enjoyment and entertainment – Mortimer does not take it but lets his chance slide quietly by.

Jem has thought of some questions to ask about photography in his aunt and uncle's homeland. The soup bowls are replaced by a platter of oysters.

Two rooms in different London boroughs. Two women – at a casual glance the same woman. Alone.

The first, bothered by an old problem that makes her tut and flap her hands to herself.

The second has busy thoughts, mundane trivialities about the following day, when she discerns a coaxing voice, male, whispering humane words. She sighs on hearing it. Flinches.

The first, her twin, stands in a room with her arms open, takes deep breaths, looks within, appeals to the darkness for answers.

The second hears his benevolence and love. He emerges. Wants to converse. He is thankful for his life, reluctant to let go, to depart. She tells him, You must.

The first banishes her doubt, her previous disappointments, the last traces of envy rubbed away – will come to this as new, refreshed and yes, receptive this time, feels her heart beat lower, and the distant echoes of the ages that are beyond her touch draw near.

The other: You were always so thoughtful and considerate; you shall do me this one last kindness and go. Do go. Please go.

While the first is saying: Come, come. I urge you. Alight. Enlighten me. Show me.

He is sad. The other replies, I am sad too, but we will soon see each other again, and I have such a lot to do until then. Really now, this is the last time, the very last.

The lady's palms are moist from effort, she knows her own weakness, despair saps her conviction. Why not? Why always this way? Why do you never come when I ask? It is the unfairness of it – the unfairness!

The lady's familiar pressure in her chest. Worse. It hurts her arm. Can you guess what I am going to do? I am going to see a doctor. That's right. You know how I abhor doctors. He recedes for the last time, she hopes. It has become too much like being tested. She is needed, has work to do.

The first knows there is only emptiness here. Here and

everywhere, and each and every time. True silence. Ordinary silence. It has never worked for her. Not once.

Highgate Cemetery, draped with vegetation, bitten with early frost, cloaked with grief. The stone angels cower and cry over their charges, the obelisks strike heavenwards, the imperial mausoleums stand firm with the strength of centuries marking the entrances to eternity. A hewn grey scene of gothic ornament. A shroud of fog disguising and revealing. Symbols clamour to be understood and indelible writings to honour, to make sense of loss, to endure. Steps and footpaths and shrubs and trees. Last destination, a home for the deceased, and a refuge for smaller lives, for foxes, birds, creepy-crawlies, flowers waiting to grow in the spring. Names and dates carved upon headstones, sarcophagi and the hearts of mourners. Cold. Souls flitting and compressed and dispersed. Thoroughfares for the dead and pilgrimage for the living. Mineral and organic matters coalesce. All of its jaggedness, hallowedness, drama and transition. Sanctuary, but not from oneself.

Here rests Isabella Gault.

By it, one of her daughters – a lady in a hat, coat and gloves. Which twin?

It does not matter, for the other arrives presently.

Each brings a tussie-mussie – one of harebells and one of heartsease (subtle blue, bold purple, presumptuous yellow) – and the tokens are placed on their mother's grave. Fallen leaves rotting and crumbling underfoot. The women link arms as they walk.

Will this be the last time we see each other? It is Florence who asks. Their voices make mist.

No. There will be others.

I thought it might be the last.

Because Amos is gone, and spouses of a certain age follow suit? Not I. Nor you, if you were in my shoes.

Why did you marry him, Rosie? It is one of life's puzzles.

There you go again, divining a mystery where there is none. I liked him for being unassuming and sensitive. I married him because he asked me so sweetly, and because I knew he would never let me down. And he never did.

Bullseye, as always. Not like the mess I made first time around. I have never got anything quite so wrong as I did that day—

Hush. None of it was your fault.

Florence ruffled: You warned me about him. You said he was selfish and unpredictable, you said he was trouble.

Rosemary gives her sister a severe glare. It was not your fault, it was his.

Still, I ought not to have married him in the first place.

You did your best. And what does it matter now? Mortimer is not like that.

No.

He cares for you.

Yes, he does.

You do dishonour to him and to yourself by fretting over what cannot be undone.

What else do you think of him?

Well. He is garrulous. He is adventurous. He is dashing.

Admit it, the age difference shocked you.

Rosemary raises her eyebrows. The phantom of scandal is always nearby when you are around, Flossie. I cease to be shocked, for I do not have many shocks left.

Stop talking like that. Remember we are the same age, you and I.

Au contraire: you have the distinction of being the older sister.

Florence smirks at this, pulls closer to her twin.

I hurt you, didn't I? Rosemary drops the question like a pebble into a pond.

I don't know what you mean.

You do. You never let on because you were protecting Mama, carrying on without me. All the same, I put myself first, and you felt I had betrayed you.

Florence is impassive. I was surprised. It was a change. And it was very long ago.

Nonetheless, I want to make amends, for both our sakes. I want you to have the post-mortem photograph. Truly. Flossie, I am giving it to you.

No thank you, I have no need for it. You were right in the first place, I will do without and be content.

Please take it. It will be evidence. It could be good publicity.

Florence sighs. On consideration, it is of limited use to me. It does not quite look authentic enough. I would be ridiculed. I choose my battles, and have done very well so far. Your offer is generous, but I decline it.

Then, how may I serve you?

Florence can see her sister is in earnest. Very well. I shall forgive you for leaving to make a life of your own – if you will forgive our mother for whatever wrongs you continue to blame her for. And that is the last favour I am going to ask of you.

For once, Rosemary is surprised by her twin. I have.

Good. Then there is nothing left for any of us to feel pained by.

A blackbird hides among the naked twigs of a tree, his feathers bristling, the vivid orange of his beak and eye contrasting with the sobriety of his surroundings.

Florence announces, We are setting off for the West Country tomorrow.

Rosemary answers, Give one of your *cartes* to Jem before you leave, will you? He would enjoy that.

I shall write a message on it for him.

Flossie, do you remember Our Secret?

186

Oh— She hangs her head and smiles. Yes—

Rosemary strips off one glove, holds up her hand in the crisp air.

Florence is cautious – is frightened it will not work, is frightened that it might. She takes off her own glove and touches her fingertips – little, ring, middle, index, thumb – to her twin's.

They can see Isabella binding the wrist of one of their brothers after an accident at the factory; can see their father carving a cockerel in wood; can see the outline of the church at the top of the hill at sunset and themselves eating gooseberries, juice running down their chins. They are in the halls and parlours and clubs and theatres and filled rooms once more. Isabella is stepping out to introduce them. They are on the steamship, catching their first sight of America on the horizon, in their dressing room which smells strongly of mildew, befuddling the invited sceptics from an empirical science society and drinking coffee in pink cups—

Rosemary can see Flossie shopping for hats to match a chequered dress; can see her reading the *Illustrated Lady's Companion* in a train compartment; see her removing her make-up at the end of the night. She is choosing wallpaper and throwing her wedding ring off a bridge and opening a letter from a desperate young woman and singing along with a group of friends around a piano and eating the flesh of a pomegranate with a silver spoon and making a donation to a children's charity and having a sleepless night in the height of summer and listening to a Mozart horn concerto and walking through New York with the man she will eventually marry—

Florence can see Rosie admiring Amos's first portrait taken at the new shop, realising she is pregnant again and crying, opening a present of lace from her daughter Winifred, having cramp in her left foot, decorating a Christmas tree with her four children, being persuaded to join her daughter Mary and her soon-to-be son-in-law in a boat on the Serpentine. She is saying a prayer for her twin on their birthday and stepping off an omnibus in the snow and meeting a solicitor to make a will and consoling Amos when Robert died and dancing a polka with Jem and asking the price of some crockery in Brighton and pruning roses and weighing tea and tying a key on a ribbon for safe-keeping and—

This is how the years dividing them shrink away, how their empathy is elevated.

It does not seem fair. You wanted it, I didn't. If it had been possible to swap . . .

But we could not, which is probably for the best.

Their arms linked, they draw closer to each other against the cold and walk further on.

Unknown

For Pleasure, 1916

Ivy clings to Arnault. Not Arnault Lodge or Arnault House, just Arnault, according to the plaque. Occasionally in conversation, Old Arnault. And once, Monsieur Arnault, but thankfully that did not stick. The house has been so named since before Cynthia Everard's childhood summers, and is now hers. Arnault has seen Cynthia at her happiest. Seen her leaving wet footprints across the floor after a dip in the Lagoon (not really a lagoon), has seen the owl pellets and snails and pine cones and wild flowers collected and displayed on this very table for – for whatever purpose was in her mind on that particular day. Seen Cynthia in new hats. Heard her recite poetry, complain of stomach ache, lie about how she lost five bob she was given as a present, cry when she was stung by a wasp. Is the Cynthia Everard of today recognisable as the same girl?

Cynthia the intellectual. Cynthia the drab academic.

189

Cynthia Everard, editor of Professor Norman Creegan's *Selected Writings* (a work in progress) and, if his son Charles has his way, Creegan's biographer. The son argues that no one else living understands his father's works better than she does. She agrees. And that nobody within his professional sphere was as liked by him as Cynthia. Entirely probable. And if she does not consent to do it, there will never be a definitive biography. On this Cynthia is noncommittal, but suspects it to be the truth.

Let me work on his legacy first, Charles, she said, postponing the day when she will have to refuse, ensuring for the present she has access to her mentor's essays lecture notes letters scribbles. The son cannot be accused of withholding. No. She is grateful for that. But the message about not commencing the biography has not been listened to, and she must have in her kitchen every paper and publication Professor Creegan ever owned in his eighty-eight years of life. Piles of it. Towers of it. Work and life, life and work mixed together. By teasing out the components of one, she will necessarily tease out the components of the other. It is a tactic and it may be working for Cynthia finds herself drawn into travel journals, lists, theatre programmes, appointment diaries, correspondence with his mistress; even the guides to angling and rambling hold some fascination because she only saw him indoors at the college – imagine the old man with a fishing rod or a walking stick! There was more to him then than mere philosophy, and that alone would fill twenty volumes. But why must he cram every space with his ideas? Why whole paragraphs written in the margins of a letter from the bank? Why whole synopses written across the sky in *Pleasant Highland Walks: A Guide for the Adventurous Gentleman*? Why is she starting to see coded notations in his diaries which suggest he was considering amending, if not reversing, one of his most renowned theories? The tantalising

190

glimpse of an unpublished essay developed over not less than nine years – she is convinced she has found four and a half pages of it with more surely to be discovered.

Whether or not she does the biography, the selected writings must take precedence. The labour, then, of deciphering a life's work, of separating what should be included from what should be left out, of deciding somehow upon a reading order, of hundreds of annotations to write.

Cynthia. Unmarried. Badly dressed. Her skirt crumpled and her silk blouse faded. Her crocheted shawl. Fair-haired (it is tied back with a scrap of fabric). Long neck, long limbs. Heavy shoes – hideous. Yet she bothers to wear rose lipstick, a gold pendant, a sapphire ring. Perhaps the child Cynthia is not so far away. Here she is, scruffy and oblivious.

What boxes and what files. What mess. It will take weeks longer than she allowed for it – and she is not displeased. The responsibility is worthy of her. The work is to her liking. Today is one of the good days, and she must make the most of these. She is invigorated. She has the edge from feelings of superiority, an impatience to succeed, her thoughts are sharp. Creegan's materials bestow their favours, disclose their content, drop their nuances before her like dogs fetching sticks. She is making progress. Yesterday is yesterday, it has gone. Today, and a clutch of similar days – though numerically fewer than the ones of slog, tedium, cross-referencing, indexing, weighing, disregarding – are the hours of inspiration which imbue a project with permanent light. It shall be a principal work. Students will have this open on their desks for hundreds of years to come. Arnault is the scene for this event. Reading matter spreads like the petals of a flower with Cynthia at the centre – on the kitchen floor and dresser and draining board. Food is less important than work. Comfort is less important than food.

If this forward motion continues, she will almost lament the arrival of Alec Worsham. Dear Alec . . . but she cannot pause long for him when the work is flowing. You will have the others to entertain you if I am busy.

As though summoned by the thought, one of them inter-rupts her now but she is only passing through and does not bother to speak. Gwen. Cynthia does not lift her eyes from the pages until Gwen is on her way out again, striding elastically, her boyish form illuminated through her cotton dress by the sun, her head covered with a summer hat, the cloth bag she is never seen without slung across her body as though she is going fruit-picking. Whatever foolishness Gwen is embarking upon this morning, Cynthia has no time for it and reasserts her concentration.

Gwen steps into the garden and breathes the luxurious air. It is filled with pollen and makes her sneeze, *choo*. She grips the brim of her hat to prevent it from falling off, checks that no one saw. No one did.

A day for love. No, for seduction, why deny it? why be afraid of naming it truthfully? Her conquest does not know it yet, does not know today is the beginning of their affair. They will induct one another into the mysteries of heart and flesh. She is giving him permission to court her as of *now*. He said, pointedly, he would be alone near the pond so she goes there in a hurry, pauses – ought not to seem eager or uncouth. A lady, how does a lady behave? A lady would not hike to her beau and appear to him perspiring and out of breath. Gwen will walk serenely. Beautifully. It will be the most elegant of gaits. A sway of the hips, which will wake within him ecstasies of passion. Unrealised passion. Hitherto unknown passion. Layers and layers of passion.

Oh, Venus, we are bringing you the gift of ourselves.

Of course – and here Gwen flattens some of the jumble in her head like a drawer of knickers – he may already have some acquaintance with the mechanics of male and female: being a man and ten years older than she it would be unusual if he had not. Gwen has reconciled with this. It is a relief, a man ought to have more experience than a woman. Ten years may sound long, but (she does a calculation) in five years, four really, when she has reached 20 he will still only be 30. When she comes of age he will be but 31. Who can call that gap significant? This thought pleases her. And – building on her theme – do not people say, interminably, how mature Gwen is for her age? She will soon catch him up. Her logic fires her enthusiasm.

She trips along the path, pushing aside low-hanging boughs fat with foliage until the trees thin and a space opens, revealing the pond (Cynthia has a childish name for it). It is shaded by bending and swaying perennials that repeat upside down in the pool, hidden from view to one side by coppice and obscured by a woodland incline to the other, away from local thoroughfares. The water probably deep. It is secluded and has drunk centuries of rain. It is made of the fresh greens and earth browns of nature's England, and its sounds are the staccato chiffchaffs and excitable wrens, the hum of damselflies and the plop of invisible fish kicking the surface with their tails. Leaves answer with hushed applause.

Gwen sees him. Visualises her appearance in this place like the entrance of Titania.

Laurence Fern is painting the scene with intensity, like sickness, holding a stub of cigarette in his mouth. He attacks the canvas with his brush and palette knife, works quickly, the strokes going on in thick globules, raises his glance briefly to confirm some detail and attacks again. It is the stippling of the Impressionists, but with less regard for form and an arbitrary use of colour. 'Expressive'. He works with speed and can make a picture in a day or two.

Gwen had never seen anything like it until he showed her. At first she thought it infantile, but having it explained to her so richly, so fiercely, has come to the conclusion that Laurence might – just *might* – be a genius. He does not look like a genius, to be sure, if geniuses are hoary, wrinkled men grown pale with obsession, grown withered with deep thought. Virility usually precludes talent; attractiveness is the compensation of a mediocre mind. Yet here is Laurence, with creativity and the physique of a boxer, a man who combines artistic sensibility with latent brute force. That Laurence is unaware of his attributes makes him more charming. That he paints with personal disregard, that he gives his art to the world selflessly . . . rapture.

He does not look like a conscientious objector either (the first and only one she has knowingly met). Gwen had preconceived ideas of how they ought to look: pallid little boys, trembling weaklings. Not this. Not a specimen like him. It had not been easy to accept but accept it she did, although she still does not fully understand it.

It definitely has something to do with some men being too good to fight in wars (she likes the sound of that, even if she cannot make up her mind what it means). Perhaps, when you are touched by enlightenment, you have to take a contrary and lonely road. It is the lot of the tragically gifted, and all part of Laurence Fern's mystery. And would it not make – she thinks to herself as she steps down to the edge and nearly falls in – would it not make their journey together, as two halves of the same being, one of mutual discovery and therefore the sweeter for it? As long as Gwen is able to know him and his thoughts in the end, however complex they are, however long it takes, every one.

Good morning, Laurence.

Miss Watts.

Miss Watts? I think it is time for you to call me Gwen, like everyone else.

Laurence does not reply.

I often come to this spot to read my book. You don't mind, do you? (This is not exactly true, Gwen has never read here before but resolves to do so frequently from now on.) It's *Emma* by Jane Austen. (This is important to say aloud, so she does.)

She takes his silence for consent. Laurence works on mutely.

Can I see it please, even though it is not finished?

If you like.

She steps behind and announces, It is your best, Laurence, your very best. Really it is.

I am most dissatisfied. It is average. It is repetitive, I have done it all before. I have not the inspiration today.

Oh but you do. I love it.

Laurence Fern makes an expression which Gwen interprets as pleased embarrassment. He paints on.

Gwen finds a seat where she can watch. She takes off her hat so the sunshine can play on her hair, and tries to find her book absorbing. Indeed, Austen usually moves her and induces sighs of admiration, but today she reads it barely at all, only the same lines over and over, never coming to the end of a paragraph or needing to turn the page because there is some sound or movement to take her interest, some stone digging into her rear that makes her rearrange. The game of predicting when Laurence will speak next is as distracting as thinking of things to say which he might find fascinating or witty.

She pipes up, You know, people tell me that I am the best at drawing in my class.

He does not seem to hear. No matter. She is certain they will have plenty to talk about when they have found the words. She must be patient with him whenever he is working, and while their relationship is new and tender. She shall be no shrew.

The heat is overpowering. She leans back on her elbows, for thinking can be work. She tilts her face to the sun.

Like a daisy, I am a daisy basking in the warmth of the sun.

Gwen reminisces about herself as a child pretending to be a bride. That is too *bourgeois* for us, she now concludes; I will simply live with Laurence as his mistress and there will be a terrific scandal.

She raises herself, shields her eyes. Is there anything you would like? I can go back and fetch it for you.

Not right now.

She frowns.

He wipes his hands on a rag, screws it up, then takes a new cigarette out of a silver case and mutters, It is not working, I am going to have to – I don't know, maybe try to salvage it, maybe abandon it.

Gwen sits up, worried. It isn't my fault, is it?

Why should it be?

No reason. (She senses this as an opportunity to show her worth.) Don't abandon it, that would be dreadful. Perhaps just take a break? do something else this afternoon? have some fun and try again tomorrow. It's like when you're stuck on an algebra problem: best to leave it for a while, and then when you come back to it, you have it figured out.

Laurence sticks out his chin as though impertinence will shame the picture into shape. You could be right there.

You have been working non-stop. There ought to be a balance.

Ought to be, but there isn't. Who knows how long the weather will hold? If the light is different tomorrow – you have heard the phrase striking while the iron is hot, Miss Watts?

Gwen has heard it. It is a sign of their growing intimacy that she empathises with his frustration. To leave a painting incomplete would be torture for him. He must finish it.

He adds, Anyway, I have to meet Sinclair from the train station tomorrow.

Who?

196

Sinclair.

Yes, she remembers him now. Laurence has already mentioned it. Another guest at Arnault; another conchie that Cynthia is giving asylum to; another artist, perchance. I could go? She offers without thinking.

Could you?

Gwen would like nothing better than to do a favour for him, but she shrugs as though she does not care.

I would appreciate it. In fact, that would make it easier. Thanks. He smiles a small, odd, delicious smile like a sip of wine.

But you must do a good turn for me and call me Gwen. No more Miss Watts, it is too fusty. Sinclair should call me Gwen, too. We are all friends here, aren't we?

Yes, I suppose we are. Laurence begins to dismantle his equipment. At Gwen's insistence he gives her the easel to carry back.

Gwen runs. She runs fast. She is good at running, can outrun most boys her own age. She runs from the station, avoiding pedestrians, crosses a road and down the lane. She runs past the Cross Keys and St Peter's Church – hair, hat and skirt streaming behind her as if she is being chased by wolves, bag swinging at her side. Her blood rushes, she rushes – the exertion like a lashing for some transgression or a reward for the endurance of some trial. It feels good to expend the tension, the energy, to be doing this instead of thinking. She runs away from the image. Runs the short cut to Arnault, will get there first. Knows she will, without having tried it before. The house is in sight.

Within Arnault, Cynthia is bowed over the table. She acknowledges it is not the way it was yesterday. What had seemed clear is now muddy. What had seemed obvious is now uncertain. And the thoughts, the unwelcome thoughts, have

197

come back. The wavering between existence and nothing. The mental vertigo. Whirling. Dizziness. When life and silence smear into one. It makes her irritable.

The hefty thump of approaching feet up the path – it is Gwen.

What are you doing here? I thought you went to the station to meet Laurence's friend.

I did.

Then where is he?

Gwen pants for breath.

Did something happen? Was the train cancelled?

There is something you should know about Sinclair . . . he's a woman.

Cynthia opens her mouth, partially. I can't help that.

Gwen leans against the wall, feeling her exhaustion – and because this is a disaster and one makes such a pose during disasters.

You didn't just leave her there . . . ?

Gwen rolls her head over one shoulder, then another. She'll be all right, she'll find a taxi.

She thinks someone's going to meet her.

Gwen has an answer for this, but knows it is unbecoming, so she whispers it to herself: Tough toads.

Cynthia has never known the agony or elation or perils of love, cares only for her studies and was to be pitied until this morning . . . now Gwen envies Cynthia her ignorance, her frumpiness, her dreary life isolated from the politics and pitfalls of human relations. Cynthia has never had a rival, and if she did, would faint at a rival like Sinclair.

Gwen has spent her life willing her hair to grow into luscious locks, has fought battles with her mother over it, thought it a badge of femininity. Her hair is longer than most but insipid, she is still waiting for the swishing tresses of her imagination. It would have been hurtful to find a woman who was Laurence's friend and had such a gloriously long curtain of hair, but Sinclair is worse than that; for she is a crop-head. The first feature which struck Gwen about Sinclair as she stepped off the train carriage and on to the platform was her short, androgynous haircut, and that she wears it with the unmistakable air of sex. The woman is divine, simply too divine, and predatory. The clip of her heels, the insolence of her red lips, her nipped-in waist. Detestable. The vacant face, oh how empty of serious thought. Her nose and forehead powdered, wearing dark blue as though it were autumn, not the height of summer. Gruesome. A piece of heavy luggage and a man in uniform assisting her with it gave Gwen the opportunity to abandon this monstrosity unobserved – if it cannot make its own way to the house, then what exactly is its purpose?

Gwen wants Cynthia to hate Sinclair as much as she does, for them to be allies, but already Cynthia has lost interest and gone back to her work. Her drudgery.

What of Laurence? He cannot mean to like this interloper, this miscreant? Gwen shoves away the thought. No, he will certainly see through it – the tailoring, the cosmetics, the reek of fragrance – it shall not impress him, it shall not penetrate. He will find it for what it is: laboured, common, obvious. Laurence is a man of substance, his taste is more refined, his mind on higher matters. Gwen ought not to be afraid of Sinclair; Gwen can still win.

She sniffs her fingers. They have the smells of bacon fat and pencil sharpenings on them, have cuts healing, the nails and cuticles bitten down. Sinclair's will be graceful, as pale and even as milk, have buffed nails with tinted polish, the scent and slipperiness of lotion. Even Gwen realises, through her agitation, that Laurence may prefer those pampered hands on him to her own. Can it be that bad?

Laurence has returned to Arnault to meet Sinclair; Gwen realises he may be annoyed at her for breaking her promise.

He is not annoyed, though, because he has forgotten it, has expunged the gesture from his memory – does not notice Gwen hiding in the parlour and peeking out of the window, notices instead the unflustered outline of Sinclair paying the cab driver. He goes to her with a secretive smile and, here is perhaps the worst, kisses her full on the mouth – greedy kiss, public kiss – and Sinclair is almost bent in half backwards from the pressure of it, then rebukes him with a tap. To apologise – flippantly, ironically – he opens his cigarette case and offers it to Sinclair (he has never offered it to Gwen before), lights one for her. Sinclair smokes it smugly.

This is terrible.

Gwen slides to the floor in a heap, for there is nowhere on the ample furniture to rest a spirit as battered as hers. Armchairs are too good for her. She must feel the woe and discomfort in her whole body, even in her knees. She must assume the position of melancholy. She is suffering, her heart is in shreds. Laurence Fern, behold your greatest work.

Is she overreacting?

Gwen carries a basket of eggs from Mr Bolingbroke's back to Arnault (all her eggs in one basket; if she drops it, it will be some sort of poetic warning).

Perhaps it can be explained. Perhaps Sinclair has a hold over Laurence that he resents, for Gwen detected some contrivance on his part. A stiffness. A definite strain. Indifference, even. Or is he playing a game with Gwen's affections by testing her fidelity, knew somehow that she was watching? Will she be unreasonable? Possessive? Will she give in to her tantrum? Will she show her disgust at the trespasser, at her shoddy treatment, at the injustice of it? No, that is not Gwen.

Be as carefree as he is, is the key. She will twitch lightly on the line for fear of its breaking. Actually, she should behave no differently from the way she did before Sinclair got here; he said himself they were all friends. It is Sinclair who will have to fit in. She does not know their ways, their rituals, has missed days of conversation and shared experiences. Gwen has got a head start, and shall simply act as if nothing has changed. (What a relief.)

Laurence has picked some tomatoes from the vines and put them in a pottery dish to paint as a still life. Some of them are green, while others are bright red and beginning to split.

Men like to be taken care of, therefore Gwen has offered to make omelettes for lunch. She makes splendid omelettes, fluffy, golden on the outside, runny in the middle.

Laurence, what would you like me to put in your omelette?

I don't really mind.

Shall I give you some choices? You can have potatoes and cabbage from last night, or salad onions or ham, or have it plain. Unfortunately we don't have any mushrooms, but I can go out and buy some if you want them desperately. I do like mushrooms myself. Eating them makes me feel quite pagan— Gwen laughs at her own imagery and flicks her hair, which has become a trophy once again (it took simply ages to grow). I suppose one could put whatever one wanted into an omelette, pickles or broad beans. What about jam? We could invent the world's first sweet omelette, wouldn't that be exciting?

Whatever the others say will do for me.

Gwen did not intend to ask each person staying at Arnault what they wanted in their omelettes, only Laurence, otherwise she will be making four separate dishes.

Laurence takes out his cigarette case and slots one between his lips.

I should like to – have one. (Gwen prevents the words 'try one' from coming out.)

I didn't know you smoked.

Occasionally. Mummy doesn't know.

Laurence appears to like this admission, extends them towards her. She fumbles, then holds one up between two fingers as she has seen other people doing, her wrist open. When Laurence clicks his lighter she puts the fag in her mouth and enjoys the seconds of close proximity with him while the flame takes. He comes nearer than the action necessitates and this, or the concoction of tobacco, makes her warm, makes her tingle. She drags a little, swallows the urge to cough and remembers to smile in thanks. If he watches for signs of unfamiliarity she does not betray any. Quite ordinary.

She resumes, I hate to be the one to tell you, but you are working much too hard. Isn't this your third picture this week? You will wear yourself out.

He drops a brush into a cup of several, clatters them around, subtracts another, inspects the bristles, applies it.

Gwen admires the painting. Oh but it is rather good, so edible-looking, so round and ripe. How I should like to gorge myself on your tomatoes, Laurence, and consign the real ones to the rubbish. I bet yours taste delicious. (Gwen paces absently, taking a puff or two.) I do worry about you. Do you understand? I think you do – what it is like to worry about the welfare of a friend, someone you care for and think highly of. It is human nature to have sympathy for one's fellows. Our sympathy sets us apart from the animals. Come to think of it . . . we once had a small dog which was quite good at reading emotions. If you were crying, or even if you weren't, if you were just sad about something and keeping it to yourself, he would scamper in and put his head in your lap as though he was trying to speak. Isn't that funny? He ran away, of course. (Gwen compares the painting to the subject and sucks some more on her smoke, finds it has grown easier, tastier.) I declare you work harder than Cynthia, and that is saying something. She rather neglects herself. Mummy says

Cynthia will never marry. She looks so ghastly all the time. For what, precisely? Some crusty old university scholar who no one has heard of and who is now dead. At least you are sharing of yourself through your art. You are reaching out. I think it's noble. But it can't be all work, can it? You ought to enjoy yourself sometimes. Part of me thinks I should do you a kindness and cook these tomatoes so you can't paint them any more—

And Gwen has been pacing the room while she speaks—

Emboldened by the success of the cigarette and its stimulating effects, she playfully lifts one of the fruits from the bowl.

What the hell are you doing?

Gwen stops at the voice, at the venom in it.

Put it back. Now.

She does so, wounded, mortified.

I am trying to finish this, will you leave me alone?

That would have been bad enough, but as she goes she hears him mumble behind her—

Fucking pest.

Gwen finishes the rest of her cigarette outside, drawing some comfort from it. Indeed, they are perfectly habit-forming. She is in full view of Cynthia in the kitchen who is standing, reading, separating one folio from another. But if Cynthia sees, she does not rebuke her.

You are an oddment, Cynthia Everard, Gwen murmurs to the vision through the grey windows and interior gloom. I wonder whether it would occur to you to spill the beans to Mummy about anything here? You must miss out on so much. Poor Bluestocking.

Sinclair materialises at the other side of Arnault, heads in the opposite direction away from Gwen and towards town. She minces down the path, does not shut the gate after her.

Gwen narrows her eyes.

*

203

As it happens, Cynthia has *not* paid any attention to Gwen. She has shooting pains down the back of her neck and the start of a headache. She berates herself because she cannot spare a day lying on her bed with the curtains closed and a moist cloth over her eyes. It has gone wrong wrong wrong.

This is how it was when she was an undergraduate. The despair of knowing – literally – nothing. Of feeling that her presence is subversive, that her calling is a nonsense, that she must be grateful for her place. Fed up of being beaten by concepts that are bigger and cleverer than she is, let alone by small revolting men with flaccid penises. If only it were a case of learning it the way one learns the date of the Battle of Waterloo or the lines of a sonnet. Why must one's ineptness be laid bare? Why must one's limitations be exposed? And what exactly does one, *Cynthia*, want?

Cynthia slams a book on top of another.

She might as well rearrange and tidy the work of a mind better than her own, consolidate it to ensure its survival, and that can be her contribution, not an inconsiderable one – and then write a biography which will sell in reasonable quantities. If what she wants is universal acceptance in her own right, she shall never get it.

Gwen's straggly shadow appears in the doorway.

Are you actually going to help me at all? Cynthia is referring to the original intention of Gwen's stay, to assist her at least some of the time with her research.

What do you want me to do?

A space is cleared and Cynthia puts two unopened boxes in front of her.

Put these in date order. Separate out publications from private writing. If you find any loose pages, match them with the documents they belong to and make a note of anything which is incomplete or missing.

Gwen finds they are almost entirely loose pages, some of them unnumbered or constituting the middle of a longer paper which could belong to more than one source. The handwriting is appalling, and all of it is *very* boring. Nonetheless, she makes an effort because Cynthia has been a good sport, has given Gwen the liberty to do as she pleases until now.

Cynthia is writing, underlining a word, marking a paragraph with an asterisk, clipping corners together. Is tired. They work this way for over an hour and a half.

Gwen finds in one of her boxes the dead man's scrapbook (all sorts in here). She turns through it looking for fragments of letters among the miscellany. She wants to ask Cynthia, who is ancient and must be able to remember, whether everyone in the previous century was as po-faced as the trollop on this calling card?

By the time she comes to the end of the album she has lost interest, instead makes the announcement which will rattle even Cynthia's poise: I fear I have fallen in love with Laurence Fern.

Who hasn't?

Gwen is quietly scandalised. What makes you say so, Cynthia?

Everyone falls in love with Laurence; he requires it of them.

She states it. Detached. Matter-of-fact. Gwen grips the side of her own face as if she has been struck and exclaims, How savage you are! Just because you have given up on love, why spoil it for the rest of us? You are such a baggage.

Running off to cry in private seems like the appropriate gesture to go with this speech, so Gwen does.

Sinclair reclines in the shade. She is as glamorous as the film star on the cover of her magazine, which she prefers to the newspaper (folded, ignored) and its reports of war. It is, if possible, hotter today than yesterday, but the heat does not affect Sinclair like other people; she does not shine, she does not burn. Her nerveless face is without expression. Her body is still and enveloped by a printed silk kimono. Her movements – a yawn – when they do happen are slow, as though she is on display. If she is surprised to find herself no longer alone, she hides it with perfect nonchalance.

It's you.

I brought you some cider. Gwen balances the two glasses on a tray, lowers it like a servant so Sinclair can take one and place it on the table beside her.

How thoughtful.

May I join you?

Sinclair flexes one eyebrow but replies, Of course you may.

Gwen sits, does not remove her bag, rests it on her lap. She pats it because her large notebook is inside (plain pages, with a useful line guide made of card to insert between them). She intended to take notes; now fears this may inhibit their conversation, it being the first on their own. Gwen has come to make a scientific study of Sinclair, to find out:

i   *Whether S is romantically involved with L.*

ii   *Whether S would like to be romantically involved with L.*

iii *What S's Christian name is & why she goes by just her surname.*

iv   *What S's weaknesses are & how to use them against her.*

v   *Whether S has any redeeming features whatsoever.*

It is harsh but necessary. The list had only been four items last night, but this morning Gwen added a fifth to show anyone, in the future, who might find it by accident and think badly of her, that she really is (or rather was) a very good person. On paper at least, Sinclair has the benefit of the doubt. Sinclair has withdrawn into her magazine, and Gwen struggles with how to begin gleaning the required information. Neither speaks, and Gwen boils inside—This is terribly rude of you, especially when I have brought you some cider and come over to make friends. Well, not to make friends, but you aren't to know that, you should be being nice to me.

Sinclair turns a page and rests a single finger on her cheek.

This is too much for Gwen – how false! She is surely pretending to read it, is probably only looking at the pictures. The longer their mutual silence endures, the more awkward it will be to break. Gwen dives in: I thought it would be nice to get to know each other. Us girls have to stick together. You don't know anyone, apart from Laurence Fern, of course . . . you don't know us, Cynthia and me, or the local area. I thought I could help out, answer any questions you may have. Do you have any questions?

Sinclair genuinely appears to give it some thought, then shakes her head.

Plus, I don't know anything about you, where you are from? your background?

There is not much to tell. I am originally from Oxfordshire, and was glad to leave it. I live in London. I am what you can see.

Gwen tilts her head interestedly. Oxfordshire. London. Remarkable. What do you do there?

Do . . . ?

Gwen can almost hear Mummy's reproaches, and backtracks. Some people are volunteering, given the state of current affairs, and some people have plans for after the war, and whatnot. I wondered if you were like that, if you had any plans, or hobbies?

Sinclair smirks. I let biology take its course. I plan to be looked after when I am married, and to get my own way quite as often as I get it now. When does the charlady come?

Oh (a question). Tuesday, Friday and Saturday. Her name is Agnes Rumford, but you must call her Mrs Rumford, Cynthia is quite particular about that, because she is ancient and has taken care of Arnault simply for ever.

I have some clothes I need her to press for me.

Mrs Rumford is excellent at ironing; makes the straightest, sharpest creases you have ever seen.

I will settle for her getting rid of the squiggling creases I don't wish to see.

Gwen's brain jars and grinds, then she realises a corner of Sinclair's red mouth is elevated and it was supposed to be some sort of joke, and a response was expected. Too late, Sinclair is elaborating—

I shall commandeer Mrs Rumford in the morning.

If you want to get in her good books she does love boiled sweets, especially lemon and lime flavour.

That is useful to know; I shall acquire some before I speak to her. Thank you for the suggestion, Gwen.

And though it annoys her, Gwen is almost pleased to have been able to help. She makes a mental note, *S; maybe not all bad?* (She will write it up properly later.) In fact, this helps Gwen relax slightly, and she sips her cider with gusto.

Sinclair drinks, too. Mm, reminds me of holidays. Funny the way a smell or a taste can do that to you, drop you in the middle of a memory.

I have the same with cigar smoke. The smell makes me think of Daddy's cigar on Christmas Eve. He always lets me take a puff before bed.

My Christmas smell is the paste we use to make paper chains.

Is it . . . ? I can picture it exactly. Aren't we funny, talking about Christmas in this weather? It's all topsy-turvy.

208

Rather. (And though they do not laugh as such, there is at least mutual pleasure.)

So . . . tell me how you know Laurence . . . *Mr Fern*. Did you meet in London?

More collided than met.

Have you known him very long?

Sinclair sighs as though the topic is dull to her. No. Though I don't think one needs to know Laurence for long to get the measure of him. He picked me, you see.

Picked?

Yes. Laurence chose me out of a group of sisters, girlfriends and cousins of mine. Not because I am the greatest prize, although I am, but because I am the hardest to crack.

To . . . marry?

Sinclair laughs a silvery, tinkling laugh. Goodness no, he hasn't any money. Poor boy is a fourth son, which is virtually the same as being born on the wrong side of the blanket, if you ask me. If he proposed he knows I'd turn him down flat. No. He is charming, very charming, and of good breeding, which can carry you pretty far, but those are not necessarily good qualities without an income to match. Laurence picked me the way you would pick a plum from a plum tree. He wants to have me and, while it amuses me, I shall permit myself to be had.

Gwen is uncertain what this means, but does not wish to show her ignorance. If Laurence, Mr Fern, did have pots of money, would you want to marry him then?

Darling, if you had pots of money, I would want to marry you.

I say. How shocking.

Sinclair smiles impishly. One likes to be able to shock now and then. You don't know how lucky you are, Gwen.

Am I lucky?

Why, yes. You have lots of blissful years ahead of you

without all that cant about love and marriage, which is just too boring for words. 'What the heart desires', 'what fate has written', birds tweeting and all that bosh . . . *Jesus* it never ends. Men can be so bloody pompous. I admit I am exquisitely jealous of you.

Right. I suppose.

Cigarette? Sinclair offers a slim feminine case, beautifully engraved.

Yes please.

Shall I light it for you?

Gwen says she will do it, Sinclair lends her the lighter and she takes a couple of snaps to make it burn. Gwen finds even Sinclair's fags to have a perfumed taste. *Thanks.* Gosh, I don't know how to say it, but I have been wondering, just now and then since you arrived . . . Do you mind my asking what your first name is? I assume Sinclair is your family name.

It is. I utterly loathe my given name. Loathe it. Can't bear to be called it or to hear it said out loud. It grieves me even to write it down.

Can't be that bad.

Hah. Sinclair sucks in and exhales the smoke like a sailor.

You don't have to tell if you don't want to.

See if you can guess it. If you were me, what would be the most rotten name someone could give you?

You promise you'll say if I'm right?

Sinclair promises.

Well, I suppose Claire Sinclair would be pretty bad, or Clara. Nope.

No, I didn't think so. Then, something twee. Eudora? or Philomena? Then you might want a good nickname of your own. (Gwen tries not to appear uncomfortable discussing it.)

No, nothing like that.

Um. One of the virtues, perhaps. Hope? Joy? Faith? Chastity?

Sinclair shakes her head at each of these.

My last guess would be a name that you thought of as dismal, a dismal sort of name. What about Maud?

It's Joanna.

Joanna . . . ? But Joanna is a perfectly lovely name.

Sinclair pretends to shiver. Yuck. I despise it.

To call Gwen disappointed would be an understatement. She would swap her *Gwendolen* for Sinclair's *Joanna* any day. She once had a doll called Joanna (has still got a doll called Joanna, but decides at this moment to give her away to a needy child), had considered naming one of her daughters with Laurence *Joanna Jane*. Sinclair is not to know this, has retreated back into the gossip columns of her magazine. If Gwen had, during the course of their encounter, altered her opinion of Sinclair, this has reverted back. Sinclair is haughty, grasping, pretentious and vain.

Gwen retrieves her notebook and a pencil, writes in it surreptitiously.

i   *Whether S is romantically involved with L. – 'romantic' is wrong word; what is right word? not 'picked'!*

ii   *Whether S would like to be romantically involved with L. – no because S is haughty and grasping &c.*

iii *What S's Christian name is & why she goes by just her surname. – Joanna / because S is stupid.*

iv   *What S's weaknesses are & how to use them against her. – numerous faults, why has no one noticed??*

v   *Whether S has any redeeming features whatsoever. – none (honest) but I do like her Chinese robe.*

Seems reasonable. Yes, and balanced. She checks Sinclair cannot see.

*

Cynthia jabs at the typewriter. It is a cumbersome machine with letter keys that stick. Nonetheless, Cynthia is fond of it and perseveres. If inanimate objects have personalities, then this typewriter is an old friend, loyal, clumsy, prone to getting into a pickle like an elderly woman trying to untangle her knitting. Kind. It is a kindly typewriter. You tell me what to put, and I will type it out for you . . . it has a helpful temperament, and Cynthia cannot blame it for the defects of age.

It is my typing which is at fault, she tells herself, rather than facing the prospect of replacing it. She uses a pen to release some of the character bars that have snarled together.

Gwen stands before her, mouth an O, seems to expect her attention.

Cynthia tinkers. What's wrong?

The girl shakes her head and closes her eyes. I might just faint, Cynthia, I really might. I think fainting must feel a lot like this.

There is a snap, and the typewriter is mended once more. What has happened now?

I don't think I can tell you. Although I was not exactly sworn to secrecy. Rather the opposite, actually; they didn't seem to care who saw them.

Who didn't?

Laurence and *her*.

Ah. Them again.

Yes, and under your roof. I think it is very disrespectful to you to be carrying on like that when they are your guests. If I were you, I would put a stop to it immediately.

Cynthia stares longingly at her papers, spreads one hand on them to reassure herself they are real. Real and hers. Her thoughts and her work. She has such a lot to do, and prefers work infinitely to—

It's her more than him; I'm sure she leads him astray. I just . . .

I just wanted to show him something. I thought Sinclair had gone out for the morning because she usually does. Dipso-maniac, I expect. Anyway, I went looking for Laurence because he hadn't told me where he was working today, and I found him in the music room. (Gwen's mouth goes dry.)

And . . . ? He was there with Sinclair?

The girl turns paler. If you went right now, you would see—

Gwen, I shall do nothing so undignified.

It is sinful. If it is not sinful, it certainly isn't decent.

Were they making love?

Gwen blanches, No! (How can Cynthia do it? How can she be so phlegmatic?) He was painting her. She was being his model. His *nude* model. Right by *your* piano. Someone might see it in the painting and say, 'That there is Cynthia Everard's piano, and she allows naked people to parade around in front of it.'

Is that all? Cynthia turns back to her typewriter and clatter-clacks out her exasperation.

Aren't you going to do anything?

And what precisely would you have me do?

(The pointed nipples, the exposed armpit, the belly button like a dimple, the triangle of dark hair . . .) Someone must do something. She wasn't wearing a stitch! Naked people at Arnault, Cynthia! What if someone else sees? What if Mrs Rumford sees? The poor dear would probably keel over and die.

Gwen, has it occurred to you that you're the one at fault? That perhaps it would be better to get past this infatuation of yours? Why not develop some interests of your own while you are stay-ing here – make some friends of your own age? What will I tell your mother if I return you to her in this state?

Gwen concentrates on these words. Then, as though the scales are falling from her eyes, she whispers, Do you mean Laurence has a touch of lavender?

This makes Cynthia pause in her typing and look hard at her. Gwendolen, you do say the most ghastly things—

And that is that.

Then Cynthia tells Gwen she has one of her headaches coming on and Gwen had better leave her alone. Which means Gwen is powerless to prevent it – whatever it is – and were Cynthia to trouble herself, she would probably be powerless too.

Gwen can hear her typing from the garden over the sound of her heart being trampled on. So she runs further on, down the road towards the village—

– and almost into a man carrying a suitcase.

I beg your pardon, young lady. I'm looking for the house called Arnault, is it near here . . . ?

Alec, it's you! And Gwen hugs him hard.

Alec Worsham permits it awkwardly, pats her on the back.

She pulls away. It's Gwen Watts, do you remember? I'm Bill and Betty's daughter.

Of course I remember, how are you?

Oh I'm . . . I'm just . . . I'm so glad to see a friendly face.

Has something happened? Is Cynthia all right?

No, she's in a foul temper.

I say, that is too bad. Should we check on her?

No, no, I don't think that's a good idea. (Gwen cannot endure the thought of Alec's seeing Sinclair's nakedness.) She's fine, very busy. We had bit of a spat.

Ah. Is Laurence there?

Yes, but I can't go back, not now. I will. I just need some time. I say, Alec, would you take me out to luncheon?

Alec has a warm heart, and cannot tolerate seeing Bill and Betty's girl in distress. He agrees.

They lunch outside the pub, Alec drinking stout with his sandwiches and Gwen drinking ginger beer with her pie.

Gwen does most of the talking as Alec is recently back from Punjab, and wants to hear about his friends. He asks after her parents.

Mummy is well, still making quilts and playing the clarinet, badly. Daddy lost a leg, you know.

Yes, I heard. It's too bad.

But he's alive, and we're ever so thankful for that. Mummy wanted to nurse him at home and Taid knows someone at the War Office, so he arranged it.

Taid . . . ?

Grandad on Mummy's side.

Is that why you are staying with Cynthia?

Gwen squints into the sun. Mummy thought it would be better. Give him space to heal without too many hens clucking. I bet they'd both love to see you before you leave, though, do you think you could manage it?

I will try. And how is Cynthia?

Oh, she's fine.

Alec leans over his pint pot. Really?

Gwen screws up her face while she tries to think objectively: She works frantically. She seems to like it. It's to do with that professor of hers who died.

Norman Creegan.

Yes, him. She is doing some kind of book. Honestly, I don't think even she knows what it's about. There's an absolute mountain of paper. I tried to help out, but I don't have the . . . you know.

Aptitude.

I was going to say brain cells. She plugs away at it all day, then drinks and smokes all night; and sometimes she is in a good mood, and sometimes she is horrid to be around. I entertain myself, mostly. There's only us, Laurence and the harlot.

I say, that's a bit strong.

215

She's called . . . Joanna. But you ought to be careful, you are just the sort she would go for – that's some friendly advice for you. She has already got her claws into Laurence.

Alec nods confidentially. How is Cynthia in herself?

Well, she still gets those headaches, but that's nothing new.

Does she ever mention me?

Gwen smirks.

Or any of us from the old days?

No-o. No, sorry. I didn't even know you were coming. But she never tells me anything, probably because I'd get the wrong end of the stick . . . Gwen looks at Alec meaningfully, who in turn finds something of interest to look at by the post office.

He asks, Are you having a nice stay?

I was. Gwen pushes away her almost empty plate. If it weren't for love.

Aren't you a bit young to be having trouble with the opposite sex?

I'm really not.

Is it serious?

Not to him. To him I'm a joke. And he's right, I am a joke.

Don't be despondent. Love makes fools out of all of us.

Which is not very encouraging. Have you been made a fool of by love?

Plenty of times.

That's absurd, no one falls in love more than once.

No one falls in love *for the first time* more than once.

But I want the first time to be the only time. You aren't very good at this shoulder-to-cry-on business, Alec Worsham.

Don't I know it? He sips his stout and searches in his pockets for cigarettes and matches.

Alec, do you think – do *you* think – that some people require everyone around them to fall in love with them?

What a heavy question for a bright afternoon.

But is it true? Are some people that . . . selfish?

Alec strikes a match and takes his time to light his fag. When it burns he shakes the match to extinguish it. I didn't offer you one . . . ?

No thanks, I'm not keen.

He dwells upon it, then answers, Yes. Some people are in love with being loved.

Does that make them bad through and through?

Alec smokes and considers. It can be bad for those around them, but what a man does to himself is nobody else's concern.

But they can be changed, if the right woman tried to change them?

He laughs. What is this about?

Nothing in particular.

Laurence got to you, has he?

Gwen could scream and stamp her foot – instead hangs her head in defeat. Am I so bloody transparent?

Language. (He intones it.) I guessed.

If one wanted to make an impression on someone such as Laurence Fern, how might one do it?

One could pretend he doesn't exist, I bet no one has tried that before—

Gwen huffs and puffs (Mummy would call me The Wolf).

Alec goes on: I have to admit, I have no idea whether or not Laurence can change, but I will say this: in the years since I have known him and his brother Nicholas and your parents and Cynthia and everyone else in our old set, all of us have changed for better or worse, except Laurence, who has stayed exactly the same.

Therefore he is likely to stay the same?

The empirical evidence seems to support it. You, on the other hand – what a fascinating project we could make of you,

217

recording your journey and how you change over the years ahead.

Gwen blushes at this. What about you? I haven't even asked you where you've been and what you've been up to. Or can't you tell me, is it secret?

Alec withdraws at the mention of his work, grows stern before her.

Is it secret? Because if it is you're probably better off not telling me about it, I'd just let the cat out of the bag. I would be a hopeless spy. I can't help myself. If a shady character tried to recruit me on a park bench for King and country I'd have to say, 'Sorry, mister, I'm just here to feed the pigeons.' *Are* you a spy?

No.

You would have to say that, even if you were.

I'm not.

You would have to say that too, wouldn't you? Is it hot in Punjab? Hotter than it is here at the moment?

Very.

And can you tell me vaguely what you do there, without endangering anyone's life?

I make promises I can't keep.

Gosh. How unhappy.

It is, for everyone concerned. But that is there and we are here.

Alec, you're in favour of women's suffrage, aren't you?

Alec feigns ambivalence, but does a poor job.

I knew it. So am I!

How can you tell?

Because you just *would*. I say, Alec, what do you think about conchies?

We're talking about Laurence again?

Not necessarily.

You don't approve of conscientious objection?

Don't know. It does seem unfair that some people risk their lives while others benefit from it but sit on their hands. It seems a bit cowardly.

Many pacifists undertake difficult or dangerous work; they farm the land, or they serve as non-combatants.

Laurence doesn't. If I was allowed to, I would fight.

That's very brave of you. But you should know there are different kinds of bravery in the world. Tell me, Gwen, have you ever held a minority view?

She rolls her eyes. Every day of my life.

I mean, an opinion where you were truly in the minority? one that the rest of your peers mocked you and hated you for? one that could create problems for your family and could potentially put you in prison?

That rather depends on whether someone considered my opinion powerful or important. Would anyone ever take a view *I* held that seriously?

It's a fair point. But if it were just a matter of cowardice and courage, don't you think the army has enough ways to scare men into service?

You're probably right but I don't know enough about it, Alec. There is no debate I can possibly have with you which I could win.

He pauses before he responds. I did not realise one of us had to win and one of us had to lose; I thought we were just having a conversation. I don't know precisely why Laurence has chosen to do what he has, but I can assure you it must have been extremely difficult for him. If you are so curious about it, maybe you should just ask?

Maybe I will. But you didn't answer my question before: what do you think about conscientious objectors?

I think the world is imperfect. I think wars have many

victims, not just the obvious ones. I think pacifism has the ring of sanity about it. And we need them. We need the minority view, if only to remind the rest of us why we believe in what we believe in, and because sometimes the minority view is the right view but its time hasn't come yet.

Like women's suffrage.

Indeed.

Gosh. You are surprising. And when you say something clever you turn all grave and handsome.

He flusters at this. Miss Watts, is that entirely appropriate?

But it's all right to say it to you, isn't it? Are you going to be Prime Minister one day?

Goodness no, I can think of several professions I would have to fail in first. What about going back now? Assuming that you are ready to face the displeasure of Miss Everard.

I am ready. Thanks awfully for being a brick.

Candle stubs sit in glass jars and melt on to saucers, along the wall and on tables in the garden. It is a mild enough evening to cover bare arms with thin sleeves – the dancing and the whisky provide extra warmth, when needed. Gwen has some, her first taste, and finds after the revulsion has subsided that it is quite as nice as vinegar, which she has always liked though never considered drinking on its own. The men savour it, so do the women, therefore Gwen will if only in small sips. So this is what getting tight feels like.

She wants to crank the handle and change the records on the gramophone, realises too late that this is a liability which impedes her chances to speak or dance with Laurence, who is partnered with Sinclair (typical). Alec is dancing with Cynthia, and seems disinclined to switch. Nevertheless, it is fun.

The recordings and the insects click and hiss.

Perhaps it is the drink or the stars appearing or the strains of songs, which have to be replayed or replaced when they come to an end. Perhaps it is the war, and that the night is precious because the world beyond Arnault is fluxing. Perhaps it is because they have spent hours talking through the people they know fighting or contributing to the effort. Gwen loses count of how many, their names and their backgrounds and their ages, who has already bought it and who is still alive. It makes Gwen feel vulnerable. Her body, still in so many ways a mystery of itself, seems to shrink at the mention of death – so it ceases to be Gwen Watts and becomes instead just organs and meat, the way Daddy's leg must have looked in a bucket. It is the presence of Alec which has reintroduced discussion of the war to the house, for he seems to know a great deal about it, is subtle in his observations and careful in his reports. Cynthia agrees with Alec on many points; Sinclair disputes a few hotly. When Alec uses phrases such as 'the moral imperative' and 'collective responsibility' Gwen becomes anxious on Laurence's behalf, despite Alec's remarks this afternoon.

Gwen knows she is ignorant. For example, she has to ask Alec which side the Indians are on.

Alec Worsham's expression turns sombre before he confirms that many thousands of Indian soldiers are fighting alongside our troops.

How super, she answers.

Not exactly— Alec explains that they want independence in return, and she finds the melancholy in his manner unsettling.

Gwen thinks hard about it, willing her useless mind to trundle to its conclusion. It does seem a fair and straightforward exchange to me.

Yes, Alec replies. Yes, it is more than fair, but I am afraid it is not remotely straightforward.

Then three words materialise in Gwen's consciousness, the definitions of which huddle close together in her head and play

221

tricks on her. Enormity. It is the enormity of the war that she cannot fathom, that there are corpses and destruction and family grief in unknowable numbers, and travesties of justice. Enormousness. It is the enormousness of the war that overwhelms her, the way it spans the globe, and she cannot visualise the edges of it because they have disappeared into countries she has barely heard of. Intricacy. It is the intricacy of the war that is baffling, the invisible threads of purpose and consequence criss-crossing in multiplicity over oceans and continents, so that a quiver on one alters life and death at the end of another. Because of the enormity, the enormousness and the intricacy, Gwen will never understand it, never. If she lives to be a hundred, the war will still be there as a blemish of uncertainty on whatever fabric of knowledge and experience she acquires in life.

I will jolly well enjoy this whisky, despite the way it burns my throat. I will jolly well enjoy playing records, despite my not having a dance partner.

After a random approach to the music collection, Gwen becomes more selective, picking out the best titles, repeating her favourites. 'Dreaming'; 'Somewhere a Voice is Calling'; 'I Don't Suppose'; 'I Lost My Heart in Honolulu'; 'In the Glory of the Moonlight'; and then 'Dreaming' because she liked it so much the first time round; and then 'I Lost My Heart in Honolulu' again.

Laurence holds Sinclair close, sways with her in and out of shadows. Her teeth are straight, white, she shows them when she shows her amusement at being spun or dipped or at some remark he whispers into her ear which pleases her. They pause to replenish their glasses and make a private toast, then resume.

Alec dances more formally with Cynthia, and they giggle less. They have an ease, they match like a saucepan and its lid. Alec wants to know about Cynthia, puts a question to her on this or that; she answers, using more description than normal.

Gwen tries not to stare at the two couples, and at Sinclair least of all. Tries not to think of Sinclair as graceful, as stylish, as refined. Sinclair leans into Laurence, rests her head on him, would purr if she were a cat.

Gwen pretends to study a label on a shellac disc. If Sinclair had not come, Laurence would be dancing with *her* right now. If Sinclair picked up the scent of a richer man, she would drop Laurence in a beat. If Sinclair suddenly left, Laurence would be devastated . . .

And if he was devastated, he would need to be comforted . . .

By the woman whom he has been aware of as a gentle and stable presence, the woman a part of him has silently worshipped from a distance since they first met. Emotions which he has suppressed out of respect might suddenly burst forth. Maybe he is simply waiting to be a free man again, and for the right occasion to present itself—

Sinclair breaks away from Laurence. I rather want a go of the gramophone myself. I'm sure I can find some music which isn't so soppy. (She flicks through some records, then notices Gwen.) We've had rather a lot of the same, don't you think? I say, Laurence, why don't you dance with Gwen for a bit? It's hardly fair that Cynthia and I have been hogging the men. Is there any ragtime?

Gwen can hardly control the sensation of plummeting, from the moment when Laurence extends his invitation to her until the moment she is on her feet in front of him. She wobbles, has managed more of the whisky than she thought. This is it, she thinks. This is actually it.

Laurence has never been closer to her than he is now, apart from the day when he lit her cigarette.

He smiles, Have you danced before, Gwen?

Plenty of times, but usually I'm the boy because I'm taller than the other girls.

Would you like to lead? (He is teasing her, and she finds it attractive.)

Oh, no. You can lead.

The music starts again. Gwen realises that Laurence has put his hand round her waist, his finger hitching some of the flimsy material of her dress, is holding her hand and that she is touching, *squeezing*, one of his shoulders. It is a strapping shoulder that wants to be squeezed. He is breathing on her and gazing into her eyes. She can smell his sweat, see the freckles on his face. There is no gap between them, their noses almost meet. They dance.

Gwen fights to stay upright, tries not to avert her eyes or allow her cheeks to flame. She hears the music as though it is far away; is aware of Cynthia, Alec and even Sinclair as shapes behind frosted glass. They are harmless, they cannot interfere, they do not matter. The war does not matter. What Mummy would say matters least of the things that do not matter. Only this matters.

You and I have discovered what lovers through the ages already know, that in times of chaos and decay, truth is a constant and truth is beauty. What is truer than two halves making one whole? What is more beautiful than fulfilment? Being in love *definitely* feels like this.

She remembers to chat and to laugh along with Laurence in a natural way – the words come easily. It is all easy. Gwen belongs here. She wishes they could live inside this song and dance up to the sky, beyond it, be lights among the spheres. The candles are like stars.

The short hours of darkness will soon dissolve into dawn, and Cynthia takes one of her walks. She does not know where it will lead; perhaps to the end of the road, perhaps to the end of her life. For if, one day, she gives in to the temptation, she will not have planned it nor written a goodbye letter nor settled her affairs. She will do it when it seems to her a good idea and the opportunity presents itself. Were the opportunity to present itself within the next mile she may be inclined, for it is night and she is alone and she is only a quarter deep into her research after all, and the drinking has given her courage. And this will have been a pleasing last evening. She follows a lane, a path, the fingernail moon. She follows her thoughts, which sink and rise in waves, which ascend and dart like birds; some of them settle on Alec.

She has got lost on her walks, found the way back several hours later or stayed out all night until daybreak, when people appeared she could ask directions of and signposts became visible. She has taken a train to the seaside wearing the clothes she left the house in, and had just enough money left over to buy a cup of tea. She has been molested. She has awoken in the door-way of a shop. She has been stalked by the disembodied phantom of the future, pale and iridescent, in the guise of a naked girl. She has been asked whether she was in need of assistance? by a lady of colour, as it happens, smartly dressed, warm, human, in contrast to Cynthia's presentiment before – she scrutinised Cynthia's face, touched her forehead with the back of her hand, pressed money into Cynthia's palm and dashed away as if late for an appointment.

More often than not she simply takes a stroll, goes back home, sleeps in her own bed. These walks are the ink-blot patterns where random and unconnected ideas merge into solid concepts, into theories worthy of being written, into structures that can withstand force.

Alec is in her net, and what ought she to do with him? The trouble is, he thinks he is a liberal, is attracted to the bohemian life, but in reality he would not cope. He would grow to resent Cynthia because she would hold him to his promises. He has been artful in his approach, she has to give him that. Stating and offering nothing specific, is handling her the way he handles his diplomatic work. All hints implications possibilities. All of it can be denied or reinterpreted, if the outcome is against him. Dear Alec, you think you are being modern.

Cynthia comes to a bridge and stops halfway across to look over the side.

Dear Alec . . . it would destroy you.

A fling, then? He alluded to it. Cynthia is not averse to the idea, but she senses danger comes with it. Alec is the sort of man who could not take a mistress without trying to save her, and she would quickly tire of his good intentions. He kept mentioning a year, but he did not call it that. He called it 'twelve months'. Twelve months is 'short', twelve months 'soon goes by'. Oh yes, I see it now, you would have us make a commitment for this length of time and no hurt feelings at the end . . . ? I know you, Alec, and I know myself, and in one year you think you could change my mind for me, and in one year we would be further apart than we already are.

These are good arguments against, but she can refute it entirely with a mere statement of fact: I am not prepared to share. There are aspects of my life which you may not be a part of, I shall not allow it. And I am not leaving Arnault. Arnault is mine, and there is nowhere I would rather be. This clinches it.

She hums a little to herself. Pinpricks of yellow light are visible in buildings across the fields.

Alec's hypothesis is flawed, and it took Cynthia only half an hour to prove it. Now she must devise a method of conveying her conclusions.

She has gone past the need for sleep and is feeling adventurous. She could walk through the night, has some money in her pocket for a train or a bus back. She should get a bicycle. What a good idea, why has she never thought of it before? Yes, she will definitely look into buying one, and this decision makes her sure she will not kill herself tonight. A walk will suffice, to a place that is unfamiliar, but she will definitely come back for breakfast.

Cynthia.

She is being called – she has been followed. She does not reply because it annoys her to have her privacy invaded and he is coming over to her anyway, clasping her body through her clothes, is kissing her.

Thirsty and hot. Gwen kicks off the covers. It is early, the sun has risen with the amber glow of arid morning. There is no water by her bed; she will have to go to the kitchen to get some. Her head throbs. She slips her dress over her and attempts the buttons with sleepy fingertips. She pushes her feet into shoes without stockings, and because it is habit, because she is not thinking about what makes sense, only about the dryness which needs to be quenched, because the kitchen seems at this moment miles not yards away, she hangs her faithful bag across her the way she does on any expedition.

Arnault is still asleep. She tries to avoid the squeaking parts of the landing which will be audible to people in their bedrooms. She takes the stairs one at a time, step-stop, step-stop, cautious of tumbling. At the kitchen sink she forces the tap and swallows a whole glass of water without rest, wipes her mouth, forces the tap again to refill it. This is worse than having flu.

She is quite awake now, even though it is some two hours before she would normally get up. Like a present. Gwen, here you are with two extra hours in the day, what are you going to do with them? Nice, really. She could go out, would be curious to see how different the world looks at this time of day. She drinks the rest of the water, then pauses at a sound—

– or was it? Does Arnault make different noises while its occupants are in bed?

227

She ignores it, then hears it again, or one similar. It is like nothing, like a bird trapped in a room. Sound, no sound.

Gwen leaves the glass on the draining board and retraces her steps with care. The disturbance, a flutter, draws her through the house towards the music room, where instinct makes her hesitate outside the door. (If it is a burglar, she will shout.) It is open a fraction, and human rustling emanates through it. She peers in.

It is a pile of cushions, rugs, hair – Cynthia's hair, Cynthia's arm, Cynthia's hand wearing Cynthia's sapphire ring. She is sleeping here on the floor, among the fabric textures, her head tucked into her elbow. She stirs, brings her other arm up to her chin and a third embraces her, the arm of the man she is with, and Gwen discerns two separate breathing rhythms, a male and a female, the signal to her sensitive ears that something unexpected has occurred. Their intimacy is mammalian, their entwined limbs have not the curves of poetry but the angles of prose. Gwen decides she must leave, and in the time it takes for this conclusion to form, he moves protectively towards Cynthia in his sleep and shows his face.

It is shame-making, creeping away hoping not to be discovered – but for the best. Gwen goes out into the garden, turns towards the sky, inhales the air sweet with pollen and sneezes.

She has a handkerchief in her bag, and dabs her eyes out of formality because one does so when one is brokenhearted, and this is betrayal, if ever Woman was betrayed. The life she pictured them sharing has been stolen by a rogue to whom she gave the flower of her regard. Yes, here are the shoots of her anger, they are pale and weak but they will grow and spread and harden into resentment. (Won't they?)

Surprisingly, this is not how she imagined it would feel. Where is the misery? Where is the despair? Where is the crying out of his name, and the beating of her breast? Gwen does not feel them. She is *miffed*. She is thoroughly *put out*. Apparently, a love spurned feels about as painful as finding out Emily Dibner has been named hockey captain. Pretty bad, but not too bad.

And *Cynthia* . . .

Cynthia is different. Gwen cannot be mad with Cynthia in the same way she is mad at Laurence (and Emily Bloody Dibner). Cynthia is not a rival in love, but practically family. Gwen has known her all her life. Cynthia is a spinster . . . who has cut herself a peculiar existence and is not undeserving of companionship when she finds it. Cynthia got to Laurence first, plain and simple.

Tough toads on me.

Gwen grasps her handkerchief in case she sheds her tears – the grass surrounding her rustles and she sneezes loudly, abruptly, blows her nose like a bugle.

Bless you. Alec is beside her, groomed and dressed.

From behind her mask of hand and hanky Gwen stares at him, certain he must have seen what she saw, yet his dapper demeanour suggests not: neat, genial, *untroubled*. You're up early, Alec.

Always am.

Er, is anyone else about?

I expect they're still in bed, nursing their hangovers. We got tight last night, didn't we? (He seems to mean it, seems at ease.) Something the matter?

Gwen falters, fights the instinct to blurt what she knows because this is what she would normally do. She grows aware of a new pressure, the urge to protect, to stand in front of a human heart and spare it suffering. The subtle navigation of human relations. Gwen has been aggrieved, but it would be much worse for Alec if he knew. Why does she think this? Yes, for his attentions upon Cynthia, for their dancing and that he found reasons to be close to her, for the journey to Arnault which is out of his way, and which his schedule of work does not strictly permit. That he wants continually to know about Cynthia's welfare, and finds the driest details of her research riveting, that he tries in his way to intrigue and impress her. And Laurence . . . ? There is history between Alec and Laurence, even Gwen knows that.

She swallows the unfairness, bitter as it is, and says, You won't tell Mummy I got squiffy, will you?

Alec laughs, and assures Gwen her secret is safe.

She thanks him profusely, telling him he is a good man – and adds in a flash of inspiration, Does the bakery open early, I wonder?

I'm sure I don't know.

Shall we find out? We can bring back a loaf for the others, and I could really do with a cream cake.

At this hour?

Yes!

If you say so. I'll fetch my wallet.

No, let me buy it, I would very much like to.

That wouldn't be proper of me.

I *insist*. (I hate it when I sound like Mummy!) I'm sure I've got my purse with me, at least I thought I did. Hold these, will you? She takes a hairbrush out of her bag and some yarn and her notebook with pages curled back over the spine and some hair slides . . . roots around for her purse at the bottom.

I say, that's rather good. It's Cynthia reading, isn't it?

What is . . . ? Oh, that. (Alec is referring to a drawing on the top page.) Supposed to be. I made it to show Laurence but I never got round to it.

I like the title.

It's a sort of joke and a sort of wish for her. I don't know. It's silly.

It's terrific. May I buy it from you?

No need to buy it; you can have it if you want, not that I understand why you would.

Because it will remind me of Cynthia, and of my stay here, and of you.

Then it's yours, and I'm glad. Look, here it is (Gwen holds up the purse). I say, it's such a beautiful morning, why don't we go *this* way.

So Gwen leads Alec away from Arnault, and any risk of discovering that the people he loves best have done him wrong.

A shouting woman, as if a murder is happening, and a man shouting back.

Alec and Gwen can hear it before they see Arnault. They stop by the gate and he murmurs, Trouble in paradise.

It is Laurence and Sinclair.

Laurence: It's all in your mind, Joanna.

Sinclair: It is not in my fucking mind.

You're just upset.

Yes, I am fucking upset. Get out of my way, you fucking dandy.

Sinclair appears with her case, and dumps it on the path.

Laurence comes after her, Just stay for an hour or two and let me explain . . . ?

She about-faces and marches back in, though not because he wants her to.

He follows after her. Joanna? Joanna?

More shouting within, then Sinclair comes back out with her handbag, coat slung over her arm, scarf draped about her shoulders, carrying her hat.

Laurence appears at the doorway, hands at the back of his head like a man watching his house on fire.

Sinclair strains to lift her luggage.

Please, Joanna . . . ?

She sways with the weight and the momentum of her rage. I hope your bollocks drop off. And don't call me Joanna!

Sinclair spins with the suitcase and trots past Gwen and Alec without acknowledgement, away from Arnault and out of their lives.

Laurence watches the space she has left behind, gazes heavenward in disbelief.

Gwen and Alec do not look at each other. Not even when Gwen says, I'm going to eat Sinclair's cherry tart.

Of course, Alec had no intention of remaining at Arnault for long. Before he goes he spends an afternoon alone with Laurence, and whatever transpires between them makes Laurence decide to leave too. Cynthia is unperturbed by their departure, relieved to have Arnault almost back to herself. She types pages of her book with a pencil between her teeth, has taken to wearing a pair of men's pince-nez, which she found in one of her professor's boxes.

Keep working, keep thinking, keep being—

Cynthia's ghosts. She never shares them, they are hers to tame or to be consumed by. Her life is her mind, it is the superior part of her, the best and the most fragile.

To Gwen, she has become quite as dull as before, leaving the girl to puzzle over whether the incident in the music room was an anomaly or had been taking place constantly beneath the surface. She cannot ask without revealing how she knows. It frustrates her, God how it frustrates her. Not because Gwen once loved Laurence, although she did, and not because Cynthia misled her, although she has. It is a separate problem which needs to be solved: the way Cynthia is blasé about love, the way she isolates herself from the warmth of intimacy, rejects the stirrings and urges (surely within her) as juvenile and superfluous.

Gwen follows the route to the Lagoon, mulling it over.

Indeed, Cynthia chose Laurence and not Alec because Laurence is expendable. Laurence is a physical being, which does not count for much to Cynthia. And she would fight any deep feelings she had for Alec because he is more her equal; because she would have a responsibility towards him, towards herself; because it might be more than just *intercourse*, and to Cynthia that detracts from—

From what, Cynthia? From work? From loneliness?

Gwen decides it makes no sense at all, and it will not be good enough for her.

My man will be an Alec *and* a Laurence; he will have the best attributes of both, and nothing shall keep me from him.

She arrives at the pond, and watches the flecks of sun on the surface.

Even if he is not . . . if he is a safe and regular soul I demand that he loves me passionately and treats me like a queen . . . or at the very least, I want him to be a kind and entertaining fellow – then we shall be one of those couples who are still laughing into old age and die within a month of each other . . . but if he turns out to be a tormented genius, I will cure him of his daemons . . . unless he is mature and wise and lavishes me with affection, then he can care for me and cure me of *my* manias instead . . . or he could be an honest, decent man with big strong hands who is content to work all day and to sit with me by our fire at night. I think he is in a trench at this very moment planning our life together, the prospect of it carrying him through, I hope. Yes, I know he must be somewhere, but I don't know exactly where or how I shall find him or who he is.

She picks up a pebble and lobs it in – *ker-splash*. She watches the ripples expand in circles, repeat, dissipate.

Then she lifts her bag off her shoulder and drops it on the ground, twists her feet out of her shoes, undoes her buttons and pulls her dress off until she is wearing only her white slip. She takes some steps backwards, inhales a breath, runs and jumps in – the water a fantastic shock to her body. She comes up for a gasp of air, to see how far she went, and dives into the depths again where it is cool and shadowy. Weeds and creatures tickle her and retract their tentacles. Beams of light are filtered and split apart. Algae bacteria invertebrates fish molluscs. There is a world under here, and Gwen never knew it. There is a world under here, and it is completely different from how she dreamed it.

Immaterialism

Reader in a Shoreditch Bar, 2008

Britain's Jeannine Okoro steps on to the ice to compete in her first Winter Olympic Games. *Deafening applause.* At eight years old, she is Britain's youngest ever figure-skating champion. She was spotted at the tender age of six by Torvill and Dean when she came to this very rink for Big Sister's birthday party (obviously). The rest, they say, is history. Now she's the favourite for an Olympic gold medal. She waves and smiles to the crowd, especially to her dad, who is sitting by the drinks vending machine with a cup of chicken soup.

She glides and performs the perfect twizzle.

Dad, watch me.

She does two more in rapid succession, twizzle, twizzle. The judges are thrilled.

Jeannine is wearing a fetching Betty Boop sweater and her new ice-skating skirt – bright green with polka dots, it twirls and flutters with each and every swish and turn – and her bestest leg warmers. She has also borrowed a pair of Big Sister's gloves because hers had tea spilled on them and are in the wash.

Now she's going for the toe loop jump. Can she do it? She builds up speed, bends her knee, launches from her toe pick, brings in her arms and lands – finishing with a sweeping gesture to acknowledge the cheers from the stands.

Dad, did you see that?

She glides. She gliiides. Another brilliant toe loop jump. The judges are in awe.

And she's going for the parallel spin. She spirals into the centre of the arena and extends her torso and leg into a T, hands thrust back, she spins faster, faster. She's doing it. She grabs the blade behind her and brings her foot up towards the back of her head in a Biellmann spin – making it look easy – releases it into an upright spin – this girl is amazing . . . and out. No wonder the judges are on their feet.

Dad, I spun. Dad, I'm gonna do a Salchow. I said a Salchow. *Sal-chow.* You watching?

Jeannine Okoro circles the rink, her arms spread like wings. She zooms. Six, three, nine, is all she has to remember. She does another twizzle, just to warm up. Six o'clock, three o'clock, nine o'clock with her free leg and her body will do the rest. She skates. She skaaates. Her leg comes up behind her at *six o'clock*, then right, *three o'clock*, swings over to *nine o'clock* and she jumps turns lands wobbles . . . *oh no*, the judges won't like that. If she still wants the gold, she'll have to pull out her star move.

Sorry Dad, that was rubbish. I'm gonna do an Axel instead. *Axel.*

The Axel is the most difficultest jump in figure skating. You take off going forwards, *which is mad,* and make one and a half rotations in the air; the trick is timing – don't twist too early. All the limbs have to work together to get you there. One arm early, or late, messes it up completely. Will the years of practice pay off? Jeannine looks calm as she skates past the fans, who have travelled all the way to north London to support her. She needs to jump *out* with arms stretched *out*, then pull 'em *in*. But whatever you do, Jeannine, don't pull into the jump too soon.

The crowd holds its breath.

She's moving. She's going. She's going to do it. Backwards then *forwards* to make the leap . . . gets scared . . .

She has only managed it once in training, when she had help; doubts whether she can make it. Her instincts anticipate the unnaturalness of the jump, she knows she is bringing her arms in quicker than she should and by then the whole move is already lost.

Twisting early taking off late sends Jeannine down *hard*. She feels the disappointment before she feels the physical pain as her body makes contact with the ice, automatically she pushes out one hand to break her fall remembering to tuck her fingers in so they don't get sliced off by someone else's skates. *Bang* like an explosion. She is winded by the impact. She is hot and cold, doubled in two, the sound of the crash buzzes in her ears. She shakes her head at her own stupidity, at the shock.

Dad saw it all, is up out of his seat, flat against the transparent barrier still clutching the vending-machine chicken soup. Jeannine, are you all right?

Jeannine can't bear to look at him. She doesn't care that other people saw her but why did she have to fall in front of him? She wanted to show how much she'd improved, how the money spent on lessons and kit wasn't wasted. Jeannine hardly ever falls, and certainly never hurts herself. She's good at skating, she knows she is, practically ready for local competitions, according to her coach.

She spends several minutes slumped over in the middle of the ice, her knees and buttocks wet. Skaters zip around her, dodge past, dangerously near. Plenty of people fall over when the rink is this busy. Little girls should learn not to show off.

Are – you – all – right?

Yes Dad, I'm fine.

Now a supervisor is helping Jeannine up and her wrist is killing her. Ow ow ow. It *kills*. She holds it to her chest with her uninjured hand.

Please let it be a sprain. If it's broken, Mum will never let her skate again.

Saturday night, light pollution bounces off wet pavements and coats the buildings in orange fur. A couple walk through Clifton hands and arms entwined, round his waist, round her shoulders. They stop to kiss. Hurry on.

Not a couple, though: two individuals who met in a hectic nightclub the music rumbling the walls vibrating an assault of beats and bass. She likes a sweet man. If she didn't, she would be out of his reach.

Leaning on the bar he smiles weakly, persuades himself she is a lost cause, someone has put her up to it; until she is linking her fingers through the loops of his jeans, until she is pressing his earlobe in her divine mouth, he can't really believe the overtures are genuine. Why is she showing him her key ring, a large letter J made of sparkles? She isn't. She is showing him a set of house keys, that they have somewhere private to go, and is now leading him through the dirty streets, clearly expert in these matters. It is captured on CCTV.

At a terraced house she struggles with the front door, works the lock back and forth as if she is unfamiliar with it. Shared accommodation, she explains and takes him upstairs past the potted plant, the tangled phone, the smell of curry and strewn junk mail. The bedroom is a female student's, filled with cosmetics, CDs, ring binders, handbags, floppy discs and a boxy computer with wires trailing from it. Several issues of *Fields of Science* magazine have been left in a heap on the carpet. One is open at a feature about natural language processing: *NLP-based information access technologies will continue to be a major area of research and development in the new millennium, but will computers ever accomplish human-like language processing?* (An illustration of a stern reader absorbed in her book disputes that such a thing is possible or desirable.) The notice board is cluttered ... handwritten notes and eclectic leaflets, a 2-for-1 restaurant offer (expired). Slotted into the frame is a snapshot of a girl in a spangled outfit clutching a tiny trophy in the shape of an ice dancer in mid-flight.

Is this you?

Oh ... a very long time ago. Don't look at it.

I think it's adorable.

She takes it from him, turns it over and reattaches it blank side out. There's Absolut and some shot glasses on the windowsill.

It is an instruction. He finds these and pours two.

Lip-glossy grin— She sinks her vodka in a single swallow, then takes off her shoes and stretches on the bed, revealing a jewelled piercing at her navel.

The textbooks are about computer science, and one detail from their hasty half-conversation rattles in his skull; he thought she was doing a politics degree, in fact, he was certain of it.

No one's coming home unexpectedly, are they?

It's my sister's place. She's away for the weekend. Lets me stay whenever I need to.

You need to now because ... ?

She kneels up on the bed and gives him kisses where he is standing.

His hand strays to the bare gap between her vest and her trousers and the peep of a pretty thong, but the caresses he places there are lukewarm.

239

She sighs, What's the matter?

Nothing.

Something is. Do you have a race problem?

No.

Some men do. Sometimes I get the signals wrong.

Not me. I think you're stunning.

What is it, then?

Usually I do this with a girlfriend. Not with someone I just met.

You've nothing to be afraid of . . . She kisses him again.

What if we just chilled tonight, spent the day together tomorrow?

Don't you want me?

Ye-es. But we could get to know each other first, maybe, do this another night. You can tell me all about your course and your family and your dreams and . . . your name.

There isn't going to be another night.

Right. I see.

She takes one of his hands, gently, pulls back his sleeve to reveal a distorted plastic wristband. What's this?

Glastonbury.

It's *filthy*. You must have been wearing it for weeks.

He picks up a pair of scissors from the desk and snips it off.

I didn't ask you to do that.

I could see it was annoying you.

Despite his good intentions, he gives in to her mouth and her inviting breaths and runs his hands over her body. As his confidence swells, he whispers a little question into her ear, Is there anything you would like me to do? (It was never important enough to ask before.)

Actually, now you come to mention it . . .

He is surprisingly good at this, her sounds, her shaking, she arches her back, one hand caressing her own breasts, the other gripping the bed frame. He is good at this.

But there is a moment which subdues the mood between them. She assumes control, becomes businesslike. His pride is stung by the implied criticism—

I'm not like that, I can take care of you.

Let me take care of myself. (There will be no careless mistakes.)

Then it is done. They pass over the awkwardness and fall back into their rhythm.

She does not let him cuddle long afterwards, does not allow him to settle for the whole night, can't stand his compliments or sentimental murmurs, these gestures are unwelcome. Has put her top and knickers back on, becomes brusque and impatient.

I like you.

She laughs. You don't like me. You don't know me.

I want to. Do you live in Bristol?

Nope. Neither do you, Essex Boy.

I had a friend's stag do. Not really a friend, we went to the same school. What brought you here, anyway?

A bad break-up.

I didn't know you were breaking up with someone. I thought you were single.

I am single.

How bad was it?

She licks her lips, then smiles. Does it matter?

Do you want to talk about it?

I've got absolutely nothing to say. She picks up his clothes from the floor, chucks them at him without making eye contact.

He puts on his T-shirt under duress. I'd like to phone you, sometime.

No. Thanks.

Then let me leave you my number?

I'll throw it away, you know I will. Don't look offended; I didn't make any promises.

I know. I think you should have told me, though.

She frowns. About?

Your ex.

It's none of your business.

True, but now I can't help wondering if you're still vulnerable. What if I've taken advantage of you?

How thoughtful . . . and yet how patronising.

I didn't mean it like that.

Do I look upset to you? Do I look like I need rescuing?

He flattens his hair and decides to try a different strategy. Spend the day with me.

I'm sorry, I can't.

Nothing serious, just a bit of fun.

She appears to consider but replies, Stop being ridiculous.

You're going back to him, aren't you?

I'd like you to leave now.

Please? Just one day together? It'll be great. We'll do whatever you want.

Make sure you're quiet on your way out, other people are sleeping.

He finishes getting dressed.

She ignores him, picks up a compact mirror, reapplies her lip gloss, snaps it shut. Her parting kiss is chaste, almost maternal, she pats his bum.

He's all wrong for you. You should be with me.

She should feel insulted. Instead, she has the urge to giggle. *Go away, Essex Boy.*

The Member of Parliament for Bexhall South decides this applicant will fill the post. He reclines in his chair, occasionally fingers his tie, rubs his chin stubble as he listens. The young male opposite is wearing a pink shirt and a whiff of Hugo Boss, has spiked hair and pitted skin from acne during adolescence. Went to a top university. Is polite and talkative, right of centre and a believer in the green agenda, confident, has a *keen* interest in journalism and PR which will be useful . . . his main weakness is that he has not been a member of the party for long, appears to have had no specific involvement in politics until five months ago.

And why is that?

I always wanted to join, of course. However when I was pursuing my career in journalism I was advised by someone, who I'm sure was entirely well meaning, that I shouldn't join any political party as it could cast a shadow on my impartiality. Then when I realised it was more honourable to become (he mimes the quote marks in the air) 'part of the solution' instead of just being a critic, I felt it was time to 'come out of the closet', so to speak. On reflection, I regret I did not become a card-carrying member sooner.

If the politician has another worry it is that this metrosexual man presents too well. His slick speech has the squeaky timbre of rehearsal. This chap likes to impress, but if he is as good as he says he is, if he is even half as good—

The last interviewee is shown in, extends a slim hand adorned with nail extensions and nail art, wears a flattering pencil skirt and fitted jacket, a vintage brooch on her lapel.

He is moved to cover their handshake reassuringly, be avuncular with her. Don't be nervous. Make yourself comfortable. You are Jeannine Okoro? Did I say it right?

Yes, fine.

I'm Jonathan Ewan. It's good to meet you. Have you been to Parliament before?

I've protested nearby.

Excellent, that's what we like to hear. Talk to me about your own political outlook.

I'm a Thatcherite.

That's not an especially popular thing to be. Would you care to elaborate?

I believe in a light touch by government, first and foremost, and for that reason I am a Eurosceptic. I believe in personal freedoms and personal responsibilities. I believe in free markets and the power of strong economies to have positive effects in communities. I think ours is the natural political party for entrepreneurs and working families, and we should be here for those people, advocating their needs, making them feel safe at night. I believe completely that aspiration and choice are intrinsically linked. I am in favour of letting people decide how to spend their own money as far as is sensible, only to tax what is necessary and not a penny more. Government exists to help people in need, and when people are doing fine for themselves, government should back off.

You have not mentioned schools and hospitals.

I like schools and hospitals. Actually no, I don't like hospitals.

You will be aware that education and health are cornerstones of public debate: these issues dominate.

Certainly.

I suppose my question to you is how do you think we, as the Opposition, should be setting ourselves apart from the government on public services?

As I said, by backing off. Public services are groaning under the weight of targets and monitoring. Ask any nurse, teacher or police officer and they will tell you they did not sign up for an admin job.

You think we should reduce bureaucracy. Haven't we been saying that for ages now?

Ye-es. But I am talking about more than mere red tape. The current level of interference can be characterised as paranoia. The legacy of this government is one of spin and megalomania, and I personally have a problem with it. Confident leadership means delegating responsibility further down the chain. You need to trust people because they're the professionals, you should give them space to do their jobs. That is what we should say in debate, and that is what we should do when we get in.

Anything else?

Jeannine thinks. I'm in favour of blocking up the Channel Tunnel.

Tell me more.

We simply have to stop the influx of immigrants and refugees because the way I see it, it's a free-for-all.

The politician's mouth convulses as though he is going to snigger or make an objection painfully obvious to him. The party has run on that sort of message before, haven't we? We got clobbered.

We sounded hysterical. And racist. We didn't make the proper arguments. We didn't say, 'Look, the Immigration Nationality Directorate isn't fit for purpose, and you have had a decade to improve it, why haven't you?' Or that Minister for Immigration is a job nobody wants, that no one does properly or stays in for any length of time. We come across as unsympathetic, but the irony is it's even more inhumane to string people along with unresolved status, sometimes for years and years. If a case doesn't stand up, then send them back to their own countries immediately. Don't ask them nicely to leave and then be surprised when they resurface eighteen months later cleaning cars for a pittance, sleeping in a squalid bedroom with six other people and having a nervous breakdown. I'm not saying foreign nationals have an easy life here, actually it's a huge mistake on our part to suggest they do, but the added pressure on housing, on healthcare, on the public purse . . . voters are dismayed by the sheer numbers, and government is complicit in a black market of cheap labour, exploitation and trafficking. We ought

245

to be ashamed. Retaking control of our borders would be a start. Then fix the system which allowed it to happen in the first place.

Ewan taps one of his teeth while he scrutinises the letter it took her an entire weekend to write. Let's talk about your previous experience—

Jeannine describes her first job at a local authority and her current job at the Chamber of Commerce.

It strikes me that, for a fan of capitalism, you didn't go into business yourself?

I still might if I don't get this job. Jeannine adds a smile.

What sort of business?

I'm not sure, but it's going to have a fantastic website. She shrugs. I am more suited to this.

What do you think of our leader then?

Jeannine exhales. I think he came along at the right time.

Do you like him?

I've never met him.

You have a vote, though. Voters have to reach a conclusion one way or the other about people standing for office, usually without the benefit of meeting them. You're entitled to your views. Based on what you have seen and heard, I ask again, what do you think of him?

For the first time during the interview, Jeannine hesitates. Jonathan Ewan presses his fingertips together and waits. She says, He has good qualities. He is articulate, engaging, enthusiastic, appealing . . . the party has been in opposition for a while; we need a leader who is appealing in order to win back a majority and he fits the bill.

But . . . ?

He reminds me of a manager at the Carphone Warehouse. I see him on the news and I think yes, I could definitely buy a mobile-phone upgrade from you.

Jonathan makes a noise which sounds like *Huh* and he turns his attention back to her CV.

Jeannine senses she should have been more circumspect, wonders if it is too late to walk it back. Her strategy was to be truthful, to speak with conviction, to be unafraid of showing her cards – it was slightly reckless. The MP has moved on to her activism at university and volunteering locally, a chance to redeem herself: On the doorstep obviously; I've been a teller a couple of times because they struggle to make up numbers. I've done a bit for some newsletters, things like that. I like going to events, so I do try to stay in touch even when I'm busy.

Jonathan describes some likely scenarios the role would bring to gauge her reactions. Finally he says, Today I have to make a decision on who I wish to employ, and I will do so based on these interviews and relevant skills and experience. Out of interest, was there any special reason why you applied to work for me? I'm asking all the candidates. (This is a lie; he thought of it just now.)

Because of your Private Member's Bill. You were trying to help small businesses.

That was three years ago.

I think you'll find it was four years ago.

And it wasn't successful.

I know. But you tried.

The meeting ends. Jonathan likes the sound of it: My assistant Jeannine will take care of it; ask for my assistant Jeannine Okoro; let me spell it for you . . . Yes, it looks good, too. She went to a former polytechnic, though. Oh pish, he mutters to himself. He has made the right choice.

Erica! He shouts for the Parliamentary Assistant of his colleague.

Erica Twycross, today in a houndstooth suit, comes in and

gives a withering look at the MP who is young enough to be her son.

Sorry, are you on the phone?

Not this very second, Jonathan.

Good. I wanted to thank you for your help today. Seeing as you will be sharing an office with my new assistant, any thoughts? Anyone strike you?

Erica has outlasted numerous elected members and parliamentary staff, cannot be fazed, answers, The black woman.

You mean the last candidate?

Yes Jonathan, the last candidate. (The only candidate who was a woman and black.)

Why her particularly?

She was the best.

Did you talk to her? Do you know her from somewhere else?

We spoke a little. No, I don't know her.

He shifts in his chair, uncomfortable at the thought of challenging Erica on how she has come to her conclusion. What about this one? He proffers the CV of his favourite.

Erica speed-reads the pages. At one point her eyes flick up, then resume their progress. Have you checked these dates for accuracy?

Jonathan does not reply; they both know he has not.

She gives the sheets back. Anything else I can do for you?

No thank you, Erica.

It is the next working day when Jonathan Ewan comes into the office, greets Erica at her desk, says yes, Jeannine was the right applicant, has accepted the job, is starting in three weeks. He has not yet taken advantage of Erica's connections, but he may wish to one day. Until then he is building up his credit, demonstrating how he values her opinion, affording her respect. He does not mention that the boy wanted more money, that despite his assertions during the interview he dithered when he

248

was offered it, then turned it down. That Jeannine was content with commencing at the bottom of the pay scale.

Jeannine Okoro wakes to the radio news report about the Wenchuan earthquake. Coffee first, toast with Marmite and deciding what to wear – grey trouser suit and pink blouse with ruffles, gold hoop earrings and DKNY bag. And suddenly the day has a shape, details, accessories. During this, an item about SATs and whether these are bogging down the curriculum; the interviewee points out they were introduced under the previous administration. Then business news.

She showers during stories about selling British nuclear-power stations to a French company and possible candidates for a European Council president; apparently there is only one contender (she smiles splashily, rolls her eyes at the name) though this assumes the Lisbon Treaty is ratified by member states. Never going to happen, she answers from behind the shower curtain.

Jeannine perches in front of the full-length mirror to style her hair with the GHD straighteners and do her make-up. Good days, favourite days, start with this part going well – when it goes badly, inevitably a stressful or mismanaged day follows. The presenters are describing the newspaper headlines now, and her interest is sparked by more concern on the declining economy, increases in energy prices, decreases in house prices. Not low enough for me yet, and she drinks what is left of the coffee gone cold.

The inevitable update on the US election; voters in West Virginia are saying many Americans will not vote for a black presidential candidate. But Jeannine thinks Obama is running a good campaign, that Obama has kismet. McCain will look unimpressive when they are standing together, debating together, will have to work hard to earn it. The visuals of a black first family. The symbol. It is better reality television than *The*

Apprentice, a better political fight than Boris and Ken— She is dressed, a dab of perfume. These shoes match her outfit, though they let in the rain, but the weather report assures her it will be dry and fine and she is going to risk it. Has her purse, her mobile, her Oyster, her pass, her keys, her—

Down into Old Street station, touches in, London is going to work. On the escalator she checks her mobile, Liam has texted her.

Morning baby. Luv u. Cant wait to see u l8r. XO

Jeannine glows. Then she takes out *Never Let Me Go*, which she will finish today on the Northern or the Jubilee line. She is a Londoner, and skilful at reading standing up on public transport during peak hours. And later, in a random act of kindness, she will BookCross it for someone else in the women's changing rooms or in one of London's green squares. Commuters shake open their newspapers magazines bend back thrillers nod along to their iPods.

At Westminster station she separates from the flow of footfall to swipe into Portcullis House through the underground entrance, and crosses the atrium where assistants and politicians, police and public, are loitering and assembling, grabbing coffee to take away, chatting, lost en route to one of hundreds of rooms. A former Home Secretary draws the gaze of some newbies – Jeannine disdains them for it, strides past with purpose.

In the office bay, Erica's computer is on but she is away from her desk. The member Erica works for can be heard making a call in his office. As ever, the light on Jeannine's desk phone indicates waiting voicemail. She starts her computer before taking her jacket off, begins sorting the wedge of letters and memos. There are forty-four new emails in the inbox since she left the office late yesterday evening, of which ten are marked high importance, and more pinging in all the time.

*

250

Erica, are you getting much traffic on the Human Fertilisation and Embryology Bill?

Erica's rapid typing is uninterrupted. Bit. On various aspects. Why?

We are. Jeannine casts a glance at the mustard cardigan and grey updo. She would have preferred to share an office with someone nearer her own age. Still, Erica is OK, has worked for politicians since the eighties, is the embodiment of those who know but don't tell. But sometimes, sometimes—

Her colleague rotates the chair and looks over her spectacles at Jeannine, schoolmarmish. What is it, Jeannine?

Has Terry given any indication to you . . . ?

Erica takes the glasses off and lets them hang from her neck on a string of beads. I put things on his desk, he gives them back . . . God knows what goes on between the ears. These issues (the lady dismisses invisible insects from the air) they come round every so often, and suddenly it feels as if we are in an elaborate and well-funded debating society, not a place of serious work. And then it dies down. You and I are here to help them.

Yeah. Are you going to the seminar today?

Which one?

Community Responsibility for Social Something-or-other. I've got the email somewhere. (Erica never bothers but Jeannine always asks, makes an effort to be friendly.)

You should go. Erica turns back to her screen, slides her specs on, resumes her wicked fast typing.

Hazel sips her mineral water, twists the cap on the bottle.

They are at the venue, both clip their event ID badges on their Palace of Westminster lanyards. Jeannine has yet to find out why Hazel is so thin. If she has a medical condition she has not talked about it, no oblique references to clinics or appointments with doctors; does not mention a strict diet or a regime of exercise, either. Jeannine Okoro goes to the gym at least twice a week (and eats what she likes), but has never seen Hazel there. Allergic to dairy or to gluten, maybe?

Hazel has short hair, adding to her boyish appearance, is talking about her sister again: I always have to phone her. I don't get angry any more, I just accept it. And she's always all, Hey, how are you? What have you been doing? keen to chat. Sometimes I can hear her almost . . . I don't know what. She never rings me, never texts. I say, 'Didn't you get my message?' and she says No, it's not working, or Yes, but she couldn't get back to me for some reason, or she tried to and I didn't answer. But I check, and there's no missed call on my phone or anything. I don't know. She doesn't even email any more.

Did anything happen?

I've asked, and she swears it's nothing. We used to go to the cinema every week, just to watch whatever was on, or go for a bottle of wine at the pub. I think she's punishing me, only fuck knows what I've done.

Jeannine takes a tissue out of her handbag, gives it to Hazel. Have you told her how this is making you feel?

Hazel blows her nose, shakes her head simultaneously. Would you?

Yes, I would tell my sister to get her act together. Jeannine has a forthright relationship with her older sibling; as children, this manifested as screaming and pushing and occasional hair-pulling.

I don't want to be needy, but it's as if she doesn't like me any more. It's what you do to someone when you're trying to get rid of them. I know sometimes sisters and brothers are estranged, but I never thought Lucy and me would . . .

Hazel sips her water again.

The delegates are networking over tea and coffee cups after

speeches and questions. Business cards are exchanged. Groupies of both sexes congregate around a frontbencher and a newspaper columnist. There are tables with displays and literature, freebies. Political conversations are conducted in raised, brassy voices. Someone makes a beeline for the two women, introduces himself.

Hazel has met him before, remembers him from another function, gives him air kisses as though they are in show business.

He describes an online project where they need people to make video clips – would Hazel and Jeannine be interested in taking part? They agree, give him their email addresses and extension numbers.

Hazel says, Do you need to go back to the office?

Just to check Jonathan's messages.

I need to check Maureen's. Are you free to do something after? go shopping? A few people are meeting for drinks later. I didn't fancy it before, but it will be good if you come – unless you have plans with Liam? Is he training tonight? Sorry, you hardly get to see him, do you? Don't feel like you have to.

Hazel's pleading is blatant, the offer not to go forced out unwillingly. Jeannine replies, Yes, I'd like to. I'll phone him, he won't mind. It's nice to go out on a school night.

In the high-street bookshop, Jeannine takes a deep breath. The booky smell. New books smell good; second-hand books smell better. She peruses literature and fiction while Hazel looks for power-reading about China, buys *The Poisonwood Bible*.

In a department store, Hazel heads for the changing rooms to try on boho dresses and tight-fitting jeans. Jeannine lingers in the shoe section. It would be useful to buy some flats, smart shoes for work and to do her commute in. Some people wear trainers for the journey, leave office shoes under their desks or carry them in a bag. Jeannine won't, for several reasons. She picks up a high-heeled court in red, turns the elegant design over in her hands, £80. A satin pair in taupe has a bow strap detail, is cheaper at £59 but Jeannine suspects the material will scuff and age quickly. Then a black zipped ankle boot with a wedge.

At the till a customer is returning a purchase, wanting her money refunded. Clothes hangers are pushed back and forth, squeaking like old bikes, a tweed jacket with oversized buttons is pulled out by another shopper, That's nice, I like that, bet they haven't got my size. An angular white mannequin is posed on a pedestal garishly lit like a science fiction prop, there is a surge in power, a technical fault, which causes Jeannine several seconds of blindness and an illusion of motion.

A floor assistant, a girl wearing a cat design top and a store headset, offers Jeannine help. She declines (spots fading from her vision); she's just browsing really, keeps looking along the shoe shelves, picks out some styles and then replaces them. She glances back at the girl, casually, is her heritage Japanese? Thai, maybe? Indian? Jeannine can't tell, and for some reason would like to know. She is a teenager with a youthful complexion, anyway – too pretty to be believed – and Jeannine Okoro goes in search of solace among the belts and clutch bags, though she does not need these.

We are for all of Britain: for communities, for families and for individuals. It is time to celebrate what I have always known in my heart, that we are members of an inclusive party. Our values are Britain's values—

He paused for applause. Jeannine also applauded.

Common sense and vigilance, a shared sense of responsibility and fairness, these are the qualities that British people possess and are the components that will make our streets safer for all of us—

He praised the residents' groups, the have-a-go heroes, the parents who set clear boundaries and good examples to follow (what about a cinch belt? Jeannine has confident taste, could she carry it off?), the numerous young people not reported in the news who reject gang and knife culture. Then, there was no doubt about it, the speaker was advocating stop-and-search.

Jeannine catches her image in a store mirror. Then she catches herself in the driver's mirror of her dad's Ford Cortina. Her legs are not even long enough for her feet to touch the floor, and she has her special ice-skating bag on the seat next to her. She waits until he gets back into the car and has revved the engine.

Dad, what did that policeman want?

His grave eyes answer her reflection. Nothing, he was just checking we're both OK, and I told him we were fine. I told him, thanks for asking.

She pouts and dares not contradict him, won't say there is a funny feeling in her tummy and she might need to stop for a wee on the way home if she can't hold it in.

Then Dad turns round and snarls over his shoulder as though she is being argumentative: He's just doing his job, Jeannine. You have to respect the law, it's one of the things we do. Understand?

She nods yes. Though she doesn't.

She takes out her lip gloss, reapplies it. (Would Keith say the same to Yasmin? I wonder.) Better.

And afterwards, being approached by the young man with the retreating hairline, his forehead gleaming in earnest, to take part in – what did he call it? – an engagement tool for the YouTube generation. There was a whole roomful of people to ask.

Hazel pulled a face, but said she didn't mind helping out.

Great, I promise you won't regret it, and he switched his focus to Jeannine because it was Jeannine he most wanted. He was polite and ingratiating, but there was an element of greediness, a twinge of desperation.

I don't mind either. And she sincerely meant it, but Jeannine is not naive.

She tries calling Liam, it goes to voicemail.

Me again, in case you didn't get my message. I'm going out with Hazel for a few hours, but I won't be late and I can't drink much because of work tomorrow. Anyway, just wanted to check you didn't mind, and you're OK. And to tell you I love you, I really do. Ring me, it will be nice to hear your voice. Bye.

In the shoe section once more, Jeannine finds a design in indigo suede with a stub toe and a metallic pointed heel, £110. She loves it immediately. When she tries on the pair she feels queenly and they will go with everything – not 'with', not 'everything', but they are exactly her style, will match what they will match, and be striking when they intentionally clash. She puts them on her credit card.

The assistant, the same girl, folds them in tissue paper, fits the lid on the box, puts them in a rigid store bag. *There you are, Madam.*

Madam. Seething silently, Jeannine slips it over the crook of her arm, but the new-purchase high has had the shine taken off it.

Hazel says her friends have called, have named a meeting place.

About time.

As they go, Jeannine turns back. The shop assistant thanks her once again and bids her a guileless goodbye.

It isn't her fault, Jeannine knows this. And *didn't I have my turn of being skinny and beautiful?* Her body heats to recall what she used to get away with. She bites her nail while she listens to Hazel's next problem (it's to do with a call centre), gnaws on it. Jeannine's *degree, relationship, job*, have recently begun to feel, what? not unsatisfactory? not unexceptional? No, she is pleased with them, pleased she can buy a pair of shoes without asking anyone's permission. A woman can take pride in what she has achieved so far, and also be aware she has yet to meet her potential. She nips the nail off.

The venue is white cubes and retro-vision feature walls, the spirits on glass shelving backlit in purple and pink. Tea lights waver in sculptural holders too big and heavy to snaffle, the music is broken beat, the staff in studded jeans and faded-print T-shirts of the Ramones and the Boomtown Rats.

It is surprisingly difficult to meet new people at Portcullis, where the offices can feel like cells. Only by being proactive, by joining one of the societies, by receiving and accepting sideways invitations from the socially promiscuous, can you develop new relationships. Jeannine meets six people this evening, all colleagues from the Whitehall bubble. She drinks dark rum while Hazel drinks bottled beer with a wedge of lime in the neck. Hazel has forgotten her distress from earlier, is friendly to the men with her physical contacts: a peck on the cheek, a ruffle, a flirty shove.

Jeannine finds herself in conversation about postgraduate courses with a civil servant, puts on a sceptical persona, asks, Wouldn't you have been better off staying in employment for that length of time?

It flew by very quickly, one year, even two years, is actually nothing in the world of work. Maybe if I had been happier in my last job . . . ? When I consider how much I benefited personally—

I thought the point was to study something in a specialised field relevant to your career.

Yes, you certainly can, but mine was more out of academic curiosity. Some people travel. Some people do pottery or play in a band. This was my thing, this was what I wanted. On the whole, employers view it positively, it shows commitment and skills development, and if one person has an MA and the next person doesn't (takes a drink), it's something else to throw in the mix. I got to explore a subject I care about.

What about money?

I didn't have any. Listen – it's Jeannine, isn't it? – if you're interested, even if you're *half*-interested, you should look up some courses, send an email to test the water. That doesn't cost anything. I mean, you are considering studying again . . . ?

Jeannine shakes her head. I like the job I have.

Well, good for you. Not many people say that about their work.

I like hearing you talk about it, though.

If I'm becoming a bore, tell me to stop.

Back at the flat, a bit tipsy, Jeannine finds it dark. This surprises her as Liam would normally wait up. She switches on a lamp in the bedroom but he is not there, all is as she left it this morning. She checks her mobile but knows already no messages no missed calls, has checked it periodically during the evening.

And while she is at it, being irritated by people who don't stay in touch (Jeannine drops her keys and her bags, looks stubbornly at the lit display of her phone again), when was the last time Tess, Naomie or even Gina bothered texting or ringing her?

A couple of hours pass and the alcohol wears off. Jeannine is reading in bed when he comes back.

I thought you would be asleep.

I'm not.

Why aren't you asleep, baby? Liam climbs over the bed to her, embraces her clumsily.

She reciprocates but answers, You didn't phone me.

I missed you, though. I missed you today. You look gorgeous like this. I love this top, it's very slinky. Did I buy you this top? He starts to kiss her shoulders and chest.

No, I bought it. Liam, didn't you get my messages? Liam?

I got them. I was with the boys, we were playing some pool.

Didn't you take your mobile?

I knew you were with people, I thought you would be having a good time. He persists in his attentions.

Before we do that, can we do this please?

He ceases, moves away, starts taking off his shoes with his back to her. He has a rumble in his breath as though he is cross with her.

She says, I don't mind you going out. You work hard, of course you should. I just want to be told about it, that's all.

You wanted to check up on me.

No, not like that. I wanted to hear from you, and roughly what time I'll see you so I don't worry about you.

Liam looks at her askance.

Do you think I'm being unreasonable? Because I don't think I am. I think it's completely normal to worry about the other person.

No, baby, you're not unreasonable. And you work hard too. You're entitled to go out whenever you like.

Jeannine did not mean for this to be about her. She did her part, and as a matter of fact rarely socialises any more. She lets it pass in order for the quarrel to be over.

Liam sighs. You're right. You're absolutely right. I'm sorry.

She does not reply immediately. They are the correct words, and he whispers them with big open eyes, but she does not like the way he drops them in; they have the smooth texture of over-use. Even if you can't phone me, just a text—

Next time, I promise. He kisses her hand as if she is a princess. Is it good? He indicates the book she is reading.

She sighs. I just started it, but yeah. And I bought some new shoes today too.

Why don't I make you one of those disgusting teas you drink, then you can show them to me and tell me about your day?

Well . . . that would be nice of you. She likes that they have this time together, that they share with each other the small and mundane parts of their lives; it is one of the ways she loves him. You and I should do something special. I'll take you somewhere expensive, we'll make a big evening of it. Would you like that? I'll even wear my suit.

She subdues her cynicism, it must be important to him if he wants to dress smartly, and merely nods so she doesn't say anything stupid.

Would you like peppermint or camomile?

Surprise me.

In the kitchen she can hear him singing Stevie Wonder, and it soothes her heart temporarily.

The sweetness of magazine pages, perfume samples absorbed into high-quality printed paper. Jeannine holds them to her face and inhales. She keeps glossy magazines, keeps them in order like an archive, gazes at the spines with fondness. She likes catalogues and brochures too, but is more inclined to get rid of these at intervals (puts a few old ones in the recycling box). It is the weight of them, getting something hefty and colourful for little money or for free, their slipperiness, that they are filled with beautiful objects she can fantasise about owning.

Some of the publications are pages and pages of writing set off with a few arty photos – attractive people relaxing in green spaces, attractive people on tiered seating, attractive people in libraries – and architecture. Some are as long as novels and filled with possibilities, possibilities of possibilities, as desirable and as far out of her reach as a Gucci handbag.

Time to get rid of them.

Then she makes a neat tower which she hides at the back of the wardrobe, unable to part with them (it would be too painful). There are men who hoard pornography, compulsively growing their collection over years, developing emotional fixations with

the sexy models they will never acquire in real life; Jeannine
Okoro hoards university prospectuses.

The weekend. So Jeannine takes the bus to her sister's, for
there is a conversation she has to have—

Look who it is! Sophia addresses this to both her children, to
Josh the infant she cradles across her denim shirt front, to
Yasmin the little girl clutching her mummy's leg. Her gold jewellery swings and jingles. Thank God someone's here, now I can
sleep.

Jeannine is used to Big Sister's lack of ceremony, used to putting the kettle on for herself, used to being given jobs to do
whenever she comes over: peeling, ironing, running to the shop,
emptying the dishwasher. Sophia is like their mum – to get on
with her you need to do your share, be bossed by her. Jeannine
is more like their dad, generally self-sufficient but will take
instructions from stronger personalities to maintain the peace.

Josh is laid on the baby mat, his eyes and fingers interacting
with the jungle animals on the play gym. Yasmin positions herself on the carpet between her brother and the television,
showing *Charlie and Lola*, curls herself into a knot so her head
droops on her knee. Sophia and Jeannine sit in adjacent armchairs, mugs of tea balanced. The mother updates the aunt on
how the children have changed in the past week. Not much, by
the sound of it.

Still, Jeannine is patient, can see Big Sister is tired, gets lonely
for adult company, wants to express her thoughts. If Jeannine
gives way first, then she can talk about what she needs to talk
about.

Sophia lowers her voice. Somebody had a bad dream the other
night (she points at Yasmin's back), screamed the whole place
down, I'm amazed the neighbours didn't complain. I thought
she was being attacked, I honestly did, even though I know there
is no way anyone could break in without us hearing before they

got to the children. Seriously, you don't know what it's like to worry about literally everything, every rash, every sharp edge, spiders in the bathroom, the whole world becomes deadly. She was in such a state, and I was calming her down saying it's nothing, bad dreams can't hurt you la la la and all the time I'm the one who's shaking. Then she's back to sleep (clicks her fingers) like that but I can't because now I'm on edge and I have to check the door and the windows and the cooker.

What did she dream about?

I've no idea. She's learned the word lorry – yellow lorry, rubbish lorry – but she confuses it with bus.

Jeannine can't tell whether this is a clue to Yasmin's dream or if it's incidental.

Sophia yawns. Josh and me need to have a nap. You don't mind, do you?

Jeannine does mind, has to hide her irritation. It is one thing not being waited on so her sister can focus on the children; it is quite another being in charge of one of them, at least before they are old enough to be bribed.

Sophia assures her Keith will be home in a minute, and of course Jeannine gives in. To aunty and niece's displeasure, the television is turned off.

Yasmin is on Jeannine's lap for Farm Puzzle.

What is Josh doing now?

Sleeping.

And what is Josh going to do when he wakes up?

Crying.

He cries a lot, does he?

Yeah.

There is a lot Jeannine likes about her little niece: her chubbiness, her tiny perfect nails, her hair in black twists with pink bobbles. (Her revulsion at the unwanted responsibility subsides a bit.) Why did you have a bad dream? There's nothing to be afraid of. We'll look after you, Mummy, Daddy, Grandma and Gramps. Me, for what it's worth.

Yasmin plugs and unplugs the wooden shapes, the duck and the sheep and the cow – will make their noises when asked.

What noise does this one make?

Quack-quack-quack.

That's right. And what noise does this one make?

Oink. Oink.

That's right.

And what noise does this one make?

Woof-woof?

And how can you tell when a dog is happy? Because-it-wags-its-tail.

Jeannine likes the way her body reacts to her niece and nephew when they are occasionally dumped in her arms: her muscles increase their strength and snap round the child of their own accord, mould to the lumpy form, and the babe clings to her in return with a tough, squishy grip. She likes their miniature features, that they are warm and squirmy.

It's not your fault you're so boring, is it? (The suggestible child shakes her head.) And you'll be very big very soon. (The child nods in agreement.)

Yasmin wriggles, catching Jeannine off guard, her tiny shell ears sensitive to her daddy coming home, to his footstep and keys before they reach the front door and the hearing of big people.

Keith comes in without calling, for fear of disturbing his wife and son, takes off his hi-vis jacket, his height and shoulders blocking the daylight in the hallway. He greets Jeannine, offers to relieve her of her burden, lifts his daughter, raising her into the air. Despite his bulk he has a gentle nature, asks how long Sophia and Josh have been resting, asks after the boyfriend because they haven't seen him for a while.

Jeannine exhales. Really great. Actually, he took me out for dinner. It was very romantic.

Glad to hear it. What about work? (That's fine too.) Keith plants his daughter on the floor, takes out the stickle bricks, encourages her to play with them. I meant to say to you Jeannine (Keith and Yasmin sort through the pieces, What are you making? a dolly?), if you ever need a place to stay, you can always stay with us.

Why would I do that?

Just in case. I thought it was worth reminding you, you could if you needed to.

Jeannine laughs because she does not know what else to do. Thanks, but you guys only have two bedrooms the last time I counted.

And a sofa that folds out.

It's nice of you to offer, but we've got our own place.

Remind me why you're still renting? Liam said ages ago that you ought to buy while you could afford it, that even if you hadn't made up your minds to get married it would be worth having some cash from a sale to split. If I remember rightly, Liam said renting was throwing money away.

He didn't say that, I did! Jeannine emphasises it hotly, then glances in the direction of the room where mother and child are napping, lowers her voice, We aren't breaking up, if that's what you think.

Who said you were? (Keith helps Yasmin to make a doll with a square head.) If you decide to study again you might need somewhere to live, that's all. Staying here would save you money. Come to think of it, you haven't mentioned it recently.

Me and not Liam . . . ?

It's a meaningless gesture if he's able to support you both from what he earns at the leisure centre.

It's a health club.

Is he able to support you both?

Jeannine scowls at her brother-in-law. You don't know what you're talking about.

You've changed your mind?

Yes, I've changed my mind.

A few weeks ago—

Well, I've gone off the idea. And I'd prefer you not to mention it again.

Jeannine pretends to admire Sophia and Keith's wedding photo, the bride and groom had a fit of the giggles outside the church, their expressions frozen for ever in exquisite laughter. Sophia had just turned twenty-five when they married. Jeannine is now twenty-nine. She twiddles her necklace (Accessorize, spur of the moment, £12.99).

Besides, it wouldn't work, she says. You, Sophia, the kids, there isn't enough space here—

Keith scratches the back of his head, It wouldn't be ideal but there's room for you to eat and sleep. For a year it could work, just about, or until you found an alternative. We would manage somehow.

Jeannine goes very quiet. Why are you saying this stuff?

Because we're family.

I can take care of myself, you know.

Yes. I know you can. (And this at least has the ring of sincerity.) Call it reciprocity. If something happened to one or both of us, I know you would make sure Yasmin and Josh were OK. Nothing *is* going to happen, but maybe we can do something to help you out? If you don't want to stay here, that's different, that's a choice. But you deserve to have a choice to begin with.

Jeannine taps her empty mug. Thanks.

Then he says, We're proud of you. We really are.

Keith was not overt in his disapproval when she got her job with Jonathan, but he hardly hid it successfully, either. Jeannine should set him straight, tell him he has no reason to be proud, remind him why he hates the man she works for. *I work in an office.*

Yes, and you're very good at it. You have chutzpah.

She snorts and stretches her arms. I'm going for a run later. A looong run.

Have you thought about asking your parents . . . ?

Ugh. Jeannine clenches her jaw at the thought of it.

Perhaps not. And for your information, we would take Liam in too, if you wanted us to.

I bet you would.

Ye-es we would, you'd only have to ask.

She hasn't got a clue we're talking about this, has she? (No need to mention Big Sister by name.) You don't even like him. You don't say anything bad about him in front of me, but I've known you for long enough.

I like *you*, and so does Sophia, and so do the kids.

The kids don't like me. They'll like me when I put ten pound notes in their birthday cards.

Yasmin rolls over in her effort to make herself heard, sucks in her bottom lip. I do, Neen.

Liam goes to work while Jeannine is still in bed. His parting kiss disturbs her. He has done this a couple of times recently, instead of letting her sleep for the extra hour until the radio comes on, knows insomnia is a problem for her.

The presenter gives a cursory greeting to the guest on the line, *Can we conclude from these findings that we have reached the limits of survivability . . . ?* The medical expert attempts an answer which summarises the findings, qualifies what the research actually might indicate.

There is no bread for toast. Opens and closes the fridge. Not enough milk for porridge. Opens and closes the cutlery drawer.

The news reporter fishes for the bullet point he needs while the other is cautious, she almost shies away from the moment, shapes the answer delicately. *Well, it depends on your definition of viability.*

The presenter does not like that much, even his calibre of listeners will be confused. *Meaning what, exactly?*

Jeannine pours her coffee, savours the smell. Now to choose what to wear, to find the groove for the day.

The other explains why viability is a complicated matter in language lay people may understand.

He persists, wants something concrete. *What do these conclusions tell us in a way that is useful in today's debate?*

That despite people's best efforts—

Jeannine is pulling a print skirt and cowl-neck sweater from her wardrobe, holds them against herself in the mirror. She remembers she was going to wear the new shoes, forgot to before and then waited for a clear London sky. She takes the jewels out of their box, positions them, admires them, gets the full effect of today's outfit.

– and the association I am a member of does not therefore support a reduction in the current twenty-four-week time limit.

The interviewer pauses for a beat. *Thank you very much indeed.*

This morning Jeannine's hair is ludicrous, the irons are not working their magic, she burns herself, ow ow ow.

People are watching.

Jonathan Ewan says this to Jeannine after she gives him the two files of correspondence. The folders bulge with unanswered letters, and Jeannine makes top sheets (*in favour* and *against*) so they will not get muddled. Jonathan has decided to wait until after the vote so some wording about the outcome can be included. There will be two versions: one to show solidarity with the constituents who agree with him, one to placate the constituents who disagree. Jonathan considers himself a Communicator. In letter-writing, in meetings, in interviews, in publication, in public debate. He has the ability to soften and to persuade. Jonathan Ewan, MP is moving Bexhall South out of the marginal column and into the safe column. The replies will be done by close of play tomorrow, Jeannine's other work is being pushed back.

He intends to go through the files personally, checking for groups and organisations, for acquaintances and names from the past, for anyone he should be checking for. He has other reading to do, phone calls to return, the summoning of the division bell.

Jeannine repeats her question.

What?

This one should be given to the police.

What is it?

The one I pulled out. It's incendiary.

What does it say?

It says that, basically, this person is likely to attack someone. Jeannine shows him the letter which she has put in a document pocket in case fingerprints can be taken off the paper, DNA off the envelope. (No one told her to, she just assumed.)

Jonathan skims through it. It's a Green Inker.

It isn't. It's far worse. The police ought to see it.

Why? What specifically bothers you?

Jeannine did not expect Jonathan to challenge her. The tone of the letter is vicious. In her opinion, the police should decide whether a crime has been committed or could be prevented, whether the writer of it is a danger to anybody, whether there needs to be a referral to social services. She thought Jonathan would think so too, thought he would tell her to use her discretion in future.

The politician says, To be fair, the language isn't directed at you or me. He takes it out of the plastic pocket, jeopardising the

268

chance for forensic science to have its way, inserts it into the folder to be answered the next day.

Jonathan, that's a threat of violence.

I'll look at it later.

Even if we don't actively report it, you can't condone it by replying as if it's an ordinary letter. (In so saying, Jeannine realises her error; no need for forensics when the author has included a name and address.)

He sighs. The trouble is, people like this are very vocal and probably use their vote, and probably have twenty friends who hold similar views and also vote.

Jeannine doubts it.

I said I would look at it later, didn't I?

Yes. And she tries to decide whether to keep arguing or to give in.

And in the instant before she makes up her mind, Jonathan says, *People are watching.* Then he waves her away, turns his attention back to his work.

If he means the two of them should not be seen disagreeing with each other (or more precisely, she should not be seen disagreeing with him) this is unnecessary, they are alone apart from Erica in the other office who pays them no attention.

Then she thinks he means people generally, in the constituency, for example; after all, it is in Jeannine's interest as much as Jonathan's that he maintains his majority.

During controversy the media are always watching, of course.

Back at her own desk, the syllables just uttered, fresh in her mind, an odd thought—

Her shoes are hurting her, she slides her finger inside them to relieve the pressure. The suede looks flawless, the design elegant. No one has complimented them yet. They will soon give a little.

Erica taps at her keyboard, the cursor invisible as it zips across the screen leaving a trail of perfect spelling in its wake. She is in apricot.

Erica, what do you do with letters which are unacceptable?

Depends what you mean by unacceptable. I have seen some horrific grammar in my time – Erica engages the brakes, turns her chair to face Jeannine. You aren't having difficulties, are you? If anyone is saying or doing anything you don't like, you tell Aunty Erica about it and I will set it straight. That includes (she jabs her finger towards Jonathan's office door). I shan't tolerate it. Believe me when I say I can make things happen they wouldn't like.

Jeannine is grateful to have Erica's battleaxe on her side. She assures her it is nothing like that, explains about the letter and its contents.

The older woman rolls her eyes. First, whatever you do, don't take it to heart. Second, it sounds as if it could have been worse; be thankful it was written on paper and not on something sharper or wetter. Those ones certainly can be dealt with by the police. You were right to show it to him if you had concerns, and remember that a reply will have his name on it, not yours. If Jonathan asks you to do anything you don't want to, you should just say no, because you're sensible and your reasons will be sound. I will back you up. Jonathan is young. Not to you, obviously, but he is, and the gaps between general elections can feel very short. Your job is to help him, and that can mean keeping his desk clear of the 'rubbish'. Some people out there are very dissatisfied with their lot and looking for ways to express their rage. Members are in the public eye, are perceived as persons of power and influence. The public has no idea how much effort goes into making a tiny little change, let alone a big one. Even keeping things the way they are can be an uphill struggle. They get thousands of letters and emails on hundreds of subjects, it is inevitable . . . But you know, don't you, that sometimes it's the respectable-looking ones you have to be most careful of?

Jeannine knows it well, has seen for herself what some people do to spoil their ballot papers in the privacy of the polling booth. It occurs to her Erica would know what Jonathan meant, might be in the mood to tell if asked.

Or Jeannine could ask about the other matter, the shock of which is finally starting to wear off. But Erica does not invite confidences of that kind, for she keeps her own private life intensely private, has managed to conceal if she has children, whether she is married or has ever been married. That information is effectively off limits.

Instead the younger woman alights on, What do you think will happen today?

It's going to be close.

Jeannine realises she does not know Erica's position on the issue, had presumed it was the same as her own but it could easily be the opposite, does not want to fall out with her over it.

Erica speaks as though she guesses Jeannine's thoughts. What concerns me is that we may be headed in the direction of the United States, where people's opinions on this influence their voting behaviour, that this one question becomes more important than pensions, or foreign policy, or law and order, or taxation, and so on. I find the thought distasteful. There is something distinctly un-British about it. I think it will be a close-run thing, and then it will be gone and then we'll get our knickers in a twist about the next thing, hopefully worthier of our attention. A recession, I expect.

Soon?

Erica shrugs once. That would separate the men from the boys. Are your shoes rubbing, my dear?

Jeannine admires her feet. They're new but they're fine.

Her colleague does not take the hint. Remember, anyone who

gives you a hard time will have me to answer to. Erica goes back to work.

To give her mind a rest, Jeannine Okoro phones the Department of Work and Pensions. She puts on her competent, authoritative voice when she explains who she is: Jonathan wrote to you over two weeks ago and the letter was clearly marked as urgent. Is somebody looking into it, please? Then can I talk to someone who knows, please? The next stage for Jonathan would probably be an FOI request regarding all cases of this type – but I am sure it would be better if you could just chase the progress and get back to me. Today? Thanks.

In between her typing, copying and phone calls, Jeannine sends three succinct emails: two to her university friends, Tess and Naomie, and one to Gina whom she has known since school. She sets a reminder on her calendar, *Lunch w. H at 1pm.*

Jeannine can't remember how Hazel became her closest work friend, but if socialising with one person more than anyone else is the definition for it, she is. Before Hazel was Alexandra Douglas, a researcher for another MP. They started their jobs around the same time, went to the same inductions and orientations, met up occasionally at the beginning.

Alexandra spoke first, Are you new? I'm new too. Can I sit here, please?

Of course. I had a top just like that, you know, I love the button detail.

Thanks. People call it red but I think it's sort of orange. It's a bit too nice for work ...

My boyfriend washed mine on the wrong temperature, it came out a funny shape and I had to throw it away.

Oh *no*! Alex recalled how much she paid for hers, and shared Jeannine's grief momentarily. It's a big place, isn't it? Who do you work for? (Jeannine told her and she frowned.) It's not a name I recognise—

272

Then Alexandra realised what Jeannine had already guessed would be the case.

But everything else was a match. Their taste in music, their love of fitness and training, though Alex preferred the swimming pool to the gym, they had read some of the same books and both liked horror films. It transpired they used to live in the same borough and went to the same ice-skating rink as children. They spent some time trying to work out if they had met before.

It is unclear why Alexandra Douglas dropped off the radar.

Someone, probably Hazel, told Jeannine that friendships across party lines could be viewed as subversive. She found the suggestion hilarious ... But what if someone else had said the same to Alexandra, and she had not? Jeannine gets a pang – like from childhood, like in the playground – uptight – despondency of isolation. She liked Alexandra, and not just because they had the obvious things in common; Alex was warm and funny and considerate. Not as self-centred as Hazel, not such a flake.

Jeannine considers this as she walks along the corridor, dreamesque for its eerie repetition, tremulous lights, audible hum of equipment, low ceiling. More corridors of the same, above and below the offices, like cabins of a cruise liner. Imagines the walls closing in.

They lunch at the café in the atrium. Hazel is talking about a new man in her life, one from the bar last week, but Jeannine cannot remember which. They have been out four times (how did she manage *that* and keep it quiet?). All right, three and a half times.

During a pause, Jeannine asks about Hazel's sister, who has not been mentioned since.

Hazel's face falls into its worry mask. Lucy's not herself. We had coffee at the weekend, and it's the first time since we were about twelve I have seen her without make-up on. She says her fiancé doesn't like it. I said, Lucky you, you don't have to bother. Of course she has beautiful skin and it makes her look ten years younger, but she didn't seem too happy about it. I asked her if she wanted to go out one evening, but she brushed me off. Again. She dresses differently, too. I reckon she's found God, what other explanation could there be?

Jeannine has a pasta salad, presses the rocket on to her fork. It is perfectly tasteless.

Hazel eats her jacket potato with veggie chilli, which looks more appetising.

Jeannine mutters casually, What's your opinion of the Fast Stream?

I think you should watch out if you were appointed, because folks who got their jobs in the usual way could easily resent you for it.

Jeannine gets her own prick of resentment; Hazel intuitively makes a good point. Clearly she's got skills Jeannine hasn't.

And now her friend starts explaining what she knows about the application process (it's tough), how she's heard of really good people who didn't even pass the exam, and the nonsense questions they put on the paper to profile you. I'm sure you'd pass, though! But wouldn't you kick yourself if Jonathan ended up on the front bench after you'd gone . . . ?

Jeannine Okoro lets the commentary run on.

Are you leaving, Jeannine?

Whatever gave you that idea?

I thought you said . . . ?

No. No. I'm not leaving, just thinking out loud.

I'm getting muddled. Are these the new shoes, then?

Jeannine shows them off.

They are fabulous. You always have such beautiful clothes. Are they Italian? I might start learning Italian. I fancy the idea of a second home in Tuscany one day, buy somewhere dilapidated and do it up, drink the local wine, eat vegetables from the market. Sounds ideal, don't you think?

How is she dressing differently?

Hmm?

Lucy . . . you said she's dressing differently.

Oh. Um. Well. She used to wear short skirts and dresses, she's very slim, you see. Practically size zero, it makes me want to puke. Tiny little tops. And since, you know, the fiancé, she's become more . . . Hazel furrows her brow in effort.

Demure . . . ?

Yes. *Demure*. Prudish. She's taken to wearing clothes that are baggy and frumpy. Concealing jumpers and tracky bottoms. She's not the girl I once knew. Apparently, he wants Lucy to put the wild days behind her, start being more of a 'lady', whatever that means. Made her get rid of her old clothes. (Hazel stares down at her plate.) Sort of peculiar really, she came home one afternoon and found he had shredded all the clothes he didn't approve of with a pair of scissors, because he thought they were too slutty. Isn't that weird? Hazel rests her knife and fork.

An episode from Sophia's past jogs Jeannine's memory, a passage from a charity briefing paper comes back to her. Is Lucy's fiancé hitting her?

Her friend goes pale, goes quiet. In the absence of their conversation, the echoes of other people's amplify to the roof, the trickle of the water feature. Hazel's eyes take on the glassy appearance of partial tears.

Jeannine leans closer, embraces her friend briefly.

Hazel whispers into Jeannine's ear that she doesn't know what to do, is frightened for her sister.

Jeannine replies it will surely be OK, you just have to be there, support her when she needs it, when she's ready for help.

Wretched platitudes. What else can she say?

*

On the treadmill after work, Jeannine reflects: at no point did it seem like a good idea to confide in Hazel, either.

Naomie was pleased to hear from her, sent a long reply sharing her news and suggesting some dates for an overnight visit to London, or equally, Jeannine is invited to stay with them in Birmingham.

Gina said she would love to meet, but because of half-term and the children . . .

And Tess has never yet answered an email the same day. Jeannine should have phoned Tess, that would have been better.

This is her own fault.

She runs past five kilometres, thinking it might not be such a bad idea to drop Alexandra an email.

Hi Alex, I saw you the other day but you were with colleagues, and I didn't want to interrupt. How are you? Have we really been here for over a year? Mental. I wondered whether you wanted to meet for a drink? Not in this dump, we'll go somewhere better!

Or what about: *I'm pathetic and totally pissed off, everything is falling apart and I can't cope. I think I'm cracking up! *lol* When are you free?*

Jeannine increases her speed, will run six kilometres, seven kilometres, eight kilometres and see how she feels.

Liam has left a sticky note on the microwave. *Out for the night. Luv u.*

She is unsurprised. Has not got the energy to be annoyed. Is, if anything, relieved to be on her own. After her workout Jeannine put her new shoes back on to come home in, has blisters on the backs of her heels to show for it. She eases them off now, exhaling at the pain ow ow ow, collapses on the sofa in front of the television with one of her teas to console herself, changes the channels like a teenager. The dirge is hypnotic, sends her into a stupor and she wishes she could have a proper drink, but there is no alcohol in.

Does not move.

Liam has given her space to think. Maybe. Or maybe he has simply done what he would have done anyway. He wanted to go out, so he went out. There you are.

After ten o'clock she watches the live broadcast from the House of Commons. An hour or so later, Jeannine Okoro decides she must get wine from somewhere (it's London, for fuck's sake, if you can't find a drink in the middle of the week in London . . .), gathers the contents of her handbag and, because they belong to her, because she is irrational, because she cannot accept that objects of such unequivocal beauty and expense would break their promise of perfection, because she is a woman, wears the new shoes to go out again.

Chilean Merlot, 250ml, 13% ABV, three units, 170 calories. Medium- to full-bodied with flavours of plums, berries and mocha. The venue radiates muted colours, lilts with the weekday crowd. One wall is covered in peeling posters cartoons foreign language newsprint bare bricks graffiti. Mao, Banksy, Hepburn and other icons vie for prominence. Jeannine sits at the granite bar and tries to read, as a distraction from her messy thoughts. She is obscured to one side by an arrangement of cut flowers, red and green spikes like claws in a vase. The interior is reflected back by the street-facing window, the traffic island and the furniture shop and the euphemistic sauna lit in the night. Jeannine's reversed outline is visible on the glass, an otherworldly creature.

A man sitting nearby is pointing a camera at her.

Are you taking a picture of me? Jeannine stops just short of yelling.

He makes wary eye contact with the woman sitting near him.

No. I was viewing the photos I've already got. He turns the Cyber-shot over revealing a frame taken during the day in a London park.

She looks, relents, softens her tone to concede haughtily, Well, that's all right then. She resumes her reading to salvage some dignity and fails, she hardly recognises herself (*shouting at strangers in bars?*). That was very rude, I apologise.

He scratches his nose, perhaps forming a sharp response, but he only mumbles, I can see how it happened, sorry to have intruded.

He has the knowingly untidy appearance of someone who once went travelling and never grew out of it. Scruffy and clean. And wears an old concert wristband, grimy, faded, the lettering bleeds. She thinks to herself, If I was your girlfriend, I'd make you take that off, and the idea causes her to smirk.

He catches her watching. Excuse me, did I sell you a house once?

Actually, I've never bought property, I'm still renting.

Did we meet at a wedding, or something?

No. Jeannine is vexed because her apology has been misconstrued. No, I don't think so.

My mistake. It's time for me to leave you to your book, isn't it?

Yes. Thanks.

Jeannine goes back to reading for half a page, aware she has made a bad impression, makes no progress. He is spinning through the pictures on his camera, a rucksack on the floor, is drinking on his own. Dad would say it is up to us to have good manners, to set high standards, to contribute, it is how we get on in life. Before she can change her mind—

I'm Jeannine Okoro, by the way. And I am sorry about before.

I'm Christopher Rhys. They shake hands as if the whole

prickly encounter has not taken place. After the introduction there is a lull. He ventures, Some women would feel funny about sitting in a bar alone, reading. Not that they should, of course, I just mean it's quite . . . unusual. Is this your local?

Sort of. (Jeannine looks around thoughtfully.) I don't think I've ever been in here before. There's, like, fifty of these in this area, they merge into one after a while. Necessity drove me out because there was no wine at home.

I see. Tough day?

More like tough week. I thought I would allow myself this luxury, I'm sure I've earned it. What about you? How was your day?

Oh. It was OK, thanks. I was visiting my brother. Half-brother, to be exact. He's studying fashion and this is his first year. I promised I would come, but I put it off for ages, I avoid London if I can.

Where did he take you?

He showed me round his halls of residence and his college. Then all the tourist traps, I'm afraid: Covent Garden, Trafalgar Square, Hyde Park. We went on the London Eye this afternoon.

One thing about living here is you never do all that stuff. I see the Eye virtually every day, but I haven't been on it. Because it's there you tend not to bother. Are you doing more sightseeing tomorrow?

No, I'm getting the train back to Colchester tonight. I'm just killing some time.

Oh, an Essex Boy?

I've never heard that before.

Of course you haven't. Jeannine fiddles with one of her earrings, then makes herself stop. I love fashion. Your brother is going to be a famous designer, then? Milan, Paris . . . ?

I think if he just earned his living by it, had a shop in Camden or an online business or whatever, that would make him happy.

He's determined, and very talented. I think so, anyway, not that I know much about it.

I bet he was glad you visited. It's a big deal, moving away, going to college. Your approval would make it feel official. What's his name?

He's Jasper. Would you like to see a photo? Chris finds one and shows Jeannine on the LCD screen, the boy is grinning, wearing guyliner, a black and yellow check scarf with a white shirt, looks pretty enough to be in a boy band.

She remarks, Ahh, he has a baby face. You don't resemble each other.

No, but we get on – now. Do you have brothers?

One sister, Sophia. She has children, Yasmin and Josh, so the pressure is off me . . . She sips her wine. You're a property developer, are you? because you asked me if I . . . ?

Christopher looks uneasy, confirms he is. I do places up. I was a carpenter before, but now I'm also a decorator and a plumber and a whatever.

And how do you get into all that?

In my case, it was just a matter of going to an auction and buying a house which needed some work done . . . without actually having any of the finance in place.

You did *what*?

Yeah, that was a pretty stressful few weeks, and involved talking to a lot of mortgage companies.

But why?

Because the house had potential. And it paid off. It had to, or I would have been in trouble. I got better at it after that.

How's the property game, then?

Slowing down, the proverbial bubble was bound to, *you know*, sooner or later.

There are always going to be people who want to buy. Like me.

He rests his chin on his hand, Could we talk about something else? I feel like this has been the only topic of conversation for the past ten years.

We are a bit fixated, aren't we? Jeannine winces, leans down to hold one of her shoes, shifts her foot inside it.

Are you all right?

Yeah. They're just new.

They're very nice, but you probably shouldn't wear them if they hurt you.

Mum used to make us wear new shoes with thick socks around the house, called it 'breaking them in'. I hated it at the time, but . . . Jeannine straightens. Did it – when you were being shown around his college by your brother – did it make you want to go back? be a student again yourself?

Chris Rhys folds his arms. I didn't go to university, as it happens, I stayed on at school initially but I wasn't sure what I wanted. And seeing what Jasper has to cope with – the fees and the loan and the overdraft – if I was his age, I wouldn't be going today either. He's stoic about it, but I worry for him. If I had studied, I like to think I would've done graphic design or photography, something like that. Actually I'm on Flickr, have you heard of it?

Yes, I know the site.

Photography is something I became interested in when I went travelling for a few months.

Oh *really*? (She dials down the condescension, he doesn't know how transparent he is.) I never travelled myself, I had too much else I wanted to do, career-wise. Where did you go?

Thailand, Australia, New Zealand, all those places.

Did you find what you were looking for?

Not really, but I went to some great parties.

And why haven't you pursued photography professionally, if you love it?

Christopher taps the digital camera as though testing it for authenticity. Maybe I flirted with the idea, but I'm not good enough, plus it's a perilous career path.

As is the one you chose.

True enough, I suppose. Nonetheless, I don't mind being an amateur. There's something pure about being able to please myself. And it's the only art form where you can make accidental masterpieces, which I think is quite special.

Good for you. And Jeannine genuinely means it, feels happy for him. What's your user name? I'll look you up.

He blushes. Immaterialism.

Like Berkeley, right?

Um, yes. You're the first person I've met who knew that.

Well, I did do some philosophy modules, as it happens . . .

So . . . Jeannine (he says her name gently, as if picking up something delicate), what do you do?

I work at Westminster as an assistant for an MP. He's a back-bencher, no one you'd recognise. Jonathan Ewan, MP for Bexhall South. He's good. He's in the constituency a lot, very active.

You work at . . . ?

Parliament, yes.

And this is the job which has caused you to . . . ?

Go out in search of a big glass of wine. Kind of. Opposition, not government, before you ask; don't judge a book by its cover.

Chris is about to comment on this, possibly even joke about it, but the words escape him, die on his lips.

Jeannine Okoro reads something into his reaction, and forms her own conclusions. She gets enough grief about her job as it is, and sometimes lies about it, thought this was one occasion when she didn't have to. She glares at him, then turns away, stares at a couple at the opposite end of the room for a while. They seem in love.

He coughs before continuing, Why did you assume I'd criticise?

Her voice is shrill. I didn't.

(The double and triple layers of female communication, he sets this to one side.) I think it's admirable to do something you believe in.

Yeah, I suppose it is. Jeannine finishes her drink with a flourish. I wasn't a very good philosophy student. My talents lay elsewhere. I enjoyed it, though, the bit I did. If I were to study again, I would do something completely different like that, random and fascinating, something just for me.

You still could.

Mm . . . maybe.

Christopher glances at his mobile phone, then comes to a decision, flips it shut and hides it in a pocket. Can I buy you another?

Jeannine closes her eyes and opens them. Have you got time?

I'm in no rush. The trains run from Liverpool Street all night. (His palms are moist, so he runs them over his jeans.)

Thank you. (Clears her throat to speak more clearly.) That would be very kind.

He catches the attention of the barman, also enquires after a first-aid box. Jeannine protests, but the barman efficiently locates and offers blue sticking plasters in various sizes. Grateful in spite of herself she applies two, they take the edge off the soreness, prevent further friction. The drinks are served and they resume their conversation.

In case you haven't guessed, I want to be a Member of Parliament. One day.

That's incredible. Though now you come to mention it, I probably figured it out.

Did you? (Disbelieving.) What makes you so sure you had me worked out?

You strike me as a person who decides what she wants and then gets it.

That isn't a completely flattering description.

It's meant to be. Following an ambition is a responsibility, if you have got one. Not like me, I just want to pay the bills, I'm not cut from that cloth. But Jasper is, he's like you, he knows what he wants and has the ability to follow it through. It would be scandalous not to.

You don't think it's a stupid thing to want?

No-o. It sounds difficult, but you should have a go. There is great beauty in risk.

That's sweet. Sometimes people are turned off when I tell them because . . . for many different reasons.

I think it's worth drinking to. Christopher touches glasses with her.

There was an important vote in the Commons this evening. I don't suppose you heard about it?

He shakes his head slowly.

Of course not, because you're normal. I don't want to give you the wrong idea, my family aren't affluent or anything, but my parents are fairly right wing. Dad set up his own company, like you, printing shops and copiers. He made it from scratch and was constantly afraid of a lefty government squeezing it dry. Mum just loved Thatcher because she was fierce. Most people tend to have the same politics as their parents, but I actively chose the party that was best for me. The one that wants to give people real choice over their lives. My sister and me were the first in our family to go to university. I don't say that out of vanity: it was Mum and Dad's achievement as much as ours. They made it possible for us, for me, to have more than them, to go further in life than they did. That's the way it's supposed to work over the generations, especially in families who start out with nothing but conviction. I know politics can be dry, but I wanted to be part of the machinery that makes things possible. I was resilient when I was younger. Headstrong. No one could talk me out of anything or stop me doing something I wanted to do. Recently I have begun to have doubts. Recently I've realised that that version of myself has gone away. When we were kids we weren't wealthy, but we were secure and we knew right from wrong, and we didn't want for anything because it was all out there to be earned by those who worked hardest for it. We were encouraged. I do believe that choice and aspiration are necessary for each other. I think proper governing is about making opportunities for people to help themselves, giving power and responsibility back to individuals. But if we promise that, then we have to deliver that. My little niece, Yasmin, I see so much potential in her which has to be safeguarded. And I never want for her to be tyrannised by society . . . or by a man. I want better for her. I'm sorry, I'm rambling. I'm in a funny mood.

I don't mind. You encounter bumps when you're on a journey; it's part and parcel of it. It sounds like they need you.

Jeannine casts her eyes down, the tip of her tongue moistens her lips. It's complicated.

It usually is when it matters.

Jeannine fingers the cover of the paperback, traces the title in relief. They sit in silence for a few minutes, and it is not unpleasant. She says, I haven't asked you if you're happily with someone? or happily single?

I've been in a relationship for three years, but it's coming to an end. I mean, we're doing a trial separation.

I'm sorry to hear it. Did she instigate it, or did you?

If I said it was mutual you'd guess it was her idea, so we better just call it what it is. It took me by surprise, I have to admit. She said I was distant, that I backed away from the important decisions. I suppose I didn't want to upset the equilibrium. I was satisfied; evidently she wasn't.

285

You won't patch it up . . . ?

Not now.

What a shame. My condolences.

I'm not a total loss yet. Are you in a relationship, or . . . ?

I live with my boyfriend – and then she mutters it, offhand, throws it away – a couple of days ago he asked me to marry him.

Chris marshals the flutter of disappointment: Congratulations.

Jeannine toys with the stem of her wineglass: I haven't said yes. I'm considering it. We've been a couple for a while. Not childhood sweethearts, but not far off.

He must love you very much. Do you love him?

I do. Jeannine appears to hold her breath. I have.

Christopher Rhys hesitates, but surely it begs to be asked: Why are you sad, Jeannine Okoro?

Honestly? It's just . . . there are so many things I want to achieve, but I get the feeling if I marry Liam, none of it will ever happen for me. That will be the end of it, the end of my life as I know it.

He gives her a bar napkin which she accepts, but to her credit does not need to use. Why on earth would he prevent you from doing what you want? Doesn't he know?

Oh, he knows all right, I've talked about it plenty.

Then I don't understand . . .

Jeannine frowns, pouts, blinks. I don't know. If I was trapped in a burning building he wouldn't think twice about running in after me, but I don't know why he wouldn't (Jeannine composes her thoughts, speaks carefully, deliberately). He did something about four weeks ago that I found kind of odd. He told me . . . I don't know, maybe I've blown it out of proportion . . . he told me he wanted me to come off the pill, stop using any contraceptives because it would prove I loved him. He said it's what real couples do.

What did you say?

When I'd picked myself up off the floor, I just explained I didn't want to risk falling pregnant. He didn't like it. He reacted *badly*. Took it personal, as if I'd insulted him but I swear I didn't mean it that way, only that now isn't the right time. We made up afterwards, and I thought the whole subject was closed. Then, the other day, he proposed.

The barman calls time. Jeannine and Christopher fall silent again.

She murmurs, I'm sorry, we don't know each other, and that was inappropriate of me. God, I'm so embarrassed, I shouldn't have said anything.

It sounds like it had to be said. And you've nothing to feel embarrassed about.

If Liam had popped the question a year ago, I'm positive we'd be married by now. It used to be me chasing him all the time, me complaining he wouldn't commit. What am I going to do?

I can't advise you on that.

You're the only one here. You're the only person I've told, as it happens. My friends are all, you know, busy with their own shit. And babies. When did I become old enough for all my friends to start having babies?

I bet they care about you more than you know.

I'm not very good at staying in touch with people because I like to work. I like work. I'm good at it. Jeannine touches her eyes and nose with the napkin. Sorry, this is too weird for you, isn't it?

No-o. It's just none of my business.

Is it normal? Do men do this to their partners? Have I got it totally out of perspective?

No it's not normal, we aren't all like that. I think it's quite a tricky place you've arrived at.

Yes, it is tricky. It's a nightmare, actually. And I'm sick of thinking about it. I know I had a future with Liam, once. What do you think? (No reaction.) Please, I'm asking for your help, it's burning me up.

Christopher sighs, treads cautiously, the path ahead irregular but discernible if he goes gently and bravely. He wants above all to do his best for this person, or at least not to fuck it up. You have—

Yes?

— excellent judgement and instincts; whatever you decide will be right because you will make it work. You just need to choose the life you want and get over the rest.

Sometimes I think I'm not very good at making choices. Sometimes I think I'm unhappy because I brought it on myself.

It's never too late to start making good choices.

Jeannine meets his humble gaze, regrets that there is only a short time left to share with him.

This sentiment is communicated somehow. It sends a spark, it causes a ripple. He is compelled to take her hand to lean towards her to place a kiss on her precious mouth. It feels acceptable to miss some steps somehow, no boundaries have been transgressed, he is confident the gift will be received as it was intended. Their contact is of itself, whole and perfect. Their physiologies leap with chemical intimacy, and then it passes.

What was that for?

Because you can do whatever you put your mind to, and I wanted some of it on me.

Her glow returns, her energy. She thinks of something nice to say but keeps it a secret.

Jeannine, it crossed my mind ... I noticed when you got here ... I swear I never would without asking your permission, but it might make a very beautiful—

Are you asking my permission?

Ye-es, I think so.

All right.

Are you sure?

Sounds like fun. Shall we do it now, before they kick us out?

It only takes a minute. Jeannine opens her paperback, her features natural, controls the urge to giggle, continues to follow the thread of the story. Chris makes a couple of quick adjustments and takes two rapid shots. Done. Would you like to see?

I'll look it up online. I should go, I've got work in the morning.

Shall I walk you home?

She raises an assertive hand to prevent him.

Right. You know my user name?

I shan't forget it easily.

Feel free to post a comment. Also there's a link if, you know, you ever want to view a property or just make contact.

She smiles. Jonathan has a website.

Who does?

Jonathan Ewan, MP, Bexhall South. My email's on there too. Or you could call the Commons switchboard and ask for his office. Jeannine gathers her handbag and puts her jacket over her arm. Thanks for the drink, and for the plasters.

Thank you for the photo, and the conversation and everything.

They pause, then part.

As she is leaving he calls her name, adds he would love to know how it turns out.

She does not indicate one way or the other, waves, is gone.

Christopher Rhys exhales, his heart thudding. He locates a pen from the zipped section of his bag, jots *Ewan / Bexhall* in a space on the Liverpool Street to Colchester timetable. Not her phone number, but close enough.

Then he makes a call from his mobile. Jasp? It's me, I've done a stupid thing and missed the last train home. Can I sleep on your floor after all? You're a star. I'll find a cab.

Reader in a Shoreditch Bar
Uploaded on 21 May 2008 by Immaterialism

+ Immaterialism's photostream
- Women and Girls Reading (Pool)
  422 items
  browse

This photo also belongs to:
+ Shoreditch (Pool)

Tags
  reading
  reader
  book
  woman
  london
  shoreditch
  bar
  wine
  wineglass
  night

Comments
Miss Labelled says:
Yes.

Sincerity Yabuki

Sibil, 2060

He says, Are you too hot?
　　She says, No.
　Tell me if you are, and I'll open a window.
　No, don't go anywhere. Stay here. Look – I can fit my whole hand inside your hand.
　What do you want to do tomorrow?
　You mean today.
　Is it? Today, what would you like to do today? We should make the most of it.
　Can I have an arm, please? Maybe drive somewhere, take lunch with us. Take the chess. Are there any castles nearby? I haven't seen one since I've been here.
　I haven't been to a castle since I was a kid. All right. We'll find a castle to visit, or some alternative ruins.
　I like ruins. Real ones, not pretend. Places with atmosphere. And haunted. Somewhere murder and treason happened.

291

Obviously.

I was wondering, will your mum come to your graduation?

Don't know. I invited her. The journey could put her off.

She ought to see you graduate. Someone ought to see you graduate other than me.

Dad will.

Yes.

Are you humouring me?

No. No, I'm being serious. I promise I'm not teasing, I'm really not.

I can see you aren't. Sorry.

That's OK.

I wish I had known you back then. I could have done with this.

This?

Us.

She makes a noise like *Hmm*, then says, We've found us now, that's what's important. Some people wait for years. Some people never find it. Isn't that sad?

Or find it and lose it later on.

The timing could have been better, but heaven knows it could have been worse.

Will your parents come?

Should do, don't see why not.

Will you introduce me?

I don't know, that sounds like a big step. (She laughs.) The real question is: will we introduce them to each other?

I never thought of that.

Don't you want them to? our parents, to meet?

I just think of them as inhabiting two parallel universes which never – he mimes – cross.

Don't have to. We don't have to do any of it. We won't be sitting together for most of it anyway, we can just wave at each other from across the room.

292

Certainly not. I want to spend the day with you. I want to spend every day with you. We'll just have to plan it out, make it as painless as possible. Do you think this is weird?

What's weird about it?

Does it make you feel like a grown-up?

No, not really. It's just the stuff distracting us from us. It doesn't touch what's within. In here . . .

Your skin's very soft (he kisses it).

I was just getting comfortable.

When Cloud Yabuki-Varma takes off her heart-shaped glasses all manner of items disappear, and when she puts them on they come back, and when she holds them out in front of her nose she can see stuff in the lenses but not around the edges. Spooky. The dinosaurs in Reptile Republic, the instruments in Music Corner, the entirety of Cupcake Garden, the floating mathematical models which can be manipulated to score points: now you see it, now you don't; now you see it, now you don't.

People do look silly in mesh when you are real world. Her classmates interact with invisible beasts, gesticulate at empty space, laugh in unison when nothing funny has happened. Some big trick. Every child is wearing i-specs in various designs like Cloud's, or helmets with visors; these are generally for boys who have not yet learned to avoid real-world walls.

Discovery Play, DP, is a highlight of the week, for it is an opportunity to engage with the more elaborate mesh programs. Pupils are encouraged to experiment with their personas in DP. Other lessons are more restricted – 'no pets', for example, not even well-behaved ones. Cloud always brings sim-kitty to DP, and sim-kitty instinctively seeks out other pet simcarnations to play with, currently a penguin, a bunny rabbit and a piglet.

Cloud and some other girls have been growing giant sunflowers today. It is possible to make them reach twenty feet high if the children select the correct weather systems, the correct food and sing songs to them. When she peers beneath her glasses her friends remain visible (in somewhat plainer clothing), while the magnificent sunflowers disappear altogether.

Feels *funny*.

She is not getting the headache adults threaten children with when they treat their i-specs like toys – rather, something has struck her as out of place, like when you put the wrong shoes on the wrong feet, though she does not know *precisely* what, and did not notice it until *absolutely* this very second ago. Everything seems normal . . .

There is another girl, the new girl, by herself kicking randomly at the ground. Nothing strange about that. The new girl is nice enough; earlier, she and Cloud shared a gluepot when they were tasked to build a bridge out of tubes, but the girl was shy and spoke little. Maribel is her name. Maribel has a mass of fair curls falling about her shoulders, the exact opposite of Cloud's hair, which is fine, dark, short and straight.

As brilliant as a detective, Cloud spots what is unusual about her and is intrigued enough to suspend her sunflower game, although hers is second-tallest already. Maribel is the only child not wearing i-specs.

Do you wear i-ris like an adult? (No need for preamble, just ask outright.) You were wearing specs earlier, I saw you.

Maribel pouts, hangs her head, shakes it briefly.

Are yours broke? Does Teacher know?

No, they're fine. It's just . . . Maribel's voice trails off.

If they're not broke, why aren't you wearing 'em?

Maribel turns resolute. I just don't like being in mesh all the time. It's very boring, you know.

Cloud has never come across anyone her own age who thought being in mesh was boring; on the contrary, children love being in mesh. You reckon? That's a pity. I think it's terrific.

We're playing a good program at the moment, growing flowers like *Jack and the Beanstalk*. They're massive. Plus, I have a cat in mesh so I like DP because I get to play with her. (She checks: sim-kitty is crouched by the sim-penguin sniffing at it sceptically.) I love animals. I want to be a vet when I grow up. What do you want to be?

Maribel frowns at Cloud suspiciously.

Cloud sighs the way she does when a jar will not open. You must want to be something? At least have an idea? Don't tell me you never thought about it before.

I've thought about it, I just don't like telling people, that's all, because I don't like being made fun of.

I won't make fun of you, cross my heart I won't.

Heard that before. People say they won't laugh, then they do. It's upsetting.

Who likes to laugh at you?

Mean kids.

Cloud Yabuki-Varma, not a child who has had much experience of unpopularity or being the object of a joke, perseveres: If I make fun of you, you can make fun of me. You can say I would be a rubbish vet, that I would give cat medicine to a dog and I would mistake an iguana for a guinea pig.

Maribel thaws – it sounds like a fair swap – mumbles, I want to break world records.

Cloud opens her mouth, the image of amazement. This timid and rather sullen schoolgirl does not come across as an adventurer. What sorts of records?

Sailing records. Going round the world in the shortest time. Crossing oceans and winning races. That sort of thing. We've got a sailing boat, you see. Boats are friendly.

I never heard of a friendly boat before. What makes 'em friendly?

You wouldn't understand.

I might! Try me.

Oh, just that they do whatever you tell them, and they're reliable, and they can be peaceful, or you can get everything right and then they take you really fast over the water. And they have their own names and feelings.

What's yours called?

Cormorant.

Fancy! I never did meet someone who knew so much about boats. Do people get paid for it? for breaking world records?

Maribel replies uncertainly, Some do.

Cloud is thoroughly impressed. I can't think why anyone would want to be mean about that, it sounds wonderful to me. You'll be famous.

Maribel graces Cloud with her first smile of the day.

Cloud is determined to maximise her good work. Do you like our school?

It's OK.

Do you miss your old one?

Not very, because – Maribel reddens – I never had a best friend there, so no one minded when I left.

I prefer good friends to best friends. Best friends can let you down but good friends are always good to you, no matter what, and you can have loads.

I didn't have many good friends, either.

That is a shame. People are nicer here, you just have to get to know them.

Maribel withdraws again.

Hey, why don't you come over and grow flowers, it's really fun.

No thanks.

Go on. It's not boring, I think you'll like it when you've had a go. You can make it rain on them and they *bong.* Cloud jumps and throws her arms open in a circle.

No, I shouldn't.

Why not? Why don't you want to, Maribel?

Thing is, I'm not allowed.

'Course you are, everyone is.

I'm not. Mum says.

At last, Cloud understands. She has heard of parents who limit their children's time in mesh, or forbid it completely. Cloud's father has been known to take the mesh away for several days, as punishment, when she is very naughty. Evidently Maribel's mother only permits it when necessary for lessons. When Cloud asks Maribel what she does for DP, Maribel has no answer and, without thinking about it, Cloud folds up her i-specs and pockets them. She plunges back into their conversation because there is no point in messing around. You know, I think my mummy is famous, but she never broke a world record that I know of.

You *think* she is? Aren't you sure?

Cloud will not admit it outright. Dad says she is.

What is she famous for?

Well ... Cloud hesitates, then says limply: She built something.

What did she build? a bridge, like we did today? or a skyscraper?

No, nothing like that because it's mesh, but people think it's quite good. It's a machine of a lady.

What does it do?

That's the question! What do it do? Cloud flattens her hands in a gesture of exaggerated ignorance. I dunno! She's away, anyway, because she's got to work on it – you know, she's got to.

Have you seen it?

Loads of times. She let me try it once, just for a teeny bit. Only adults can use it, you see.

Maribel raises her eyebrows, her turn to be impressed. What happened? Did it hurt?

Cloud twists her mouth while she thinks how to describe it. No, it doesn't hurt much. (Truthfully it did not hurt in the slightest, but somehow it is expected that Cloud should appear heroic for having had a go on Mummy's invention.) Well, the lady moves, you see, and then looks in her book and then you can see stuff. But it isn't exactly like the mesh, although it *is* like it. And I saw . . . a girl, an orphan who was very nice and pretty and lived in olden times, except I think she was sad about something. And she had to do a sort of modelling job.

Maribel replies it sounds good, though it doesn't really, she just wants to make a friend out of Cloud. What does your dad do?

He's a shrink.

What's a shrink, then?

Cloud repeats her emphatic gesture. I dunno, but he isn't very good because he has to practise every day.

Maribel sniffs and wipes her nose with her sleeve. Um, what shall we do now?

Cloud suggests they make up their own game for DP, one which involves Maribel showing her how to sail a pretend boat and Cloud showing Maribel how to perform lifesaving operations on pretend mice, using extremely small pretend surgical knives.

Director Fernand's violet i-ris twinkle. He is the kind of man who does not make many changes to his mesh appearance. His skin tone is accurate and blemish-free, his jaw only slightly improved. His real-world clothes are bespoke, so he can afford to let them show through. The room is filled with experts, dignitaries, celebrities from the international community. Some to see and some to be seen. A disorientating array of body shapes, manipulated facial features and fashion statements. A super-model, a superhero, a hypnotist, an invisible man. Decorated masks, skin adornment, hairstyles like architecture. A woman holds a baby dragon in her arms. A minotaur sips espresso. A vampire converses with a 1940s film star; they conclude their point about monetary policy as the speaker raises his hand and the applause dies down.

Colleagues, guests, representatives of the press, welcome to the European Museum of Art. I must start by thanking you for being patient because the journey behind us has indeed been long, and there is a long way left to go. I am extremely grateful that you are here to share this special event with us, in person, in mesh or onscreen, and I promise you will remember today because what you will see is truly extraordinary. This is a unique project, one of a kind. We hope to inform you, we hope to enthral you, and we look forward to exploring the future *and the past* together with you, our partners and friends. I will not keep you waiting any longer, so please join me in welcoming the head of the Sibil project, and its creator, Sincerity Yabuki.

There is a stronger surge of applause as people scan the hall to see who Sincerity Yabuki is. The fabrics of several garments flux into new designs, colours running like liquid. A lady with green hair and fairy wings flutters these expectantly. A snake necklace worn by another guest comes to life, slithers down its owner's torso, rearranges itself as a belt. The clapping stretches out arti-ficially for several seconds until, finally, a woman who is slim and conservative in persona appears on the stage, smiles waves shyly her gold i-ris sparkling, shakes hands with Director Fernand who, acting the part of gracious host, invites her to sit with him.

Sincerity, you and I have known each other for some time now. I have said it before but I would like to say it again, publicly, that the Sibil is a remarkable achievement, and this museum is the envy of galleries and spaces around the world because you have made your home here with us.

Sincerity speaks steadily, taking a breath at each pause: You are being kind, Fernand. It is a great honour for me to work in this beautiful and prestigious building, which so captured my imagination when I was a little girl even before I saw it in mesh. It gives me deep satisfaction that my project will continue to be hosted by the European Museum, and that the museum will be a guardian of its development. Sibil will be the catalyst for a new era in the study of art. Through Sibil, we will rediscover aspects of our culture, and nature, which progress has made us forget. What better place for her to be than here?

More avatars appear in the gallery, some in formal evening-wear.

Take us back to the beginning. How did it all start?

Sincerity tilts her head as though remembering what happened a lifetime ago. I was an undergraduate. I was a young engineer experimenting with mesh programming, to see what it could do and what its limitations were. The mesh is data . . . vast, complex, magnificent; vibrating, infinite data . . . that we have put there. We fill it with our knowledge and numbers and theories, our visuals, our music and our beliefs. The problem is one of orderliness: organising it, searching it, teasing out what is relevant. And being in mesh as frequently as we are now, we have become liable to synchronistic accidents, open to little acts of serendipity. So it was when I came across a pre-mesh photo of a young woman in a bar, made by an amateur artist. In many ways it was not an unusual image, except that I was rather taken with it, with the product of the union between these two people, artist and sitter. What I wanted, back then, was to know and to experience this particular artwork – or any artwork that touched me, for that matter, be it a painting, sculpture or photograph. I think it is important to emphasise that I wanted to know about it, really to understand it, on an aesthetic level and on a human level; in a sense, to get close to it. Who was this person? Why was she in the bar? Where was this location? What turn of events brought her there? How did she know the photographer? Were they strangers, or were they intimate? That was my objective, but also a lot of my work around this time was unconscious, I suppose. As I said, I was experimenting and had nothing to lose. So on the one hand we have a work of art, an object of great beauty and curiosity, a historical artefact with a story to tell; on the other hand we have chaotic data, all the resources and capabilities in mesh . . . (there is a blip: Sincerity's voice sinks to nothing, her persona wobbles, then the link is restored) . . . the information is already there, captured in the image; the picture, the objet d'art, has the potential to tell us everything about it, we just need to unlock it.

You were trying out different mesh programming?

Yes, different coding, various mathematical equations. Some of it was ordinary and familiar, some of it was guesswork, or following my intuition. I had a few hunches, did many trials. Of course, nearly all were unsuccessful, though some turned up interesting results, interesting enough for me to carry on.

Did you have an expectation of what a working prototype might be like? Were you aiming for a particular format?

Oh yes. I had this old photograph, and what I expected to make from it was a profile, a collection of facts and dates and names about the picture; or alternatively, perhaps a referencing system which would point you to potential research pathways, something you would pick up and explore manually, following your areas of interest. I was aiming for something fairly low-tech.

And what did you actually find? What did you *see* and what did you *hear*?

Sincerity Yabuki pauses. She closes her eyes and opens them again before she answers, gold invisible then returning. There were people and voices. There were environments and events. The photo came to life, as it were; it started to reveal its story – *a* story, at any rate. The history of the picture was shown to me as if it had always been there, waiting to be discovered. It appeared in fragments and glimpses, at first. There were echoes of conversations between these people, hints as to their relationships and tribulations. It was like I was alone in a theatre, and the ghosts were putting on a play just for me.

Sibil makes mesh content?

In a manner of speaking.

Without the need for writers or engineers or anyone to input any mesh coding?

Sibil makes you experience, in mesh, real or fictionalised aspects of what is already there embedded within a real-world object. The artwork is the starting point; from that, it weaves an extended portrait of sorts, showing us this art piece in a new way.

Fernand brings a finger over his smile. It sounds incredible when you say it.

It is.

Is it a tool or a toy?

You mean, can we rely on what Sibil shows us as being factual material, or is it just for entertainment? (Sincerity shrugs emphatically.)

Fernand laughs and turns to the delegates. Sincerity is being coy because she and I have had several fraught conversations about this, haven't we?

Some of it is factual and can be verified.

Some of it is blatant fabrication.

We can't be entirely sure what we are seeing, can we, Fernand?

No, we can't. But whether it's true or false, people might still argue that this is impossible: original mesh content does not just appear out of thin air.

I have never said it was original content; it is *organised* content. These audio-visual narrative portraits experienced by Sibil-users are elicited from information cues present within the artwork, combined with data in mesh, which is, in effect, infinite.

How is it done? Sorcery?

No magic I'm afraid, Fernand, just plain old mathematics and programming.

In a potent cocktail. I should explain to the audience that I have personal experience of the Sibil, and it was sublime and startling.

And I should explain that the director is literally paid to say that! (This admission is rewarded with polite laughter.)

There is an additional component, isn't there?

Yes. The final element is the user themselves, because what we have found is that each person experiences something specific and unique to them. Sometimes the differences between cases are subtle, and key aspects stay generally the same; whereas sometimes the whole environment or story changes, warping into another form altogether. There is a shift in tone or emphasis. How much is revealed alters from user to user: they might witness just a single moment out of many hundreds; or a whole event might spin out before them into a completely new direction, contradicting what has come before. It is as if the individual brings something of their own to Sibil, a personal interpretation, as though Sibil is responding to their sensibilities and collaborating with them. It's like when a reader of a book imagines the characters in their own way, or the viewer of a

303

painting has a personal aesthetic response to it. We don't understand this phenomenon yet, but we will.

Part of the work of your research team is to record these
'immersions' . . . ?

Yes. We tend to call them sensory immersions, rather than
sim, or VR, to differentiate what is spontaneous from what has
intentionally been made by design. We do not build these mesh
events; they manifest independently. I wish to make it clear that
there has been no creative input by anyone on my team. In fact,
we have no control over what Sibil shows us. We just observe it
and try to piece it together.

I think, Sincerity, some reports have misrepresented that.

I agree. This is a new technology, so perhaps there has been
confusion.

And the full acronym is . . . ?

Sensory Immersion Bioscript Interface Locus, affectionately
known as Sibil.

So you select a photograph or a painting, and through Sibil
someone can experience in mesh the story buried within it?

Sincerity smiles, her i-ris bright; no one would notice how her
hands have twisted together in her lap.

He adds, Why don't you tell everyone the bad news?

The bad news is that currently the program only works on six
preselected images.

Only six out of thousands upon thousands?

I'm afraid so. The earliest is fourteenth century. The most
recent is twenty-first century.

Do these six pictures have anything in common with one
another?

No, not really. (Avatars in historical costumes have begun to
materialise.)

Well, they have *something* in common, wouldn't you say so,
Sincerity?

Yes, all right then ... they are all representations in one way or another of the literate female.

Fernand rephrases for clarity, Of a woman or a girl reading a book?

Yes. But they are not connected to each other in any meaningful way, as far as we can tell.

Did you have any particular reasons for choosing those portraits?

They were selected quite at random. We are experimenting with others, and in due course more will be added so users will be offered a larger choice. That is the goal.

How is it going, this process of adding images to the Sibil portfolio?

Um. We are working on it at the moment.

Director Fernand links his fingers as though this is all fascinating, even though his involvement with the project has been over several years. I have not asked the obvious question yet: *why?*

Why did I do it?

Why dedicate your life to this bizarre creation?

Definitely not for the attention. (Sincerity Yabuki pauses to sip pink liquid from a glass.) Let's say, I did it for beauty. I did it because we humans intuit that beautiful objects can tell stories. We believe they have power. It is why we cherish things, because of the way they move us. They have voices, and would speak to us. They are imprinted with the past.

And your invention *makes art talk?*

She helps us to be better listeners. And I think it was only a matter of time: if I hadn't invented Sibil, someone else would have. We have not yet discovered her full potential – she has so much more left to give.

Spoken like a proud parent.

It is not the way it used to be, Director Fernand. We cannot now walk into an art gallery and encounter for ourselves an original masterpiece like previous generations did. It is true that in mesh we have instant access to detailed reproductions of practically all art objects held in trust by governments, and many more besides from private collections. But by protecting these works for posterity they have been lost to most of us. I wonder whether we are not the poorer for it? Have we become the prisoners in the cave? In that sense Sibil is, in perpetuity, inferior to her objective, because we are still removed from the work itself, and moving ever further away from it, deeper into shadows.

Director Fernand's next question is drowned by a smatter of clapping, which builds in momentum into full-scale applause. More people appear in mesh, and there is a spike in onscreen viewers. Fernand allows the excitement to run on, his eye on the audience figures displayed in the corner of his vision. As the rumble dies into anticipating silence, he announces it is time to unveil the Sibil. He leads Sincerity Yabuki, hesitant until Fernand places his hand at her back, away from the platform. The house lights are dimmed.

A dot hovers in mid-air, which widens into a gash cut through space, and out of it flows a black curtain which forms an enclosed cube, tastefully done. The material looks authentic, quivering from its own momentum and a faint draught. The curtain opens itself.

Sibil is white. Not Caucasian but *white*: as sheet ice as new paper as porcelain, from her braids to her bare feet. Not a blemish, not a variation, every feature of her – hair, skin, pupilless eyes – smooth like the inside of a shell, dazzling like a torch, as though carved from a single radiant white stone. Likewise her ornaments, her beads and star pendant, diadem, hoop earrings, the pedestal she rests on, are made of the same ghostly matter. She clasps in her casual hand blank pages, a

306

skinny book with its cover torn off. She appears at first glance to be wearing a gown, the folds of her skirt enveloping the forms of her legs, one crossed over the other, but this is only the effect of the seamless block of whiteness; she is naked from the waist up. She sits, chin cupped in hand, elbow on knee, awaiting instruction.

The audience show their appreciation with more applause and cheers; rainbows thread themselves like ribbons around the room, rose petals fall like snow, writing appears across the ceiling offering congratulations in several languages, birds butterflies bunches of flowers burst into colourful movement, their lives decorative and brief. It is the mesh community's way of conveying support and encouragement.

Sincerity Yabuki does not enjoy the moment. There must be only several dozen people actually present in the hall with her; the rest are avatars. Why exactly should she share Sibil with them? It is tempting to drop out mesh – just *pop* and gone, right now – she worries the pearl processor shimmering on her ring finger. Spirit herself away, and let them think whatever they want.

She does the mental exercises Dinesh taught her.

Better now.

The swell of noise rises reverently, then it dips, then dies. The scattering and flying and unfurling salutations have settled and are at rest; cease and disintegrate.

Sibil moves barely, for she does breathe, does blink. Like a statue and not a statue, less realistic and more convincing than regular simcarnations. Sincerity Yabuki knows what is happening, has witnessed it many times. The audience are unsure precisely what they are seeing, for Sibil seems neither of mesh nor of real world. As though she comes from a third, inexplicable place.

There are disturbances of people in the crowd touching their

307

processor lapel pins, bracelets, torcs, ear cuffs – a few avatars start dropping out, but many remain. Intrigued. Bewitched. Exchanged glances lose their impact in mesh, but a few attempt it. This rarely happens any more, the arrival of a technology which is unfathomable.

Director Fernand rocks on his heels. I am afraid Sibil does not speak. For reasons not yet fully understood, a language application has never operated successfully. Each previous attempt has set the research team back around two weeks to make repairs. Why don't we take a few questions before we continue?

Sincerity digs her nails into her palms. Her work is too good for them.

Later someone writes on their journal, *It looked like it was thinking.*

It was a triumph. Don't you think so, Sincerity?

I thought you were going to jump in at one point.

When?

You know when.

Ah, you refer to the 'original masterpieces' patter. I have heard it before.

Concerns are genuine, Fernand, and justified. No one really knows what has happened to our treasures. Whether they have been sold in secret auctions, whether they have been irreparably damaged through ignorance or malicious intent, whether they are being used as bribes for corrupt officials, criminals and despots.

Fernand laughs. I am sorry your suffering is so great. How terrible for you that you must carry these worries everywhere. But of course there *are* people who know these answers. And I can personally assure you, as one of the 'despised' heritage custodians, such travesties could never occur. Protection means protection. It is not ideal, but it is by far the best system we have at present. Who knows? One day it may again revert back to the way it was. Then anyone who wants to will be able to molest the Venus de Milo.

Where is the accountability? That's what people want.

You think that secrecy means there is no accountability? You think I don't have to obtain three signatures from the Board in order to shave each morning? You should see the rigmarole they put me through whenever I choose a tie.

Sincerity has liked Fernand since the day they met, likes his relaxed nature. Aren't you angry with me?

Why should I be? You have earned your right to say what you think. You are an artist. You should be encouraged to express yourself. I have no wish to censor you.

I am not really an artist, Fernand, I'm only an engineer.

I say that you are an artist, and the museum is lucky to have you. I have told you before, I will stand by you. I shall always be your advocate to the Board, should you need one.

You are kind.

No, I am selfishly motivated. This is what I am in it for — these discoveries, to be at the centre of the cyclone. Do you understand?

I haven't got you into trouble, then?

Don't dwell on it any more. Enjoy your success.

Sincerity makes a smile. In mesh it looks genuine.

How is that little girl of yours?

She is fine, thank you. She wanted to come, but she had school. I told her she could watch onscreen afterwards.

This is a big day for her too, seeing you out there—

Yes, in a way I suppose it is.

I did not see Dinesh, though; I meant to say hello to him.

He had patients, and it wouldn't have been fair to them at such short notice—

Fernand nods sympathetically. Both of you are so busy. Sometimes I don't know how you manage.

She does not answer that.

You're tired, Sincerity. I can hear it in your voice. Will you take the day off tomorrow?

Sincerity starts to object.

Fernand persists. If there is anything urgent, he will call her: It has been hectic recently, you will work better if you are refreshed, if you have given to your family the attention they are deprived of. Please, I beg you, take the day off?

She detects implied criticism, folds her arms against it, then marvels at her own negativity. Perhaps Fernand is right; she is just too tired.

Cloud nudges her sashimi with her chopsticks. A miniature white and red koi trembles into life, turns its head and flicks its tail, floats off her plate and into the air, swims about above their table as though in a real pond. Cloud watches it, then prods her nigiri next – a bright yellow fish soars from her plate and at once makes a beautiful arc around the first, as she hoped it would. The fish intermingle, gracefully dancing together. Now if only she can get her dad to do the same to his, then they will have maybe five or six fishes up there, and that will be lovely. But he is eating his maki rolls already—

Dad, you haven't made any of your fish swim.

Dinesh Varma pauses mid-mouthful and looks up to where Cloud is pointing. Oh, sorry. He taps one of the sim-fish in front of him, a creature patterned in white and black, but it stays obstinately still.

You're doing it wrong.

You do it for me then. He pushes his bowl nearer to his daughter.

Cloud grins through her i-specs and touches the fish with the tips of her own chopsticks. As before, the fish twitches into life and scoots up to swim in circles with its friends. Throughout the restaurant, aquatic creatures are floating diving soaring – the waiters, made to look like mermaids and mermen, levitate above the floor, their feet only just visible if you look closely, tails streaming behind.

He comments drily, I remember when dinner and theatre were separate. Your food didn't look at you in the way it does now.

Cloud tuts. They aren't *real*, Dad.

Aren't they? Mummy's real.

Sincerity's avatar breaks into a smile.

Dinesh leans over. *Are* you real?

Cloud chides him, Of course she's real.

Good, because if my fish doesn't come back I can eat Mummy instead.

Cloud finds this hysterical. You can't eat Mummy!

I don't see why not, if my sushi has run off. Dinesh bunches his fist at the sim-fish, Hey, you lot! I paid for you. Come back, or I will be forced to eat somebody. Perhaps Cloud as a starter, and Sincerity for a main course.

More giggles from Cloud.

Mm, sounds delicious.

Sincerity puts up her hands plaintively, Please don't eat me, I don't taste very nice. (But it sounds forced, even to herself; she is no good at these jokes.)

Cloud exclaims, I'm not a starter!

No? Dinesh feigns thinking. I'll have you for dessert then, because you're so sweet.

He pops a kiss on his daughter's cheek and she wipes it off with the back of her hand. Cloud has just begun a new phase where she dislikes public displays of affection, and is still in a previous one of using long words she does not completely under-stand. Both of these now come to the fore: Honestly, Dad, you're so *extravagant*.

Dinesh and Sincerity make eye contact through mesh. They

share their first moment of perfect unspoken unison in days while Cloud prods the rest of the fish into simmy-swimmy motion. He says, You were brilliant.

You were watching? I didn't see you.

Only onscreen between appointments. I didn't want to be pinging in and out while you were talking, I was worried it might distract you. I was with you, though.

Thanks.

I was.

I believe you.

They fall into mutual silence. Dinesh eats another roll, though it occurs to him this might make one of the fish disappear.

What is it like? Does it taste good? (Sincerity always asks when Dinesh and Cloud are eating a meal, always wants to know.)

He shrugs. Not the best ever. Not like the time we made it ourselves.

We didn't make it properly.

What are you talking about? That was the best sushi I've ever had.

Sincerity repeats herself, We didn't make it properly, and we made a big mess in the kitchen.

I liked it, the sushi, and the mess, come to that. I liked it because it was ours. Our sushi. Our mess.

Well, I didn't like the mess, and I didn't think the sushi was that special.

Then we should have kept on trying, shouldn't we? We should have made it every week until we got it right.

Their conversation pauses again.

Dinesh decides to leave this topic and try something else. I had another mail from Astrid today. She asked after you, and sends her love. I sent her some pics of Cloud.

What did you do that for?

She wanted to see them, I guess, see how our baby's grown.

She never mails me.

Perhaps she thinks you're too busy.

And she thinks you're not? Why doesn't she contact both of us together? that's what I wonder.

Dinesh sits back in his chair.

Sincerity elaborates, I'm just saying that she was my house-mate too, and, you know . . .

What?

Well . . . she was my friend first. (Pathetic.)

Dinesh speaks acerbically, If it means that much to you, why don't you mail her yourself? I can give you her new address.

Sincerity will do no such thing: but she doesn't want to be the villain, either. So? How is Astrid, then?

Very divorced.

Stung. Sincerity knew it, she fucking well knew it, but if she says anything now she will sound paranoid (even though she's probably right). She fiddles with the pearl on her finger – it would be disastrous to drop out mesh now – it will hang over them, make it worse.

Cloud exclaims, Look!

One of the fish has swum down by Cloud's chair, where sim-kitty was dozing. The kitty is now wide awake and interacting with the flying fish, head turning to and fro as the fish sails past her, tries to bat it with her paw when it gets close enough, lunges for it.

Look, she's trying to catch the fishy. I'll help her. Cloud makes a giggling grab for the fish, but of course her hands only close round thin air and pass through the simcarnations, ruining the illusion.

Can you just stop that, please? (It is Cloud's mother using her grown-uppy voice.) You can't touch things in mesh, you might spill or break something which is real world.

313

Cloud knows this already, but still makes a half-hearted reach for the fish in case this time is different.

Dinesh prevents it firmly. He tells Cloud to listen to her mother, threatens not to take Cloud to nice places any more if she is naughty.

Cloud sulks.

Sincerity wishes she could sulk too; instead, asks about his work.

Dinesh shrugs. He normally has a piece of news to share, a patient with an unusual problem, something he's read in a journal.

She presses gently, Is anything the matter?

No, nothing. Work is fine.

Doesn't sound fine.

I am having a slump, that's all.

Making too many people better, are you?

No, not that. It's complicated. It's been going on for a while.

You haven't said anything. How can I help?

You can't. Thank you.

Tell me about it, at least?

Dinesh glances briefly at Cloud. Best not to. It would take too long, anyway. We'll talk about it later, when you come home.

Later. Sincerity and Dinesh should keep a list of all the conversations they will have later. She says, I do believe you.

About what?

That you were thinking about me. I was thinking about you, when I was speaking in front of all those scary people.

Well, you were fantastic. I was so proud of you. We both were.

Sincerity's pleasure does not show through her avatar. She prompts, Did you hear the part about art protectionism?

Yes, Plato's cave, very clever.

You did hear it, then? I put that in for you.

314

For me?

Well, for us. I wanted to show I'm independent.

Dinesh nods.

I thought you would be pleased.

I am pleased.

Sincerity scrutinises him. You don't sound it. You sound singularly unimpressed.

Dinesh Varma rests his chopsticks beside his dish. I don't think it actually matters.

What doesn't matter? It's all we talked about when we were at university.

Yes.

Not *all* we talked about, but we believed in it. I believed in it.

Yes, I know you did.

She hesitates, then presses on. We were never going to have jobs in mesh, were we? We were going to live as much in real world as we could, out of principle. We were going to help save real paintings and real books – track them down, keep them safe for our children and our grandchildren, because hard formats are the only ones which survive in the long run. You published about it. Your position was that diplomacy had suffered a mortal blow, that hostile governments can at least communicate through cultural objects. That from shared beauty and appreciation of history, trust can grow and peace can be fostered. Dinesh, you said the mesh was ultimately unreliable and unsustainable as a resource. *You* convinced *me* we're too reliant on it, and that one day terrorists will undermine it and swathes of literature and art and music and knowledge will be wiped out – gone – lost for ever, and with no way of retrieving them. You said—

I know what I said.

– untold damage has been inflicted upon the mental and emotional health of society, and who knows what the long-term effects will be on people of Cloud's generation who cannot remember a time when the art in museums was real? *We have impoverished ourselves beyond reckoning.* Those were your words.

I don't disagree.

Then I don't get it. I've done something about it. I stood up there and risked everything to say what we believe in, to keep it alive.

No you didn't, Sissy. No. You didn't. You are a mouthpiece of the museum.

I am not a mouthpiece of the—

Please can we stop?

You just called me—

They want you to say those things, they *want* you to, because you are brilliant and they have you in their pocket, so it doesn't matter. It makes them look edgy to have their darling talking like a rebel, but nothing will really happen; nothing will change. You didn't *do* anything.

Cloud watches both her parents withdraw into amazed silence.

Her mother whispers, I thought I did something good.

Her father relents. Of course. You tried to.

Well . . . Sincerity's tone is not accusing any more, but genuinely bewildered. What have *you* done?

Nothing. I haven't done a single bloody thing.

Cloud turns her mouth into a comma. There's a girl at my school who's never in mesh. Her parents don't let her, unless she absolutely has to for lessons.

Sincerity makes an effort to show interest. Really? Is she nice?

Yes. She's called Maribel and she's my friend. Sometimes I take my specs off so we can play together.

That's kind of you.

To demonstrate her ability to be kind, Cloud lifts her i-specs

316

on to her forehead, revealing eyes scrunched into a big grin. She glances around the real-world restaurant, which is dull in comparison. Most of the moving fish and a number of avatar customers disappear, including her mother. She can also see real-world people beneath their mesh skins: a strapping man in leathers, zips and cobwebs turns out to be bald, round and middle-aged in life. Cloud raises and lowers her glasses several times, fat man muscle man fat man muscle man fat man muscle man.

Cloud hears her mother's voice: If you keep doing that, you'll give yourself a headache.

Mesh mummy no mummy mesh mummy no mummy mesh mummy – it's spooky. Cloud looks down at sim-kitty and makes her disappear reappear once. Dad, when can I have a real-world kitty?

Dinesh sighs. You won't like it.

I will like it, Dad, I will.

Real animals need a lot of looking after.

Da-ad. Please?

Sincerity Yabuki gets a familiar ache. Anything to do with real world, and Cloud's default is to ask her father about it. Dad is the tangible parent, Mum is the insubstantial one. She intercedes, Why exactly do you want a real cat, Cloudy?

Because it's nicer. Because they're cuddly and warm. When they purr it travels in your body.

You know real animals get sick, don't you?

I know. When I'm a vet I'll make her better myself.

And you know real animals don't last for ever?

Cloud frowns. Yes. (She does know.)

But sim-kitty doesn't get old. And you can take her wherever you like, and no one minds.

The father speaks next: Don't you love sim-kitty any more? Don't you think she's pretty?

317

Cloud stares at the simcarnation feeling like a traitor. Sim-kitty gazes back, is designed to react to attention from her owner, gambols playfully. The child mutters, Why can't I have both? I've thought of a good name already.

Dinesh sighs. Maybe when you're older.

How old, exactly, do I have to be before I'm allowed?

He turns to Sincerity for support, who tilts her head, mulling it over.

She says, I think we should let her have one.

Pardon?

I think she should be allowed a pet if it's what she genuinely wants.

Cloud gasps, Oh, really Mummy?

Sissy, if we are going to discuss this we should do it properly, in private, and tell our daughter our joint decision afterwards so she knows we are united.

She hates it when he does that, when he pulls out some family-therapy technique and applies it to them as a couple – pretends she did not hear him. Cloud has been asking for a cat for ages, and nothing we have said has put her off. She's older now, she knows her own mind.

Yes, but I'm the one who'll end up looking after it.

Sincerity had braced herself, takes the hit, it hurts her but she does not show it. When I'm home I'll help. In the meantime, we can both make sure Cloud takes her full share of responsibility. And you know what else? She's right. A living cat is infinitely better than a fake one, especially to an only child. I don't want her to be afraid of doing difficult things in real world. Teaching her how to look after a pet is a good idea; that's my opinion.

Cloud knows it will not happen while one parent still refuses. She holds her breath, wishing for her father to agree.

Dinesh is unconvinced. I shall have to think about it . . . and you will have to be an extremely good girl.

318

How good, exactly, do I have to be before I'm allowed?

As though it can hear them, sim-kitty jumps up on to mesh mummy's lap and arches flirtatiously. Sincerity does not attempt to stroke her in case her hand runs through it and spoils the effect.

Dinesh is composed, attentive.

His patient paces around the office, has yet to remove his i-ris for their sessions, although the only item in the room active in mesh is the patient's own persona. Is this the reason he keeps looking down at his shoes? In life, they are a utility style and colour, but to their owner they are an accurate replica of a pair once worn by Noël Coward. Then he sighs unevenly.

That bastard was trying to show me up. After taking credit for what I had done, he was trying to humiliate me in front of the whole department, in front of everyone, colleagues who respect me – some of them have known me for ten years. I wanted to tell him I felt betrayed, I wanted to protest, and I didn't because I was flabbergasted – for the first time in my life I knew what the word truly meant. I was so flabbergasted at what he was coming out with I just couldn't speak.

The psychiatrist is sure there is more to come.

The effort I have made, the work I have put in for that company, doesn't matter. I don't matter. They care about results, not who gets crushed in the process. It's malicious. Calculated. They would poison our drinking water if there was a profit to be made, and they thought they could get away with it. Leeches.

Why is their recognition important to you?

That is a good question, Doctor Varma. I don't know. They're the ones with the low self-esteem.

What makes you say that?

Because if they had any sense of self-worth, any decency, they wouldn't be the way they are. They're addicted to money, can't get enough of it.

Dinesh resets his expression from attentive to receptive.

Doctor Varma, in your professional opinion, do you think I need validation in the workplace because I didn't get enough love from my father?

Dinesh knows what to do. He counts to ten. Then he replies in a measured tone, Would you like to explore this issue together?

(Like clockwork.)

At home, Dinesh does something he has not done for almost a year: goes into the spare room crammed with cardboard boxes and opens a few of them, peruses the contents. When they moved in, this was set aside as a library, not a guestroom (Our friends can sleep on the futon, Cloud's friends can sleep in her room). They planned to cover two walls in bookcases, floor to ceiling, to nurture their collection, savour it in special reading chairs. They bought the chairs, but no books have been read in them yet. To reach one, Dinesh has to make space, the boxes have a film of dust on top which he disturbs into flurries.

Sissy, we are better than other people. We're different.

He whispered it under the sheet after they had made love. He meant it, he meant it. Their love was unusual, extraordinary, corny, they were going to make an eccentric life together. Be true to their teenage selves.

Conventionality crept up on them and then leaped. Dinesh is still reeling from it. They lost the slivers of perfection they once had. No more whole days in bed together, no more flowers given without occasion, no more Pack a bag we're going to Prague for the weekend . . . *to surprise you.*

They live apart. They went from making plans to putting plans on hold to indifference about their future, their neglected ambitions dying quietly like plants. For a while he blamed Sincerity because she was the talented one – she brought this upon them. Simple (synonymous with 'easy' and 'foolish'). He blames himself now, a much harder and heavier burden. Doctor Dinesh Varma did not fight it. He should have. He let it happen. He should not have. Consequently, this mess.

I wouldn't know us.

Cloud goes to bed without a fuss.

Dad, you know my friend Maribel? Well, she has a picture on her wall of a beach. Painted on it, so it's still there in real world.

A mural?

I think I would like one. If I'm not quite good enough for a cat, could I have one of those, a *mural*, instead, please? Not of a beach, though, that would be copying.

In your room? Which wall would it go on?

Cloud points to the wall opposite, which apart from a desk and floor cushions has few objects obscuring it.

If you had one, what would you like your mural to be of?

In the way of children, Cloud has left some salient details out of her plan. She was so taken with the idea of having a mural and getting parental agreement, choosing the subject had been overlooked. And, in the way of children, she hits upon a favourite theme instantly: Trees with woodland creatures.

Dinesh tucks her in. Should he leave her door ajar in case she has a nightmare? (His nightmare is that Sincerity will soon realise leaving them is now only a matter of degrees.)

No, not any more.

If you're sure. *Shh-leep*—

Cloud echoes, *Shh-leep*.

Another mail from Astrid. Seeing her name in his inbox gives Dinesh the sensation of swallowing neat bourbon.

*

Sincerity Yabuki's avatar stands at the end of the bed, a phantasm. In daylight, avatars blend convincingly into their environment, while in darkness they give off a lurid glow. Commercial and public buildings balance this with artificial lights, but in private dwellings you usually put up with an intrusive and sickly glare.

Dinesh lies with his hands behind his head. They maintain the tradition of saying goodnight to each other, but the sex games they used to play to keep the relationship passionate have long since faded. He stares at her in a way he would never do if she were actually here.

Sincerity's projected face is hard. You can't expect me to stand by a promise I made two years ago, not when so much has happened, *is* happening.

You mean three years.

We are at a delicate juncture, the next few months are crucial. You surely see that?

I do.

We talked about this together. We agreed that if I had to stay on to finish what I started . . . don't you remember?

Yes, I remember. In exceptional circumstances—

Then what is there to fight about?

The trouble is, exceptional circumstances come along with monotonous regularity.

This is my life's work.

No. It isn't.

Oh stop it, Dinesh. Does it hurt your ego so much you have to resort to clichés?

No. It doesn't. Seeing what you have achieved makes me immensely proud of you. If you don't know that by now . . . I merely meant that your research team, if you decided to leave, would get on just fine without you.

Rubbish.

I'm not suggesting you completely give up what you care about, but working in a more advisory capacity might be good for you, give you an opportunity to try something new for a while. I am thinking of your well-being as much as anyone's. I wasn't trying to make you feel guilty.

Do you think my child is my legacy? Cloud is not me.

I know that. Sissy, I'm losing track.

Of what?

Dinesh fumbles with the unfinished thought.

Sincerity musters, Are you having problems with her? Is she all right?

She's perfect. She wants a mural in her bedroom.

Right. Sounds interesting. You'll both have fun with that. Actually, I ought to tell you more often that you are a splendid father.

Thanks. (He is grateful, but his reaction is too faint to be conveyed over the distance.) You sound quite tired.

I'm nearly done.

Did you eat?

Yes.

Dinesh can tell she is lying, wishes he could make her some shio ramen.

She says, We should talk about this later.

He says, I think that's an excellent idea.

I'm sorry for snapping at you.

I know you are. What have you got in the morning?

Oh – Sincerity's avatar ruffles her hair – the usual. Budget meeting, a report to write, catch up on some mail and if I have time, I'll look at my data. What about you?

Nothing special. I thought I would get a sitter in, go out for a drink after work for a few hours.

Yes, you should do that.

I will. Sincerity?

323

Yes, Dinesh?

You don't need me any more.

The ghost at the end of the bed shivers – once, a glitch – then the connection strengthens. No, I don't.

No. I thought not. I was just making sure.

Goodnight Dinesh.

Yes.

Sincerity drops out mesh and the room goes dark. Dinesh turns on his side, does not remove his i-ris or draw the blinds. I wish I could smell you, Sissy, I wish I could wrap myself around you to keep you warm.

Sibil shines like a jinn. Luminescence, purity. Sincerity Yabuki has finished for the night, takes a stroll around the deserted galleries where the paintings hang in mid-air. Her installation is here, too.

In the European Museum of Art one can view a Rembrandt from the back as well as the front; one can lift the layers of a Titian effortlessly to uncover the genius clumsy restoration has hidden; one can grow a Gwen John until precision flecks on the canvas become unwieldy ridges and fissures. One can crawl over these pictures like a beetle, strip them bare, split them apart.

Time alone with Sibil is rare and brief. Usually visitors stream past the glass partition while Sincerity is doing maintenance or running tests with one of her subordinates. This solitude is the way it used to be when she was younger, when it started, when she was seduced by its complexity and elegance.

Sibil's appearance is a rudimentary simcarnation based on a design from archives (Sincerity responded to a mail). *I chose it for its simplicity*— followed by firm assertions about retaining creative control.

In fact, Sibil selected her own appearance. Lying about it is unpleasant but necessary, and the engineer takes comfort in the certainty no one would believe her anyway.

I did not invent Sibil. I am not an inventor in the conventional sense. I have shown what has always existed, what lay waiting to be discovered like a prime number. Send.

Her reply is construed as modesty. Whenever Sincerity Yabuki explains that Sibil was revealed, rather than created, that Sibil's true realm is accessible by the mind, people think she is speaking figuratively. Observe, even if she tries to be honest she is not listened to.

I would be delighted to give a demonstration to your faculty, please liaise with my assistant to arrange it.

There have been times, lonely times, when Sincerity has permitted herself a thought experiment – a strange and absurd thought experiment which she would never share with anyone. It is far-fetched, ludicrous. But in this private moment with her work, it creeps back, a sinister idea waiting to see daylight or be put out of its misery. Hypothetically, what if Sincerity Yabuki was chosen? Hypothetically, what if Sibil chose her?

Earlier, Fernand squeezed her elbow, a gesture he has adopted recently, spoke confidentially. I hope you will be pleased, Sincerity. It took more wrangling than I anticipated, but I have finally negotiated you access to the vault.

What vault?

Don't be silly, our vault.

Sincerity gazes with love at her masterpiece and is ashamed of herself, a lady of science, for contemplating it. It is a sign of stress, surely, entertaining these irrational thoughts, these delusions of grandeur. Of an unstable mind.

Fernand enjoyed her astonishment, that he was able to bestow on her what she could not have obtained by herself. I think perhaps they fear losing you to a rival institution. I said we would be the last to know if you were being courted by a foreign government. The Board wants to give you every resource to develop your work further. Obviously, they want you only to include pieces from the European Collection! If you can view the originals, it will inform your choices of the most suitable, the best. (She did not disabuse him, but her team has had difficulties – big problems – adding pieces, as though Sibil will not accept any more.) I said that my directorship was about this, about revolution in art, new ways to experience it post-protectionism. I explained I can only remain director as long as you, and your team of course, are with us, under our jurisdiction, being nurtured and encouraged here.

You threatened to leave?

I implied a bit. To lean on them.

Sibil does not return her stare, never acknowledges the presence of anybody unless instructed to. She sits and sits and sits. A blank. That Sibil might have some kind of *consciousness*. That Sibil is some kind of *being*. That Sincerity Yabuki has some special quality, or place in the world, which has led to a *meeting* between them. Outrageous.

She said, That was generous, Fernand, but you shouldn't have risked your own position. He said, A trifle, do not think on it. She said, Won't they resent you? He answered in a musical note, No-o.

Is it possible we have opened a window into the world of archetypes? Delete.

The media chatter has begun to bother her. Pressure, unending speculation: What is the next phase? What is the three-year plan? the ten-year plan? When will you announce S2?

I put it to you that Sibil is like a thread connecting different points across centuries. She is the Zeitgeist, literally 'time ghost', or more accurately 'the spirit of the age'. Finally humanity's mysteries will be revealed because historical artefacts have begun to surrender

326

their secrets. They are calling out to us . . . Delete delete delete. It is her workload talking. Pull yourself together.

S2! How she loathes them for that. Technology is by nature transient, a stepping stone, it exists in order that what comes next can exist. (Blind eyes. Abused book. White light.) But Sibil will not conform to this model. Sibil is unique. She will thwart any attempts to make her obsolete, Sincerity can guess it the way a mother predicts the behaviour of her child. Furthermore, the insult will cause Sibil to vanish – blink out of existence – become mesh noise. Lost. (And what will that do to Sincerity's reputation?)

These thoughts she keeps to herself; even Dinesh does not know.

Sometimes Sincerity Yabuki is frightened. Frightened for Sibil. Frightened by Sibil. At least she has never publicly let slip her fear, her sense, that Sibil has a life of her own. At least no one can hear her talking to Sibil the way she is now.

I do not know how much longer I can protect you. Maybe it would be better if you went back to wherever you came from.

The woman in the gallery turns away from the reading girl, to take in other paintings and sculptures surrounding her. She stops before a Picasso, yearns to see it in real world. The empty real space makes her shiver, and she wraps a loose end of her pashmina shawl close about her.

Fernand smelled strongly of cologne. You have lamented that originals are hidden. *Voilà*, you have your heart's desire. Your research will be unrestricted. You will be entitled to see as many as you like, whenever you like, for as long as you like. You do not seem pleased . . . ?

I'm overwhelmed.

The Sibil machine is dangerous, one particular critic is fond of repeating.

She cannot deny it. To deny it, Sincerity would first have to

327

understand it. The magical interaction between viewer and art manifested, a vortex of contradictions—

When a user approaches, Sibil stirs into life. An image is chosen by the participant. Sibil flicks those tatty pages and the immersion commences. Not always entertaining, not always educational, not always truthful. Always *different*.

Other commentators declaim it for a hoax, a manipulative publicity stunt.

Why me?

After mental repetition, Fernand's answer has taken on a high, slippery polish. Because we are kindred spirits. Haven't I told you often that you are exceptional? Don't you hear me when I speak?

He touched his thumb to his own lips, then to hers. The jolt of real-world contact sent her heart thrumming. She was suddenly reminded of her own body, its organs, its impulses, its uses. Has not been aware of this for a very long time. Can taste the richness of it.

Perhaps the Picasso would disappoint her in real world. Perhaps its abrasive transcendent imperfection is a lie. (To someone else, possibly, not to her.)

Sincerity touches the pearl ring processor – all the art objects in the gallery and many of its embellishments zip out of sight, leaving two colonnades supporting a dramatic glass roof open to the night sky. The stars are hidden by city pollution; dawn will arrive in a few short hours. In another time zone, her family are partway through their morning routine.

Yes, she hears him now. Sincerity Yabuki sees clearly what her life might yet be like.

Astrid has one blue i-ris and one orange, is experimenting with her appearance to improve her figure and her cheekbones, wears a plunging dress and astrology tattoos down her back. She talks about how *he* never let her true personality blossom because his identity dominated their relationship. *He* is never mentioned by name, but spoken of in italics. Dinesh is a professional listener, and Astrid takes advantage of this.

I'm not bitter, no, definitely not. I am stronger. Definitely stronger. Some people might say those years were a waste, but I don't think so. I'm like the inventor of the light bulb or the telephone, I have found out how not to be in a marriage. I shan't make the same mistake, shall I? I succeeded in choosing the wrong person to devote myself to, and now I am better prepared, more learned, in the ways of picking a mate. I'm very artistic, I have creative sensibilities, I like things to be just right. Not in an obsessive way, but I would describe myself as a perfectionist. *He* didn't understand that about me. *He* was intimidated by it. What's wrong with having a vision, I ask you? with liking beautiful things? A home shouldn't be totally masculine – straight lines and right angles. I will miss the lifestyle, though, I have to admit, I will miss the lifestyle. Who doesn't want security and a nice house? But I am happier now than I have ever been. I feel free. (Astrid uncrosses and recrosses her legs, revealing knee-high boots with a pointed heel.) I'm still terribly vulnerable, and I think it's a sign of strength to acknowledge it. I cry in the shower every day – that is my crying time, and afterwards, no matter what I'm doing or how bad I feel, I can't cry again until the following morning. I'm also extremely spiritual, but I haven't explored that side of myself before because, well, I wasn't allowed to. I can now, though. I started learning calligraphy about two weeks ago, and I write up these maxims and mantras. The New Astrid gets that stuff, and is assimilating wisdom into her life. I want to be my own best friend because I treated myself badly before. And I want to share the New Me with someone. I do. I want to share this person with somebody who values her, somebody intelligent and warm. I'm glad we

329

met up again, Dinesh. We should make it a regular thing, so neither of us gets too lonely.

Turning away from Sincerity and towards Astrid: Dinesh can visualise it.

Visualise it, yes. To do it – is that the kind of man he is?

An affair with her would be easy to handle; she would be a compliant, pleasing companion, but in his heart the prospect is tasteless, tawdry. It is not so much the example of his patients (their disastrous forays, the aftermath) which puts him off, or that he would hurt Sincerity's feelings, or that one day he will have to explain himself to Cloud, although these are factors. It is the knowledge that no affair would match the best of his relationship with Sincerity, that by doing so he would once and for all reduce the worth of what they have together to something commonplace and expendable. Infidelity with a needy and attractive woman might be a welcome distraction, but he would be selling his greatest asset very cheaply.

He says nothing instigates nothing acts on nothing, takes a taxi home after a friendly platonic parting. Poor, cloying Astrid is easy to put out of mind.

What consumes Dinesh instead is the excruciating possibility that he and Sincerity are past mending, that he has left it too late. This cuts to the bone, gives him feverish sweats, makes him grieve the way he did for his father.

From her room Cloud hears her dad come home, pay the sitter; the clunk of glass against bottle and he goes to bed. Quiet. Quiet.

Her sheets smell of clean cotton.

She likes her toys and her clothes.

She used to be afraid of the dark, but does not mind it any more because some animals prefer the dark and are called *nocturnal*. If it's OK for animals, then it's OK for her.

A boy at her school cried when his parents were getting

divorced; it means they were married before but are not any more. His face pops into Cloud's head, like it's mesh. Trouble is, he cries a lot anyway, it *is* tiresome.

Cloud's parents can't get divorced because they aren't married in the first place, she explained in return.

He said his argue.

Well, Cloud's parents argue – arguing out their clevernesses – they like An Argue.

The boy was upset because his dad had left already, and would have nothing to do with his mum, and, and . . .

And what? You'll never see him again? (Cloud was moved in that moment, but it transpired she shouldn't have been because he *was* still going to see his dad, quite a lot actually - actually more often than she sees Sincerity.) *What?* Why are you making such a fuss, then? No point being vague when she just wanted to know.

He wailed, They can't stand each other, they shout, they smash plates!

Cloud has a beautiful straight fringe which she can fluff upwards if she blows from her bottom lip. She did this when he said that, and answered him, If they can't stand each other, and they're breaking things, they're probably better off divorced, aren't they? How many plates, exactly, have you got left?

Then Cloud got told off by Teacher for being insensitive, which hardly seems fair, even in retrospect.

Her pyjamas are very comfy and yellow. She has another set like this in lilac.

And now she feels like *shh-leep*.

Cloud decides it is time to invite Maribel over to spend the night. They will do only real-world things like baking and swimming – and Maribel has already promised Cloud she can visit her on her boat.

Cloud reckons her parents will marry one day, because that

would be very like them. Animals don't marry. Many species form attachments, though, are loyal and loving for their whole lives. What is OK for animals is OK for her.

She dreams of a graceful crane which flies a great distance over wilderness over cliffs over the sea, which she greatly enjoys and instantly forgets. The bird becomes a muddled feathery impression in her memory.

On love: always the great gestures, or that it is incompatible with ambition and individuality. Rarely the small gestures, rarely that these make the other accomplishments possible. A work in progress. A chain of kindnesses fashioned a link at a time. Clumsy effort, but effort nonetheless.

It means – what?

That I will have breakfast today because I would want you to have breakfast today; I put on my good underwear; also, that I dress appropriately for the weather; I can do the activities of adults, which seemed mysterious to me when I was small; I know just what to pack in a suitcase without making a list because I can remember it in my head from our trips together (you taught me tricks like these); I pay for things out of an account with both our names on it, big things like flights; I am likely to treat myself to a new lipstick on the way, to know when a purchase is good value and when it is expensive and should be left in the shop (you would be exasperated if I spent unwisely, but you would be horrified if I began asking your permission); I am not scared to take public transport on my own because you don't want me to go through life being afraid of what might happen; I use the minutes I am made to wait as an opportunity, I listen to music or I read something worth reading – on this occasion the film reviews, in case there is something on we both would like; I smile at people because I hope they are as loving as you, as lucky as me – when they reciprocate I know they must be our comrades; I am capable of following signs and instructions and monitoring announcements without your help, but when I am by myself I am more conscientious, because if I got stuck that would worry you; I buy your favourite coffee and drink it for you; I can guess roughly what you would say about the sim-models advertising luxury brands strutting around the airport – you would be scathing and rather insecure; I go to the gate at around the same time we would normally go; when I am alone I have the window seat, whereas when you are here I tell you it does not interest me and you can have it; I watch the safety demonstration and I identify the exits which I did not do before; though I am a woman of science I want to get there in one piece for you, and on occasions like this I send out a plainly worded prayer; I will not bring you a plastic present, but at the other end, even though I am almost home and I want to get there quickly, I will take a detour so I can arrive with something good to eat.

Outsiders will consider what I have done inflated and roman-tic – you will repeat this story in future – because it was impulsive and involved a journey and some expense but, hon-estly, this is nothing special. I am not feigning modesty or being humble or trying to confuse you. I am aware in an ordinary way that this is a day like the rest since we met, where you exert your tender influence on me directly and indirectly. I am being myself. Without you, life is entirely feasible but hateful.

Dinesh wakes, sheets tangled around his limbs, to find Sincerity standing at the end of their bed in the illumination of morning. Unusual, though unsurprising. The hangover is horrendous, dulls his wits, slows him down. A lucid part of his brain forms the notion she has been waiting for him for some time, while another part, befuddled by alcohol, perceives an alteration in her appearance he cannot identify. A second sense perks into life, smell: there is coffee nearby.

She says, Good morning.

Morning.

Did you sleep well?

Like the dead. Dinesh rubs his eyes.

Sincerity comes close to him, lowers herself beside him on the bed, the mattress gives way beneath her weight—

Christ! You're actually here (never so sober so fast in his life). I thought you weren't.

Not wearing her gold i-ris and the natural brownness of her eyes revealed, her body firm and fragrant and complete, how can he have mistaken it?

Dinesh embraces her quickly, then retreats from her with equal vigour. Why are you here? Has something happened to Cloud?

'Course not.

Are you sure? Where is she? God, I didn't mean to sleep in so long.

She's fine. I gave her breakfast. She's doing some drawing.

He replies with mute astonishment.

Out of character for Sincerity Yabuki, she fills the gap with further explanation: Cloud asked me whether owls lived in woods, and then she wanted some pictures to copy from. I know we have an ornithology book somewhere – I couldn't find it though, that room's such a mess. So we looked up photos onscreen of different species and ... that's what she's doing. Drawing owls.

Research for her mural?

Yes, that's right. 'Just in case.'

Sissy, why are you here?

Because it was time. Sincerity scans the surfaces and the floor – the bottle of Jim Beam left on the bedside table with a used glass and a third of its contents missing; his untidy habits and personal effects have asserted ownership of the furniture and the carpet, shirts mainly, shoes, products; this, and his appalling appearance, as though he has been ill. Sincerity thinks privately it will not take long to put right.

I would have collected you from the airport.

I know. I wanted to surprise you. Aren't you happy to see me?

I'm bowled over.

Good. I'll bring you coffee. She goes out to the kitchen, and by the time she returns with two cups, Dinesh has splashed water on his face, arranged the pillows so they can sit next to one another, flattened his hair after a fashion. She places them down on either side and climbs on to the bed, tucking her feet beneath her. Now Dinesh gives her the deep, longing hug he has waited for, kisses her repeatedly on her neck cheek ear – she responds with physical relief, informs him there are croissants for breakfast.

Still Dinesh Varma finds it unreal, as though some crisis has visited them, says he is sorry their library is a disaster.

It's just unfinished business.

You haven't changed your mind?

Sincerity blows on her drink, confirms between breaths it is still what she wants.

Has anything happened at the museum?

She shakes her head no, then amends it to, Nothing that can't wait, we'll talk about it later.

He sees it now: she has come back unannounced in order to break it off, to pack her possessions and move out. This is the charade to spare his feelings temporarily (his patients have told him all about it). A play. A palliative. Look, why don't we discuss it now?

Because I don't want to.

It's about the other night, isn't it? You can say if it is, I won't be shocked or angry. I promise. I won't intentionally make it worse. I'll be as understanding as I can.

335

Sincerity glances at him sideways.

You told me you didn't need me any more.

Yes. That's right.

You meant it, then? I didn't misconstrue it. You aren't here to take it back and make it better. I secretly hoped you would do that. I secretly believed you might.

She puts her cup back down, turns to face him. I am here to make it better, but not take it back. Dinesh, I don't need you. But I do want you, I want you desperately. Which is not quite the same.

You aren't leaving, then?

I was never leaving. Do *you* want to leave? I won't fight you about it. People leave over less, don't they? I know I've been away for a while. It wouldn't be totally unexpected to find your life had moved on, and I don't want to be unreasonable.

I'm not going anywhere.

It crossed your mind, though. It would be peculiar if it hadn't. I put this off for longer than I intended.

Has anyone harmed you while you've been gone? If they did—

No, they haven't.

I worry when you're out of my protection.

But I'm not.

He says, I'm not making you happy, am I? It's clear now.

She says, I'm not unhappy. Neither am I content. What's more, I don't think you are, either. We seem to have lost sight of what's in front of us – I have, at any rate. You gave me good advice before, and you know how I detest it when you're right. I'm suffocating. I thought I would come home so we can – I don't know – talk, prioritise, be together. Make plans, the way we used to. I didn't have anything specific in mind. We can just do nothing, if you prefer.

I see. Right . . . and that's all?

Yes, that's all.

Well then, OK.

She says, Have I given you a fright?

He says, A small one.

Sorry, that wasn't my intention. How dreadful of me, how horrible for you. I deeply apologise, Dinesh, there's no excuse for it. I'm truly sorry.

It's forgotten.

Each is struck by the resemblance of Cloud to the other. By the vibrating strings which join them.

Dinesh presses on, Besides, you're right, I for one don't want Cloud to be dependent on anybody. I would be a hypocrite if I wanted less for you.

No, but she shouldn't be careless, either. She should value what is important, cherish what needs to be cherished. Are we broken, Dinesh? Did I break us?

No, we're just rusty.

She nods in agreement. Yes, that is nearer the mark; he is good that way.

Are you sure there's nothing wrong at the museum?

More of the same, I'm afraid. You tell me about your work first. You said you were in a slump, but you never explained why.

We should resolve this absurd cat situation first. She goes on and on about it since you mentioned it.

Sincerity nearly gives in, but there is no point being falsely deferential, just be herself – that's for the best, normality will restore their relationship faster. Their minds will rediscover old patterns; their bodies will fall back into step. Cloud can wait. Sincerity asks, How is your practice? I want to know about that uppermost. I want to know how it pleases you, and if it does not, what can be done to change it?

I'm afraid that could take all day.

I've nothing better to do.

*

337

Phoebe stretches, elongating her limbs. When resting in one spot such as this cushion, this room, she can stay put for several hours then suddenly, unexpectedly, it is time for action, time for some attention, time to go. She likes to be left alone and she likes company, and she herself does not know which she wants until she wants it. What was tranquil becomes dull. What was private becomes insufferably remote. This chair and that chair and these bookshelves are now monuments to her isolation, cannot be eaten, are not lavishing her with compliments – no fuss when fuss is urgently required. She jumps expertly, lands expertly, is absorbed into the house she knows, its floors, its steps, its smells, it textures: it is her terrain. Her tabby coat would give splendid coverage in nooks and corners if her white chin white bib white socks did not give her away. She craves outside. Outside! Outside! Miaows it until the back door is opened for her, trots into the garden to find her favourite, here at ground height – rolls against her, rubs her head against her. This is what she wants. The rest of her desires vanish.

Dinesh Varma's affection for the cat is tested daily. Phoebe is a vain and greedy creature. And competition. She has discovered Cloud lying on her front on a blanket on the grass, leaning over her open textbook, the other hand automatically reaching to acknowledge and stroke her beloved pet. Phoebe has never lost the appearance of a kitten, remains lean and cute and playful and therefore spoiled by the two women. Tart. Dinesh tries to recollect why he gave in, remonstrates with his past self. Gradually this gives way to a newer, deeper, altogether more serious anxiety and he shouts for Sincerity—

– who immediately appears and calmly asks what the matter is.

You were lurking.

I really wasn't.

He gestures accusingly at their daughter.

Sincerity, quizzical. Why? What's wrong?

Don't you see?

Sincerity checks, for she may have missed the obvious; answers blankly that Cloud is studying for her course and what is the problem with that?

Not *that*.

Sincerity looks again.

Cloud's sandals have slipped off, she has crossed her feet in the air behind her. Tidy, painted toenails. She is wearing one of her flimsy vests, a strap lifting though not fallen from her shoulder. Engrossed.

A Note

Simone Martini, *Annunciation*, 1333, Uffizi, Florence; and *The High Priestess (II)* in the traditional tarot deck.

Pieter Janssens Elinga, *Woman Reading*, 1668–70, Alte Pinakothek, Munich. Also Pieter Janssens Elinga, *Still Life with Citrus Fruit*, 1623–82, Ashmolean Museum, Oxford; Pieter Janssens Elinga, *Still Life 'Toebackje'*, c.1650, Museum Bredius, The Hague.

Angelica Kauffman, *Portrait of a Lady*, c.1775, Tate Collection. Also Angelica Kauffman, *Ellis Cornelia Knight*, 1793, Manchester Art Gallery, finished 'out of friendship'; Angelica Kauffman, *Poor Maria*, 1777, The Burghley House Collection.

Horatio Nelson King, *Giulia Grisi*, 1860s, National Portrait Gallery, London. Also Julia Margaret Cameron, *Portrait of a Sybil (Mary Emily ('May') Prinsep)*, 1870, National Portrait Gallery, London.

Duncan Grant, *Vanessa Bell (née Stephen)*, circa 1916–17, National Portrait Gallery, London. Also Heinrich Vogeler, *Martha Vogeler*, c.1905, VG Bild-Kunst, Bonn; and reading nudes such as: Félix Vallotton, *Reading Abandoned*, 1924, Musée des Beaux-Arts, Paris; Théodore Roussel, *The Reading Girl*,

1886–7, Tate Collection; Suzanne Valadon, *Female Nude*, 1922, Musée d'Art Moderne de la Ville de Paris.

Flickr.com, *Women and Girls Reading* pool, in particular photos of commuters on the subway and the tube.

William Wetmore Story, *The Libyan Sibil*, 1861–8, Smithsonian American Art Museum, Washington, DC. Also Kimbei Kusakabe, *Woman Writing with Brush*, 1890s, oldphotosjapan.com; Correggio's *Mary Magdalene*, which was lost during the Second World War, though it was much emulated and these works survive: Friedrich Heinrich Füger, *The Penitent Magdalene*, 1808, Neue Pinakothek, Munich; Jean-Jacques Henner, *Woman Reading*, c.1880–90, Musée d'Orsay, Paris.

Acknowledgements

Thank you to Bill Hamilton and colleagues at A. M. Heath, for your expertise and professionalism. Thank you to Ursula Doyle and colleagues at Virago (and Little, Brown), for your talent and support. Thank you to Julie Stokes for your friendship. Thank you to Hilary Mantel for everything.